Shuttered Schools

A volume in
Research on African American Education
Carol Camp Yeakey, *Series Editor*

Shuttered Schools

Race, Community, and School Closures in American Cities

edited by

Ebony M. Duncan-Shippy
Washington University in St. Louis

INFORMATION AGE PUBLISHING, INC.
Charlotte, NC • www.infoagepub.com

Library of Congress Cataloging-in-Publication Data

A CIP record for this book is available from the Library of Congress
http://www.loc.gov

ISBN: 978-1-64113-608-2 (Paperback)
       978-1-64113-609-9 (Hardcover)
       978-1-64113-610-5 (ebook)

Dedicated to those marginalized youth and their families who suffered the consequences of neighborhood school closure.

CONTENTS

SECTION II

IMPLICATIONS

CHAPTER 1

THE RISE OF SCHOOL CLOSURES IN THE 21st CENTURY

Ebony M. Duncan-Shippy
Washington University–St. Louis

In recent years, mass school closures have reshaped public education in cities across the United States. Increasingly, urban districts are grappling with declining enrollments and financial deficits, challenges traditionally associated with rural districts (Bard, Gardener, & Wieland, 2006). In response to these challenges, education officials shuttered approximately 24,000 K–12 public schools between 1999 and 2013, displacing on average a quarter of a million students each year (NCES, 2016). Recent reports on school closings in Detroit, Chicago, Philadelphia, and other cities suggest that stringent accountability policies, new achievement benchmarks, urban depopulation, redevelopment, municipal budget deficits, charter school expansion, and a host of other political and contextual factors drive contemporary closure trends (de la Torre & Gwynne, 2009a; Dowdall & Eichel, 2011; Engberg, Gill, Zamarro, & Zimmer, 2012; Fine, 2012; Han, et al., 2017; Hurdle, 2013; Kelleher & Wisniewski, 2013; Lipman, 2013; Sunderman & Payne, 2009).

Shuttered Schools, pages 1–6

1

Mass closure has uprooted the lives of the tens of thousands of marginalized students as school districts struggle with the political legacies of racial inequities. Given their overrepresentation in many urban school districts (Snyder, de Brey, & Dillow, 2016, p. 111, 185), African American students experience school loss at higher rates than students of other races (Burdick-Will, Keels, & Schuble, 2013; de la Torre & Gwynne, 2009b; de la Torre et al., 2015; Han et al., 2017; Nathanson, Corcoran, & Baker-Smith, 2013; Sunderman & Payne, 2009). The alarming rates of public school closure in U.S. cities and their disproportionate impact on Black students have garnered global attention. After touring several major cities (i.e., Washington, DC; Baltimore, Maryland; Jackson, Mississippi; Chicago, and New York), delegates from the United Nations Working Group of Experts on People of African Descent (2016) deemed the rise in urban school closures an affront to the human rights of Black youth. Furthermore, they interpreted closure practice as a mechanism of ongoing racial discrimination rooted in the legacies of slavery, Jim Crow, and failed desegregation efforts.

Communities across the United States—especially high-poverty African American ones—are not losing public schools due to school factors, but rather due to social, economic, and political ones beyond school walls. Within equity-based frameworks, the social significance of school closures extends beyond the primary purpose of education. Schools are key social organizations that allocate status and facilitate opportunities for upward social mobility. From this perspective, school communities not only transmit skills, training, and knowledge, but also organize the daily lives of youth. For example, schools integrate young people into broader communities, instill values and shared beliefs, provide physical and psychological safety, shape identity and meaning-making processes, and grant access to social opportunities. Urban school closure deprives communities of essential social institutions, which are detrimental to youth's immediate educational opportunities and to the institutional relationships forming their school communities.

School closure advocates assert that these strategies can improve test scores and resource allocation, but opponents highlight the considerable costs to educational communities. Understanding education as a primary social institution, students, families, and school staff lose much more than neighborhood schools: They lose *school communities*—the magnitude of which is reflected in the considerable public resistance to school closure decisions (Brummet, 2014; de la Torre et al., 2015; Green, 2017; Han et al., 2017). While schools were once institutional fixtures in most communities across the nation, they are now disappearing to such an extent that some neighborhoods no longer have district-operated public schools (Demby, 2015; Kamenetz, 2014).

The resurgence of school closures is largely overlooked in contemporary education scholarship, and much of what is known about this phenomenon stems from popular media coverage and research reports. *Shuttered Schools* is an interdisciplinary volume that integrates multiple perspectives to study the complex phenomenon of school closure—an issue not confined to education. These rigorous new studies situate recent school closures in broader social, economic, and political contexts in order to discuss the implications of these decisions for students and their families, teachers, and communities. Research in *Shuttered Schools* accounts for the disproportionate impact of contemporary closures on African American students and examines the implications of these decisions for school communities.

This two-part volume focuses on the patterns and processes of school closures in Section I, before turning to the implications of these decisions in Section II. Chapters 2 and 3 describe the racial and socioeconomic contexts of contemporary school closures. In "School Closure in Strained Cities: Implications for Racial Equity in U.S. Education," Duncan-Shippy examines how changes in school communities advance contemporary school closures in U.S. school districts. Based on analyses of national school and district data, she finds that ecological characteristics (e.g., school racial and economic composition, population decline) and institutional conditions (e.g., charter school growth, financial strain) contribute to closure practice in ways that have implications for racial equity in education. In "School Closings...Atlanta Style: The Convergence of Poverty, Segregation, and Achievement," Davis, Oakley, and Stover analyze public school and census data to examine these patterns more closely using Atlanta, Georgia as a case study. Based on their socio-spatial analyses, Davis and colleagues find that schools in high poverty and predominantly Black neighborhoods are more likely to close compared to schools in more advantaged areas, and conclude that racial and economic segregation are primary drivers of contemporary school closure.

Chapters 4 through 7 focus on the processes and experiences of school closures in major districts across the United States. In "The Consequences of School Governance Change in Detroit: From Proposal A to the Education Achievement Authority," Kang and Slay trace shifts in school governance over a 20-year period, and their implications for education policy and contemporary school closures in Detroit. They demonstrate how state intervention—namely, changes in Michigan's school funding formula and the development of a state-run recovery school district—fractured the Detroit Public School system and undermined local control of public education. The peak in school closures in Detroit coincides with substantial changes in governance, which the authors interpret as evidence of a broader political shift toward neoliberal governance.

In Chapter 5, "An Open and Shut Case: Gentrification and School Closure Decisions in Washington, DC," Syeed contrasts community efforts to retain neighborhood schools across the District of Columbia. Race and class advantage are key to explaining outcomes, as gentrifying communities are able to wage successful bids for keeping schools open through an emphasis on neighborhood development. In contrast, demographic shifts in high poverty areas often thwart the efforts of African American residents to save local schools.

In "Complicating 'Sector' Agnosticism: Relational and Spatial Displacement and Dispossession through School Closure in Cleveland," Galletta situates the contemporary school closure experiences of African American students in Cleveland's historical context. By providing an extensive description of changes in the city's educational context, this chapter demonstrates how public policies intersect with social conditions, to create the "perfect storm" for dispossession and displacement through school closure.

Finally, in "Race, Class, and Education in North Little Rock, Arkansas: The Process and Impact of the Closure, Renovation, or Rebuild of (Almost) Every School in the Pursuit of World Class Schools," Lowery connects school closure decisions with the allocation of educational resources. She analyzes school closings in the unique case of North Little Rock, Arkansas—a district that consolidated, closed, or rebuilt nearly all of its public schools. Emphasizing the decision-making processes of education officials, Lowery concludes that district leaders employ colorblind strategies to justify school closure decisions, while ignoring the impact of the legacy of racism in the city.

Section II of the book emphasizes the implications of school closure for myriad outcomes—including its association with housing values, teacher political attitudes, public trust, and student test scores. In "The Effects of Public School Closures on Neighborhood Housing Values in U.S. Metropolitan Areas, 2000–2010," Brazil uses national data to model the effects of elementary school closure rates on median property values in suburban and urban census tracts. Findings support the assertion that school closures depress the economic welfare of neighborhoods—especially when those neighborhoods have greater proportions of African American residents. Chapters 9 and 10 centralize the political attitudes and responses of residents and teachers experiencing school closures in Chicago and Philadelphia. In "'A Spoke in the Wheel': School Closures and the Continued Violation of Public Trust," Nuamah draws from policy feedback scholarship to examine public reaction to school closures in six neighborhoods in Chicago. Combining content analysis of public school board meetings, interviews with parents, as well as additional ethnographic data, this chapter demonstrates that previous experiences with school closure shape community members' suspicious interpretations of the district's motives as well as their considerable and continued mistrust of education officials in Chicago. "School Closures and the Political Education of U.S. Teachers" considers the effects of closing schools on teachers. Ware and Maton track changes in teachers' political attitudes and activities after experiencing or witnessing school closures in their districts. They find that school closures politically activate many teachers, who engage in various form of short- (e.g., participation in collective demonstrations) and long-term (e.g., membership in local caucuses) resistance efforts to protest closure decisions. Finally, Welsh and Hill assess the disruptive effects of closure-related mobility on student learning in "Closing Costs: Examining the Impact of School Closures on African-American Students' Educational Outcomes." Drawing evidence from post-Katrina New Orleans, the authors describe the prevalence of closure-related student mobility and model the effects of closures on student achievement. In the concluding chapter, "Education Reform in the Racial State: The Costs of School Closures for Marginalized Communities," Duncan-Shippy speaks to the broader implications of school closure research and highlights ways to advance scholarship on the topic.

REFERENCES

Bard, J., Gardener, C., & Wieland, R. (2006). Rural School Consolidation: History, Research Summary, Conclusions, and Recommendations. *Rural Educator, 27,* 40–48.

Brummet, Q. (2014). The effect of school closings on student achievement. *Journal of Public Economics, 119,* 108–124.

Burdick-Will, J., Keels, M., & Schuble, T. (2013). Closing and Opening Schools: The Association between Neighborhood Characteristics and the Location of New Educational Opportunities in a Large Urban District. *Journal of Urban Affairs, 35*(1), 59–80.

de la Torre, M., & Gwynne, J. (2009a). *Changing schools: A look at student mobility trends in Chicago Public Schools since 1995.* Chicago, IL: Consortium on Chicago School Research.

de la Torre, M., & Gwynne, J. (2009b). *When schools close: Effects on displaced students in Chicago public schools.* Chicago, IL: Consortium on Chicago School Research.

de la Torre, M., Gordon, M. F., Moore, P., Cowhy, J. R., Jagešić, S., & Hanh Huynh, M. (2015). *School closings in Chicago: Understanding families' choices and constraints for new school enrollment.* Chicago, IL: Consortium on Chicago School Research.

Demby, G. (Performer). (2015). What we lose when a neighborhood school goes away. *On Code Switch Race and Identity, Remixed.* Washington, DC: National Public Radio.

Dowdall, E., & Eichel, L. (2011). *Closing public schools in Philadelphia: Lessons from six urban districts*. Philadelphia, PA: The Pew Charitable Trust, Philadelphia Research Initiative.

Engberg, J., Gill, B., Zamarro, G., & Zimmer, R. (2012). Closing schools in a shrinking district: Do student outcomes depend on which schools are closed? *Journal of Urban Economics, 71*, 189–203.

Fine, M. (2012). Disrupting peace/provoking conflict: Stories of school closings and struggles for educational justice. *Peace and Conflict: Journal of Peace Psychology*, 144–146.

Green, T. L. (2017). "We felt they took the heart out of the community": Examining a community-based response to urban school closure. *Education Policy Analysis Archives, 25*(21). http://dx.doi.org/10.14507/epaa.25.2549

Han, C., Raymond, M. E., Woodworth, J. L., Negassi, Y., Richardson, W. P., & Snow, W. (2017). *Lights off: Practice and impact of closing low-performing schools (Volume I)*. Stanford, CA: Stanford University, Center for Research on Education Outcomes.

Hurdle, J. (2013, January 28). Education department to hear school closure complaints. *The New York Times*. Retrieved from https://www.nytimes.com/2013/01/29/education/education-department-to-hear-school-closing-complaints.html

Kamenetz, A. (2014, September 2). *The end of neighborhood schools*. Retrieved from NPR ED website: https://apps.npr.org/the-end-of-neighborhood-schools/

Kelleher, J. B., & Wisniewski, M. (2013, March 21). Chicago announces mass closing of elementary schools. *Chicago Tribune*. Retrieved from https://www.chicago-tribune.com/news/ct-xpm-2013-03-21-sns-rt-us-usa-education-chicagobre92k-1ci-20130321-story.html

Lipman, P. (2013). Economic crisis, accountability, and the state's coercive assault on public education in the USA. *Journal of Education Policy , 28*(5), 557–573.

Nathanson, L., Corcoran, S., & Baker-Smith, C. (2013). *High school choice in New York City: A report on the school choices and placements of low-achieving students*. New York, NY: New York University, Research Alliance for New York City Schools; New York University, Institute for Education and Social Policy.

NCES. (2016). *Table 216.95, digest of education statistics, 2015 (NCES 2016-014)*. Washington, DC: National Center for Education Statistics, U.S. Department of Education.

Snyder, T. D., de Brey, C., & Dillow, S. A. (2016). *Digest of Education Statistics 2015 (NCES 2016-014)*. Washington, DC: National Center for Education Statistics, Institute of Education Sciences, U.S. Department of Education.

Sunderman, G. L., & Payne, A. (2009). *Does closing schools cause educational harm? A review of the research*. Bethesda, MD: Mid-Atlantic Equity Center.

The Working Group of Experts on People of African Descent. (2016). *Report of the working group of experts on people of african descent—visit to United States of America, 19–29 January 2016*. Geneva, Switzerland: United Nations Human Rights, Office of the High Commissioner for Human Rights.

SECTION I

PATTERNS AND PROCESSES

CHAPTER 2

SCHOOL CLOSURE IN STRAINED CITIES

Implications for Racial Equity in U.S. Education

Ebony M. Duncan-Shippy
Washington University–St. Louis

Urban school districts are subject to the well-documented challenges of concentrated poverty, racial segregation, uneven economic development, community disinvestment, collective trauma, limited political capital, and countless other social ills (Anyon, 2005; Condron & Roscigno, 2003; Dixson, Royal, & Henry, 2014; Hinze-Pifer & Sartain, 2018; Howard, 2008; Orfield, Ee, Frankenberg, & Siegel-Hawley, 2016). As a result, many city schools operate in contexts of pervasive resource strain, which delimit the educational and occupational prospects of youth. In recent years, pronounced social strain in urban communities has resulted in more public school closures. Between 1999 and 2013, for example, government agencies across the United States closed approximately 24,000 public schools, uprooting on average 255,000 students each year (National Center for Education

Shuttered Schools, pages 9–56
Copyright © 2019 by Information Age Publishing

Statistics [NCES], 2013). Although shuttering schools is not exclusive to urban school districts, rates of closure nearly doubled in large central cities since the late 1990s (NCES, 2013b). From 2000 to 2010, approximately 30% of school districts in large and mid-size U.S. cities closed public schools, with an average of 11 school closures per district (Engberg, Gill, Zamarro, & Zimmer, 2012, p. 189).

Public school closures in urban areas is significant for a number of reasons. First, while closed schools are often those with low test scores (de la Torre, et al., 2015; Han et al., 2017b; Sunderman & Payne, 2009), a complex array of factors from beyond the school walls appear to drive contemporary closure patterns. Growing economic inequality (Duncan & Murnane, 2014; Noguera & Pierce, 2016), dwindling public school enrollments and municipal budgets (Arsen, DeLuca, Ni, & Bates, 2016; Penn, 2014), faltering tax bases (Galligan & Annunziato, 2017; Owens, 2018), segregation (Orfield & Frankenberg, 2014; Owens, Reardon, & Jencks, 2016; Penn, 2014), and a host of other factors exacerbate inequality in urban school communities where closures are increasingly common. In addition, broader contextual changes like the 2008 global recession only further constrained access to public resources and services, thus deepening inequities in these areas (Yeakey & Shepard, 2012).

Second, school closure is associated with color- and class-blind educational policies that hurt students and communities (Noguera & Pierce, 2016; Wells, 2014). Research to date indicates that school closure certainly affects learning, but such research rarely considers the relationship of closures to factors beyond school walls. For instance, school closure practice raises equity concerns, especially for young people living and learning in economically depressed and socially marginalized communities. Indeed, the decision to shutter schools often occurs to the detriment of African American youth. Third, school closure raises equity concerns because it not only dislocates students with limited educational opportunities, but there is little evidence that these decisions improve education. Closures displace a quarter of a million students per year (NCES, 2016) with scant evidence that they improve student outcomes (Burdick-Will, Keels, & Schuble, 2013; de la Torre & Gwynne, 2009; de la Torre et al., 2015; Han et al., 2017a; Nathanson, Corcoran, & Baker-Smith, 2013; Sunderman & Payne, 2009). Although officials and policymakers often prescribe and justify closures as education reform, there is little evidence that they benefit students, their families, or their broader communities.

Reports indicate that school closures are increasing in Chicago, Philadelphia, New York, and other major U.S. cities, and many former industrial centers in the Rust Belt (Green, 2017; PACER, 2013; Yatsko, 2012). Furthermore, research indicates that urban school closures are often concentrated in the most racially and economically deprived communities within these districts (Deeds & Pattillo, 2015; Lee & Lubienski, 2017).

Although case studies of urban districts suggest that closures occur in local communities marked by significant economic and social strain, there is limited attention to national patterns in school closure contexts. While case study research provides rich insights into the political and social contexts of the closure of a sole school or closures in a single district, it is important to account for broader patterns. Case studies conclude that school closure is an urban problem, but fail to compare school closure patterns in urban districts with those of other localities. Research comparing the conditions of closure in school communities across the United States can identify factors driving closure practice—and the extent to which those factors concentrate closures in urban contexts.

Inequality in school communities, the racial contexts of concentrated poverty, and colorblind policies facilitating mass closure confirm the continued significance of social contexts in understanding the efficacy of purported education reform. This chapter argues that social processes form the institution of education such that school closure originates in the ecological and institutional contexts of a school. It maintains that recent school closures are the result of a confluence of contextual factors that have detrimental effects on the educational opportunities of marginalized youth in contexts marked by strained resources and institutional relationships. Therefore, consistent with early case study research, this chapter considers school–community relationships when accounting for closure patterns. However, this work contributes to education research by using national data to compare school closure patterns across locale types to capture the extent to which variation in school–community relationships explains closure patterns.

School–community relationships are especially complex; both community resources and problems traverse school boundaries. The social, political, and economic disparities that pervade education are rooted in the indelible intersection of race and poverty in education policy and practice. Thus, educational challenges not only arise from the immediate school context, but also from societal problems like poverty, institutional racism, and resource strain. Given the social and demographic composition of cities, these social problems shape education in urban districts to a greater degree than those in other locales. Rampant social problems rapidly expend community resources in distressed urban schools and districts. Because resource strain also operates in a racialized manner, it is important to consider the far-reaching effects of race and poverty when accounting for the rise in contemporary school closures in U.S. cities. School closure is especially harmful for African American students, who experience it at higher rates than their peers, in part because mechanisms of inequality consign them to economically distressed communities (Burdick-Will et al., 2013; Carlson & Lavertu, 2015; Nathanson et al., 2013). This chapter emphasizes the implications of closing predominantly African American schools for educational equity in urban districts.

Drawing from national data sources, this chapter examines the racial and social significance of closures as education reform and its intersections with longstanding disparities in school communities. Research questions are as follows: (a) To what extent are common measures of ecological and institutional contexts associated with school closure patterns?; (b) Do closure patterns in urban districts and schools differ from those in suburban, town, or rural areas?; and (c) What implications do these patterns have for racial equity in education? Subsequent sections describe the theories that frame the interpretation of school closure patterns. In contextualizing school closures, this chapter incorporates sociological perspectives of inequality to explain how school–community relationships influence contemporary public school closures. The first section discusses the organization of school resources and communities, and traces the shift from ecological to institutional definitions of community in sociology. It is followed by a theoretical discussion of how and why community problems become school problems. An overview of the racialized dimensions of this process and its significance for educational equity is presented, before demonstrating how theoretical perspectives on race and social institutions advance our understanding of the social significance of school closures in U.S. cities.

Original analysis in this chapter identifies key social correlates of closure as a way to describe patterns at the national level, and to identify points of intervention that may disrupt the reproduction of social inequality in education. Findings imply that the disproportionate effects of closure on African American students is due to the persistent ways in which racial and economic inequalities stratify and strain local school–community relationships. This chapter demonstrates that school closure is associated with population change and enrollment decline, schools' racial and socioeconomic composition, educational spending, and the growing charter school sector. These factors appear to be even more influential in explaining closure patterns for urban schools and districts. The conclusion emphasizes ways that school closures across the United States exacerbate inequities in social opportunity and mobility for Black youth.

SCHOOL CLOSURE IN CONTEXT: THE SIGNIFICANCE OF ECOLOGICAL AND INSTITUTIONAL DIMENSIONS IN SCHOOL–COMMUNITY RELATIONSHIPS

A careful conceptualization of school community is necessary for adequately contextualizing the racial complications of school closures. For the purposes of this chapter, school community refers to the geographic, demographic, institutional, and organizational dimensions that comprise the social context of a school. This definition integrates institutional and ecological perspectives in the social sciences in ways that incorporate the immediate geographic and social contexts of the school as well as the set of organizations that are connected to it through various social processes (e.g., regulation, cooperation, competition—see Arum, 2000). Ecological perspectives in education indicate that schools are essential organizations in community life because they influence social interaction and individual development. Institutional perspectives emphasize the organization and administration of educational resources, the operation of schools, educational policy implementation, and the effects of these factors on teaching and learning contexts.

Previous research has asserted that school closures are concentrated in urban districts, without corresponding analyses of other contexts. This chapter compares school–community relationships in urban, suburban, town, and rural districts to account for closure patterns. Such comparisons are necessary because the ecological and institutional contexts of schools and districts differ considerably by urbanicity. For example, schools and districts in urban areas tend to be larger and enroll more students than those in other locales. Urban districts are also more racially and economically diverse than those in other areas (NCES, 2013a; 2018). In contrast, rural districts often have fewer schools and students. Unlike many urban and rural schools, suburban schools rarely operate in high poverty contexts. Although poverty is becoming a suburban problem (Allard, 2017; Kneebone & Berube, 2014), suburban districts are typically more affluent and generate more revenue for funding education than other types (Erikson, 2016; Lewis-McCoy, 2016). With respect to variation in institutional contexts, state and federal policies are often limited to certain districts. For example, many states restrict where charter schools can operate, often limiting them to major cities where the need for education reform is perceived as more immediate and apparent. Additionally, state agencies may have a weaker presence in suburban and rural districts, which tend to be more isolated and geographically dispersed than urban ones. Comparing school closures in these different types of districts can reveal whether and how the contextual factors associated with closures influence patterns across different types of districts.

School–Community Relationships: From Ecological to Institutional Perspectives

Traditional Ecological Perspectives

Until the 1960s, dominant sociological conceptualizations of school communities have emphasized the local ecological contexts of formal education. This has reflected the influence of localism in education governance, as the development of mass education in the United States began as a deeply local process in the 18th century. Although this localism produced marked differences among the colonies with respect to educational practice, schools primarily served wealthy, White, Protestant males and focused on meeting aristocratic and religious ends during the colonial period (Spring, 2011). Nevertheless, democratic localism became a significant force in the development of mass education after the American Revolution and well into the subsequent centuries (Arum, 2000; Spring, 2011).

The development of mass education in the United States coincided with industrialization and urbanization in the 19th century. Shifts in attitudes and ideologies in the post-Revolution period set the stage for the Common School movement (Arum, 2000; Labaree, 1997; Spring, 2011). This movement undermined local control, but could not prevent localism from remaining an influential and controversial force in education policy throughout the 20th and 21st centuries (Arum, 2000; Hochschild & Scovronick, 2003). By the early 20th century, the United States was the world's leading industrial nation with a growing public education system. More than half (51%) of 5- to 19-year-olds were enrolled in public school in 1900; that number rose to 75% by 1940 (Snyder, 1993).

As cities grew to accommodate increasing labor demands and workers' families, sociologists became more interested in urban social organization. Robert Park became a renowned sociology professor at the University of Chicago for his contributions to the study of urban life, human ecology, and race. In the early 20th century, he helped establish the "Chicago School" approach to understanding social life and interactions in cities—developing the human ecology perspective within the discipline (Gross, 2004). He viewed the city as a product of human interaction, with a complexity that could be captured only through analysis of its physical organization, economic order, and culture (Park, 1915). Park maintained that sociologists should interrogate the forces that shape the city and its residents. His work examined how these forces played out in neighborhoods and the myriad ways in which human interaction maintained neighborhood boundaries and influenced institutions. The Chicago School approach to understanding the influence of local communities on individual behaviors and collective urban social life has remained influential in the discipline (e.g., see Drake & Clayton (1945/1993; Pattillo, 2007; Wilson, 2001).

The popular neighborhood effects perspective derived from the Chicago School approach. Neighborhood effects studies have emphasized the relationship between the demographic characteristics of urban communities and the social integration and opportunities of its residents (e.g., refer to Wilson, 2001). Consistent with the Chicago School tradition, neighborhood effects research asserted that local contexts influence human behavior and interactions, as well as the operation of institutions within cities.

While this perspective has also influenced conceptions of school–community relationships in education research, prominent sociologists of education abandoned it in the 1960s. The discipline returned to its theoretical roots, as competing mainstream approaches described schools as either reflections of societal needs (functionalist interpretations) or problems (conflict interpretations). Both popular perspectives intimated that local community contexts mattered little for understanding school conditions and educational outcomes. This shift away from ecological sociology in education research continued well into the late 20th century, when a new conception of school–community relationships emerged.

By the 1980s, sociologists of education became interested in understanding whether organizational characteristics informed teaching and learning in schools (Bidwell, 2001; Gamoran, Secada, & Marrett, 2000; Hallinan, 2001). This shift reflected the development of institutional theory in the social sciences. Institutional theories of schools have been concerned with how social forces structure schools and how organizations affect school characteristics and operation (Bidwell, 2001; Meyer, Scott, & Strang, 1987). As evident by topics like governance and classroom organization (Hallinan, 2001), institutional theorists have emphasized how organizational factors influence variation in educational access and outcomes as well as the academic and social behaviors of students (Bidwell, 2001; Hallinan, 2001). Historically, institutional theorists studied schools in two key ways: (a) through analyses of teachers' workplaces (Bidwell 2001), and (b) through investigations of the influence of social capital (see Arum 2000 for a review). Studies of faculty workplaces included interests in teachers' work, the social organization of schools, and how these contexts affect student learning (Gamoran, Secada, & Marrett, 2000). They also explained the extent to which students are provided (or denied) the opportunity to learn (Barr & Dreeben, 1983).

New Perspectives on School Communities

More recent institutional perspectives (i.e., neo-institutional theory) have continued to emphasize the relationship between education and society. Neo-institutional studies of education have examined how state practices influence the administrative processes, organizational behaviors, and political legitimacy of schools and associated agencies (Arum 2000; Bidwell 2001; Gamoran et al. 2000). Consistent with institutional theory, this perspective has emphasized the organizational environment of mass education, arguing that focusing on a school's ecological context misses how policies and organizational practices also shape educational contexts (Arum, 2000; Scott, 1994). Furthermore, it has conceptualized school communities such that they do not simply reflect residents in immediate neighborhoods, but in larger institutional environments, wherein laws, regulations, governing agencies, state authorities, and other organizations influence the allocation of educational resources and delivery of services. To this end, organizations (e.g., state regulatory bodies, teachers unions, professional schools, universities, other school sectors, etc.) that are connected to a school through regulation, cooperation, or competition comprise its "organizational fields" (Arum 2000; Scott 1994). This new articulation of institutional theory has identified organizational fields as central to a school's institutional community.

From a neo-institutional perspective, school closures have reorganized institutional communities—as students, parents, staff, and resources are shifted across uncertain educational contexts. Closures have forced families and staff to scramble (sometimes mid-year) for transfers to other schools and local businesses to adjust to resultant changes in the commercial rhythms of neighborhoods and communities. Closure has affected other schools in the organizational field, as it has reassigned students and resources to other schools that then must manage the disruptive adjustment of accommodating dislocated students. Additionally, reassigning students from closed schools has altered relationships among families, government agencies, schools, and staff. In short, closures have removed students from institutional communities as well as ecological ones—with the former representing a more significant disruption considering that public school assignment is increasingly decoupled from residence.

A neo-institutional perspective suggests that the institutional community of a school provides access to social resources and opportunities, and represents the domain where power dynamics play out and where social (in) equity is constituted or challenged. Under this framework, the causes and significance of school closures derive from both social and political determinants. A neo-institutionalist, for example, might attribute the growing number of closures to governance and economic changes such as municipal and state retrenchment following the 2008 global recession, or neoliberal policies and practices undermining the traditional public school sector. While institutional perspectives provide a partial explanation of how closures stem from broader forces like economic conditions and policy initiatives, an emphasis on institutions can easily become colorblind when they are decontextualized.

School closures have racially disparate impacts. When institutional theorists have acknowledged racial disparities, they have often treated race as secondary to organizational practices and relationships (Bonilla-Silva, 1997; Omi & Winant, 2008). However, to represent reform, school closure must fundamentally disrupt patterns of racial inequality operating in school communities. Racial inequality in the ecological and institutional contexts of schools has influenced the efficacy of education reform—especially in urban communities. Whereas institutional theorists have shied away from the explanatory power of human ecology in favor of an emphasis on school organizational fields, minimizing the ecological context misses the devastating effects of school closures in racially and economically marginalized communities.

The Reproduction of Racial Inequality in School Communities

Race matters for both the ecological and institutional dimensions of school communities. School closure research requires frameworks that conceptually bridge ecological and institutional considerations while treating race as a fundamental axis of social inequality. As a theoretical framework, racialization has offered a way to situate school closure in social contexts, and to explicate how ecological and institutional factors relate to racial inequalities in education. Racialization perspectives have accounted for the continued significance of race in collective life, as well as the ecological, ideological, interpersonal, and psychological mechanisms that facilitate or hinder access to social resources and shape experiences in social institutions. For the purposes of this chapter, racialization refers to the dynamic process that extends racial meaning and significance to social institutions, space, practices, intergroup relationships, identities, and social resources (Bonilla-Silva, 1997; Feagin, 2006; Holt, 1995; Miles & Small, 1999; Omi & Winant, 1994; Small, 1994). In racially hierarchical societies like the United States, racialization has operated as a form of social reproduction—that is, it systematically and unequally distributes social status as well as material and immaterial resources (e.g., money, credentials, employment, wealth, power, and prestige, etc.) within or among social groups. In other words, it has been conceptualized as the process by which the social advantage and disadvantage of one generation is conferred to the next—which has reflected cycles of inequality that have been difficult to disrupt.

From a racialization perspective, institutions have reproduced racial inequality such that institutional access, experiences, and processes have racially specific patterns (Omi & Winant, 2008). These patterns have comprised racialized contexts, in which pervasive racial inequalities in social institutions like education (Ladson-Billings, 2018; Orfield & Frankenberg, 2014), housing (Small, 1994), the economy (Shapiro & Oliver, 1995), and the legal system (Alexander, 2010) comprise everyday life. As a result, race has influenced the composition of social networks and other forms of social capital (Hampton & Duncan, 2011; McPherson, Smith-Lovin, & Cook, 2001), physical well-being (Brown, 2018), and mental health (Brown, Donato, Laske, & Duncan, 2013; Turner & Avison, 2003).

Closures are just one of the many ways that public education is racialized. Ecological and institutional factors like school and neighborhood demographics, racial differences in the material resources of parents, schools, and local and state educational agencies (e.g., district); racial patterns of student achievement and outcomes; and racially coded curricula and policies have all imbued public education with racial significance. Racial disparities in access (e.g., school assignment mechanisms and school choice policies), experiences (e.g., tracking in school and disciplinary experiences), and outcomes (e.g., high school graduation) have exposed the inherent racialization of schooling—no matter how colorblind it may seem (Miles & Small, 1999; Omi & Winant, 1994).

Summary and Research Questions

Understanding education as a primary social institution (Baker, 2014) makes the consequences of school closure extend beyond disrupting student learning.[1] While teaching and learning are fundamental aims of schools, these educational organizations provide more than knowledge. Schools sort students into social statuses, distribute material and immaterial resources (e.g., capital, prestige, and school access), foster psychological and physical safety, and facilitate familiarity through routines. Furthermore, this chapter has argued that schooling and education policy are subject to the macro-economic, political, and social forces that shape society. As a result, school closure originates in the ecological and institutional contexts of education. To this end, three research questions guide analysis in this chapter:

1. To what extent are common measures of ecological and institutional contexts associated with school closure patterns?
2. Do closure patterns in urban districts and schools differ from those in suburban, town, or rural areas?
3. What implications do these patterns have for racial equity in education?

DATA AND METHODS

To examine trends in school closure, this analysis drew federal data from the NCES Common Core of Data (CCD). The NCES compiles the CCD from demographic, administrative, fiscal, and geographic data for the universe of public schools and districts in the United States and its territories. Education officials respond to annual surveys about schools and districts that provide free elementary and secondary education (Chen, Sable,

Mitchell, & Liu, 2011). The analytic sample for this chapter was comprised of 14,919 school districts and 104,307 unique public schools operating for at least a year between 2000 and 2013. Additional analysis examined closure patterns for 3,753 charter schools; but, charter schools and all-charter districts were otherwise excluded. The sample also excluded districts or schools without location or closure information, those that were in U.S. territories, and those operated by the Department of Defense.[2] This analysis included 14 years of school and district data and combined 70 data files: 11 district dropout files (2000–2010), 14 district universe files (2000–2013), 14 district finance files (1999–2012), and 31 school universe files (1999–2013).[3] School and district data were linked and datasets were combined across years using unique school and district identifiers provided by NCES.

The CCD provided information on the closure status of schools as well as their location and demographic composition. These data also provided information about district finance and student enrollment and completion. These variables were selected as common indicators of the academic and social contexts of schools and districts. Measures at the district level were included in the analysis to provide information about the contexts—especially institutional—outside of the schools themselves. Analyzed in conjunction with compositional data at the school-level, this chapter identified key correlates of closure in schools and districts. Ecological correlates included measures of school and district urbanicity and enrollment. The number of schools was disaggregated by closure status at the district-level. Measures of school racial and economic composition were also included.[4] Institutional variables were limited to district expenditures and revenue, dropout rates, and payments to charter schools. Charter status was also included as an institutional correlate of closure at the school-level. Because they were collected annually, each independent variable was time varying (i.e., they changed from year-to-year). The most recent information was used when conducting analyses across years. When comparing annual averages or proportions, analyses used data from that year (or most recently available in case of missing data or closure).

School closure status was complicated in two ways. First, a school's closure status varied from year to year. In this analysis, a closed school was one that closed and remained closed during the study period. If a school closed and later reopened (either as a public or charter), then it was assigned open status. Second, coverage error was a particular concern with respect to school closure status, as reports of new schools or closed schools might have contributed to overcoverage (i.e., a school or agency was counted more than once) or undercoverage (i.e., a school or agency was omitted). The CCD compiles annual survey responses from school and district officials. In the case of school closure, the individuals responsible for submitting surveys may have left the school or failed to respond before it closed. Amid the tremendous administrative effort that closing a school requires, completing a federal survey might be of low priority—especially considering that there is very little incentive to do so if a school will not be operational in the subsequent year. In addition, a school may have closed before it received the annual survey request from the federal Department of Education. As such, NCES survey analysts at the Department of Education do not guarantee the accuracy of state agency reports regarding the addition or deletion of schools. However, they conduct extensive reviews of these reports each year to preserve the longitudinal consistency of the data (Glander, 2015). Since it is likely that closures are underreported, this analysis offers conservative estimates of the prevalence of school closure.

Analysis in this chapter described school closure patterns at the district and school levels. Using statistical significance tests, it compared means and proportions of key institutional and ecological variables by district closure practice (i.e., whether or not a district closed schools between 2000 and 2013) and school closure status (i.e., whether or not the school closed and remained closed between 2000 and 2013). It also compared these patterns across school and district urbanicity, and emphasized racial variation in the composition of displaced students and closed schools. For interval variables, two-sample independent t-tests were used to compare means. Otherwise, these analyses used two-sample tests of proportions. Null hypotheses—that is, no difference in means or proportions—were rejected at the $p < 0.05$ level.

FINDINGS: CONTEMPORARY SCHOOL CLOSURES IN UNEQUAL SCHOOL CONTEXTS: INSTITUTIONAL AND ECOLOGICAL DIMENSIONS

This descriptive analysis examined the correlation of closure with ecological factors such as enrollment decline in urban districts, as well as institutional factors like corresponding changes in tax revenue for public education and competition for students from the growing charter school sector. Analyses considered correlates of district closure practice—that is, whether a school district closed at least one public school during the 14-year study period. District-level analyses examined the prevalence of closures, where they occurred, changes in school funding, and finally academic measures.

Trends in District School Closure Practice

Prevalence of Closure Practice

This chapter traced school closure trends in a national sample of approximately 15,000 U.S. school districts ($n = 14,919$). Public schools closed in 18% of U.S. school districts ($n = 2,684$) between 2000 and 2013

(Figure 2.1).[5] District closure practice varied during the 14-year study, as the share of districts closing schools declined steadily from 18.1% in 2000 to 15.3% in 2013 (Figure 2.2). Districts typically closed no more than two schools during the study period. Close to 70% of districts closed a single public school, while an additional 19% closed two schools (Table 2.1). Fewer than 100 districts closed five or more schools (Table 2.1)—which placed these districts in the 95th percentile for school closures. All of the districts

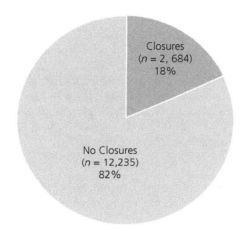

Figure 2.1   U.S. school districts by closure practice, 2000–2013.

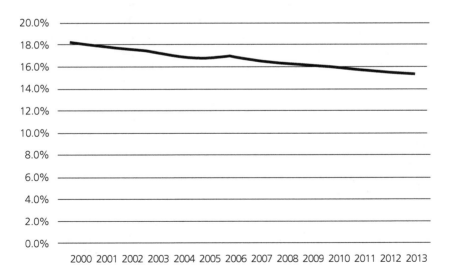

Figure 2.2   U.S. districts with closed K–12 public schools by year, 2000–2013.

TABLE 2.1 Number of Closed U.S. Public Schools per District 2000–2013			
Schools (n)	Districts (n)	%	Cum. %
1	1,836	68.4	68.4
2	509	19.0	87.4
3	161	6.0	93.4
4	80	3.0	96.4
5+	98	3.7	100.0
	2,684	100.0	

Note: Counts exclude charter schools and all charter districts.

in the 95th percentile for closures were urban districts. New York City Public Schools closed the most schools ($n = 204$), followed by the City of Chicago ($n = 59$) and the New York State Office of Mental Health ($n = 30$). Ogden City District (Ogden, UT) and the Milwaukee School District (Milwaukee, WI) completed the top five districts (Table 2.2).

District Urbanicity

District closure practice varied considerably by urbanicity. More than half (52.9%) of all districts in the sample were located in rural areas; in contrast, 6% of districts were in cities.[6] School closures occurred the most often in city districts. Although there were fewer districts in urban areas relative to suburban and rural ones, a significantly higher share of city districts closed schools each year (Table 2.3).[7] While 23% of districts in cities closed at least one public school during the study period, significantly lower shares of suburban and rural districts implemented closures (16 and 17%, respectively). The share of districts closing schools declined for all locale types across the 14-year study period (Figure 2.3). City districts consistently displayed the highest share of closures; suburban and rural districts closed schools the least often. Rates between cities and towns were statistically indistinguishable.[8]

District Size

Depopulation has devastated school communities. Shrinking urban populations result from broader societal shifts like suburbanization, deindustrialization, and globalization (Beauregard, 2013; Cunningham-Sabot, Audirac, Fol, & Martinez-Fernandez, 2014; Wiechmann & Pallagst, 2012). Population loss has demographic and institutional consequences for communities and schools. It has been associated with urban decline, which, in the worst cases, results in neighborhood abandonment and widespread commercial and industrial building vacancies (Cunningham-Sabot et al., 2014). Population decline and building vacancies have weakened economies

TABLE 2.2 U.S. Districts With the Most School Closures, 2000–2013				
Rank	District Name	City	State	Total Closures
1	New York City Public Schools	Brooklyn	NY	204
2	City of Chicago 299	Chicago	IL	59
3	New York State Office Mental Health	Albany	NY	30
4	Ogden City District	Ogden	UT	18
5	Milwaukee School District	Milwaukee	WI	16
6	Boston	Boston	MA	15
7	Charlotte-Mecklenburg Schools	Charlotte	NC	15
8	Detroit City School District	Detroit	MI	14
9	Albany City School District	Albany	MI	12
10	Grand Rapids Public Schools	Grand Rapids	MI	12
11	Columbus City School District	Columbus	OH	11
12	Turlock Joint Elementary	Turlock	CA	11
13	Warren City	Warren	OH	11
14	Minneapolis	Minneapolis	MN	10
15	Pontiac City School District	Pontiac	MI	9
16	Pittsburgh	Pittsburgh	PA	8
17	Syracuse City	Syracuse	NY	8
18	York City	York	PA	8
19	Oklahoma City	Oklahoma City	OK	7
20	Beaumont ISD	Beaumont	TX	6
21	Duluth	Duluth	MN	6
22	Hickman Mills C-1	Kansas City	MO	6
23	Holland City School District	Holland	MI	6
24	Seattle	Seattle	WA	6
25	Toledo City School District	Toledo	OH	6
26	Alton Community Unitary School District 11	Alton	IL	5
27	Auburn School Department	Auburn	ME	5
28	East Baton Rouge Parish School Board	Baton Rouge	LA	5
29	Greeley 6	Greeley	CO	5
30	Maricopa County Regional District	Phoenix	AZ	5
31	North Carolina Schools for the Deaf/Blind	Canton	NC	5
32	Pocatello School District	Pocatello	ID	5
33	San Diego County Office of Education	San Diego	CA	5
34	Troy City School District	Troy	SD	5

Note: Counts exclude charter schools and all charter districts.

TABLE 2.3 Means and Standard Deviations of Total Schools by District Closure Status and Year, 2000–2013

Year	Closures			No Closures			Total Districts
	n	M	SD	n	M	SD	N
2000	2,604	7.0	26.9	11,786	5.4	9.9***	14,390
2001	2,616	7.0	26.1	11,814	5.5	10.1***	14,430
2002	2,597	7.2	30.9	11,862	5.5	10.3***	14,459
2003	2,575	7.1	27.4	11,911	5.5	10.3***	14,486
2004	2,541	7.2	27.3	11,931	5.6	10.6***	14,472
2005	2,475	6.8	13.6	11,888	5.8	10.9***	14,363
2006	2,412	7.0	13.5	11,921	5.8	11.0***	14,333
2007	2,322	7.4	14.0	11,813	5.9	11.2***	14,135
2008	2,283	7.4	13.9	11,846	5.9	11.2***	14,129
2009	2,254	7.3	14.0	11,853	5.9	11.1***	14,107
2010	2,219	7.2	13.8	11,812	5.9	11.1***	14,031
2011	2,184	7.1	13.8	11,826	5.9	11.1***	14,010
2012	2,151	7.0	13.2	11,832	5.9	11.0***	13,983
2013	2,119	7.0	13.2	11,808	5.9	10.8***	13,927

* $p < 0.05$, ** $p < 0.01$, *** $p < 0.001$

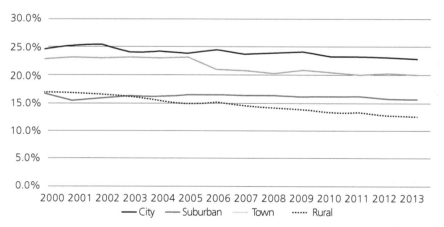

Figure 2.3 U.S. districts with closed K–12 public schools by urbanicity and year, 2000–2013.

(Wiechmann & Pallagst, 2012), as state and local governments not only lose property tax revenue from vacant commercial and residential buildings, but also sales and income tax revenues due to a lack of commerce and employment in blighted areas. Further, local infrastructure maintenance has comprised greater shares of municipal budgets, thus creating additional economic and social strain. With respect to schools specifically, depopulation has led to enrollment decline and the related issue of building underutilization—that is, when public school buildings operate below capacity. Education researchers have noted that underutilization is a common justification for closures (Engberg, Gill, Zamarro, & Zimmer, 2012; Sunderman & Payne, 2009). Indeed, when enrollment falls short of expectations, district officials have emphasized the costs of using school building space inefficiently to justify school closure decisions (PACER, 2013).[9]

In this national sample, districts with closures were larger than those without—they generally had more schools and enrolled more students. Districts with closed schools had an average of 7.1 schools, compared to 6.3 in those without closures (Table 2.4). Districts with closures had between seven and eight schools on average for the study period (Figure 2.4). Statistical tests indicated that districts without closures had significantly fewer—between

TABLE 2.4 Means and Standard Deviations of Total Schools by District Closure Practice, 2000–2013			
	n	*M*	*SD*
Closures	2,710	7.1	18.4
No Closures	12,209	6.4	16.4***
	14,919	5.8	

* $p < 0.05$, ** $p < 0.01$, *** $p < 0.001$

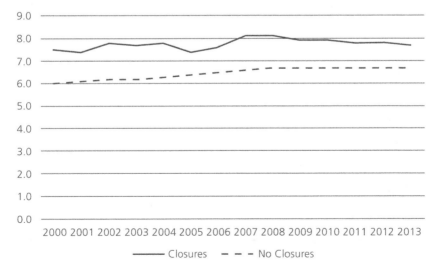

Figure 2.4 Average total schools by district closure practice and year, 2000–2013.

six and seven schools. District size also varied by urbanicity, as significant differences emerged between districts with and without closures for all locale types except cities. Among districts with closures, those in cities had the highest average schools (27.9)—more than double the total schools in suburban districts with closures, five times that of towns, and eight times that of rural areas (Figure 2.5). However, city districts with and without closures were similar in size.

Although closure practice was often associated with declining enrollments, the average number of students grew in districts with and without closures between 2000 and 2013 (Figure 2.6). However, districts with closures had more students on average than those without them for each year.[10] The size of city districts, along with differences by closure practice in town and rural districts, likely drive these national patterns. City districts with and without closures enrolled more students on average than suburban, town, and rural districts (see Table 2.5). Although average enrollment declined in urban districts with closures over time, it was statistically indistinguishable from that of districts without closures (see Table 2.5, Figures 2.7a and 2.7b).[11] Similarly, suburban districts with and without closures were similar in size, with no observable changes over time. Enrollment was also larger in town and rural districts with closures.

District Finance

Globalization led to drastic shifts in the 1970s and 1980s that collapsed local work processes and changed the economic base, spatial organization, and the social structure of cities across the world (Sassen, 2001). This global

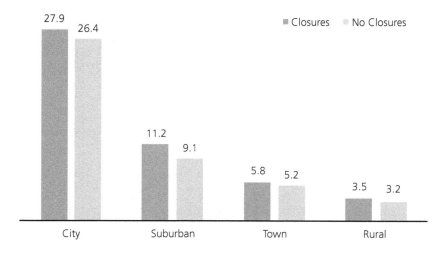

Figure 2.5 Average total schools by district closure practice and urbanicity, 2000–2013.

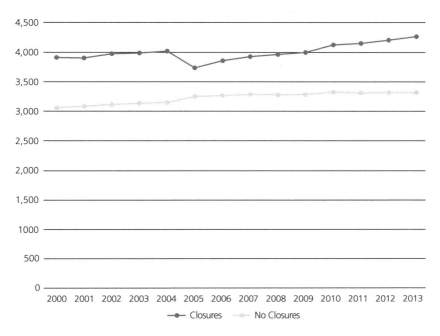

Figure 2.6 Average total students by district closure practice and year, 2000–2013.

TABLE 2.5 Average Enrollment District Level, by Urbanicity and Closure Practice, 2000–2014						
Closures				**No Closures**		
	n	*m*	*SD*		*n*	*m*	*SD*
City (ref.)	206	13,160	32,457	City (ref.)	673	11,609	17,203[b]
Suburban	570	4,225	7,464[b]	Suburban	3,092	5,039	9,712[b]
Town	551	2,341	2,406[b]	Town	1,897	2,002	2,044[ab]
Rural	1,360	1,070	2,565[b]	Rural	6,524	1,042	2,107[b]

[a] Statistical significance tests assess differences between district practice within locale
[b] Statistical significance tests assess differences between locale within district practice, city is reference.

integration also shaped the 2008 recession—which severely disrupt local economies, often compounding the effects of uneven development and social inequality. These broader changes were particularly devastating for schools in communities with high unemployment and unstable tax bases, where resource strain has been associated with rampant class and race inequities. Because public school funding is distributed on a per-pupil basis, depopulation and corresponding declines in enrollment have pervasive

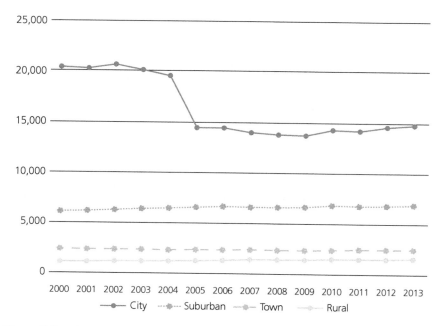

Figure 2.7a Average student enrollment in districts with closures by urbanicity, 2000–2013.

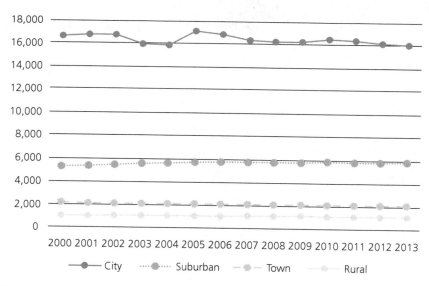

Figure 2.7b Average student enrollment in districts without closures by urbanicity 2000–2013.

effects on local public education systems. Lower enrollment has strained local educational budgets; fewer students means decreased funding, and underutilization translates into a larger share of a budget's allocation to the fixed cost of maintaining district facilities.

Oftentimes, budget concerns have superseded equity concerns, and district officials have justified school closures as a way to address deficits and other economic challenges (Billger & Beck, 2012; Jack & Sludden, 2013). For example, in 2011, Detroit's mayor argued that closing a third of the city's public schools would reduce the school district's operating costs by $75 million (Wasko & Mrozowski, 2011). In this analysis, district finance measures captured the political and economic contexts of schools during the study period. Expenditures increased for all districts between 2000 and 2013—but the rate of increase was higher before 2009—suggesting that the global recession slowed education spending (Figure 2.8). Expenditures were significantly higher in districts with closures for all years under observation. In 2000, for instance, average spending in public school districts with closures was $32.4 million, and grew to $58.4 million by 2013. Average expenditures in districts without closures grew by half as much over the period, from $25.3 million in 2000 to $39.9 million in 2013. Regardless of closure status, average expenditures were highest in city districts (Figure 2.9). Statistically, closure status matters for expenditures in rural districts only, where districts with closures had higher mean expenditures than those without them. Patterns in rural districts were consistent with national patterns.

School funding in districts with and without closure also varied by revenue source: more federal, state, and local revenue went to districts with closures (Figure 2.10). For the entire sample, local taxes accounted for

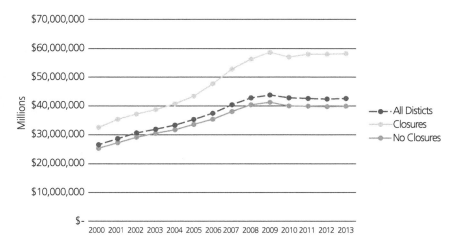

Figure 2.8 Average total district expenditures by closure status, 2000–2013.

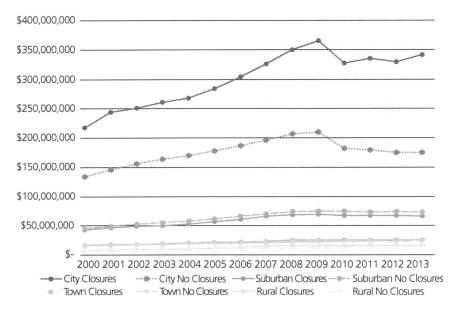

Figure 2.9 Average total district expenditures by urbanicity and closure status, 2000–2013.

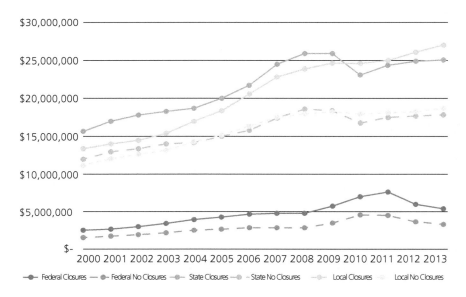

Figure 2.10 Average district revenue by funding source, 2000–2013.

approximately half of school revenue on average, while state sources provided 40% and federal the remaining 10%. Consistent with spending patterns, revenue from all three sources increased between 2000 and 2013. However, state revenue in districts with and without closures declined slightly between 2009 and 2010, and federal revenue declined in both district types between 2011 and 2013. These patterns indicated that education costs were higher in districts with closures.

Dropout Rates

The emergence of school accountability policies has been a key mechanism driving the recent upsurge in public school closures (Deeds & Pattillo, 2015; Engberg et al., 2012; Lipman & Haines, 2007; Sunderman & Payne, 2009). Accountability policies have shifted the institutional contexts of education, as they have redefined school–community relationships. Those advocating for school closures have viewed these policy decisions as a way to hold education agencies accountable. Prior to political shifts, academics and activists alike attributed public school closure to deteriorating facilities, low enrollments, and financial challenges. At the federal level, the passing of the controversial No Child Left Behind Act (NCLB) of 2001 tied school closure decisions to academic performance indicators in an effort to hold schools more accountable for student achievement. Under the Bush Administration, NCLB required states to test students (Grades 3–8, 10–12) in reading and mathematics each year and publicly report test results (U.S. Department of Education, 2003). Schools that failed to meet proficiency standards were subject to school improvement interventions, including school choice options, tutoring services, school restructuring, and closure. Closure and restructuring policies continued under the Obama Administration—and were included in both the Race to the Top competition and the Every Student Succeeds Act (ESSA; U.S. Department of Education, 2016, 2017).

This analysis examined high school dropout rates as indicators of district academic contexts. Comparisons of rates in districts with and without closures demonstrated that those with closures have worse academic outcomes than those without. On average, districts with closures had higher dropout rates than those without them (Table 2.6). Again, district-level patterns varied by urbanicity. Regardless of closure status, mean dropout rates were highest in cities (Figure 2.11). In 2000, the dropout rate in urban districts with closures was nearly three times the average for the overall sample—and more than double that of urban districts without closures. Dropout rates were higher in suburban and town districts with closures as well. In contrast, dropout rates were identical in rural districts with and without closures. By 2009, mean dropout rates were lower in all district types. In 2009, closure practice mattered for rates in suburban districts only—where

TABLE 2.6 Average High School Dropout Rate District Level, by Closure Practice, Select Years						
	Closed			Opened		
Year	n	M	SD	n	M	SD
2000	2,054	3.6	10.4	9,434	2.6	4.9***
2009	2,120	2.6	5.7	11,241	2.2	5.3***

$^{*}\, p < 0.05,\, ^{**}\, p < 0.01,\, ^{***}\, p < 0.001$
Note: Statistical significance tests compare within year differences in closure practice.

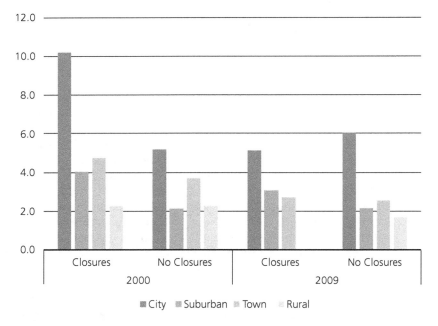

Figure 2.11 Average high school dropout rate district level, by closure practice and urbanicity, select years.

those with closures had higher rates than those without. Rates in city, town, and rural districts were statistically similar across closure practice. These patterns suggest that the academic correlates of school closure were stronger and more consistent in the early 2000s than in recent years.

Charter Payments

District spending on charter schools is another measure of school accountability as charters have become more prevalent in the institutional contexts of public education. In many urban districts, charter school enrollment grew as traditional public school enrollment shrunk. Because these schools are publicly funded, and because they operate as schools of choice, districts must include payments to charters in local budgets, as tax funding must accompany students who practice school choice. As such, analysts and activists have ascribed public school enrollment decline and closure to the outsized growth of the charter school sector. In addition, parent dissatisfaction with public schools and public school failure have been associated with charter school growth. Thus, examining district spending on charter schools in this analysis not only captures the considerable growth in this sector, but also provides insight into local academic contexts.

Average charter school expenditures increased in all districts, from $10,005 in 2000 to $211,860 by 2013 (Figure 2.12), reflecting the rapid growth of this sector in the early 21st century. While charter school spending was similar in the first 2 years of the study period, it surged in districts with closures thereafter. In 2002, districts with closure spent an average of $64,000—double that of districts without charters. By 2013, closure districts were spending more than $714,000 on charter schools—about six times of districts without closures. City districts likely drove the upsurge in charter spending, although it grew in all locale types. Charter spending in city districts with closures grew the fastest, exceeding one million in 2003—4 years before those without closures (Figure 2.13). By 2013, city districts with closures spent $7.5 million of expenditures on charter schools compared to $1.26 million in districts with none. This precipitous growth in urban charter spending was consistent with the overrepresentation of charter schools in cities.[12]

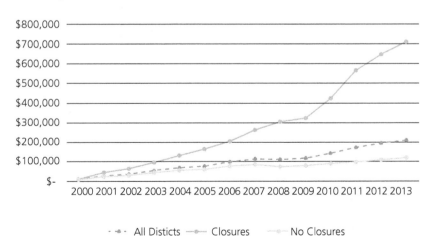

Figure 2.12 Average district expenditures on charters, 2000–2013.

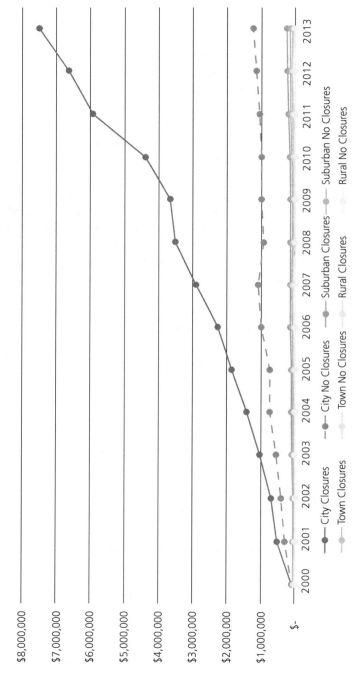

Figure 2.13 Average district expenditures on charters by urbanicity and closure status, 2000–2013.

Characteristics of Closed Schools

The preceding analyses indicated that the ecological and institutional contexts of districts differed considerably by closure practice. Urban districts in particular often had distinct patterns relative to those in other areas. School-level analyses of the ecological and institutional correlates of closure compared schools that closed with those that remained open. In particular, these analyses examined the racial and socioeconomic characteristics of public schools to understand the extent to which differed by closure status. In addition, analyses examined enrollment differences by school closure status, as well as the significance of charter school status for closure patterns. Interpreting school-level patterns in conjunction with those at the district level demonstrated that the closure of individual schools is generally consistent with district level patterns. These findings also indicated that districts often closed schools serving disadvantaged students.

Prevalence of School Closure

School-level analyses include 104,307 unique public schools. Overall, one in six schools ($n = 16,650$) closed between 2000 and 2013 (see Table 2.7).[13] There were approximately 90,000 schools operating annually, and an average of 2,225 (or 2.5%) closed across the nation each year (Figure 2.14). On average, the share of closed schools peaked at 3.5% in 2003, but remained close to the average thereafter. By 2011, the number of closed schools dropped to early 2000 levels. While the total number of schools in the sample grew by only 4% between 2000 and 2013, the number of closed schools grew by 31%.

School Urbanicity

Closure patterns also varied by urbanicity. Suburban areas had the most schools ($n = 31,958$), and towns had the least ($n = 14,743$). While city schools comprised 26% of the entire sample, 31% of schools that closed were in cities—a significantly higher proportion than the 25% of schools that remained open (Table 2.8). Similarly, rural schools were slightly overrepresented among those that closed. In contrast, suburban and town schools, which comprised 31% and 14% of the sample respectively, were underrepresented among schools that closed. Generally, city schools closed

TABLE 2.7 U.S. Public Schools by Closure Status, 2000–2013		
	n	%
Closed	16,650	16.0
Operational	87,657	84.0
Total	104,307	100.0

Note: Counts exclude charter schools and all charter districts.

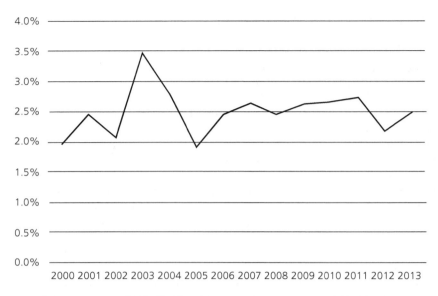

Figure 2.14   Percent of U.S. K–12 public schools that closed, 2000–2013.

TABLE 2.8   Percent Distribution of Schools by Closure Status and Urbanicity, 2000–2013

	All Schools		Closed Schools		Open Schools	
	n	%	*n*	%	*n*	%
City (Ref.)	26,816	25.7%	5,178	31.1%[a]	21,638	24.7%
Suburb/urban	31,958	30.6%	3,736	22.4%[ab]	28,222	32.2%[b]
Town	14,743	14.1%	2,492	15.0%[b]	12,251	14.0%[b]
Rural	30,790	29.5%	5,244	31.5%[a]	25,546	29.1%[b]

[a] Statistical significance tests assess differences between closure status within locale
[b] Statistical significance tests assess differences between locale within closure status, city is reference.

at the highest rates for nearly every year, and the share that closed ranged from 2.3% in 2000 to 4.4% in 2003 and 2013. Closures of city, suburban, and town schools peaked in 2003, a year after NCLB went into effect and a year before this peak occurred in rural schools.

Student Enrollment

Public school closures occurring between 2000 and 2013 displaced an average of 240 students from each school.[14] Average public student enrollment declined from 2000–2013 in both closed and operational schools (Figure 2.16). However, mean enrollment in closed schools was consistently

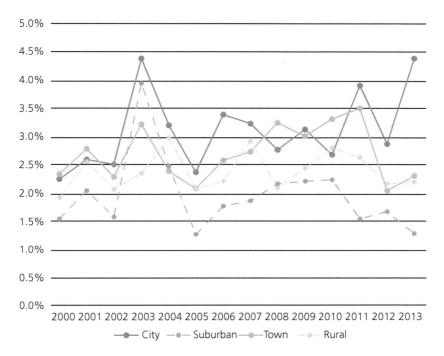

Figure 2.15 Percent closed K–12 public schools by urbanicity and year, 2000–2013.

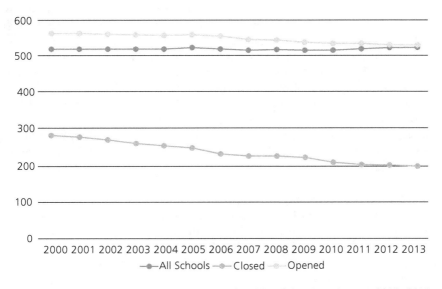

Figure 2.16 Average student enrollment school-level, by closed status 2000–2013.

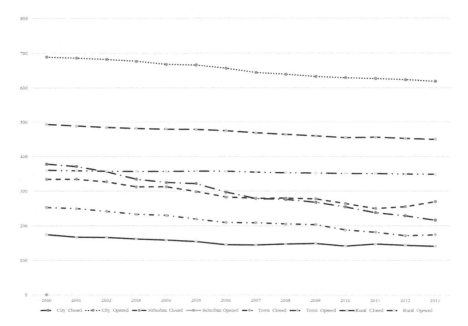

Figure 2.17 Average student enrollment school-level, by urbanicity and closed status 2000–2013.

about half of that in open schools. Additionally, the rate of decline in average enrollment was three times higher in closed schools relative to operational ones. In operational schools, average enrollment in 2000 dropped by 6% by 2013; in schools that eventually closed, however, the average enrollment dropped by nearly 20% between 2000 and 2013. Average enrollment declined for schools in all four locales (Figure 2.17). However, closed schools had lower average enrollments than open ones for all years and locales. Average enrollment was highest in open suburban schools (mean = 653) followed by open town schools (mean = 471). Among schools that closed, the highest mean enrollment was for those in cities (mean = 296), followed by those in suburban areas (mean = 291), towns (mean = 212), and rural areas (mean = 153).

School Racial Composition

Previous case studies have indicated that school closures disproportionately affected African American students (Brummet, 2014; de la Torre, et al., 2015). White students comprised 60% of the student population in all schools (Figure 2.18). At 17.4 %, Latinx students were the second largest racial group, followed by African American students at 16.3%. Consistent with prior studies, African American students were the only group overrepresented in closed

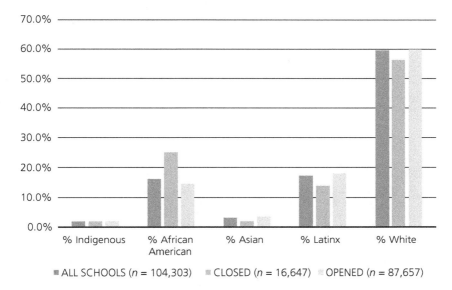

Figure 2.18   Percent distribution of student racial groups in K–12 U.S. public schools by closure status, 2000–2013.

schools—one in four students displaced by closures were African American (Figure 2.18). In contrast, Asian, Latinx, and White students were underrepresented in closed schools. Furthermore, while White students constituted a smaller share of students in closed schools over time, African Americans comprised a greater share; for example, in 2000, closed public schools were on average 61% White and 24% African American (Figure 2.19). By 2013, closed schools were 48% White and 28% African American. The average share of Latinx students in closed schools also increased over time, while the proportions of students who were indigenous or Asian remained the same.

Racial disproportionality was even more pronounced when these patterns were disaggregated by school urbanicity. While African American students disproportionately attended city schools, they were grossly overrepresented among those that closed. At 48.4%, African American students represented the largest racial group in closed city schools (Figure 2.20). In contrast, they were the third largest group in city schools that remained open (27.1%)—after White (35%) and Latinx (29.2%) students. Asian students were overrepresented in open city schools relative to their percentage of the total population, and Indigenous students were just as likely to be in open and closed schools. Regardless of closure status, White students represented the largest racial group in all other locale types. Schools in suburban, town, and rural areas had similar shares of White students—regardless of closure status (Figure 2.20). In contrast, enrollment patterns

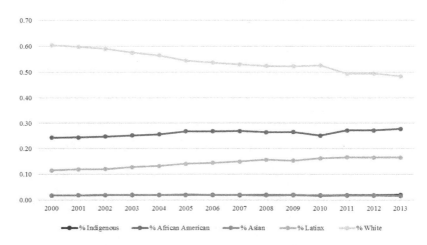

Figure 2.19 Percent distribution of student racial groups in closed schools by year, 2000–2013.

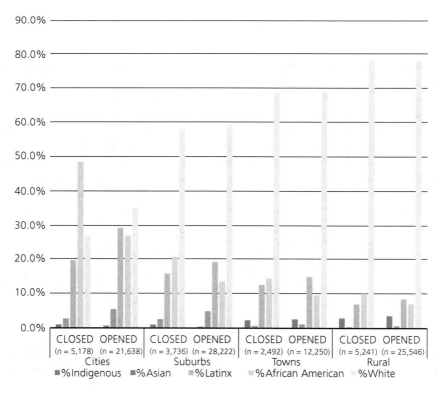

Figure 2.20 Percent distribution of student racial groups by closure status and urbanicity, 2000–2013.

for students of color varied by closure status. Similar to city schools, higher shares of African American students were enrolled in closed suburban, town, and rural schools than in open ones. In contrast, the shares of Latinx, Asian, and Indigenous students were higher in schools that remained open.

In addition to comparing the distribution of racial groups by school closure status, this analysis also used a racial composition index to assess how closure patterns varied by the aggregate racial makeup of a school. Relative to schools that remained open, greater shares of closed schools were predominantly African American or multiracial: 14% of closed schools were African American, compared to only 6% of those that remained open (Figure 2.21). Similarly, only 7.5% of open schools were multiracial, compared to 18.5% of closed ones. Higher shares of schools that served a mix of African American or White students with other groups of color or schools that primarily served students of color (excluding African Americans) remained open. Predominantly White schools and schools with a mix of White and African American students were just as likely to close as they were to remain open. Patterns varied fairly little by urbanicity. City schools were nearly identical to the overall sample, while those in suburban, town, and rural areas were also very similar.[15] Among suburban schools, slightly higher shares of closed schools were predominantly White relative to open ones (28% and 26%, respectively). A higher share of African American-White schools was

Figure 2.21   Percent distribution of schools by closure status and racial composition index.

among those that closed (11% of closed schools and 8% of open schools). Town and rural areas also followed overall patterns, but predominantly White schools were less likely to close in towns, and African American-white were less likely to close in rural areas.[16] In short, school closure was positively correlated with African American student enrollment across locale type.

School Socioeconomic Composition

Poverty in school communities has strained school and family resources. Critics of school closures have worried that these policy decisions disrupted familiar educational and social contexts for disadvantaged students. Opponents have contended that schools subjected to closure were penalized for difficult social conditions inherent in broader contexts. Chief among these concerns have been the effects of poverty on both education and the students who live in contexts marked by pervasive institutional and resource strain. Given the overrepresentation of students of color in economically depressed and socially marginalized communities, closures have raised concerns for educational equity.

Over the course of this study, the number of students receiving free/reduced price lunch—a common indicator of economic disadvantage—increased from 39.5% in 2000 to 52.9% in 2013 (Figure 2.22). Closure patterns

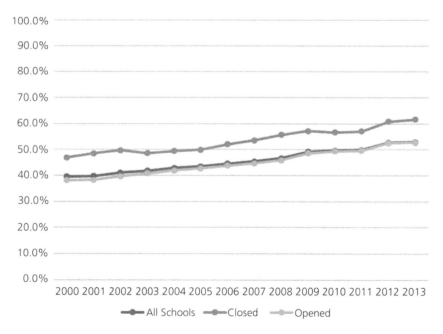

Figure 2.22 Percent of students receiving free/reduced lunch in K–12 U.S. public schools by closure status, 2000–2013.

varied considerably by a school's economic composition. Closed schools had higher proportions of free/reduced-lunch students for every year in the study. Over time, the rate of increase was much higher in schools that closed relative to those that remained open. In 2000, for example, 47% of students in closed schools qualified for free/reduced lunch, compared to 38% of students in open schools. By 2008, 56% of closed school students were eligible for lunch subsidies, compared to 46% of students in schools that remained open. By the final year of the study, 62% of students in schools that eventually closed qualified for free/reduced lunch, compared to 53% of those in schools that did not. Consistent with previously noted geographic patterns, city schools had higher shares of economically disadvantaged students—regardless of closure status. The largest shares of free/reduced lunch students were in city schools that eventually closed, followed by city schools that remained open (Figure 2.23). On average, open suburban schools had the smallest shares of free/reduced-lunch students.

Charter School Status

The final section examined differences in closure rates between the sample of 104,000 public schools and the 3,700 charter schools excluded from preceding analyses. School closures is a component of charter policies. By definition, charter schools are contracted to improve student outcomes,

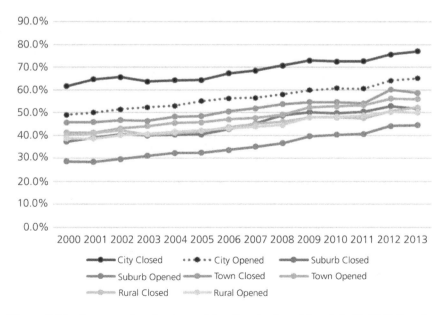

Figure 2.23 Percent of students receiving free/reduced lunch in K–12 U.S. public schools by urbanicity and closure status, 2000–2013.

usually within a three-to-five year period, or be subjected to closure. To this end, charter schools may close at higher rates than traditional public schools. On the other hand, non-charter schools may close at higher rates if charter school competition attracts students from traditional public schools.

As indicated earlier, roughly 16% of the public schools in the sample closed at some point between 2000 and 2013 (Figure 2.24). Charters schools closed at a higher rate—one in four during the study period. Closure rates dropped for both charter and non-charter schools over time (Figure 2.25). However, this decline was much faster and more substantial for charters relative to non-charters. In 2000, 36% of charter schools closed, relative to only 16% of traditional public schools. By 2007, one-in-three charter school closed compared to one-in-eight non-charters. In 2013, approximately 4% of charters closed, compared to only 2% of district schools.

The ecological patterns for charter schools also differed from traditional public schools, so this analysis compared their geographic patterns between the two types. As previously mentioned, charter schools were overrepresented in cities relative to traditional public schools. In this sample, 47% of open charter schools were located in cities, compared to 25% of district-operated public schools. However, district-operated public schools were overrepresented among closed schools in cities, while charter schools were underrepresented. Although nearly 50% of operating charter schools were located in cities, 42% of closed charters were. In contrast, 25% of open public schools were in cities, compared to 31% of closed ones.

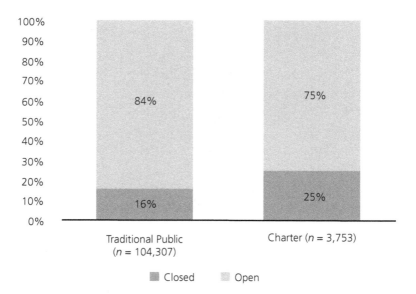

Figure 2.24 Percent distribution of charter and non-charter schools by closure status.

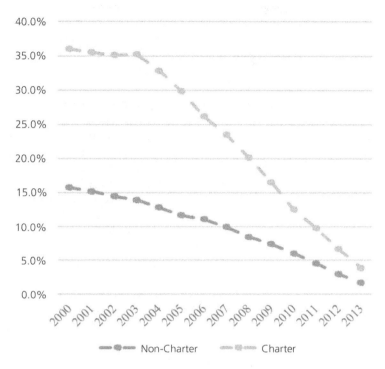

Figure 2.25   Percent of closed charter and non-charter schools, 2000–2013.

DISCUSSION AND CONCLUSION

Findings in this chapter are based on a national sample of 15,000 districts and 107,000 public schools. Analyses reveal that 16% of schools in the sample closed between 2000 and 2013—an average 2.5% of public schools across the nation each year. Public school closures displace an annual average of 240 students from each school. These closures occur in 18% of U.S. school districts. This chapter demonstrates that district closure practice is associated with considerable differences in ecological and institutional contexts. Ecological characteristics like a school's racial and economic composition and population decline contribute to school closures. In addition, institutional changes like charter school growth, academic failure, financial strain, and economic inequality are also associated with public school closure. Schools close more often in cities than in other areas, where closures shutter more buildings and displace more students on average than those in suburban, rural, and town settings combined. Although districts with closures have more students on average than those without them, mean enrollment in closed schools is consistently about half of those that remained open. One in four students affected by closures is African American; in cities, about half of affected students are African American. Furthermore, predominantly Black schools are closed more often. Closed schools also have higher proportions of free/reduced lunch students, and the largest shares of economically disadvantaged students are in city schools that eventually close.

Findings also link school closures to academic failure, increasing public education costs, and growth in the charter school sector. On average, districts with closures have higher dropout rates than those without them. Revenue and expenditure patterns show that education is more expensive in districts with closures than others. Increasing costs in many districts stem from the growing charter school sector. In 2002, districts with closure spent an average of $64,000—double that of districts without charters. A year later, city districts with closures spent in excess of $1 million on charters, and $7.5 million by end of study period (compared to $1.26 million in districts without closures).

School closures are associated with common markers of social disadvantage in school communities, which indicates they may be concentrated in marginalized areas. The ecological and institutional correlates of closure suggest that these decisions likely strain schools and educational resources even further, exacerbating social inequality in school communities. These patterns are even more concerning for youth in cities and for those who unduly bear the burden of economic inequality. Over the course of this study, the number of students receiving free/reduced price lunch increased from 39.5% in 2000 to 52.9% in 2013. Economic disadvantage was even greater in city schools that closed, where the rate for free/reduced lunch students ranged from 62 to 77%. These patterns reflect the reality that economic trends have become even more dismal in recent decades.

The relationship of school closures to social inequality is especially concerning in urban, predominantly African American schools and communities. Whether through mechanisms of social support or social control, the functions of schools as community institutions become more critical in areas *wherein* poverty, political marginality, economic decline, and other forms of inequality distress families, local economies, and social institutions. In such marginalized areas, public policy also plays an exaggerated role in the lives of youth, who are often "deeply enmeshed in the state through the provision of public housing and public schooling and matters of public safety" (Shedd, 2015, p. 5). In other words, youth of color in poor urban neighborhoods are most susceptible to changes in public policy, as shifts in their local institutional communities often directly and detrimentally affect their quality of life.

While this study advances the field through examining national patterns of school closure, researchers may address some limitations in future studies. Findings from this descriptive analysis identify some of the institutional and ecological correlates of closure at both the district- and school-levels. Confounding variables of urbanicity, poverty, and racial composition interact in ways that make it difficult to isolate their main effects. Furthermore, these dimensions of social identity and context are lived simultaneously. Because many of these variables are correlated such that their co-occurrence may account for closure in meaningful ways, future research should include interactive and inferential analyses to address the confounding effects of race, socioeconomic status, and policy. In addition, future education research that does not examine closure directly might consider including it as an indicator of school and district contexts—given that it can operate as proxy for important differences in institutional and ecological contexts.

Those advocating for school closures view these policy decisions as a way to reform education and improve student outcomes (Bulkley, Henig, & Levin, 2010; Han et al., 2017b), but with little evidence that high quality alternatives are available. Reports on school closures have indicated the opposite—many students were assigned to schools with similar or even lower test scores than the ones that were shuttered (de la Torre et al., 2015; Han et al., 2017b). Furthermore, learning is negatively impacted with just the announcement of school closures, as we see a dip in test scores (and grades) once it is announced that a school is slated for closure (Gaertner, Kirshner, & Pozzoboni, 2016). Analyses in this chapter rely on district and school-level data, and do not test these patterns directly. Researchers might consider collecting student-level data to assess how these changes in ecological and institutional contexts affect students, especially those who encounter closures multiple times. Student-level studies not only trace how closure affects displaced students, but can also examine effects on receiving schools. Additionally, research in this area might consider closure effects on teachers, administrators, and other school staff.

Schools, like students, entered and exited the dataset used in this chapter at different times. Just as students might encounter closure more than once, the closure status of schools can also change multiple times. Additional work may examine this subset of schools, as well as use time-sensitive analyses like event history models to understand how these patterns vary by time. Incorporating time-sensitive methods not only account for the effects of changes in a school's closure status over time, but may also pinpoint threshold effects of time-varying measures. In addition, some schools were identified for closure but remained open, while others were closed but eventually reopened. It may be interesting to examine this subset of schools to better understand the implementation of closures, as well as to identify effective interventions for keeping schools open.

Finally, this study was limited in the operationalization of key variables. School community refers to the geographic, demographic, institutional, and organizational dimensions that comprise the social context of a school. This chapter, however, focuses only on limited ecological and institutional variables associated with closure. Future work should include specific geographic and organizational measures. Other geographic analyses might consider how these patterns play out in communities with changing demographic or institutional characteristics—that is, gentrifying or newly developed communities. Future work in the area might also incorporate geographic methods in order to identify exactly where closures are occurring in school districts, thus incorporating an intermediate level of analysis between the district and school. GIS and other methods can identify whether closures are concentrated in certain communities in school districts as well as the characteristics of those communities. Furthermore, embracing these methods offers another way to operationalize school communities. Additional studies might include other ecological and institutional variables in large-scale quantitative analyses, or support community-based research on the experience of closure for students, families, schools, and communities. Findings from this chapter capture some social correlates of communities, but additional research could centralize it in analyses.

In accounting for the implications of school closures in the 21st century, this chapter demonstrates that racially inequitable school closure patterns are evident in cities across the United States. Various macroeconomic, political, and social factors advance this "epidemic" of school closures (Fine, 2012, p. 145) in urban communities. Ecological and institutional mechanisms concentrate closure in strained communities in ways that reproduce educational inequity—harming students who are already living and learning in the margins of collective life. Findings demonstrate that persistent social inequities especially constrain urban schools serving African American students. As a result, public agencies shutter these schools at significantly higher rates than those in other locales and those with other racial profiles. Rather than represent reform, school closures contribute to disparate educational and social experiences of African American youth.

Contemporary closure practice is especially problematic with respect to educational equity for African Americans, because it undermines essential social institutions in racially and economically marginalized communities. As a social institution, education is both a scapegoat for societal ills as well as a purveyor of them—a fundamental tension which accounts for why the causes of closure often originate from beyond school walls. While inequality is widening in school communities, political support for social welfare policies is declining. At the same time, support for privatization and public deregulation is growing in ways that further constrain access to public resources and services—especially in communities where families often rely on such resources. While education reform should be a policy priority—especially in marginalized communities—contemporary policy approaches fall short of making meaningful change. The correlates of closure demonstrate that they routinely occur in districts operating in strained ecological and institutional contexts. Further, schools that close frequently serve racially marginalized and economically disadvantaged students. School accountability policies, however, ignore the strain that social inequities place on school resources. As a result, they unduly punish schools for societal challenges and exacerbate inequality in strained communities. If the goal is to prevent school closure through true reform, then the solution is not shifting students from one high-poverty school to another, but expanding resources in ways that reduce the strain on students, families, and communities.

NOTES

1. Indeed, Baker (2014) argues that given their significance in daily life, schools are primary rather than secondary institutions, and thus play a far greater role in identity construction processes, meaning-making, and perceptions of social status, than conventional sociological perspectives indicate.
2. The national data included the universe of public schools ($n = 129,287$) and public school districts (n=19,943) operating for at least 1 year between 2000 and 2013.
3. District finance files covered fiscal years 2000–2013. From 1999–2006, three separate files comprised annual school universe datasets. Only select years were available for school district dropout rates. Consistent with NCES protocols, this analysis substituted school data from the previous year for schools that closed—which was missing in the year that the school closed.
4. School racial composition was based on a seven-category index of neighborhood racial composition: predominantly White, predominantly Black, predominantly other race, mixed White and other race, mixed Black and White, mixed Black and other race, and multiracial. In predominantly White schools, at least 80% of students were non-Hispanic White, and no other group represented more than 10% of the population. At least 50% of students in predominantly Black schools were non-Hispanic Black and no other racial group represented over 10% of the population. In predominantly Asian or Hispanic schools, at least 50% of the student population were Hispanic or Asian and no more than 10% were non-Hispanic Black. White-Asian and White-Hispanic schools were between 10 and 50% Hispanic or Asian, less than 10% Black, and at least 40% White. Black–White schools were 10 and 50% Black, at least 40% White, and less than 10% Hispanic or Asian. Black-Hispanic and Black-Asian schools were at least 10% Black, at least 10% Hispanic or Asian, and no more than 40% White. Finally, multiracial schools were at least 10% Black, at least 10% Hispanic or Asian, and at least 40% White (Crowder, Pais, & South, 2012, pp. 332–333).

5. This represents the unique count of districts practicing closure between 2000 and 2013 (i.e., a district is counted once if it had school closures at any point during the study period). Annual closure rates capture districts with school closures across multiple years.
6. Results not shown. Analyses available upon request.
7. City districts also tend to be the largest, in terms of the number of schools and students, while rural ones on average are the smallest.
8. Results not shown. Analyses indicates that significant differences also emerge between city and town districts, but only in 2008 (with patterns trending toward significance in subsequent years). Analyses available upon request.
9. Analyses also compared differences in facilities costs at the district-level. Districts with and without closures are statistically similar in the average costs to maintaining school buildings. Analyses available upon request.
10. The pattern holds for the 2005–2006 school year, but the difference between the district types was not statistically significant.
11. This may be due to the considerable variability in student enrollment in city districts. In this sample, city districts have the largest standard deviation and range of student enrollment relative to other district types. This considerable variability translates into overlapping confidence intervals for average enrollment between districts with and without closures.
12. Nearly 60% of charters were located in cities, compared to only 25% of traditional public schools (National Center for Education Statistics, 2013a).
13. The rate of closure is similar at the school and district levels because most districts closed just one school (see Table 2.1).
14. This analysis relies on district- and school-level data. Student-level data are necessary to detect whether a student encounters closure more than once. Due to these data restrictions, it is impossible to calculate the cumulative number of students displaced by school closures using this dataset.
15. Results not shown. Analyses available upon request.
16. Results not shown. Analyses available upon request.

REFERENCES

Allard, S. W. (2017). *Places in need: The changing geography of poverty*. New York, NY: Russell Sage Foundation.

Alexander, M. (2010). *The new Jim Crow: Mass incarceration in the age of colorblindness*. New York, NY: New Press.

Anyon, J. (2005). *Radical possibilities: Public policy, urban education, and a new social movement*. New York, NY: Routledge.

Arsen, D., DeLuca, T., Ni, Y., & Bates, M. (2016). Which districts get into financial trouble and why: Michigan's story. *Journal of Education Finance, 42*(2), 100–1126.

Arum, R. (2000). Schools and communities: Ecological and institutional dimensions. *Annual Review of Sociology, 26*(1), 395–418.

Baker, D. P. (2014). *The schooled society: The educational transformation of global culture*. Stanford, CA: Stanford University Press.

Barr, R., & Dreeben, R. (1983). *How schools work.* Chicago, IL: University of Chicago Press.

Beauregard, R. A. (2013). Shrinking cities in the United States in historical perspective: A research note. In K. Pallagst, T. Wiechmann, & C. Martinez-Fernandez (Eds.), *Shrinking cities: International perspectives and policy implications* (pp. 78–92). New York, NY: Routledge.

Bidwell, C. E. (2001). Analyzing schools as organizations: Long-term permanence and short-term change. *Sociology of Education, 74,* 100–114.

Billger, S. M., & Beck, F. D. (2012). The determinants of high school closures: Lessons from longitudinal data throughout Illinois. *Journal of Education Finance, 38*(2), 83–101.

Bonilla-Silva, E. (1997). Rethinking racism: Toward a structural interpretation. *American Sociological Review, 62*(3), 465–480.

Brown, T. H. (2018). Racial stratification, immigration, and health inequality: A life course-intersectional approach. *Social Forces,* 1507–1540.

Brown, T. N., Donato, K. M., Laske, M. T., & Duncan, E. M. (2013). Mental health status: The importance of race, nativity, ethnicity, and cultural influences. In C. Aneshensel, J. Phelan, & A. Bierman (Eds.), *Handbook of the sociology of mental health* (2nd ed., pp. 255–276). New York, NY: Plenum Press.

Brummet, Q. (2014). The effect of school closings on student achievement. *Journal of Public Economics, 119,* 108–124.

Bulkley, K., Henig, J., & Levin, H. (2010). *Politics, governance, and the new portfolio models for urban school reform: Between public and private.* Cambridge, MA: Harvard Education Press.

Burdick-Will, J., Keels, M., & Schuble, T. (2013). Closing and opening schools: The association between neighborhood characteristics and the location of new educational opportunities in a large urban district. *Journal of Urban Affairs, 35*(1), 59–80.

Carlson, D., & Lavertu, S. (2015). *School closures and student achievement: An analysis of Ohio's urban district and charter schools.* Columbus, OH: Thomas B. Fordham Institute. Retrieved from http://edex.s3-us-west-2.amazonaws.com/publication/pdfs/School%20Closures%20and%20Student%20Achievement%20Report%20website%20final.pdf

Chen, C., Sable, J., Mitchell, L., & Liu, F. (2011). *Documentation to the NCES Common Core of Data Public Elementary/Secondary School Universe Survey: School year 2009–10* (NCES 2011-348). Washington, DC: National Center for Education Statistics, Institute of Education Sciences, US Department of Education. Retrieved from http://nces.ed.gov/ccd/pdf/INsc09101a.pdf

Condron, D., & Roscigno, V. J. (2003). Disparities within: Unequal spending and achievement in an urban school district. *Sociology of Education, 76*(1), 18–36.

Crowder, K., Pais, J., & South, S. J. (2012). Neighborhood diversity, metropolitan constraints, and household migration. *American Sociological Review, 77,* 323–352.

Cunningham-Sabot, E., Audirac, I., Fol, S., & Martinez-Fernandez, C. (2014). Theoretical approaches of "shrinking cities." In K. Pallagst, T. Wiechmann, & C. Martinez-Fernandez (Eds.), *Shrinking cities: International perspectives and policy implications* (pp. 14–30). New York, NY: Routledge.

de la Torre, M., & Gwynne, J. (2009). *When schools close: Effects on displaced students in Chicago public schools.* Chicago, IL: Consortium on Chicago School Research. Retrieved from http://files.eric.ed.gov/fulltext/ED506954.pdf

de la Torre, M., Gordon, M. F., Moore, P., Cowhy, J. R., Jagešić, S., & Hanh Huynh, M. (2015). *School closings in Chicago: Understanding families' choices and constraints for new school enrollment.* Chicago, IL: Consortium on Chicago School Research. Retrieved from https://consortium.uchicago.edu/sites/default/files/publications/School%20Closings%20Report.pdf

Deeds, V., & Pattillo, M. (2015). Organizational "failure" and institutional pluralism: A case study of an urban school closure. *Urban Education, 50*(4), 474–504.

Dixson, A. D., Royal, C., & Henry Jr., K. L. (2014). School reform and school choice. In H. R. Milner IV, & K. Lomotey (Eds.), *Handbook of urban education* (pp. 474–503). New York, NY: Routledge.

Drake, S. C., & Cayton, H. (1993 [1945]). *Black metropolis: A study of negro life in a northern city.* Chicago, IL: University of Chicago.

Duncan, G. J., & Murnane, R. J. (2014, February 11). How public schools can fight back against inequality. *The Atlantic.* Retrieved from https://www.theatlantic.com/education/archive/2014/02/how-public-schools-can-fight-back-against-inequality/283669/

Engberg, J., Gill, B., Zamarro, G., & Zimmer, R. (2012). Closing schools in a shrinking district: Do student outcomes depend on which schools are closed? *Journal of Urban Economics, 71*, 1890–203.

Erikson, A. T. (2016). *Making the unequal metropolis: School desegregation and Its limits.* Chicago, IL: University of Chicago Press.

Feagin, J. (2006). *Systemic racism: A theory of oppression.* New York, NY: Routledge.

Fine, M. (2012). Disrupting peace/provoking conflict: Stories of school closings and struggles for educational justice. *Peace and Conflict: Journal of Peace Psychology*, 144–146.

Gaertner, M. N., Kirshner, B., & Pozzoboni, K. M. (2016). When school closures backfire. In M. A. Gottfried, & G. Q. Conchas (Eds.), *When school policies backfire: How well-intended measures can harm our most vulnerable students* (pp. 85–108). Cambridge, IL: Harvard Education Press.

Galligan, J. J., & Annunziato, A. (2017). Education funding crisis in the suburbs: The impact of the 2007–09 recession recovery policies and the New York state tax levy cap on school district financial planning practices. *Journal for Leadership and Instruction, 16*(1), 9–14.

Gamoran, A., Secada, W. G., & Marrett, C. B. (2000). The organizational context of teaching and learning. In M. T. Hallinan (Ed.), *Handbook of the sociology of education* (pp. 37–63). Boston, MA: Springer.

Glander, M. (2015). *Documentation to the NCES Common Core of Data Local Education Agency Universe Survey: School Year 2013–14 Provisional Version 1a.* Washington, DC: National Center for Education Statistics, Institute of Education Sciences, US Department of Education. Retrieved from https://nces.ed.gov/ccd/pubagency.asp

Green, T. L. (2017). "We felt they took the heart out of the community": Examining a community-based response to urban school closure. *Education Policy Analysis Archives, 25*(21).

Gross, M. (2004). Human geography and ecological sociology: The unfolding of a human ecology, 1890 to 1930—and beyond. *Social Science History, 28*(4), 575–605.

Hallinan, M. T. (2001). Introduction. In M. T. Hallinan (Ed.), *Handbook of the sociology of education* (pp. 1–14). Boston, MA: Springer.

Hampton, L. A., & Duncan, E. M. (2011). Identities and inequalities: An examination of the role of racial identity in the formation of social capital inside a voluntary youth organization. *Social Identities, 17*(4), 477–500.

Han, C., Raymond, M. E., Woodworth, J. L., Negassi, Y., Richardson, W. P., & Snow, W. (2017a). *Lights off: Practice and impact of closing low-performing schools (Volume I).* Stanford University. Stanford, CA: Center for Research on Education Outcomes. Retrieved from http://credo.stanford.edu/pdfs/Closure_FINAL _Volume_I.pdf

Han, C., Raymond, M. E., Woodworth, J. L., Negassi, Y., Richardson, W. P., & Snow, W. (2017b). *Lights off: Practice and impact of closing low-performing schools (Volume II).* Stanford, CA: Stanford University. Retrieved from http://credo.stanford. edu/pdfs/Closure_FINAL_Volume_II.pdf

Hinze-Pifer, R., & Sartain, L. (2018). *The proximal impacts of community violence on student behavior in school.* Pacific Grove, CA: Sociology of Education Association. Retrieved February 17, 2018 from https://appam.confex.com/appam/2017/ webprogram/Paper21347.html

Hochschild, J. L., & Scovronick, N. (2003). *The American dream and the public schools.* New York, NY: Oxford University Press.

Holt, T. C. (1995). Marking: Race, race-making, and the writing of history. *The American Historical Review, 100,* 1–20.

Howard, T. (2008). Who really cares? The disenfranchisement of African American males in preK–12 schools: A critical race theory perspective. *Teachers College Record, 110*(5), 954–985.

Jack, J., & Sludden, J. (2013). School Closings in Philadelphia. *Penn GSE Perspectives on Urban Education,, 10*(1), 1–7.

Kneebone, E., & Berube, A. (2014). *Confronting suburban poverty in America.* Washington, DC: The Brookings Institution.

Labaree, D. F. (1997). Public goods, private goods: The American struggle over educational goals. *American Educational Research Journal, 34*(1), 39–81.

Ladson-Billings, G. (2018). The social funding of race: The role of schooling. *Peabody Journal of Education, 93*(1), 90–105.

Lee, J., & Lubienski, C. (2017). The impact of school closures on equity of access in Chicago. *Education and Urban Society,* 53–80.

Lewis-McCoy, L. (2016). *Inequality in the promised land: Race, resources, and suburban schooling.* Stanford, CA: Stanford University Press.

Lipman, P., & Haines, N. (2007). From accountability to privatization and African American exclusion: Chicago's "Renaissance 2010." *Educational Policy, 21*(3), 471–502.

McPherson, M., Smith-Lovin, L., & Cook, J. M. (2001). Birds of a feather: Homophily in social networks. *Annual Review of Sociology, 27,* 415–444.

Meyer, J., Scott, R., & Strang, D. (1987). Centralization, fragmentation, and school district complexity. *Administrative Science Quarterly,* 186–201.

Miles, R., & Small, S. (1999). Racism and ethnicity. In S. Taylor (Ed.), *Sociology: Issues and debates* (pp. 136–157). Basingstoke, England: Macmillan.

Nathanson, L., Corcoran, S., & Baker-Smith, C. (2013). *High school choice in New York City: A report on the school choices and placements of low-achieving students.* New York, NY: New York University, Research Alliance for New York City Schools; New York University, Institute for Education and Social Policy. Retrieved from https://files.eric.ed.gov/fulltext/ED541824.pdf

National Center for Education Statistics. (2013a). *The status of rural education.* Washington, DC: Author. Retrieved from http://nces.ed.gov/programs/coe/indicator_tla.asp

National Center for Education Statistics. (2013b). NCES Figure 1. Percentage distribution of public elementary and secondary students, schools, and districts, by locale: School year 2010–11. *The Condition of Education.* Washington, DC: Author. Retrieved from https://nces.ed.gov/programs/coe/indicator_tla.asp

National Center for Education Statistics. (2016). Table 216.95. Number and enrollment of public elementary and secondary schools that have closed, by school level, type, and charter status. Common Core of Data (CCD), Public Elementary/Secondary School Universe Survey, 1995–96 through 2013–14. Washington, DC: Author.

National Center for Education Statistics. (2018). Characteristics of Traditional Public Schools and Public Charter Schools, Condition of Education. Washington, DC: Author.

Noguera, P. A., & Pierce, J. C. (2016). The (evasive) language of school reform. *Educational Leadership, 74*–78.

Omi, M., & Winant, H. (1994). *Racial formation in the United States: From the 1960s to the 1990s* (2nd ed.). New York, NY: Routledge.

Omi, M., & Winant, H. (2008). Once more, with feeling: Reflections on racial formation. *PMLA, 123*(5), 1565–1572.

Orfield, G., Ee, J., Frankenberg, E., & Siegel-Hawley, G. (2016). *"Brown" at 62: School segregation by race, poverty and state.* Los Angeles, CA: Civil Rights Project/Proyecto Derechos Civiles, UCLA. Retrieved from https://www.civilrightsproject.ucla.edu/research/k-12-education/integration-and-diversity/brown-at-62-school-segregation-by-race-poverty-and-state/Brown-at-62-final-corrected-2.pdf

Orfield, G., & Frankenberg, E. (2014). Increasingly segregated and unequal schools as courts reverse policy. *Educational Administration Quarterly, 50*(5), 718–734.

Owens, A. (2018). Income segregation between school districts and inequality in students' achievement. *Sociology of Education,, 91*(1), 1–27.

Owens, A., Reardon, S. F., & Jencks, C. (2016). Income segregation between schools and school districts. *American Educational Research Journal, 53*(4), 1159–1197.

PACER. (2013). *School closings policy. Issue brief.* Pennsylvania Clearinghouse for Education Research. Retrieved from https://files.eric.ed.gov/fulltext/ED553148.pdf

Park, R. (1915). The city: Suggestions for the investigation of human behavior in the urban environment. *American Journal of Sociology, 20*(5), 577–612.

Pattillo, M. (2007). *Black on the block: The politics of race and class in the city.* Chicago, IL: University of Chicago Press.

Penn, D. (2014). *Policy brief: School closures and redistricting can reproduce educational inequality.* Davis, CA: Center for Poverty Research. Retrieved from https:// poverty.ucdavis.edu/sites/main/files/file-attachments/cpr_penn_redistricting _brief.pdf

Sassen, S. (2001). *The global city: New York, London, Tokyo.* Princeton, NJ: Princeton University Press.

Scott, W. R. (1994). Institutions and organizations: Toward a theoretical synthesis. In W. R, Scott & J. Meyer (Eds.), *Institutional environments and organizations* (pp. 55–80). Thousand Oaks, CA: SAGE.

Shapiro, T. M., & Oliver, M. (1995). *Black wealth/White wealth: A new perspective on racial inequality* (1st ed.). New York, NY: Routledge.

Shedd, C. (2015). *Unequal city: Race, schools, and perceptions of injustice.* New York, NY: Russell Sage Foundation.

Small, S. (1994). *Racialised barriers: The Black experience in the United States and England.* New York, NY: Routledge.

Snyder, T. D. (1993). *120 years of American education: A statistical portrait.* Washington, DC: U.S. Department of Education, National Center for Education Statistics. Retrieved from https://nces.ed.gov/pubs93/93442.pdf

Spring, J. (2011). *The American school: A global context from the Puritans to the Obama era* (8th ed.). New York, NY: McGraw-Hill.

Sunderman, G. L., & Payne, A. (2009). *Does closing schools cause educational harm? A review of the research.* Mid-Atlantic Equity Center. Retrieved from http://files. eric.ed.gov/fulltext/ED543514.pdf

Turner, R. J., & Avison, W. R. (2003). Status variations in stress exposure: Implications for the interpretation of research on race, socioeconomic status, and gender. *Journal of Health and Social Behavior,* 488–505.

U.S. Department of Education. (2003, August 23). *Fact sheet on the major provisions of the conference report to H.R. 1, the No Child Left Behind Act.* Retrieved from NCLB/Overview: https://www2.ed.gov/nclb/overview/intro/factsheet.html

U.S. Department of Education. (2016). *Transitioning to the Every Student Succeeds Act (ESSA) FAQs.* Washington, DC: U.S. Department of Education, Office of Elementary and Secondary Education.

U.S. Department of Education. (2017, July 3). *Programs.* Retrieved from Race to the Top District (RTT-D). https://ed.gov/programs/racetothetop-district/ index.html

Wasko, S., & Mrozowski, J. (2011, Match 12). *DPS presents Renaissance Plan 2012 to Radically Restructure Academically Failing Schools, Significantly Reduce Operating Costs Under Model to see charter proposals for 41 schools.* Retrieved March 13 2011, from http://detroitk12.org/news/article/2267/

Wells, A. S. (2014). *Seeing past the "colorblind" myth: Why education policymakers should address racial and ethnic inequality and support culturally diverse schools.* Boulder, CO: National Education Policy Center. Retrieved September 9, 2015, from http://nepc.colorado.edu/publication/seeing-past-the-colorblind-myth

Wilson, W. J. (2001). *The truly disadvantaged: The inner-city, the underclass and public policy.* Chicago, IL: University of Chicago Press.

Wiechmann, T., & Pallagst, K. M. (2012). Urban shrinkage in Germany and the USA: A comparison of transformation patterns and local strategies. *International Journal of Urban and Regional Research, 36*(2), 261–280.

Yatsko, S. (2012). *Baltimore and the portfolio school district strategy. Portfolio School Districts Project.* Center on Reinventing Public Education. Retrieved from http://files.eric.ed.gov/fulltext/ED532896.pdf

Yeakey, C. C., & Shepard, D. L. (2012). The downward slope of upward mobility in a global economy. In C. C. Yeakey (Ed.), *Living on the boundaries: Urban marginality in national and international contexts* (pp. 3–22). West Yorkshire, England: Emerald Group.

CHAPTER 3

SCHOOL CLOSINGS...
ATLANTA STYLE

The Convergence of Poverty, Segregation, and Achievement

Tomeka Davis, Deirdre Oakley, and Shanae Stover
Georgia State University

ABSTRACT

For over a decade Atlanta has been the site of unprecedented redevelopment coupled with controversial policy implementations—lauded by some local and national policymakers, but highly criticized by others at both levels. In addition to the systematic demolition of public housing and the restructuring of housing for the poor, Atlanta Public Schools (APS) was also closing schools and merging others. APS's stated intention was to generate improvements by closing, merging, and privatizing schools due to under enrollment and low performance. Many of the school closures and mergers happened in the city's poor and lower-income African American neighborhoods, including some implicated in the widely publicized cheating scandal that recently engulfed APS. Using data from APS, the census, and the U.S. Department of Education, the purpose of this study is to provide a neighborhood-level

Shuttered Schools, pages 57–89

socio-spatial analyses of (a) what schools were closed and/or merged, (b) the socioeconomic and racial characteristics of the schools and their surrounding neighborhoods, (c) whether school performance (test scores) played a role in the closures, and (d) whether poor and non-poor Black neighborhoods were equally likely to experience closures. In other words, we are doing our analyses to inform the broader question of whether these institutional processes where racialized.

Famously known as the "The City too Busy to Hate," Atlanta's well-known moniker originated as an attempt to brand the city as racially heterogeneous yet economically prosperous. In fact, the phrase was coined by Mayor William Hartsfield in 1955 as a way of distinguishing Atlanta from other southern cities like Little Rock and Birmingham that were beleaguered by racial unrest and economic loss that resulted in response to the unrest (Bayor, 2000). Despite the image of prosperity, racial inequality in the city has been ever present, especially among schools. Like many other large cities, residential segregation has overwhelmingly shaped the context of schooling in the city. As a majority Black (about 75% of students in the 2013–2014) and overwhelmingly low income district (about 75% of students were on free and reduced lunch in the 2013–2014 school year),[1] Atlanta Public Schools (APS), like many other urban districts, has experienced White flight over the years that has left an indelible mark on the racial and economic character of the district. Moreover, given the sprawl of the metropolitan Atlanta area, APS is unique compared to other large districts in the south like Charlotte and Raleigh that have countywide districts (which APS is not) and as a result, have been able to implement integration plans that, in the past, helped curtail (though not eliminate) racial and economic isolation (Lassiter, 2013).

While recent school closings in Chicago and Philadelphia have taken on crisis proportions since 2013, closing en masse suddenly and amidst significant protest (Good, 2016; Uetricht, 2013), the nature of school closings in Atlanta have been less dramatic in terms of their immediacy and magnitude. Nevertheless, school closings in Atlanta reflect the usual dynamics of race and affluence. We contend that *school demographic patterns which are tied to neighborhood racial and economic segregation fuel lower school enrollment and performance levels—reasons which the APS district explicitly cite as the primary motives compelling recent school closures.* District enrollment levels never rebounded from decades old demographic shifts that saw Atlanta neighborhoods and schools transition from White to Black and non-poor to poor. What remains is a district predominated by many low-income neighborhoods where poverty is associated with population loss (Kingsley & Pettit, 2002) and in turn, declines in school enrollment, as well as low levels of academic achievement. Although similar demographic changes have transpired in many cities across the country, Atlanta is unique because of the size of its comparatively large Black middle class and attendant reputation as a Black Mecca and also because of the recent test cheating scandal which rocked the district. In addition to investigating the link between school and neighborhood racial/economic segregation and school closures, we also examine whether the problem of school closures extends beyond Atlanta's poor, Black neighborhoods to non-poor Black communities as well. Using data from APS, the National Center for Education Statistics' Common Core of Data, as well as data from the 2000 and 2010 Census, we examine school closings in the APS district and find that schools with declining enrollments and high levels of poverty were most likely to close, while schools with higher reading scores were less likely to close. Moreover, declines in enrollment were linked to neighborhood poverty.

Our literature review proceeds in the following manner. First, we discuss the existing literature on school closures. Next we discuss recent events in the APS district followed by residential segregation patterns in Atlanta. Finally, we present the results from our data analysis along with potential implications.

ECONOMIES OF SCALE: EFFICIENCY AS A RATIONALE FOR CLOSURES

Surprisingly, the existing research on school closings is limited. While high profile school closings in Philadelphia and Chicago over the last few years have prompted activists and scholars to question the motivations behind closures (Good, 2016; Uetricht, 2013), there is very little extant research to draw from. Declining enrollments, poor performance, and more efficient financial management are the most common reasons districts cite for closing schools (Johnson, 2014). The very small extant body of published research on school closures bears this out. Using Illinois high school data, Billger and Beck (2012) found that increasing enrollments decreased the odds of closure. Interestingly, Billger and Beck also found that high schools which received higher proportions of tax revenue were also more likely to close. Johnson (2014) found a distinctive racial and class-based element to school closings in Chicago. His findings showed that between 2005 and 2013, zip codes with less than 34% of Black residents had fewer school closings than zip codes with lower percentages of Black residents. Johnson also found that zip codes with per capita incomes of less than $19,944 experienced more school closings than zip codes with higher per capita incomes. Using data from the Common Core, Chicago Public Schools, and the Census, Burdick-Will, Keels, and Schulbe (2013) found that although schools were most likely to close in disadvantaged Chicago neighborhoods, under-enrollment and underperformance were the key reasons for school closures. Recent research by Lee and Lubienski (2016) indicate that although

Chicago Public School leaders expressed financial efficiency as the motivation behind closing schools, school closings in the district led children from poor, crime heavy neighborhoods to have to travel even further to reach school, resulting in greater exposure to crime.

Evidence from APS indicates that declining enrollments and performance were identified as primary factors in deciding to close schools. For example, language from a March 2012 closing recommendation by the superintendent's office read:

> APS traditional schools serve 47,000 students;[2] yet, we have seats for 60,000 students. Heating, cooling and lighting 13,000 empty seats consumes resources which could be put to better uses [sic] elsewhere. Not only must we reduce our costs, but more importantly, we must make decisions that are in the best educational interest of all students. Data show that the majority of empty seats are in the southern part of our district, while the northern section of the district is experiencing overcrowding. In some areas, enrollment is low because families with school-aged children have moved. In other areas, enrollment is low because of the perception or reality that the school lacks academic rigor and adequate support. Sparsely populated, inadequately supported schools adversely affect the education of children. By addressing under enrollment, as well as overcrowding, we can ensure educational equity across the district... Our proposal is to concentrate our resources by operating a more efficient and effective school district. (APS, 2012, p. 1)

While this passage illustrates an economy of scales mentality on the part of APS, it also illustrates the reality of residential segregation and White flight in the metropolitan Atlanta area. The northern section of the district is White and wealthy, while the southern part of the district is poor and mostly Black. Later in the chapter we go into detail about racialized residential patterns in Atlanta, but some introduction to the geography of the metro area is necessary here. The Atlanta MSA (metropolitan statistical area as defined by the U.S. Census Bureau) is sprawling collection of 28 counties and small "cities" that lie within them. The city of Atlanta is located in Fulton County, situated in the geographic center of the Atlanta MSA. The city lies mostly within the boundaries of Fulton County, but there is a small amount of spillover on the city's eastern border into DeKalb County. The APS district shares these same boundaries. There is a great deal of class and economic heterogeneity in the district as wealthier enclaves located in the northern parts of the city (e.g., Midtown, Buckhead) are composed of housing stock valued in the millions. On the other hand, there are a large number of poor neighborhoods in the southern and western (e.g., Lakewood, West End, Sylvan Hills) parts of this district. Outside the city boundaries, the geography of wealth and disadvantage take on a similar pattern, with wealthier suburbs located to the north of the city (e.g., John's Creek) and poorer suburbs to the south (e.g., College Park). These areas outside the city limits are served by the Fulton County School district and not APS.

The APS recommendation also states the northern and Whiter parts of the district are experiencing growth while the southern, almost exclusively Black parts of the district are dealing with decreasing enrollments. While the observation regarding the "perception or reality" that the district lacks "adequate support" appears to point to potential problems associated with poverty as a challenge to enrollment, this statement also highlights recognition on the part of APS that families residing with the district boundaries believe the district's schools "lack rigor," and in turn, choose not to enroll their children in APS schools. Whether these sentiments about "rigor' are merely coded language referring to the overwhelmingly large Black population of the district is unclear. Regardless, these statements still point to declining enrollment as the precipitating cause of school closures. Other documents from the district regarding school closures include a similar rationale. For example, a frequently asked questions memo regarding the closure of Turner Middle School, which was located between Hamilton Holmes Drive, Martin Luther King Drive, and Interstate I-20 West of downtown and closed in 2010, notes that

> Henry McNeal Turner Middle School has experienced a significant decrease in student enrollment as a result of the aging of the residents in the communities in the school's attendance zone. APS has been monitoring Turner's enrollment over the last several years, hoping that the student enrollment would begin to increase. Unfortunately, that has not happened, and the data do not indicate that there will be any significant growth in the middle-school-aged population in the area in the near future. The official October 2009 enrollment at Turner was 271 students, a drop of 170 students from October 2006, when 441 students were enrolled. Turner has continued to lose students since October 2009, and the current enrollment is approximately 260 students. Any time a middle school's enrollment falls below 300 students, the district takes a serious look at its continued viability. A comprehensive middle school in the Atlanta Public Schools offers connections classes in foreign language, band, choral music, orchestra, art, physical education, technology, etc. Turner Middle School is currently not able to offer all of these programs due to the small number of teachers at the school, which is determined based on student enrollment numbers. (APS, 2010, p. 1)

Here, APS officials acknowledge age related demographic changes to the community surrounding the school that impact enrollment and the problems associated with running a school that is below optimal capacity. Elsewhere in the memo, APS attempts to allay concern that three recent charter school openings (University Academy, KIPP STRIVE, and KIPP WAYS) may have led to Turner's closing. However, the memo notes that only 37 students left Turner to attend one of the newly opened charters.

THE CHEATING SCANDAL

In addition to declining enrollments, the cheating scandal that recently reverberated across the district points to the importance of academic performance as a possible contributor to school closings. In 2008, the *Atlanta Journal Constitution* (AJC) began investigating large increases in end of the year standardized test scores at a number of metro Atlanta area schools, including APS as well as schools in DeKalb County and the Fulton County School District (Vogel & Perry, 2008). Continued investigation by the AJC revealed strange patterns of erasure marks on the tests, which, in combination with the large increases in scores, led the state to step in and appoint investigators to conduct an independent inquiry. These results of the inquiry led to the referral of 185 teachers to the Georgia Professional Standards Commission (the body responsible for the certification and professional conduct of certified teachers in Georgia public schools) and to the indictment and prosecution of 35 teachers, administrators, and executives for racketeering and related felony charges, including the district's superintendent, Beverly Hall (Niesse, 2013).

The scandal has brought nationwide attention to the district, and it has also arguably drawn increased scrutiny to the workings of the district by state policymakers. In March 2015, around the same time teachers and administrators who stood trial were being sentenced for their involvement in the scandal, the governor's office announced plans for legislation to create a statewide Opportunity School District (Bloom, 2016a; Hernandez, 2015).[3] The Opportunity District would involve taking over schools in the state, including APS schools that earned an "F" rating on the Georgia Department of Education's accountability measure, the College and Career Performance Index, for 3 consecutive years. The idea is modeled after the Recovery School District in Louisiana (in which more than 100 New Orleans schools were closed after Hurricane Katrina in an attempt to drastically overhaul the district) and Tennessee's Achievement School district (Georgia Governor's Office, 2015; Hernandez, 2015). In an effort to thwart state takeover and maintain some degree of control, APS superintendent Meria Carstarphen announced that APS was laying out a "turnaround strategy" to preemptively close some of the district's lowest performing schools and use charter school operators and external education management organizations to take over other lower performing schools. In response to strong community opposition, Carstarphen openly stated, "Right now we have a choice. If the state takes a school, they could close it, end of story" (Bloom, 2016b). The new superintendent, who claims to favor neither traditional approaches to school improvement (i.e., in-house reforms that are often opposed to newer approaches to reform like accountability, charter schools, external management operators, etc.) nor market approaches that emphasize school closures and contracting school services out to external operators, has been adamant that the district must find solutions to help improve academic outcomes for the neediest students, regardless of the ideological perspective the solution emanates from.[4]

PATTERNS OF RESIDENTIAL SEGREGATION IN ATLANTA

As we mentioned in the previous section, the geography of poverty and race in Atlanta delineate much of the inequality in APS. Housing and schools are inextricably linked, and the patterns we see in school closings are also tied to the historical patterns of Black housing placement and movement in Atlanta. According to Bayor (1996), Atlanta established its first segregated housing ordinance in 1913. In an effort to contain Black residential growth and to create a buffer zone between White and Black neighborhoods, several similar ordinances followed through the early 1930s. Although racialized zoning ordinances were declared unconstitutional in 1917 by the Supreme Court in *Buchanan v. Warley*, city officials managed to craft subsequent ordinances to maintain racial separation. Blacks were purposefully relegated to the central business district (downtown), near industrial areas, and on the west side of the city while the northern area of the city was classified as White (Bayor, 1996). Highways and roads were also used as barriers to restrict Black residential growth. Land (2009) notes that by 1960 it was "publicly acknowledged that Interstate 20 West was established, in part, as a boundary between White and Black communities" (p. 206). *By 2000, the majority of the Black population in the metropolitan area was contained to an area south of Interstate 20 but within Interstate 285* (Land, 2009), the latter of which is the highway that encircles suburban parts of Cobb, DeKalb, and Fulton counties. Locals often refer to Interstate 285 as "the Perimeter"; it acts as both a physical and psychological barrier dividing the city and less prosperous inner ring suburbs from more prosperous outer ring suburban areas (Kruse, 2013; Land, 2009). These demographic configurations have fluctuated to some degree over the last half-century, owing in part to school desegregation as well as gentrification and urban housing policy. Overall, these changes in housing patterns have shaped the character of residential segregation and in turn school racial and economic composition in APS. Figure 3.1 illustrates racialized residential patterns within the APS boundaries. The darker portions of the map indicate areas where Whites are most concentrated. Clearly, Whites are heavily concentrated in the areas north of Interstate 20, especially between Interstates 75 and 85 and GA–400. While the northern boundaries of 285 are not pictured on the map, this pattern of heavy White concentration continues to the north, extending up through the north Georgia mountains.

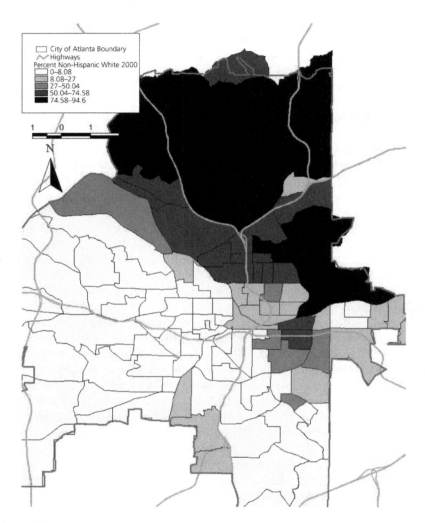

Figure 3.1 Percent White in census tracts within APS boundaries, 2000. *Note:* Interstate 285 is captured running north–south on the west side of the map; Interstate 20 runs east–west; Interstate 75 runs northwest to southeast; Interstate 85 runs northeast to southwest; Interstates 75 and 85 connect in the center of the map; GA-400 branches off north from I-85 in the Northeast section of the map.

After a long history of Jim Crow, neighborhood demographic transformations altered race and class-based patterns of enrollment in APS. These neighborhood transformations were the result of two related factors, both of which ultimately led to White flight away from the city, and in turn, APS. *First, as early as the 1940s, even before Brown v. Board of Education forced schools across the South to desegregate, Blacks had been steadily making their way into once all-White residential areas of the city* (Bayor, 1996; Kruse, 2013). As Blacks moved into these areas, Whites fled. For example, Kirkwood, formerly a working-class White neighborhood located on the eastern edge of the city limits that spills over into DeKalb County, saw Blacks move into the area in the mid-1950s. By 1964, Kruse (2013) argues that observers classified the community as "all-Negro." The same is true of westside Atlanta neighborhoods like Mozley Park, (home to the closed Stanton Elementary), Adamsville, and Cascade Heights.

Second, new policies governing school racial composition and student assignment dictated by Brown v. Board of Education led to White flight out of neighborhoods where school racial composition was changing. Atlanta, like many other Southern school districts after Brown v. Board of Education, desegregated schools by allowing Black students to submit transfer requests for enrollment at White schools. Because few Blacks made such requests, Black enrollment into White schools was relegated to a mere trickle. Instead, Kruse (2013) notes that the APS district regularly changed the "racial designation" of public schools as White neighborhoods transitioned from White to Black. Thus, swift racial transitions in neighborhoods led the Atlanta School Board to "transfer" entire schools from White to Black. For example, changes in neighborhood racial composition in the westside neighborhoods of Collier Heights and Grove Park led the Atlanta School Board to "transfer" James Mayson Elementary to Black students in 1961 amid a great deal of protest by Whites. Similarly, in Kirkwood in 1961, the neighborhood's Whitefoord Avenue Elementary was also "transferred" to Black students (Kruse, 2013). These demographic changes have laid the foundation for current school demographics. Today, many, though not all, of the schools that were "transferred" remain majority Black. Whitefoord Elementary, which is still currently open in the Kirkwood area of Atlanta, remains overwhelming Black. According to the Common Core of Data, in the 2013–2014 school year, 261 of Whitefoord's 266 students were Black. Consequently, although Kirkwood has gentrified and is now home to low-income Black families as well as middle and upper class Black and White families, the composition of the school has not changed from what is was in the 1960s after the entire school was "transferred" from White to Black.

Ultimately then, school desegregation and the movement to open up opportunities for Blacks only shifted pockets of segregation around the city and metropolitan area, as areas that were formerly White transitioned to Black or resulted in the creation of altogether new White suburban enclaves outside of the city like those outside the 285 Perimeter (Kruse, 2013). According to Kruse (2013) although Blacks and Whites had been evenly represented in the APS district during the 1964–1965 school year, by 1970 White enrollment was cut in half from its peak in 1963. Kruse notes that by 1969, the Black–White ratio in APS was two to one; by 1971 it was three to one. By the 1990s, the percentage of White students in APS was only 6% (Henry & Hankins, 2012). *Moreover, the flight of Whites out of the district not only led to a decline in the number of Whites, but a decline in overall enrollment. Total enrollment in the district has declined from a high of 102,797 in 1960* (Research Atlanta, 1971) *to 51,145 students in the 2014–2015 school year.* APS' new superintendent, Maria Carstarphen, noted that the current infrastructure of APS was designed to accommodate the 100,000 plus students of previous decades and with current enrollment figures at half that level, the district must find ways to operate in a more efficient manner.[5]

By the 1970s in some neighborhoods, and by the 1980s and 1990s in others, there were organized pockets of White middle- and upper-class resistance to White flight from the city and the city's schools, both among Whites living in established, well-to-do areas like Buckhead as well as among White gentrifiers moving to intown neighborhoods that Blacks had dominated after the White flight of earlier eras (McConnell, 1980; Henry & Hankins, 2012). By the late 1990s, their activism corresponded with increases in the district's White enrollment in areas like Buckhead, Morningside, and Virginia Highland (Henry & Hankins, 2012). In fact, data from the National Center of Education Statistics indicate the percentage of White students attending APS schools doubled between the 2000–2001 school year and the 2013–2014 school year —increasing from 6.75% to 14.33%, even as overall enrollment declined from 58, 230 students in the 2000–2001 school year to 50,131 in the 2013–2014 school year. The growth in White enrollment in the district is exemplified by the 2013 construction of a new state of the art high school, North Atlanta High School, in Buckhead, the wealthiest in-town Atlanta community. At a cost of $147 million, the school, built on a $55 million dollar 56 acre plot of land, is equipped with an 1800 seat gymnasium, a performing arts complex, a broadcast and video center, and a shooting and rifle range. The $147 million dollar price tag is almost four times the median cost to construct a high school in the region, which as of 2013, was only $38 million dollars (Severson, 2013).

In addition to North Atlanta, whose White enrollment is at 30% of the school's total enrollment, there are only 12 other schools in APS with White enrollments over 25%, out of almost 100 schools in the district. All of these schools are located north of the Interstate 20, the previously mentioned interstate highway that separates Whiter, more prosperous areas of the city from poorer, mostly Black areas (see Figure 3.1). These include Grady High School, which is located in the Midtown area, and the elementary and middle schools that feed into Grady and North Atlanta, including Morningside Elementary, Mary Lin Elementary, the newly constructed Springdale Park Elementary, and Inman Middle School, located in the Virginia Highland neighborhood, as well as Neighborhood Charter's middle and elementary school sites located in the Grant Park and Ormewood Park neighborhoods to the east (see Figures 3.2 and 3.3). The elementary schools in the northern part of the district have relatively large percentages of White students, ranging between 54% and 79%. In this part of the district, the percentages of White students decline across different grade levels. For example both Grady and North Atlanta's White enrollments are right at 30%, owing most likely to parental decisions to send their children to private school during these years. This may in part reflect wealthier parents' perceptions of the

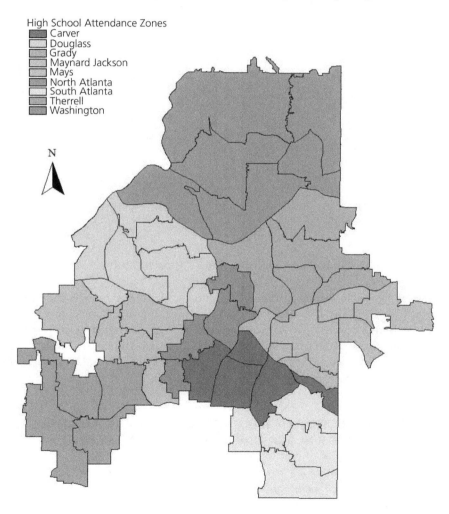

Figure 3.2 APS High School Attendance Zones (with elementary zone boundaries); 2015–2016 boundaries.

Figure 3.3 APS Elementary Attendance Zones; 2015–2016 boundaries.

"lack of rigor" described in the earlier cited superintendent recommendations (see p. 62) or the status derived from graduating from elite private high schools and the drive among the wealthy to gain admission to elite colleges. Buckhead and North Atlanta are home to a number of elite private schools like Pace Academy, Westminster, Atlanta International School, and The Lovett School.

THE INTERSECTION OF RACE AND CLASS: HAVE ATLANTA'S NON-POOR BLACK COMMUNITIES BEEN SPARED?

Little research in sociology has addressed the important intersections of race and class. Early Black sociologists recognized the peculiar position of the Black middle class (Du Bois, 1903; Frazier, 1957), and a debate has raged among contemporary scholars regarding whether class alleviates any of the disadvantages associated with race (Feagin & Sikes, 1994; Lacy, 2007; Pattillo-McCoy,

1999; Hughes & Thomas, 1998; Wilson, 1978). This debate is particularly relevant in the context of Atlanta because as Keating (2010) notes:

> Not only are there a white north Atlanta and a mostly black south Atlanta, there are also two black Atlantas. Not only is there growing economic inequality between blacks and whites, there is also growing economic inequality between middle-class blacks and poor blacks. Like many major American cities, Atlanta has a growing black underclass, and the city suffers from all the problems that attend persistent urban poverty. The standard of living of a sizable minority of the city's blacks is much closer to that of middle-class whites than to that of poor blacks. Race and class fracture the Atlanta community along several different fault lines. (pp. 8–11)

Research on the relative well-being of the Black middle class has produced mixed results, with some research asserting that although middle-class African Americans may struggle with some of the indignities and inequities associated with race, they are not nearly as disadvantaged as poor Blacks (Lacy, 2007; Wilson, 1978). On the other hand, a contrasting body of research suggests that middle-class African Americans remain "vulnerable" to the negative impacts of race (Landry, 1987; Pattillo-McCoy, 2005; Pattillo-McCoy, 1999). With regard to schooling, the small amount of existing research suggests that middle-class African Americans are exposed to similar kinds of negative schooling conditions (higher rates of school poverty, lower aggregate math and reading test scores, more teacher turnover, etc.) as lower income Blacks (Davis & Welcher, 2013). Thus, a relevant question here is whether middle-class Black Atlantans experience similar rates of school closures as poorer Black Atlantans.

In addition to the well-known "The City Too Busy to Hate" moniker, Atlanta has also gained distinction as a "Black Mecca," though that distinction has been contested. Although Chicago, Harlem, and Washington, DC had long histories as Black Meccas in the early parts of the 20th century, deindustrialization of the 1970s lead to a decline among the fortunes of all workers in these cities (Frey, 2005; Levy, 2015), but hit Black, low-skilled workers especially hard (Wilson, 1987; 1996). Many of the same industries that left the northeast and midwest during this period of deindustrialization relocated to the SunBelt. By the 1970s, Atlanta was gaining a national reputation as a regional Black Mecca ("Black Mecca of the South," Garland, 1971). More recently, Atlanta's profile as a regional economic hub has broadened into a national one as a result of a booming economy but also from global attention gained from hosting the 1996 Olympics and more recently as an entertainment hub for music, movie, and television production. Similarly, the city's reputation as a Black Mecca also expanded from regional to national primarily as a consequence of (a) a large Black business ownership (Levy, 2015), (b) a large percentage of Black white collar workers and workers in middle-class occupations (Hewitt, 2000), (c) because of the strong political power yielded by Blacks in the city since the 1970s (Levy, 2015), and (d) because of the extremely large reverse migration among Blacks to Atlanta beginning in the 1980s (Frey, 2005; Pendergrass, 2013). Reverse migration is particularly important, because as Frey (2005) notes, Georgia experienced an especially high in-migration of college educated Blacks. Moreover, Atlanta is home to two of the top historically Black colleges in the nation, Spelman College and Morehouse College, whose graduates often remain in the city as professionals in economically lucrative fields like business, medicine, or law and also as officeholders in city and state government.

In the previous section, we noted that White flight out of the city proper to the suburbs and exurbs in the greater Atlanta area led to demographic changes that significantly altered the racial and economic makeup of the APA. However, movement out of the city and in turn APS was not limited to White middle and working class residents. A portion of Atlanta's large Black middle-class followed the White exodus out of the city in the 1980s (Sjoquist, 1988). Sjoquist (1988) notes that while suburban Atlanta neighborhoods gained 536,000 Whites (a net increase of 64.2%) between 1970 and 1980, the suburbs gained a 160,000 Blacks, a net increase of 287.6% during the same period. By 1980, Sjoquist notes that average income for Black families living in the suburbs was $4,000 higher than Black families living in the city. Consequently, the movement of middle class Blacks out of the city led to further declines in the population and economic base of the city and the school district.

However, while Frey's (2005) analysis of in-migration indicates there is a level of Black affluence on a scale that separates it from other major American cities, the Keating (2009) quote suggests that poverty among Blacks remains a significant problem in the city. Moreover, because of residential segregation, poverty not only impacts the Black poor, but it also affects non-poor Black and middle class neighborhoods (Massey & Denton, 1993). Though significant numbers of middle-class Blacks migrated out of Atlanta, Pattillo-McCoy (2005) argues that benefits of Black middle-class outmigration are in effect neutralized because any Black out-migration triggers White flight and similar out migration by lower income Blacks. Consequently, Black middle-class neighborhoods gradually become class heteroegenous, exposing middle-class and non-poor African Americans to higher rates of social problems than Whites at the same economic level. Even if the immediate neighborhood (for example a census block)[6] is middle-class or non-poor, it is likely to be contiguous or adjacent to a poor Black neighborhood. Thus, because of residential segregation and the physical proximity of Black poor and non-poor neighborhoods, Black families living in non-poor neighborhoods are likely to be affected by poverty even though the family lives well above the poverty line.

This interplay between residential segregation and neighborhood poverty which inhibits non-poor Blacks' ability to fully out migrate from Black neighborhoods and ultimately fully detach from the social consequences of poverty characterize many of the Black areas within the boundaries of APS. *Westside Atlanta neighborhoods are excellent examples of this pattern, and based on our spatial results, appear to have experienced a non-trivial number of school closings.* Prior to the 1950s, Westside neighborhoods like Collier Heights, Adams Park, Cascade Heights, and Adamsville (roughly running along I-20 and bordered to the west by I-285) were all White, and like other Atlanta neighborhoods, transitioned from White to Black in the 1950s. Currently, there is a great deal of class heterogeneity in these areas. For example, in census tracts in and around the Cascade Heights area, median home values are roughly $110,000 (meaning 50% of the homes are worth more than $110,000), yet the Gini index is 0.43.[7] The area is home to some of the wealthiest and most powerful African Americans in the city, including former mayor Shirley Franklin and former mayor/U.S. Ambassador Andrew Young. Thus, while median home values are indicative of a certain degree of affluence in the neighborhood, the high Gini index reveals there is also a substantial amount of income inequality as well.[8]

Given the pattern of race and economic segregation in the city, the impact these demographics have on school enrollments and performance, and the class heterogeneity in some of these neighborhoods, we examine whether and how the confluence of these factors have affected school closings in Atlanta. We turn to our data to test these relationships.

METHODS

Data

To more closely examine the issue of school closings in Atlanta, we use data from a variety of sources. First, we use race, income, and population data from the 2000 and 2010 census to examine the demographic characteristics of the census tracts which contain schools that closed. Next we combine data from APS on closings, mergers, and openings, with data from the Common Core of Data between the 2000–2001 school year and the 2013–2014 school year. The Common Core of Data is a database of schools, school districts, and state level education agencies which details school enrollments, school racial and economic composition, expenditures, and so on. collected by the Department of Education through the National Center of Education Statistics. We use data on school enrollment and the number of students on free and reduced lunch. Finally, we use math and reading test data from the Georgia Governor's Office of Student Achievement beginning in the 2010–2011 school year (the earliest school year which test score data was available) until the 2013–2014 school year. These data indicate the percentage of students evaluated as not proficient on the annual Criterion Reference Competency Testing (CRCT).

Variables for Regression Analysis

School Closing

We use data provided to us from the APS district on school closings and openings as well as data from the National Center of Education Statistics' Common Core of Data (CCD). We started with a list of schools that were open in the CCD during the 2000–2001 school year. APS supplied data on school closings, and from this, we created a binary variable for school closings which we coded 1 if a school was ever closed for every year after the 2001–2002 school year (and coded 0 if the school remained open). We cross-checked this data alongside the CCD to ensure what year the school had actually closed, since the APS data only lists the year the closing was decided on and not implemented.

School Enrollment and Income Level

We take data on school enrollment and the number of students of free and reduced lunch between the years 2000–2001 and 2013–2014 from CCD. We assess changes in school enrollment over the time period under scrutiny.

School Performance

We use publicly available data from the 2010–2011 school year until the 2013–2014 school year from the Georgia Governor's Office of Student Achievement (GOSA) on the number of students not meeting proficiency standards in reading and math on the state mandated Criterion Reference Competency Testing to measure school performance. Test score data prior to 2010 was not publicly available nor was it made available to us after an official request, following stated protocol for data research purposes to GOSA. We suspect the lack of data prior to 2010 is a result of fallout from the cheating scandal. However, such data is likely to be unreliable for the same reason.

Analyses and Coding Decisions

Despite compiling data from multiple sources, there were still some data limitations. Over the course of the period under study, many of the high schools in APS were split into "smaller schools," following the smaller schools model that districts nationwide implemented in the 1990s and early 2000s (Schwartz, Stiefel, & Wiswall, 2013). Atlanta did this in the mid-2000s, and four of the nine high schools in APS, including Carver High School, Booker T. Washington High School, South Atlanta High School, and Therrell High School, implemented this model. As a result, these schools were listed as separate schools with separate demographic statistics (enrollments numbers, number on free and reduced lunch, teacher student ratio, etc.) in the CCD. For example, beginning in 2005, Carver High is listed in the CCD as Carver High School, the Early College High School at Carver, the School of Health Sciences and Research at Carver, School of the Arts at Carver, and the School of Technology at Carver. The other aforementioned high schools have a similar setup in CCD, though the commencement dates for this split varies. Since the closings primarily affected elementary schools and a small number of middle schools over the time period under scrutiny (with the exception of Harper Archer High School which was closed in the Fall of 2002), we chose to exclude these high schools from the analysis.

We begin our examination with a spatial analysis of the demographic characteristics of census tracts where schools closed in the district. We include the following variables in this analysis: percent Black in 2000, percent poor in 2000 (defined as the percentage of residents living below the federally established poverty line), percent of persons between the ages of 5 and 17 living in the census tract in 2000. Next, we analyze school-level data on enrollment, percent of students on free and reduced lunch, and math and reading test scores as well as the census tract characteristics with a series of regression models using panel data procedures.[9]

RESULTS

Descriptive and Spatial Results

Between the Fall of 2001 and the Fall of 2013, 28 schools were closed in APS. Table 3.1 shows the means for school and census-level characteristics by closure. Schools that closed had significantly lower enrollments (around 200 students fewer) but significantly more students on free and reduced lunch (about 12% more) than schools that did not close. In addition, although schools that closed did not have significantly fewer students missing the proficiency mark in math than schools that remained open, they did have significantly fewer students not meeting proficiency standards in reading. While the differences in enrollment between schools that closed and remained open are quite large, the differences in socioeconomic context, though statistically significant, are not substantively large. *Eighty* percent of students in schools that remained open were on free and reduced

TABLE 3.1 Means by Closure

	Overall	Closed	Not Closed
School Characteristics (Fall 2000–Spring 2013)[a]	*N* = 1,244	*N* = 178	*N* = 1,066
Enrollment	523.802	359.466**	551.243
Percent free ad reduced lunch	79.903	90.818**	78.080
Test Scores (2010–2013)	*N* = 312	*N* = 14	*N* = 298
Percent of students not proficient in math	28.896	35.607	28.581
Percent of students not proficient in reading	11.397	16.871*	11.140
Census Tract Characteristics (2000)	*N* = 1,152	*N* = 178	*N* = 974
Percent Black in census tract in 2000	77.238	81.638*	76.434
Percent Poor in census tract in 2000	28.126	37.222**	26.464
Percent of Persons 5–17 years old in census tract in 2000	19.530	19.714	19.497

* significantly different from Not Closed mean at $p < .05$
** significantly different from Not Closed Mean at $p < .01$
[a] Average from 2001 until closure for School Demographic Data

lunch compared to *90%* in schools that closed. Clearly, the district as a whole is disadvantaged. The descriptive statistics for the census tract-level characteristics also show that there is a relationship between census tract disadvantage and school closures. Census tracts that experienced school closures had significantly more poor and Black families than tracts that did not experience closures.

Our quantitative descriptive results align with the census-level data displayed in our maps. Figures 3.4 and 3.5 illustrate how patterns of racial and economic segregation influence school closings. Only two of the school closures in APS between the Fall of 2000 and the Spring of 2013 occurred in the northern, wealthier (and Whiter) part of the district. In Figure 3.4, the darkest areas have the highest percentages of Black residents. The black areas of the map are census tracts that are almost entirely Black demographically speaking—these census tracts are 90 to 100% Black. Similarly, Figure 3.5 shows that only these two schools were in census tracts that had fewer than 75% of its residents living below the poverty line. Thus, on a descriptive level, it appears that school closings are linked to the extremely high levels of racial and economic segregation in Atlanta neighborhoods.

Figure 3.6 displays the change in percentage of people in the population that were 5 to 17 years old in each census tract between 2000 and 2010. If declining school enrollments are linked to school closings, we should see a descriptive association between declines in the population of people aged 5 to 17 years (i.e., the population of school age children), and school

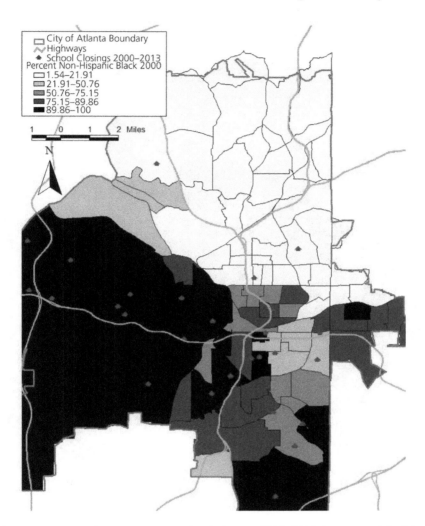

Figure 3.4 Map of Atlanta Public School closings 2000–2013, by percent Black in census tract, 2000.

closings, as suggested by the Turner School memo closing we cited earlier. As the Turner Middle School memo suggests, declines in the percentages of school aged children in a census tract appear to be related to school closings. The lighter areas indicate census tracts with the heaviest declines in the population of school-aged children, while the darker areas show areas that experienced the least loss and/or population gain. The two darkest

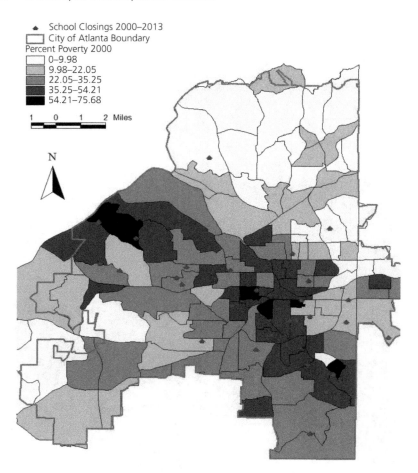

Figure 3.5 Map of Atlanta Public School closings 2000–2013, by percent poor in census tract, 2000.

shades in our delineation are located primarily in the northern part of the district, indicating that they experienced population gain. Of the two schools that closed in the northern part of the district—one was reopened as a primary center for an elementary school that was experiencing population growth and overcrowding (Margaret Mitchell Elementary in the far northwest corner of our map closed in 2003 and reopened in 2009 as a "primary center" for Brandon Elementary School which is located in Buckhead). On the other hand, the lightest areas (i.e., those experiencing population decline), are located in the southern and poorer parts of the district. Thus, we see that heavily minority and poor neighborhoods that were experiencing population decline are also neighborhoods where schools closed.

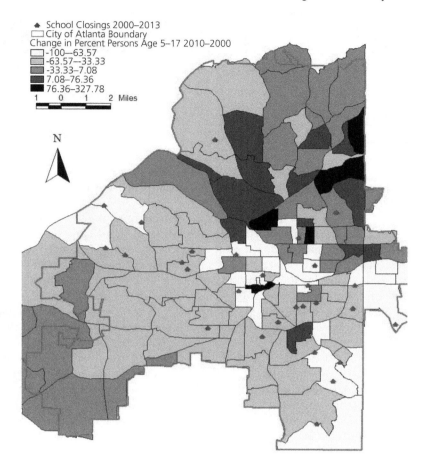

Figure 3.6 Map of Atlanta Public School closings 2000–2013, by change in percentage of persons aged 5 to 17 in census tract, 2000–2010.

REGRESSION RESULTS WITH SCHOOL-LEVEL INDICATORS

Consistent with our hypothesis that census tracts with more Blacks and more poverty were most likely to experience closure, Tables 3.2 and 3.3 generally show that school and neighborhood disadvantage are strongly associated with closure. First, Table 3.2 shows that poorer census tracts tend to have lower school enrollments. A 1% increase in census tract level poverty leads to a 6 student reduction in student enrollment. Moreover, census tract level poverty is a much stronger predictor of lower enrollments than neighborhood racial composition. After accounting for census-tract level

TABLE 3.2 Maximum Likelihood Estimates for Impact of Census Tract Characteristics on School Enrollment Fall 2000 to Fall 2013

	Enrollment	Standard Errors
Percent poor in 2000	−5.618[**]	2.092
Percent Black in 2000	−1.631	.991
Percent of persons 5–17 years old in 2000	5.613	
Constant	653.177	78.639
N	1,152	

poverty, the percentage of school age children in the census tract was not related to school enrollment.

Table 3.3 displays the results of probit regressions for school closings. Model 1 shows that enrollment has a negative and significant association with closing. This means that a one unit decline in enrollment (i.e., the loss of a single student) leads to a .005 decrease in the z-score of the probability of a school closing. Substantively, this is a very small effect. The probit regression model is a nonlinear model, so the probability of closing depends on the value of the independent variable in question. This means that a school with an enrollment of 300 students (slightly below the mean for schools that closed in our sample, see Table 3.1) has a .0000002 probability of closing. The probability of closing for a school with an enrollment of 600 students (slightly above the mean for schools in our sample that did not close) is even smaller at .00000005. Similarly, Model 2 shows that the percentage of students on free and reduced lunch has a positive and significant association with closing. Model 3 includes both enrollment and the percentage of students on free and reduced lunch in the model together; enrollment is the only significant predictor in this model. Still, including school economic context in the model significantly changes the substantive impact of closing. We can interpret Model 3 in the following manner: A school with an enrollment of 300 students and 95% of its students on free and reduced lunch (slightly above the mean for our sample) has a .072 probability of closing (7.2%). In a school with an enrollment of only 250 students—well below the mean enrollment for schools that closed in our sample but in line with some, for example, the Turner Middle School example we cited in our literature review—and 95% of that enrollment on free and reduced lunch, the probability of closing would be .1038 or 10.38%. On the other hand, a school with 600 students and with 50% of its students on free and reduced lunch (below the mean for schools that remained open) has a .0000051 probability (.00051%) of closing. Therefore, although school socioeconomic context is not a significant predictor of closing in the multivariate case, it still appears to impact the probability of closing.

TABLE 3.3 Probit Maximum Likelihood Estimates for Atlanta Public School Closings Fall 2000 to Fall 2013 (Standard Errors in Parentheses)

	1	2	3	4	5	6
	Enrollment	Percent FRL	Enrollment & Percent FRL	Math & Reading Scores	All School Characteristics	School & Census Characteristics
School Characteristics						
Enrollment	−.005*** (.002)		−.004* (.002)		−.012* (.006)	−.044*** (.010)
Percent free and reduced lunch		.089*** (.020)	.039 (.026)		.062 (.063)	.216 (.126)
Percent of students not proficient in math				−.012 (0.56)	−.034 (.071)	−.045 (.137)
Percent of students not proficient in reading				.103 (.094)	.102 (.119)	.475* (.215)
Census Tract Characteristics						
Percent Black in 2000						−.022 (.071)
Percent poor in 2000						.273*** (.083)
Percent persons 5–17 years old in 2000						−1.020*** (.267)
Percent Poor × Percent Black						
Constant	−1.784 (.002)	−11.081 (1.714)	−3.965 (2.401)	−7.060 (1.133)	−9.151 (5.790)	−11.078 (11.652)
Log likelihood	−72.018	−77.266	−84.429	−24.035	−20.023	−14.766
N	1,244	1,244	1,244	312	312	294

* $p < .05$; ** $p < .01$; *** $p < .001$

Models 4, 5, and 6 display the probit coefficients for the math and reading test scores, followed by all of the school-level characteristics and then all school and census-level characteristics. In Model 4, the percentage of students identified as not proficient on state mandated reading and math tests had no significant impact on school closings. When we include all of the school-level characteristics in a single regression (Model 5), enrollment remains the only significant predictor of school closings. However, in Model 6, when we include school and census level characteristics, reading test scores reach significance. School enrollment remains significant, and the percentage of school-age children is also significant, indicating that the likelihood of closure decreases as the percentage of school-age children in a census tract increases.

In Table 3.4, we test the hypothesis that census-tract level poverty affects the likelihood of school closure for poor and non-poor Blacks in similar ways. To examine this question, we include all our census tract-level variables along with an interaction term in a probit regression with school closure (dummy coded, 1 = census tract had at least one closure) as the dependent variable. The interaction term between percent Black and percent poor is not significant, indicating that as expected, poor and non-poor Black census tracts experience similar rates of closure. We decompose this effect in Table 3.5. As you see, the frequencies of closures are lowest in the three left columns (i.e., in census tracts with lower percentages of Blacks), *but are highest across all ranges of poverty in the highest Black census tracts.* If closures predominated in poor neighborhoods regardless of race, we would see the largest frequencies running across the bottom rows of Table 3.5, not the far right column of Table 3.5. Instead, school closures predominate in heavily Black census tracts, regardless of poverty. The — in the low Black/

TABLE 3.4 Probit Maximum Likelihood Estimates for Interaction Between Census Tract Percent Black and Percent Poor on Atlanta Public School Closings

Census Tract Characteristics	DV: Census Tract Experienced at Least One Closure (Yes = 1)	
Percent Black in 2000	−.002	(.007)
Percent poor in 2000	.020	(.026)
Percent persons 5–17 years old in 2000	.018	(.022)
Percent poor in 2000 × percent Black in 2000	−.000	(.000)
Constant	−1.591	(.486)
Log likelihood	−57.964	
N	130	

* $p < .05$; ** $p < .01$; *** $p < .001$

TABLE 3.5 Frequency of School Closings by Percent Black and Percent Poor				
	Percent Black			
Percent Poor	**0–25%**	**26–50%**	**51–75%**	**76–100%**
0–25%	3	2	0	4
26–50%	1	0	2	9
51–100%	—	—	0	3
Total	4	2	2	15

Note: Frequency indicates tract with specified characteristics had at least one closure; — Indicate no census tracts in the data fitting specified description.

high poverty range is telling in and of itself because it indicates there were no observations in the data set falling into this category within the APS boundaries. In other words, there are no census tracts in APS that are both White and poor.

What happens to the students who attended a school that closed? Does closing a school improve the socioeconomic context of schools for students who were reassigned? Table 3.6 sheds some light on this issue, albeit not a good one. It shows that the closures and subsequent reassignments did little to improve the economic conditions of the reassigned students' school environment. The mean percentage of students receiving free or reduced lunch in schools that closed was 90.08%, while the mean free and reduced lunch percentage for the school's students were reassigned is 89.80%. A *t*-test reveals that this difference is not statistically significant ($t = .127$, $df = 85$, two-tailed *p*-value = .899). Given the distribution and location of the district's wealthiest schools, few of the students who were reassigned ended up in schools with significantly lower numbers of low-income students. Table 3.6 also shows that none of the schools that were closed formally reassigned students to charters, though there was concern that this might have been the case, for example as was the case with Turner Middle School (APS, 2010). Some students were reassigned to the district's single gender academies—Coretta Scott King Academy for girls and BEST Academy for boys.

Table 3.6 also shows that in only a handful of instances, schools that had higher rates of free and reduced lunch were merged with schools that had lower rates of free and reduced lunch, thereby, improving the socioeconomic context for only a small fraction of students reassigned while maintaining the status quo for the majority of reassigned students. For example, the best scenarios for closures/mergers with regard to improving the economic context of schools appear to be the mergers of Burgess and Peterson Elementary in the Fall of 2004. This resulted in Peterson students moving from 94% of students on free and reduced lunch to the merged Burgess-Peterson

TABLE 3.6   Percent Free and Reduced Lunch (FRL) by Closure and Reassignments

Closed/Merged School(s)	Percent FRL (Last Fall Open)	Reassigned/New School	Percent FRL (First Fall Open)
Guice ES	98.57 (2000)	Parkside ES	89.50 (2001)
Slaton ES	89.05 (2000)		
West ES	90.52 (2000)		
Minnie Howell ES	93.74 (2001)	Heritage Academy	89.65 (2002)
Hubert ES	98.19 (2001)	Cook ES	89.61 (2002)
		Witefoord ES	88.10 (2002)
Harper Archer HS	64.42 (2001)	Mays HS	65.18 (2002)
		Douglass HS	47.84 (2002)
		North Atlanta HS	50.17 (2002)
Collier Heights ES	84.42 (2002)	Usher ES	87.83 (2003)
Pitts ES	87.45 (2002)	Pitts-Mitchell ES	88.71 (2003)
Margaret Mitchell ES	90.25 (2002)	Bolton Academy	88.94 (2007)
Lakewood Heights ES	90.06 (2002)	(New) Dobbs ES (new site)	85.68 (2003)
(Old) Dobbs ES	95.18 (2002)		
Anderson Park ES	61.62 (2003)	White ES	84.98 (2004)
		F. L. Stanton ES	95.04 (2004)
		Usher ES	87.83 (2003)
Arkwright ES merges with Ragsdale ES	Arkwright: 95.60 (2003)	Finch ES	90.82 (2007)[a]
	Ragsdale: 89.73 (2003)		
Rusk ES merges with M. A. Jones ES	Rusk: 86.84 (2003)	M. A. Jones ES	90.02 (2004)
	M. A. Jones: 87.14 (2003)		
Burgess ES merges with Peterson ES	Burgess: 75.91 (2003)	Burgess–Peterson ES	76.49 (2004)
	Peterson: 93.47 (2003)		
Ralph McGill ES	97.64 (2003)	Cook ES	97.95 (2011)
Oglethorpe ES	90.41 (2006)	Bethune ES	99.40 (2007)
		M. A. Jones ES	93.61 (2007)
Tull Waters ES	96.66 (2007)	Humphries ES	94.13 (2008)
		Dobbs ES	99.47 (2008)
Walden MS	90.74 (2007)	King MS	91.36 (2008)
Williams ES	85.71 (2008)	Usher/Collier Heights ES	96.13 (2009)
		Towns ES	96.11 (2009)
Blalock ES	94.25 (2008)	Towns ES	96.11 (2009)
C. W. Hill ES merges with Hope ES	C. W. Hill: 87.45 (2008)	Hope ES (Hope-Hill ES)	95.84 (2009)
	Hope: 95.03 (2008)		

(continued)

TABLE 3.6   Percent Free and Reduced Lunch (FRL) by Closure and Reassignments (continued)

Closed/Merged School(s)	Percent FRL (Last Fall Open)	Reassigned/ New School	Percent FRL (First Fall Open)
Turner MS	98.89 (2009)	Coretta Scott King Academy	89.20 (2010)
		BEST Academy	92.82 (2010)
		Harper Archer MS	96.95 (2010)
Capital View ES	92.40 (2011)	Perkerson ES	98.78 (2012)
White ES	94.42 (2011)	Grove Park Intermed.	98.63 (2012)
		Woodson	99.23 (2012)
		F. L. Stanton	98.84 (2012)
Cook ES	97.95 (2011)	Centennial Place ES	69.74 (2012)
		Hope-Hill ES	91.24 (2012
		Parkside ES	75.56 (2012)
		D. H. Stanton ES	97.36 (2012)
		Whitefoord ES	95.40 (2012)
East Lake ES	89.95 (2011)	Toomer ES	73.25 (2012)
Herndon ES	89.17 (2011)	Bethune ES	98.84 (2012)
Grove Park ES	99.17 (2011)	Grove Park Inter. (3–5)	98.63 (2012)
Woodson ES	97.39 (2011)	Woodson Primary (K–2)	99.23 (2012)
Adamsville ES	95.27 (2011)	Adamsville Primary (K–2)	99.24 (2012)
Miles ES	95.79 (2011)	Miles Inter. (3–5)	96.72 (2012)
Coretta Scott King Academy	91.89 (2009)	Opens to Citywide Enrollment	89.20 (2010)
BEST Academy	93.07 (2009)	Opens to Citywide Enrollment	95.65 (2010)
Parks MS	98.06 (2012)	Sylvan MS	99.48 (2013
Overall	$X = 90.08$		$X = 89.80$
	SD = 8.05		SD = 11.65

[a] Although both Arkwright and Ragsdale are listed as closed by the fall of 2004 in the CCD data, the APS data indicates that the students were reassigned to Ragsdale in January 2005 until Finch opened in the fall of 2007.

Elementary having only 76% of its students on free and reduced lunch. In another case, the closure of East Lake Elementary School in the Fall of 2012, which had a free and reduced lunch rate of 90% to Toomer Elementary School, whose free and reduced lunch rate was only 73%, was also an improvement for students. After these two examples, the "improvements" appear only marginally better at best. The closure of Harper Archer High School and the subsequent relocation of students to Douglass and North

Atlanta High School, but not Mays, was an improvement. Finally, in the earliest set of closures we identified, the closure of Guice Elementary in the Fall of 2001, which had a free and reduced lunch rate of 99%, resulted in the relocation of students to Parkside Elementary, which had a free and reduced lunch rate of 90%. These are best case scenarios in our data (though moving to almost 100% low-income environment to a 90% low-income environment as in the latter case seems to offer little relief). The rest of the closures/mergers show movement to a similar environment (e.g., the relocation of Slaton and West Elementary students to Parkside in 2001), the merger of Rusk and Jones Elementary in 2004, the relocation of McGill Elementary students to Cook Elementary in 2007, and so on. Consequently, we conclude that closing and reassignment did very little to improve the socioeconomic context of students.

CONCLUSION

Our spatial results reveal that school closings have largely been fueled by race and class segregation. Schools in heavily Black and poor neighborhoods were most likely to close compared to schools in the wealthier and Whiter parts of the APS district. Our multivariate results show that school closings in Atlanta are connected to declining enrollments and to some degree, school and neighborhood economic conditions (i.e., poverty). Therefore, we conclude that school closings in Atlanta have been shaped by housing and related demographic patterns in the city and the school district that have left some neighborhoods racially and economically isolated. Moreover, despite the importance of school and neighborhood poverty, we find that low poverty/high Black census tracts experienced school closures at rates indistinguishable from low poor/high Black census tracts.

Reading test scores had a significant impact on closures, but this effect was not robust and only reached significance after controlling for census tract level poverty. The (lack of) robustness of the test score results may be related to data limitations stemming from the cheating scandal. Test score data after 2010 is publicly available, but we were not able to gain access to test score data prior to 2010, even after following established protocol from the Governor's Office of Student Achievement for obtaining these data. We attribute this to concerns about the validity of test score data throughout the duration of the cheating scandal, which began by some estimates as early as 2001 (Georgia Governor's Office, 2011; Georgia Public Policy Foundation, 2015). Consequently, we have significantly fewer observations for the analyses that included math and reading test scores compared to our other school-level analyses. Low academic achievement has been an open concern of state and local APS officials in recent years. The recent Opportunity School District proposal (to take control of low achieving schools away from local districts and place them under state control) put forward by the governor was purportedly in response to low achievement in the district, even though it was ultimately opposed by voters in the November 2016 election. Still, there may be some reason to believe the governor's proposal was a response to "save face" after the cheating scandal. A few of the schools implicated in the cheating scandal, including Parks Middle School (which was considered a particularly egregious case) and Capital View Elementary School, have closed since the cheating was exposed.

Finally, we find that closures were distributed across poor and non-poor Black neighborhoods similarly and that closures and mergers do nothing to improve the socioeconomic contexts of students' schools. The existing literature on school closings does not seem to suggest that school districts are interested in improving the contexts of students' schooling (Good, 2016; Lee & Lubienski, 2016; Uetricht, 2013). Instead, districts tend to be focused on financial efficiency and economies of scale. Whether closing schools achieves the financial goal is a separate and empirically interesting question in and of itself; while closing schools may be rational in this regard, it does little to improve the context of schools. In our case, it surely did not help APS place students into better economic contexts, though it did not, as in the case of Lee and Lubienski's (2016) findings in Chicago, expose students to even greater dangers. Moreover, school closures come at great emotional costs (Logan & Molotch, 1987). Schools are places with affective and psychological value, not commodities that can be exchanged without evoking a sense of loss. While we don't examine the affective impact of school closures, the strong emotions they evoke is clear from the sentiments apparent in protests when the talk of closures is broached, as has been the case most recently here in Atlanta. When news of the proposed Opportunity School District Plan broke in March of 2015, protesters staged a march on the steps of the capital to express their discontent (Hernandez, 2015; Simonton, 2015).

While the cheating scandal may have prompted officials to consider a turnaround strategy that included closing schools with low levels of academic achievement, the negative attention it brought to the district may have contributed to heightened vigilance among policymakers to hasten the closure of schools to ameliorate the embarrassment caused by the scandal. The talk of closing schools for poor performance has increased dramatically in the years since the scandal. This is an interesting situation to follow, and we will continue to watch developments in the coming years.

NOTES

1. We define low income as students who receive free as well as reduced priced lunch. To qualify for free or reduced priced lunch, students must come from households whose income is at 130% and 185% of the poverty line respectively (U.S. Department of Agriculture Food and Nutrition Service, 2015).
2. The recommendation noted that "Counting charter schools, APS serves approximately 50,000 students."
3. In the November 2016 elections, voters rejected the Governor's Opportunity School District proposal.
4. Speech to the Center for State and Local Finance, Andrew Young Policy School, Georgia State University on February 8, 2017.
5. Speech to the Center for State and Local Finance, Andrew Young Policy School, Georgia State University on February 8, 2017.
6. A census block is the smallest size geographical unit charted by the Census Bureau. It is typically the size of a city block, but can be limited to an area as small as an apartment complex in a densely populated urban area or as large as a hundreds of square miles in a rural area (U.S. Census Bureau, 2011).
7. The Gini index is a measure of income inequality scaled from 0 to 1 where 0 indicates that all income within a geographic unit is spread equally across all members in the unit and 1 indicates that a single person in the geographic unit holds *all* of the income.
8. Average Gini for census tracts 76 and 81.02.
9. Specifically we analyze the multivariate data with the xtprobit command with random effects in Stata.

REFERENCES

Atlanta Public School (2010). *Recommendation to close Henry McNeal Turner middle school: Frequently asked questions.* Retrieved from https://www.atlantapublic schools.us/cms/lib/GA01000924/Centricity/Domain/2439/Turner_School_Closing_FAQ.pdf

Atlanta Public School. (2012). *Superintendent's final redistricting and closure recommendations.* Retrieved https://www.atlantapublicschools.us/cms/lib/GA01000924/Centricity/Domain/45/Final%20-%20Version%20Posted%20May%207.pdf

Bayor, R. (1996). *Race and the Reshaping of Twentieth-Century Atlanta.* Chapel Hill: University of North Carolina Press.

Bayor, R. H. (2000). Atlanta: The historical paradox. In D. L. Sjoquist (Ed.), *The Atlanta Paradox* (pp. 42–58). New York, NY: Russell Sage.

Billger, S. M., Frank, D. B. (2012). The determinants of high school closures: Lessons from longitudinal data throughout Illinois. *Journal of Education Finance 38*(2), 83–101.

Bloom, M. (2016a, January 6). Atlanta public schools: Worst schools to get remake. *Atlanta Journal Constitution,* p. 1A.

Bloom, M. (2016b, February 21). APS chief takes bold gamble to rescue schools. *Atlanta Journal-Constitution,* p. 1A.

Burdick-Will, J., Keels, M., & Schuble, T. (2013). Closing and opening schools: The association between neighborhood characteristics and the location of new educational opportunities in a large urban district. *Journal of Urban Affairs*, *35*(1), 59–80.

Davis, T., & Welcher, A. (2013). School quality and the vulnerability of the Black middle class: The continuing significance of race as a predictor of disparate schooling environments. *Sociological Perspectives 56*(4), 467–493.

Du Bois, W. E. B. (1903). *The talented tenth*. New York, NY: James Pott.

Georgia Public Policy Foundation. (2015). *The Atlanta cheating scandal*. Retrieved from http://www.georgiapolicy.org/2015/04/the-atlanta-public-schools-cheating -scandal/

Feagin, J., & Sikes, M. (1994). *Living with racism: The Black middle-class experience*. Boston, MA: Beacon Press.

Frazier, F. (1957). *Black bourgeoisie*. New York, NY: Simon and Schuster.

Frey, W. H. (2005). The new great migration: Black americans' return to the south, 1965–2000. In A. Berube, B. Katz, R. E. Lang (Eds.), *Redefining urban and suburban America: Evidence from Census 2000* (pp. 87–110). Washington, DC: Brookings Institution Press.

Garland, P. (1971). Atlanta: Black mecca of the south. *Ebony 8*, 152–57.

Georgia Governor's Office. (2011). *Special investigation into test tampering in Atlanta's school system*. Retrieved from http://www.courthousenews.com/2011/07/27/ APS1.pdf

Georgia Governor's Office. (2015). *Georgia's proposed opportunity school district—Overview*. Retrieved from https://gosa.georgia.gov/sites/gosa.georgia.gov/files/ related_files/site_page/Georgia%20OSD%20overview%20rev2%20March %2023%202015.pdf

Good, R. (2016). Histories that root us: Neighborhood, place, and the protest of school closures in Philadelphia. *Urban Geography*. doi:10.1080/02723638.20 16.1182286

Henry, E., & Hankins, K. (2012). Halting White flight: Parent activism and the (re) shaping of Atlanta's "circuits of schooling," 1973–2009. *Journal of Urban History*, *38*(3), 532–552.

Hernandez, E. (2015, December 02). Five things to know about Gov. deal's opportunity school district. *Atlanta Journal Constitution*. Retrieved from https://www.ajc.com/ news/local-education/things-know-about-gov-deal-opportunity-school-district/ jTEqgF5jmLRs5A2hy8ax3M/

Hewitt, C. L. (2000). Job segregation, ethnic hegemony, and earnings inequality. In D. Sjoquist (Ed.), *The Atlanta Paradox* (pp. 185–216). New York, NY: Russell Sage Foundation.

Hughes, M., & Thomas, M. (1998). The continuing significance of race revisited: A study of race, class, and quality of life in america, 1972 to 1996. *American Sociological Review 63*(6), 785–795.

Johnson, R. (2014). Where schools close in Chicago. *Albany Government Law Review*, *5*, 508–544.

Keating, L. (2010). *Atlanta: Race, class and urban expansion*. Philadelphia, PA: Temple University Press.

Kingsley, T., & Pettit, K. L. S. (2002). Population growth and decline in city neighborhoods. Washington, DC: *Urban Institute*. Retrieved from http://www.urban.org/sites/default/files/publication/60281/310594-Population-Growth-and-Decline-in-City-Neighborhoods.PDF

Kruse, K. (2013). *White flight: Atlanta and the making of modern conservatism.* Princeton, NJ: Princeton University Press.

Lacy, K. (2007). *Blue-chip Black: race, class, and status in the new Black middle class.* Berkeley: University of California Press

Land, L. (2009). *The culture of property: Race, class, and housing landscapes in Atlanta, 1880–1950.* Athens: University of Georgia Press.

Landry, B. (1987). *The new Black middle class.* Berkeley: University of California Press.

Lassiter, M. (2013). *The silent majority: Suburban politics in the sunbelt south.* Princeton, NJ: Princeton University Press.

Lee, J., & Lubienski, C. (2016). The impact of school closures on equity of access in Chicago. *Education and Urban Society.* doi:0013124516630601

Levy, J. (2015). Selling Atlanta: Black mayoral politics from protest to entrepreneurism, 1973 to 1990. *Journal of Urban History 41*(3), 420–443.

Logan, J., & Molotch, H. (1987). *Urban fortunes: The political economy of place.* Berkeley: University of California Press.

Massey, D., & Denton, N. (1993). *American apartheid: Segregation and the making of the underclass.* Cambridge, MA: Harvard University Press.

McConnell, D. (1980). Investing in neighborhood revitalization. In A. Hamer (Ed.), *Urban Atlanta: Redefining the Role of the City* (pp. 143–153). Atlanta, GA: Georgia State University.

Niesse, M. (2013, April 30). APS cheating scandal: Ex-APS teachers' job outlook dim. *Atlanta Journal Constitution*, p. 1A.

Pattillo-McCoy, M. (1999). *Black picket fences: Privilege and peril among the Black middle class.* Chicago, IL: University of Chicago Press.

Pattillo-McCoy, M. (2005). Black middle-class neighborhoods. *Annual Review of Sociology, 31*, 305–329.

Pendergrass, S. (2013). Perceptions of race and region in the Black reverse migration to the south. *Du Bois Review, 10*(1), 155–178.

Research Atlanta. (1971). The Atlanta School System–Draft Report. Atlanta, GA: Research Atlanta.

Schwartz, A. E., Stiefel, L., & Matthew, W. (2013). Do small schools improve performance in large, urban districts? Causal evidence from New York City. *Journal of Urban Economics 77*, 27–40.

Severson, K. (2013, August 7). A $147 million signal of faith in Atlanta's public schools. *New York Times*, p. A14.

Simonton, A. (2015). *Georgia school takeover plan passes despite protests.* Retrieved from http://atlantaprogressivenews.com/2015/03/28/georgia-school-takeover-plan-passes-despite-protests/

Sjoquist, D. (1988). *The economic status of Black Atlantans.* Atlanta, GA: Atlanta Urban League.

U.S. Census Bureau. (2011). *What are census blocks?* Retrieved from http://blogs.census.gov/2011/07/20/what-are-census-blocks/

U.S. Department of Agriculture Food and Nutrition Service. (2015). *Child nutrition programs—Income eligibility guidelines.* Retrieved from https://www.federalregister.gov/documents/2015/03/31/2015-07358/child-nutrition-programs-income-eligibility-guidelines

Uetricht, M. (2013). Chicago is ground zero for disastrous "free market" reforms of education. *The Guardian.* Retrieved from https://www.theguardian.com/commentisfree/2013/mar/27/chicago-teacher-strike-against-school-closures-and-privatization

Vogel, H., & Perry, J. (2008, December 14). CRCT scores surge: Miracle or masquerade? Exam results raise red flag. *Atlanta Journal Constitution*, p. 1A.

Wilson, W. J. (1978). *The declining significance of race: Blacks and changing American institutions.* Chicago, IL: University of Chicago Press.

Wilson, W. J. (1996). *When work disappears: The world of the new urban poor.* New York, NY: Vintage Books.

CHAPTER 4

THE COSTS AND CONSEQUENCES OF SCHOOL GOVERNANCE CHANGE IN DETROIT

From Proposal A to the Education Achievement Authority

Leanne Kang
Grand Valley State University

Kelly E. Slay
University of Maryland–College Park

ABSTRACT

This chapter examines the relationship between school closures and school governance change in Detroit, what is arguably (next to New Orleans) the greatest case of dismantling the traditional public school system in the United States. Our historical analysis involves the overlaying of existing data on school closures in Detroit (Grover & van der Velde, 2016) upon a narrative that details the emergence of neoliberal school governance beginning in 1994 (Kang & Slay, 2017). By doing so, we find that the greatest number of school closures occur at the moment in which efforts to institutionalize neoliberal school governance accelerate. Unlike other studies that have attributed school closures to declining enrollment or financial mismanagement, we argue that school closures signal the transition to neoliberal school governance, a fundamental change in who manages and decides. As other studies have shown the detrimental effects of school closures on communities that are predominantly Black and Brown, our study focuses on how governance change in such communities is a threat to democracy and public schooling, a look as to where we have gone since Brown v. Board. We conclude the chapter by discussing how Detroit's unprecedented number of school closures are indicative of the dilemmas of neoliberal school reform, with consequences that are situated within the particular racial, sociopolitical, and historical context of the city made visible by the creation of a statewide "recovery district," the Education Achievement Authority (EAA).

On February 7, 2017, Betsy DeVos, a billionaire philanthropist and staunch defender of charter school expansion and choice in Michigan, was sworn in as secretary of education. For nearly a quarter of a century, DeVos's million dollar contributions to Michigan's GOP party and specific educational campaigns—such as the failed effort to pass a school voucher bill in 2000—have in total contributed to the proliferation of charter schools in the state (Felton, 2016). Between 1999 to 2014, the secretary of education contributed $5.2 million to charter schools (Rizga, 2017). In 1999, there were only a few charter schools in Michigan; by 2012, charter schools enrolled more than a third of Detroit's students (Dawsey, 2012). During this period, the Detroit Public Schools' (DPS) enrollment dropped 72% (Addonizio & Kearney, 2012) forcing nearly 200 schools to close (Grover & van der Velde, 2016). DeVos's philanthropic record indicates that she views "choice and competition as the best mechanisms to improve America's education system" (Rizga, 2017). To us, DeVos reflects the remarkable intertwining of philanthropy, business, and state government in educational policy and reform in the last several decades—what scholars are calling "neoliberal school governance." The recent appointment of DeVos is not simply President Trump's pick but a culmination of broader historical tides that are explored in this chapter. Thus, this chapter also calls for a deeper interrogation of school closures in Detroit. What can the relationship between school closure and neoliberal school governance in Detroit tell us about the future of public schooling?

Detroit's staggering number of school closings is part of a "national epidemic of school closures" (Fine, 2012, p. 145). Between 2000 and 2010, 70 urban school districts across the nation—in rust belt cities such as Buffalo, Cincinnati, Detroit, Kansas City, and Pittsburgh, and in southern and western cities such as Birmingham, Little Rock, Richmond, San Antonio,

Portland, Provo, and Seattle—closed on average 11 schools per district (Engberg, Gill, Zammaro, & Zimmer, 2012). Given the epic proportion of closings, there is surprisingly little empirical research on the process of school closures and its effects (Carlson & Lavertu, 2015; Deeds & Pattillo, 2015). The literature suggests that school closures are due to population decline, competition from charters, and budgetary issues (Carlson & Lavertu, 2015; de la Torre, Gordon, & Cowhy, 2015; Engberg et al., 2012; Garnett, 2015; Sunderman & Payne, 2009). Fewer attribute the crisis to policies such as No Child Left Behind (NCLB), Race to the Top (RTT), and ensuing accountability regimes (Deeds & Pattillo, 2015; Lipman, 2011a; Sunderman & Payne, 2009). The latter authors have argued that federal legislation reinforced the use of school closures as a reform strategy for chronically underperforming schools. For instance, the Obama Administration has made turning around such failing schools a top priority for school reform with RTT, an initiative which "overhauls low-performing schools through curriculum changes, staff restructuring, and, when other improvement measures fail, *school closures* [emphasis added]" (Deeds & Pattillo, 2015, p. 478).

However, few have recognized that school closures are mechanisms stemming from policies that address both persistent low achievement and fiscal challenges at the school or district level (Engberg et al., 2012). Even fewer recognize how policies associated with school closures are part of a broader movement to change governance approaches (Henig, 2013; Kretchmar, 2014; Lipman, 2011a). This chapter contributes to the school closure literature by examining the relationship between the history of school governance in Detroit and the recent closing of schools.

Nowhere have these issues been more salient than in Detroit, although little empirical work exists on education reform in Detroit compared to cities like Chicago and New York. According to a 2011 report by Pew Charitable Trust, among six urban districts (Chicago; Detroit; Kansas City, MO; Milwaukee; Pittsburgh; and Washington) that "engaged in large-scale public school closings in the past decade" (Dowdall, 2011, p. 1), Detroit had the highest number of school closures. Since 2002, the DPS's enrollments had declined steeply; approximately 10,000 students per year left for charter schools and nearby suburban schools (Mrozowski, 2009), the highest drop in enrollment (–54%) among the six cities in that decade (Dowdall, 2011).

In many ways, Detroit has become the quintessential poster child of the deterioration caused by deindustrialization and global restructuring as the media spotlights its unemployment, poverty, and crime. Its schools have also become a prime example of urban public schooling failure; the former Secretary of Education under the Obama Administration told the press that he "loses sleep over Detroit's miserable schools" (Pedroni, 2011, p. 205). For decades the media has also attributed the DPS's problems to corruption and financial mismanagement (Henderson, 2016). What is less known and discussed, both publicly and in research, is how school reforms in the last 35 years contributed to dramatic school governance change at the turn of the century. School closings might seem obvious in a city that has lost over 60% of its population since 1950 (Angelova, 2012). Still, while the common discourse around the unprecedented number of school closures points to drastic declines in enrollment as well as the district's financial mismanagement, our historical analysis suggests a more complex story in which we argue that successive policies leading to governance change are central to the reason 231 schools have closed since 1980. Thus, this chapter explores the relationship between school closures and governance change within the neoliberal context of our time.

In this chapter, we overlay existing data on school closures in Detroit (Grover & van der Velde, 2016) upon a narrative that details the emergence of neoliberal school governance beginning in 1994. By doing so, we find the greatest number of school closures occur at the moment in which efforts to institutionalize neoliberal school governance accelerate. Thus, we argue that the shuttering of schools is symptomatic of governance change. Our exploration of the historical conditions that gave rise to school closings in Detroit is an important contribution to the literature that, with few exceptions, has cast school closings as the result of declining enrollment and budget woes without critically analyzing or interrogating the ways in which school governance change has led to such outcomes.

We begin by characterizing school governance change in the United States during the course of the 20th century, noting the gradual erosion of traditional structures and the rise of a neoliberal restructuring agenda. Next, as part of our conceptual framework, we describe the neoliberal ideology in which emergent reforms and governance models are grounded, relying on key concepts to guide our analysis of school governance change. We conclude by discussing the costs: the social and political implications of school closures in a city like Detroit, and the dilemmas of today's restructuring agenda in the second most segregated city in the nation, where 83% of the population is Black and the median income is $21,000 less than the rest of a state that is 79% White.

SCHOOL GOVERNANCE CHANGE IN THE 20TH CENTURY

Early Models of School Governance

There is nothing new about Americans tinkering with school governance. The concept of changing the formal structure of governance to improve schools has deep roots in American political and intellectual history (Henig & Rich, 2004). While there has never been a national system of schooling in the United States, there have been two patterns of school governance in the history of American public schooling: what we call *village school governance* and *traditional school governance*. Emerging in the 19th century, the village school system was a loose arrangement of rural schools managed by laypersons of villages and towns spread across the United States. By the beginning of the 20th century, traditional school governance emerged, reflecting organizational models found in the division of labor in factories, the coordination of modern businesses, and the punctuality of the railroads (Chandler, 1977).

A new generation of educational reformers at that time argued that a system of village schools no longer served citizens in the advent of rapid industrialization and urbanization in America. These reformers, an elite group of business and educational experts, set out to transform the village school system into a large, bureaucratic, centralized system. Funded by local property taxes, this new governing model—what we now consider as the traditional school model—was distinctly autonomous and self-operating, unlike other governmental units (Henig, 2013). This new arrangement, with the establishment of a school board at the top, quickly spread across the country. By mid-century, nearly all school districts, large and small, adopted this governing structure, making it the unofficial national system.

However, by the late 1960s and 1970s, racial and socioeconomic conflict ensued. In the post-WWII economy, cities like Detroit, Newark, Chicago, and New York began to experience significant financial decline and school boards competed for increasingly scarce resources; increases in the population in these cities only compounded their fiscal challenges. In addition, forced desegregation and an increase in Black migrants from the South, combined with the out-migration of second-generation White ethnics, further exacerbated and complicated existing social, political, and economic issues that had emerged after the Great Depression. These social and demographic changes in U.S. cities and attacks on the quality of education, especially among the historically disadvantaged and poor, led to major criticism of traditional school governance (Tyack, 1974). For example, Tyack (1974) wrote:

> Despite frequent good intentions and abundant rhetoric about "equal education opportunity," schools have rarely taught the children of the poor effectively—and this failure has been systematic, not idiosyncratic. Talk about "keeping schools out of politics" has often served to obscure actual alignments of power and patterns of privilege. (p. 11)

Such critiques implicated the existing governing model for its failure to educate all children well, challenging the basic foundations and assumptions of traditional school governance—nowhere more vociferously than in America's urban centers (Tyack, 1974). In addition to the inflow of various immigrant groups after WWII, Blacks continued to migrate to northern cities from the Jim Crow South, doubling the Black population in cities like Detroit and Chicago (Sugrue, 2005). Discriminatory policies such as redlining against Blacks and other racial/ethnic groups not only created "ghettos" but also a system of segregated schooling. Until the Civil Rights Movement, which put the issue of racial inequality on the nation's conscience, the leaders of the traditional school arrangement largely ignored the intensifying racial cleavages of the city (Anyon, 1997; Ravitch, 1974; Shipps, 2006). Shipps's (2006) history of Chicago Public Schools, for example, demonstrated how issues of race ultimately put pressure on traditional school governance and continues to affect school reform in Chicago to this day (Lipman & Haines, 2007; Lipman & Hursh, 2007). Herein lies a turning point in U.S. school governance history: originating from the widespread challenges faced by many large urban school districts in the 1960s and 1970s, a restructuring agenda emerged, spanning the next several decades, but, by next century, neoliberalism would co-opt efforts to address racial inequality.

School Reforms and Emerging New School Governance

The belief that the school system had not served minority groups and the poor well unleashed a flurry of new innovations, which would become what we know today as charter schools, vouchers, school choice, and so on (Fuller, 2000). New forms of schooling enabled "members of outcast groups" to put "their own people in place of the traditional corporate model of governance" (Tyack, 1974, p. 269). Yet, by the early 1980s, the early 20th century Progressive Era system was still largely intact. Graham (1995) likened the schooling system to a battleship:

> Large, powerful, cumbersome, with enormous crews, these giants of the ocean go where they are told to go by some distant authority, which presumably understands better than anyone on the ship, including the captain where and why they should go. Maneuverability is not their strength. (p. 3)

Graham's (1995) metaphor reflects that while there were many calls for change, things were moving slowly. However, by the mid-1990s, there was a rush of reforms which, using Bulkley's (2010) typology, we categorize into at least three strategies: standards-based reform, differentiation of schools, and market-based reform. Although each type has different and sometimes overlapping goals, in many ways they have ultimately worked together in breaking up the battleship, an extraordinary restructuring of the public schooling system and the materialization of neoliberal strategies.

Standards-Based Reform

The 1983 report *A Nation At Risk*, which claimed that, "the educational foundations of our society are presently being eroded by a rising tide of mediocrity that threatens our very future as a Nation and a people" (National Commission on Excellence in Education, 1983, pp. 5–6), launched the standards movement (Ravitch, 2010). Reforming schools by raising standards or implementing "back to basics" education (Fuller, 2000) was incorporated into federal policy beginning with President Bill Clinton's Improving America's Schools Act in 1994 and on through President George W. Bush's No Child Left Behind Act in 2001 (Ravitch, 2010). Over time, however, the goals of the standards-based reform evolved from establishing rigorous curricula and instruction to creating a high-stakes accountability system based on the outcomes of assessments tied to standards (Bulkley, 2010; Ravitch, 2010).

Ravitch (2010) argued that the rewards and punishment system of NCLB resulted in the "hijacking" of the standards movement, shifting efforts away from actually raising standards to codifying the testing of student performance as a way of keeping schools and districts accountable. Policymakers on both sides of the aisle had come to believe that accountability via testing would lead to better outcomes. While NCLB's goal was to improve the quality of public schooling, Ravitch argued that instead it created a culture in which teachers were punished, vilified, even fired as sanctions were imposed on schools that did not make adequate yearly progress. The other effect of NCLB was a historically unprecedented increase in the federal government's role in education (Manna, 2011; McGuinn & Manna, 2013; Reed, 2014). What were once local matters now involved both federal and state officials: from "education" presidents to "education" mayors (Henig, 2013; Henig & Rich, 2004; Wong, Shen, Anagnostopoulos, & Rutledge, 2007). In short, the standards movement gradually expanded the federal role in school governance.

Differentiation of Schools

At the same time, large urban school districts continued their experimentation with a second reform strategy that originated in the 1960s and 1970s: differentiation of schools. Magnet schools, smaller themed schools, and charter schools claimed to "service the varied needs and interests of students" and foster educational innovation by "offering a range of schools within a system of choice" (Bulkley, 2010, p. 18). Notably, the Gates Foundation pushed toward differentiation of schools through its 5-year initiative to fund the creation of new, small, autonomous high schools (Bulkley, 2010). The original purpose of charter schools, for example, was to empower a group of parents, educators, or community activists to establish an independent school that would be more responsive to the special needs of that particular community (Fuller, 2000). However, increasingly, foundations and philanthropists sought to fund the differentiation of schools, particularly charters, suggesting they were distinct from the common school model (Graham, 1995). Later, it evolved into a broader strategy for creating a new "market" of schools (Bulkley, 2010).

Market-Based Reform

Meanwhile, a third reform strategy, market-based reforms, would take hold in public schooling. The rise of Reagan and conservatism would repurpose charter schools by redefining the concept of "empowerment" to mean the empowering of parents to *choose* the schools they wished (Fuller, 2000). This shift was key to laying the foundation for market-based reforms and breaking apart traditional schooling. Influenced by Milton Friedman's ideas about the overregulation of government and the private marketplace as a solution for increasing both access to and the quality of schooling (Friedman, 1955), reformers began to envision the marketplace as a new institution to govern public schooling. Chubb and Moe (1990) argued that local school bureaucracy was the central reason for poor schooling and that local control was the problem because it was invested in maintaining the status quo. The solution, therefore, was for the market—"schools of choice"—to single-handedly disrupt this governing structure, break up its monopoly, and establish a system in which schools would improve by competing with one another in a market of differentiated public schools or of school choice.

In 1989, at the first Education Summit in Charlottesville, President George H.W. Bush and 50 governors agreed that school choice would be a major component in their national agenda to reform public education. The summit and subsequent events like it would lead to a widespread, bipartisan belief that creating a market of schools through school choice policies (e.g., charters, vouchers, and other open enrollment assignments) would lead to improved educational opportunities and outcomes. In 1991, Minnesota passed the first charter law, marking the beginning of a market-based movement that would quickly spread across the country and Michigan. Market-based reforms in combination with the differentiation of schools would promote the creation of an alternative system of public schooling, endorsed by federal and state policy, and supported by new education networks consisting of foundations and philanthropists like Gates. This emergent system led by non-education actors, more national constituents, and nonlocal decision makers was a clear divergence from the local governance model.

The history of school governance change indicates that the flurry of reforms in the last 30 to 40 years, so often studied in isolation from each other, all have something in common: they have been mechanisms for the gradual dismantling of traditional school governance, which at its organizational core is the publicly-elected school board (Henig, 2013). Henig (2013) argued that so-called "education executives" (i.e., mayors, governors, and presidents) and the increased influence of the judicial branch, Congress, state legislatures, and new educational actors such as foundations and other nongovernmental agencies suggested the emergence of a new governance model. However, dramatic school governance change by itself does not explain why such transformations have occurred disproportionately in urban school districts, nor its impact (i.e., school closures). Thus, we consider the larger neoliberal context in which school governance change is happening (Lipman & Haines, 2007).

CONCEPTUAL FRAMEWORK: NEOLIBERAL EDUCATION REFORM

Neoliberalism is a term used to describe an era of global capitalism that has occurred during the past 30 years (Lipman, 2011b). With the United States (and some parts of Western Europe) facing an economic structural crisis in the late 1960s and early 1970s, a new brand of economic theorists introduced the idea that the welfare state was to blame and that societies are most efficient when individuals are free to pursue their interests in the market without government intervention (Lipman, 2011b). This idea produced an assemblage of economic and social policies that would quickly spread beyond the United States: sharp retrenchment of public services, tax reduction and deregulation, and major waves of privatization (Dardot & Laval, 2013; Lipman, 2011b; Lipman & Haines, 2007). Beyond a period of new economic and social policies driven by capital accumulation, neoliberalism has become a new rationale, ultimately altering the ways in which nation-states govern.

Neoliberalism as a set of discourses, ideologies, and practices has developed a new common sense for how we think about the world and our place in it (Dardot & Laval, 2013; Harvey, 1989; Harvey, 2005; Lipman, 2011b; Peck & Tickell, 2002). At its heart, neoliberalism stems from a "belief in the end of the 'age of bureaucracy'" (Dardot & Laval, 2013, p. 235). The rhetoric of neoliberalism consists of critiques about how, in the context of globalization, government not only lacks efficiency and productivity but also embodies the kinds of constraints that fundamentally impede economic competitiveness. Thus, neoliberalism seeks "an expansion of the spaces of capital accumulation" (Dardot & Laval, 2013, p. 216). While this has led some to describe neoliberalism as a withdrawal of the state, Dardot and Laval (2013) suggest, rather, that it is the end of nation-states governed by nonmarket principles. In other words, neoliberalism's rationale has transformed how we govern. In place of the welfare state (a governing system that emphasized both economic progress and the equitable distribution of growth), government "aims to maximize the population's utility" (Dardot & Laval, 2013, p. 225) by creating situations in which individuals adapt to competition. Simply put, neoliberalism has altered governance by making competition central to state activity and by modeling itself after the practices of private enterprise. Thus, the ways in which neoliberalism has determined a new mode of government is key to our conceptual framework.

While neoliberals argue that a market-driven approach to policy will benefit all consumers and bring worldwide prosperity, the privatization and restructuring of public resources has been found to "benefit corporations and governments more than clients and local constituents" (Duncan, 2013, p. 3). Policies that reduce costs, such as weakening the bargaining power of unions, reflect more generally the ways in which government is lowering the quality of social protection. The establishment of new public management—a blend of public, private, and voluntary sectors—to solve community problems has permitted new voices in policy conversations and has thus transformed how power is accessed (Hursh, 2016). Empirical studies have shown that neoliberal policies further disadvantage underserved constituents and exacerbate, not lessen, economic and social inequalities across race and class in a variety of institutions (Duggan, 2003; Pattillo, 2007).

Arguably, nowhere are the damaging effects of neoliberalism more demonstrable than in public schooling (Apple, 2001; Bulkley & Fisler, 2003; Hankins & Martin, 2006; Lipman & Haines, 2007; Lipman, 2011b; Lubienski, Gulosino, & Weitzel, 2009; Pedroni, 2011; Stambach & Becker, 2006; Stuart-Wells, Slayton, & Scott, 2002). By the 1990s, neoliberalism had infiltrated school reform. Milton Friedman, among the chief intellectual economic thinkers at the University of Chicago in the mid-century who extolled the free market as an alternative to social democratic liberalism, began to argue how market mechanisms would improve public schooling (Friedman, 1955). In the late 1980s, Chubb and Moe (1988) had declared that the failures of public schooling stemmed from its institutional environment; that is, the democratic structure of public schooling—its bureaucracy and politics—were barriers to improvement. The solution, they argued, was to situate the enterprise in a new institutional environment: the market. Competition would improve efficiency and encourage innovation as schools responded to consumers rather than a broad constituency (Chubb & Moe, 1990). Since then, the notion that markets and privatization are a "natural and neutral way through which decisions should be made" (Hursh, 2016, p. 36) has become a generally accepted approach to education policy (Deeds & Pattillo, 2015; Lipman, 2011a; Lipman & Hursh, 2007).

The greatest and most obvious manifestation of neoliberalism in school reform is perhaps a system of charter schools and its accompanying school closures—the creation of a market of schools in which schools compete for enrollment, underperforming schools are closed, and parents are no longer viewed as constituents but as consumers. What is less apparent are the ways in which this new system of schooling relates to school governance change. The facilitation of a market of schools is made possible by transforming the way schools are governed; both charter schools and school governance change are symptomatic of neoliberalism in the education sector. What is key to our analysis is how neoliberal school reforms have disproportionately affected low-income, urban neighborhoods and have ultimately disenfranchised historically disadvantaged communities (Lipman & Hursh, 2007; Saltman, 2000; Stuart-Wells et al., 2002). In this regard, two themes in the literature on neoliberal education are particularly salient in our historical narrative: the racialization of neoliberal education policy and the shift from "government to governance."

Racial Logic of Neoliberal School Reform

The discourses through which neoliberal policies are justified are based on a racial narrative, a representation of Black spaces as pathological, crime-ridden, and dysfunctional (Lipman, 2011a; Pedroni, 2011). For instance, the rationale for state seizure of land through eminent domain, the dispersal of low-income people of color, and the closing of public institutions (e.g., schools, hospitals, public housing) is the need to subject these spaces to the supposed "regenerative and disciplining effects of the market" (Lipman, 2011a, p. 226). In this narrative, only private management and market-driven restructuring can correct the failure and dysfunction that is thought to be bred in the "ghetto." In the case of schooling, while school debt is the result of decades of disinvestment and other historical factors (e.g., White flight, discriminatory housing practices), the racialized logic of neoliberal school reform blames the disenfranchised for their conditions, reifying the White spatial imagery that justifies the razing of Black communities.

While neoliberalism is promoted as an efficient, politically neutral approach that will benefit all, Lipman and Hursh's (2007) study of Renaissance 2010, a neoliberal plan to recreate the city and its schools in Chicago, revealed an increasingly economically and spatially divided city. Similar studies have suggested that the closing and replacement of schools with charters—a plan that has presented charter schools as a superior option to failing traditional schools—is a plan to attract professionals for a global city; in effect, only the privileged actually have access to better options (Lipman, 2011a; Lipman & Haines, 2007; Lipman & Hursh, 2007; Pedroni, 2011). Although charter advocates argue that competition—the weeding out process—raises the quality of traditional schools, such wide-scale improvement is largely questionable (de la Torre & Gwynne, 2009; de la Torre et al., 2015; Engberg et al., 2012; Zernike, 2016). Instead, available choices to native residents are of lower academic quality (Stambach & Becker, 2006) or, due to capacity constraints, are inaccessible to a majority of local students (de la Torre & Gwynne, 2009). Finally, little thought is given to how school closures affect families as they are forced to relocate or find new schools (Deeds & Pattillo, 2015; de la Torre et al., 2015; Zernike, 2016).

The fact that communities affected by school closures are not consulted underscores the racialized logic of neoliberal school reform. For instance, there was no consultation with teachers, principals, or school employees when reformers decided to close 20 schools in Chicago (Lipman & Hursh, 2007). Increasingly, according to Lipman and Hursh (2007), communities of color like those in Chicago are implementing acts of resistance, expressing "outrage at the dismissal of any meaningful participation by the communities and people affected by these policies" (p. 174). While neoliberalism promises individual freedom and choice, in practice it has disproportionately caused suffering, particularly in African American neighborhoods, and the NAACP has recently called for a moratorium on charters (Strauss, 2016). Such blatant disregard for the opinions of the community has been perceived as racist and dictatorial. This is because the neoliberal project has also fundamentally changed government, modeling itself after the practices of private enterprise. Thus, the suppression of democracy is not incidental but a key mechanism for changing who decides for schools.

From "Government to Governance"

School closures and the expansion of charters, as policies, are related to other neoliberal school reform strategies that are changing the ways in which schools are governed. For instance, mayoral control—which Chicago pioneered—is often a tactic that is associated with the appointment of "unelected public-private bodies," without community involvement or with public hearings that are only "perfunctory in nature" (Lipman, 2011a, p. 220). Restructuring agendas, such as suspending or eliminating the school board (i.e., influence of local actors), not only diminish democratic participation but also transform the level at which schooling decisions are made, leading to a general shift from local to state to national (Hursh, 2016). Federal policies such as NCLB and RTT have incentivized mayoral takeover and school closures as reform strategies that have allowed for the emergence of new educational players. A mix of state and federal officials, philanthropies, and corporations—providing support around school closings and the expansion of charters—have exerted an unprecedented level of influence in U.S. education reform in the last several decades, (Lipman, 2011a; Lipman & Hursh, 2007; Pedroni, 2011; Saltman, 2010).

With the onset of neoliberalism, the role of school governance has significantly changed from a "democratic tradition of universal care, equity, and concerns with the social" (Saltman, 2000, p. 34) to a managerial culture that maximizes profit and individual gains. Moreover, Wolch (1990) argued that venture philanthropists who play key roles in setting policy and performing government functions with no public accountability have essentially become a shadow state. The interweaving of philanthropic organizations and city government reflect this shift from "government to governance" (Lipman, 2011a, p. 226), with the notion that it is no longer "government by the people" but rather "government over the people." One of the far-reaching consequences of empowering nongovernmental actors to make decisions about public education without public accountability is that it has delegitimized and weakened the democratic nature of the school system (Kretchmar, 2014).

Again, the discursive framing of public schools, particularly in urban areas, as failing monopolies unable to manage themselves has allowed outsiders to step in. Neoliberal school reform has increased a mix of governmental and corporate interventions in the daily lives of those especially from marginalized, under-resourced communities (Lipman & Hursh, 2007). Few have recognized that school closures are symptomatic of governance change, the redistribution of who gets to make schooling decisions in predominantly communities of color. Thus, the notion of neoliberal school reform allows us to show how the creation of the EAA statewide recovery school district in Detroit—a public–private partnership of state officials, venture capitalists, and foundations—signaled the end of traditional school governance and marked the largest number of school closures in the period leading up to its establishment. This theoretical framework also helps us to evaluate the costs of closures by exploring the social and political dilemmas of the neoliberal project in cities like Detroit, a majority Black, highly segregated city.

METHODOLOGY

Our study was grounded in historical methods: the framing of events and actors, contextualizing, and observing patterns of detail—all to make meaning of school governance change over time and tell a plausible story of the causal relationship between these changes and school closings. As such, Detroit provided a highly applicable historical case study for a closer examination of: (a) new and emerging patterns of school governance at the turn of the 21st century; (b) the implications of the explosion of school closings in urban communities; and (c) the costs and consequences of such practices for children, teachers, and communities. In comparison to the social science methods used often in the study of educational problems, in historical research the "method" proceeds from "the notion of sequence" (Stone, 1989, p. 257). As Stone (1989) explained, "Events have manifold causes, many of which we may never identify or even be conscious of. But by following events sequentially, we gain some understanding of what remains constant, what changes, and what is associated with each" (p. 255). Our primary sources consist of newspaper articles, government documents, and websites. A body of secondary sources, including previous studies conducted by the authors (Kang, 2015), informed our understanding of DPS's history. We then overlay existing data on DPS's school closures (Grover & van der Velde, 2016) upon this historical narrative. By doing so, we find the greatest number of school closures occur at the moment in which efforts to institutionalize neoliberal school governance accelerate. Thus, a historical case study approach (Yin, 2003) was apropos given our aim to understand the unprecedented number of school closings in Detroit during the past 35 years and the contextual conditions (i.e., school governance changes) that helped give rise to these closings.

Our analysis also included neoliberal concepts to support our observations around school governance change: "Good concepts illuminate significant details, and telling details point to illuminating concepts" (Stone, 1989, p. 255). We were particularly interested in analyzing school closures within the context of how policies have led to new governing arrangements—highlighting the racial resonances; the discursive framing of educational decision-making and reforms (e.g., choice, quality, efficiency); the role of nongovernmental actors in the educational landscape; and importantly, the particular types of governance arrangements enacted at different points in time.

HISTORICAL NARRATIVE

The Rise and Decline of the Detroit Public Schools (1960s–1980s)

In the early 19th century, what formal schooling there was in Detroit consisted of a few "free" schools, run privately or by religious organizations. By 1842, the Detroit Board of Education was established to manage a rudimentary system of 13 publicly-funded schools and 2,000 pupils (Grover & van der Velde, 2016). As the city's population rose, the number of school-aged children grew 20-fold to 40,000 by 1900, and 88 more schools were added to accommodate them (Grover & van der Velde, 2016). The dawn of the 20th century would see yet more exponential growth as Detroit's budding auto industry attracted tens of thousands of migrants in search of employment from both within the United States and abroad, bringing the city's total population to 1.57 million by 1930 (Grover & van der Velde, 2016). With more than 200,000 students in 1927 and 180 more new school buildings (Grover & van der Velde, 2016), this period of growth reflected not only the demand for capacity but also the need to address the new technological, economic, and social changes of the industrial era (Tyack, 1974).

While school growth—aided by a strong economy—marked the rise of the DPS, so did the transformation of a crude lay-controlled arrangement of schools into a professionalized "board of directors" that oversaw a large bureaucracy. Until 1916, the city's wards elected board members. The early school reformers successfully campaigned to centralize schools under a single at-large board, arguing that citywide elections would elevate the status of the position and result in more qualified candidates. This governing structure, the traditional governing model, would go unchallenged for the next 40 years (Mirel, 1999).

A major blow to traditional school governance—and the DPS itself—came in 1967 when a major tax increase aiding the school district was soundly defeated at the ballot. This rejection came about in no small part as a result of shifting demographics in post-WWII Detroit (Mirel, 1999). Employment opportunities attracted tens of thousands of young Black families from the South, and the city's population went from 81% White and 16% Black in 1950 to 59% White and 29% Black only 10 years later (U.S. Census Bureau, 1980). By the time the 1967 tax increase was proposed, White working class voters—still a majority of the electorate—were much less inclined to support the DPS, whose students were by this time predominantly Black. It would prove to be a major turning point in the fate of the DPS: "Never again would large numbers of white working-class voters support a tax increase for the Detroit public schools" (Mirel, 1999, p. 325). Meanwhile, the city's tax base as whole was steadily shrinking throughout this period as White families relocated to the suburbs (Sugrue, 2005). The city's efforts to desegregate its schools through busing in compliance with the 1974 U.S. Supreme Court ruling in *Milliken v. Bradley* further accelerated this White flight. With the nation as a whole entering an economic recession, the first major wave of school closures came in 1976, targeting 14 schools (Grover & van der Velde, 2016). By the end of that decade, the DPS not only had less revenue to finance itself but also fractured political support for raising taxes.

Failure to Change From Within: A Turning Point (1981–1993)

The school crisis in the 1960s and 1970s resulted in Detroiters experimenting with "community control," a brief 10-year period in which the school district was decentralized in an unprecedented attempt to reorganize governance since the beginning of the century. The perception was that an all White school board was incapable of understanding the needs of Black schools and neighborhoods. Thus, by essentially returning to a ward-based system, school leaders were elected by neighborhoods to address particular schooling issues. Community control, however, brought few improvements and on September 15, 1981, Detroiters voted to reinstate the at-large school board (Mirel, 1999). Still, 41 more schools would close in the next decade (Grover & van der Velde, 2016). Overall financial decline, dissatisfaction with the Board of Education reinforced by negative portrayals in the media, and fractured political support would create the conditions for a fiscally conservative governor to implement sweeping reforms and mayoral take-over of the DPS.

The media largely portrayed the DPS's financial troubles as stemming from corruption, featuring stories of expensive first-class trips and of chauffeurs who earned more than the average DPS teacher (Mirel, 1999). In reality, declining enrollment and an eroding tax base played a significant role in the district's financial woes. Blacks were now 63% of the population as Whites continued to leave for the suburbs (U.S. Census Bureau, 1980). By 1982, enrollment dipped below 200,000 and 15 more schools closed (Grover & van der Velde, 2016). The collapse of the auto industry, beginning in the early 1980s, was also taking its toll on the Motor City's economy. In fact, when tens of thousands of auto jobs were lost, the school district became the second largest employer in the city and a critical source for maintaining Detroit's Black middle class (Henig, Hula, Orr, & Pedescleaux, 1999; Rich, 2009). With the DPS's employees concerned about job security during uncertain economic times, the teachers' union—the Detroit Federation of Teachers (DFT)—became all the more intense in its demands. The school board bowed to these demands, which many argue was the cause of the DPS's educational malaise (Addonizio & Kearney, 2012; Mirel, 1999; Rich, 2009).

Having amassed consecutive annual budget deficits since 1978 (Addonizio & Kearney, 2012), a coalition of Blacks, Whites, labor unions, business groups, grassroots activists, and major political leaders emerged to denounce the school board's sheer lack of fiscal responsibility and promised to unseat incumbents in the next election (Addonizio & Kearney, 2012; Mirel, 1999). In 1988, all of the incumbents' seats were won by outsiders. Calling themselves the HOPE team, they effectively established a "reform board." The new board swiftly took control and balanced the budget. However, once they set out to restructure the schools (e.g., establish magnet schools), the DFT perceived these efforts as a threat to its contracts and fired back by depicting HOPE board members as union busters. Underestimating the DFT's influence in the community, HOPE members lost all of their seats in 1992 (Mirel, 2004). The collapse of HOPE signaled a turning point: the inability to break the status quo from within would be used to justify efforts to subdue the influence of the teachers' union and overhaul the bureaucratic nature of traditional school governance.

Changing Governance: Proposal A and Mayoral Control (1994–2004)

In 1990, Michigan elected Republican Governor John Engler, who had campaigned on cutting taxes and fixing education. Having been influenced by Chubb and Moe's (1990) groundbreaking ideas about how school bureaucracy was the root of all contemporary education problems, Engler set out to overhaul the state's school system and diminish the power of the teachers' unions, which he believed were the single greatest force in maintaining the status quo (Goenner, 2011). Engler had also taken to Chubb and Moe's (1990) ideas about circumventing local bureaucracy and politics by creating a "market of schools," an alternative system in which parents could exit failing schools and opt for better ones. The other notion was that competition had the capacity to transform schools in ways that reformers had been seeking to engineer in a variety of other ways. While only 15 schools closed during Engler's governorship between 1991 and 2003 (Grover & van der Velde, 2016), the governor's policies—Proposal A and mayoral takeover—were sweeping reforms that would usher in competition, neoliberal approaches to school reform, governance change, and the greatest number of school closings in the DPS's history.

Taking advantage of the public's general discontent with high property taxes, the governor successfully passed legislation that not only promised to cut taxes but also revolutionize education. On March 15, 1994, when 70% of Michigan voters approved replacing property tax with the state sales tax as the main source of school funding, *The New York Times* declared that it was "the nation's most dramatic shift in a century in the way public schools are financed" (Celis, 1994, para. 1). Indeed, Proposal A would have a remarkable effect on the future of schooling in Michigan. Changing the source of school funding shifted finance decisions from local to state government, which was now responsible for collecting and distributing school funding. Thus, in effect, Proposal A increased the state's role in public education. It is important to note that while the new funding formula purported to increase the amount of funding for districts like the DPS, Proposal A would be highly sensitive to economic highs and lows. When the recession hit in 2001, there was not only less school funding all around but significantly less for the DPS given the demands of inflation (e.g., rising personnel costs) and other costs such as capital improvements (Arsen et al., 2005; Hammer, 2011; Izraeli & Murphy, 2007). Nonetheless, Engler was satisfied by how Proposal A delivered a sharp blow against the teachers' unions; increasing the state's role in funding matters significantly decreased the unions' ability to negotiate with school boards (Goenner, 2011). With Detroit as home to the largest teachers' union in the state, this policy was arguably the first major effort to change governance by dismantling the political support around it.

At the same time, changing per-pupil funding to follow the student allowed for the launching of charter schools and "schools of choice" across the state—in effect, an alternate system of schooling (i.e., a market of schools) that would compete with the DPS. From an initial 14 charter schools in 1995, an average of seven new charter schools opened every year; by 2001, more than 19,000 students were enrolled in charter schools in Detroit (Grover & van der Velde, 2016). As parents and students left the DPS for charters, Proposal A, in effect, siphoned funding away from traditional schools while exacerbating the district's worsening budget issues (Hammer, 2011). Between 1999 and 2011, with state funding at approximately $6,400 per pupil, a loss of 11,155 students cost the DPS $71.4 million (Grover & van der Velde, 2016). By 2009, schools of choice enrolled 5% of the students across the state, a transfer of $595 million in state funds to nontraditional schools. Thus, Proposal A was greatly responsible for the DPS's downsizing and fiscal crisis, marking the beginning of extreme cost-cutting measures such as school closures and other neoliberal strategies in school governance.

After the successful passage of Proposal A, the governor began to turn his attention to Detroit. In his 1996 State of the State address, after citing the DPS's high dropout rate and chronically low test scores, the governor proposed a mayoral takeover of the district. Several other cities—notably Chicago—had already begun to experiment with mayoral control, with mayors either appointing reform boards or directly working with a chief executive officer (CEO) of schools (Wong et al., 2007). Again, the rationale was that the bureaucratic nature of traditional school governance was inclined to maintain the status quo and had been, for far too long, failing students and parents. The governor's proposal, however, was immediately controversial. Many Detroiters perceived a racial undertone to Engler's plan. By now, Detroit was a majority Black city (82%) and opponents of mayoral takeover argued that they would be the only district in the state unable to elect their own school officials (Kang, 2015). Others surmised that the governor wanted the ability to control the money designated for rebuilding the DPS's infrastructure, a $1.5 billion bond issue that Detroiters had voted for in 1994 (Black, 2016). In 1998, Detroit's mayor, Dennis Archer, a Democrat, expressed his dismay with the plan, arguing that the state should not dictate the terms of school reform to Detroit; but, in the same breath, the mayor told Detroiters to face the facts because Republicans had swept the legislature (Mirel, 2004). Indeed, in 1999, a Republican majority passed a bill for mayoral takeover and compromised with Detroiters by imposing a

5-year limit, at which point Detroiters would decide whether or not to keep the new governing structure.

The mayoral board appointed Kenneth Burnley as CEO. A native Detroiter, the appointment helped to calm some people's anxieties and the transition to mayoral control was relatively smooth. Throughout the CEO's tenure, the mayor was noticeably absent. Thus, Burnley became the face of school reform in Detroit and, in effect, acted on behalf of the governor (Mirel, 2004). It was an incredible sign of the reach the governor had in Detroit and the increased state role in school reform in Detroit. Although Burnley improved academic outcomes in the first few years of his tenure, the CEO announced a $48.7 million budget deficit in 2004 (Mirel, 2004). What many did not understand at the time was how Proposal A was creating a structural crisis; thousands of students left the system during Burnley's tenure. Despite the CEO's efforts, he could not attract new students fast enough to offset the ones who were leaving the system. Shaken by the news of the deficit, Detroiters voted to reinstate the publicly-elected school board (MacDonald, 2005).

Although the effects of Proposal A obstructed the effectiveness of mayoral takeover, the two sweeping policies had set a precedent for further tinkering with the DPS's governance. In fact, the more Proposal A precipitated a financial crisis, the more policymakers were inclined to address the problem with neoliberal strategies—extreme measures that would completely eradicate the DPS's traditional governing structure and result in the greatest number of school closures in the DPS's history.

The Rise of Neoliberal Governance: Emergency Management and the Education Achievement Authority (2005–2015)

Although Governor Engler had begun the fundamental reordering of the political dynamics around public schooling in the state, on the national front a combination of policy approaches—standards-based reform, differentiation of schools, and market-based reforms (embodied in federal legislation such as NCLB and RTTT)—sought to breakup traditional school governance on a large scale but more importantly brought new educational players onto the scene. As a structural and financial crisis ensued in Detroit, this new education regime found it an opportune time to establish public–private partnerships that could radically transform the DPS while a new governor authorized certain governmental bodies and agencies with the power to circumvent traditional democratic processes and seize schools and fire teachers without consulting local constituents.

Because the DPS's enrollment continued to drop precipitously, the reinstated school board struggled to make any significant improvements, with the deficit ballooning to $400 million in 2008 (Bukowski, 2008). This caused Democratic Governor Jennifer Granholm—who had taken office in 2003—to declare a financial emergency with the passage of Public Act 72 and appoint the DPS's first emergency manager, Robert Bobb. Once again, the school board had been suspended, this time indefinitely as the emergency manager had acquired the authority to resolve the district's financial crisis (Bowman, 2013). A growing national network of foundations, venture philanthropists, service providers, and private education industry vendors, who had been supporting reform in other cities, had been reluctant to consider Detroit. Now, sensing that the installment of an emergency manager had quelled the influence and politics of local actors, various groups began to express their interest in supporting Detroit's emergency manager (Bukowski, 2008; Reckhow, 2010). Bobb had graduated from the Broad Foundation's superintendent training program, founded by the billionaire Eli Broad and Governor John Engler in 2002. The men envisioned the program producing leaders that would transform school systems in the nation's largest districts through a market model (Kang, 2015). The Broad Foundation had, in fact, committed to funding a portion of Bobb's salary as emergency manager (Welch, 2010).

With $20 million in federal stimulus funds, Bobb's immediate strategy was to hand over schools to private educational management organizations (EMOs), beginning with the hiring of four EMOs with multi-year contracts to turn around 17 of the worst-performing high schools in the district (Schultz, 2009). Bobb then launched the Renaissance Plan 2012, an aggressive campaign to retain students and attract them back to the district. By the end of Bobb's first year, the Wall Street Journal reported that emergency management had taken the school district a step closer to financial stability (Kellogg, 2009). By 2011, however, the emergency manager admitted that his plan had been unable to bring in enough revenue while projecting the loss of another 73,000 students by 2014 (Dolan, 2011). In 2011 alone, Detroit lost 7,856 students to other school districts, or 10% of its total enrollment (Grover & van der Velde, 2016). In a last-ditch effort to eliminate a $327 million deficit, Bobb suggested closing nearly half of the DPS's schools and increasing the average size of the high school classroom to 60 students (Dolan, 2011). Facing significant criticism, Bobb resigned in June.

No amount of triage could reverse the effects of Proposal A, with the loss of per-pupil funding for each student who left the DPS. Yet, subsequent emergency managers would largely approach the fiscal crisis in a similar fashion: close schools even though such cost-cutting measures could not keep up with the rate at which the deficit was growing. Meanwhile, charter operators began to expand their offerings, advertising in areas where the

DPS's schools were closing (Grover & van der Velde, 2016). (At the time of writing, the DPS's fourth emergency manager, Judge Steven Rhodes, who oversaw Detroit's municipal bankruptcy in 2013, was managing the state's $617 million bailout for the DPS.) While emergency management did little to improve the DPS's financial condition, it was pivotal to introducing a gamut of neoliberal practices: the removal of local voices (i.e., the indefinite suspension of the school board), the development of public–private partnerships (i.e., the introduction of the Broad Foundation as a key player), and the practice of handing schools over to EMOs. Emergency management would also create the conditions for the next governor to completely seize the DPS's schools and create the EAA.

When Republican Governor Rick Snyder took office in early 2011, he inherited several educational initiatives from the Granholm administration. In 2009, the state had put together a package of bills in hopes of winning $400 million in RTT dollars, a federal incentive program for school turnaround. Although Michigan failed to win any federal money, some of the bills nevertheless became law (Murray, 2010). One of the laws established a State School Reform/Redesign District (SRRD), which would provide the blueprint and basis from which to launch the EAA. When Snyder entered office, no schools had been transferred to the SRRD; he then engineered a way to transfer the DPS's schools without any legislative action or need for consulting the public (Kang, 2015).

Reminiscent of Governor Engler, Snyder envisioned overhauling the state's education system and modernizing the delivery of education for the 21st century. Several months into his term, the governor delivered a special message on education to the Michigan legislature in which he argued for the removal of all state and local barriers that hinder innovation (Snyder, 2011). The governor also immediately expanded the powers of the emergency manager and appointed Roy Roberts, a former General Motors executive, to work closely with him (Kang, 2015; Mason & Arsen, 2014).

In May 2011, the governor sent representatives from his office to meet with Roberts, leaders from Eastern Michigan University (EMU), and the Broad Foundation to discuss how to set in motion the recovery school district. They would do it through an interlocal agreement whereby two public entities, the DPS and EMU, would agree to collaborate and share resources in providing a public service. While interlocal agreements around water or utility services, for example, are a fairly common strategy for cutting costs, the idea of creating an authority for transferring and establishing the recovery school district was unprecedented (Kang, 2015). Because Roberts had complete control of the DPS, he could immediately begin transferring schools without public consultation, virtually seizing school buildings and students from the district. While the plan faced deep opposition from locals that triggered weeks of protest like the one at Mumford, Detroiters were essentially powerless. The interlocal agreement enabled the governor to launch the EAA without relying on traditional democratic processes. Roberts announced the transfer of 15 DPS schools to the EAA on March 13, 2012 (Dawsey, 2012). Meanwhile, Snyder appointed a chancellor, a graduate of the Broad Academy, to oversee the EAA; again, the Broad Foundation would finance the chancellor's salary. Private donations would also foot the EAA's one-time start-up costs. The founding board of the EAA, to which the chancellor reported, included corporative executives and philanthropists from the Detroit area and across the state (Kang, 2015).

In designing the recovery school district, Roberts worked closely with foundations like Broad and contracted with Agilix, a company offering software solutions for schools, to provide a largely experimental technology platform called "Buzz." In the media, Roberts boasted that Buzz was the main feature in the new school district's instructional and curricular innovations (Smith, 2014). The EAA also required the rehiring of all former DPS employees, which resulted in the firing of many teachers and the hiring of new ones, 27% of which were from Teach for America (TFA; Gross, 2014). In the next several years, the EAA struggled to improve student outcomes. There were reports of fiscal mismanagement, lack of operational support, and lack of transparency, and disciplinary problems. In 2013, after the filing of a Freedom of Information request, hundreds of emails attested that Buzz was a botched online program: significant disruptions during the baseline assessment, headsets needed for audio were not available, weak wireless signals, and many students unable to log into the system at all (Pedroni, 2013). Undoubtedly, these stories drew much public attention and scrutiny, with critics arguing that the EAA was essentially a "Jim Crow District" in which African American children were being experimented on (Sands, 2012). For all its failures, the Michigan House's Republican majority still managed to pass an EAA expansion bill in 2014 (Livengood, 2014). At the time of writing, however, there are plans for reabsorbing the EAA back into the DPS (Zaniewski, 2016).

During this period, nevertheless, the EAA completely supplanted the local school board regime with outsiders, indicating the end of traditional school governance in Detroit. Thirty years of policies, both state and federal, had culminated in the gradual erosion of the school board, allowing for an unprecedented intertwining of philanthropic organizations and city government, and signaling the rise of neoliberal school reform in Detroit. While Proposal A launched the creation of charter schools in the state, it also resulted in a much smaller DPS. By 2012, the DPS enrolled fewer than 50,000 students, compared to 180,000 in 1994 (Data Driven Detroit, 2012). In 2013, the number of Detroit's pupils enrolled in charter schools had eclipsed the number enrolled in the DPS (Grover & van der Velde, 2016). "As of 2014, there were 96 charter school programs operating in Detroit, compared to 103 public school programs" (Grover & van der Velde, 2016). Ironically, the shrinking of the DPS, making it impossible to eliminate the deficit, provided a rationale for more neoliberal measures. The expansion of emergency management, the creation of the EAA in spite of mass resistance and protest, the purging of local actors, the weakening of democratic processes, and the outsourcing of teaching and learning to service providers like Agilix and organizations like TFA all reflected the neoliberal agenda of installing new "managers" and "experts" to carry out school reform in the 21st century. During this period, 175 more schools closed. Among the 231 schools that had closed since 1980, 76% of them occurred in the last 10 years when policymakers accelerated their efforts to fundamentally change school governance in Detroit. Thus, school closures, we argue, are part and parcel with governance change.

DISCUSSION

Detroit's economic boom and population growth at the dawn of the 20th century led to governance change: from village schools to a large bureaucratic system, which we have referred to as traditional school governance. Pressures to dismantle traditional school governance in Detroit began in the 1960s. By 1971, Detroit decentralized its school district. This decision to alter the school district's governance model was accompanied by Detroit's first major wave of school closures in 1976 (Grover & van der Velde, 2016). This marked the beginning of a new era. Our historical case study of the DPS after 1980 reveals that subsequent policies continued to seek governance change, strategies that began with gradually eroding local control (i.e., a coalition consisting of the teachers' union, school board officials, teachers, and constituents) and pushing decision-making into higher levels of government (i.e., the state), and eventually introducing new educational actors onto the scene (e.g., foundations, philanthropists, educational entrepreneurs, service providers, etc.). Meanwhile, when efforts to change governance significantly accelerated after 2000, 76% of all school closures occurred between 2005–2015, a rate of 13 schools per year. In 2012, the first full-year the EAA was in operation, the DPS would close 31 of its schools, the largest number of closures in a single year in the district's history (Grover & van der Velde, 2016). While school closures have been attributed to shrinking enrollment, population decline, and the recession, our analysis suggests that school closures are also symptomatic of governance change.

From an historical perspective, on the one hand, America's fondness for tinkering with governance (Tyack & Cuban, 1995) puts forward the idea that perennial changes in management are inevitable and path-dependent. In this sense, one could view school closures as an unfortunate outcome of transitioning from one system to another. On the other hand, the neo-liberal agenda, a rationality for a new type of government, have resulted in a bewildering number of school closures disproportionately affecting low-income African American communities and families, illuminating the dilemmas in our contemporary efforts to overhaul the system and the costs of school closures associated with changing governance. We identify at least two costs in Detroit: the dismantling of democracy and reinforcing historic racial and class divides.

Dismantling of Democracy

Dardot and Laval (2013) argued that neoliberal policy makers' commitment to the economic future is, ironically, something that they themselves have actively constructed over decades; that the "obstinacy" or "fanaticism" with which they pursue austerity is in fact redress for previous pursuits. Unable and unwilling to break with this normative framework, neoliberals are "embroiled in the headlong rush to adapt increasingly to the effects of their own previous policy" (p. 14). In this case, Proposal A, which unleashed Michigan's charter school movement, would create a financial and structural crisis for the DPS, but ultimately creating disaster-like conditions that permitted Governor Snyder to circumvent democratic processes, a kind of utilitarian authority unimaginable elsewhere. The establishment of the EAA, furthermore, is a prime example of this reckless rush to fix the effects of previous policy. Exploiting a loophole in the state constitution—which allowed two political entities to function as a governmental entity without approval from the state legislature or citizens—the governor utilized "closed door" maneuvers and private partnerships to implement the recovery school district as quickly as possible. It mattered little that Detroiters had little to no opportunity to weigh in and taxpayers had recently voted to pass a $50 million bond to renovate Mumford High, one of the city's most cherished schools. Rather, the new governing regime perceived the EAA as a maneuver to return Detroit to solvency. The neoliberal idea that improving schools is part and parcel of urban renewal projects permitted the takeover of 15 DPS school without consulting parents while denigrating the usual democratic processes that African Americans, in particular, have fought for so long.

Since the 18th century, Western countries have been built on the premise that elected officials answer to the governed. But the new rationale behind today's school reform efforts, like the EAA, suggests that bypassing citizens is especially acceptable under the circumstances of financial crisis (Dardot & Laval, 2013), "revitalization efforts" and the need for creating a "good business climate" (Lipman, 2011a, p. 220). The gradual relocation of power from local actors—teachers' unions, school board officials, parents, and so on—to new external and often private actors subverts the fundamental meaning of citizenship. For instance, in June 2016, the Michigan Legislature unanimously opposed a plan that would enable a local commission to oversee and manage all of Detroit's schools including charters; additionally, their decision included a provision containing punitive language regarding administrators and teachers who engaged in illegal strikes (Gray, 2016). According to Lipman and Hursh (2007), increasing acts of protest and resistance is evidence of neoliberal tactics. The demonstration at Mumford High is but one example of countless acts of protest in the last decade. Although Judge Rhodes, the most recent emergency manager, met with DPS parents shortly after his appointment by the governor, it was largely perfunctory and ameliorative in nature as he told parents that they should take up their grievances not with him but the legislature (Hicks, 2016).

The case of school governance change in Detroit demonstrate how today's efforts to reform urban schools far too often ignore community interests in predominantly low-income neighborhoods of color; the voices of parents, teachers, students, and taxpayers often go unheard (Deeds & Pattillo, 2015; Duggan, 2003; Kretchmar, 2014; Lipman, 2011a; Lipman & Hursh, 2007). Therefore, we find one of the most perilous aspects of school closures is that it signals the erosion of democracy for those that government should especially fight to protect.

Reinforcement of Historic Racial and Class Divides

"For Detroit's Children, More School Choice but Not Better Schools" is the headline on the front page of a recent edition of the *New York Times* (Zernike, 2016). In just 10 words, the headline sums up what we contend is the final cost of school closures: in Detroit, the more school closings, the more charter schools. With the vast majority of charter schools concentrated in Detroit and with little evidence that the system outperforms traditional schools, Detroit's pupils have in effect been transferred from one poor-performing system to another. In reality, choice has served as an illusion while preserving a separate and unequal schooling system between urban and suburban, Black and White neighborhoods. There is evidence that the disparities have increased since Proposal A. While there were significant disparities between urban and suburban schools in 1994, the DPS was performing on par with other urban school districts across the United States (Zernike, 2016). But, by 2009, 15 years after one of the nation's most lenient and expansive charter school laws was enacted and hundreds of school closures, Detroit was reported as the lowest-performing urban school district on national achievement tests (Zernike, 2016). In 2015,

NAEP results showed that only 4% of Detroit's eighth graders scored proficient in math compared to the state's average of 29%; in reading, only 7% of Detroit's eighth graders scored proficient compared to the state's average of 32% (DeVito, 2015). Indeed, while the expansion of charters in Detroit—second only to New Orleans—has garnered praise in some circles, some news media outlets have published stories about the extreme sacrifices Detroit parents are forced to make within a system of perpetual school closures and charter openings. In a recent edition of the *Atlantic*, it was reported that some parents have to travel 6 hours and take up to eight buses each day to get their kids to the school of their choice (Einhorn, 2016).

Finally, the EAA, which signaled the end of traditional school governance and a period of a historic number of school closings, also encapsulates a separate and unequal system and reinforcement of racial and class divides in the region. It must be noted that while policymakers promised to turnaround the lowest-performing schools in the state, only Detroit schools were selected. Without publicly elected officials (e.g., the school board) to represent Detroiters, the emergency manager made a unanimous decision to transfer schools into an untested and experimental system. Within months of opening, the 8,000-pupil district recorded 5,200 disciplinary incidents, and students were performing much worse academically—not better—than before the EAA had begun to govern their schools. Investigations would soon reveal how the system's online platform, its main strategy for teaching and learning, was essentially broken; who knows how many idle days there were in which students were not learning. Critics questioned what middle class, suburban, White family would permit their children to be taught by uncertified teachers (i.e., TFA) and by untested technologies (Kang, 2015). Yet, a discourse remains that Detroiters are largely responsible for their schooling problems.

Therefore, the cost of school closures has been the reinforcement of existing racial, political, economic, and spatial inequalities of the metro Detroit area and the ongoing marginalization and exclusion of African American, low-income, and working class residents. For decades, influential actors have touted that governance change would usher in the invisible hand of the market as the key to improving education. However, we find that in Detroit, the market is the conduit through which racism, inequities, and intransigence are perpetuated.

CONCLUSION

In this chapter, we have offered a historical case study that suggests a more complex story about school closures in the city of Detroit. We argue that the staggering number of school closings since 1980 is symptomatic of successive policies that are part of a broader neoliberal restructuring agenda. This historical perspective allows us to draw some parallels between governance change in the 20th century and the 21st century, while highlighting some key differences that expose the dilemmas of today's school reform efforts. Decline, not growth, characterizes our time and the conditions in which policymakers perceive neoliberal strategies as making perfect sense for addressing educational problems. Thus, new school governance and its coalition of supporters are indifferent to the effect of school closures on real people and neighborhoods when neoliberalism promises to theoretically address issues of economic decline. But the consequences of governance changes and its associated school closures are grave. In Detroit, we see how school reform in the last several decades have pitted locals against state officials, reinforcing deep racial and political divides in the region; we see the futility of protests, signaling the loss of democracy; and, we see the DPS's financial debt and budgetary crisis far from being resolved. Most damaging of all, the state of education for Detroit's children has hardly changed, if not worsened. NAEP test scores and college readiness rates rank Detroit among the lowest in the country. Because Detroiters themselves are often blamed for school closures (e.g., financial mismanagement or corruption), this chapter seeks to reveal how non-local actors who have engineered governance change are responsible for Detroit's historic mass number of school closures. Time will tell whether governance change was worth it, but the costs and consequences strongly suggest otherwise.

REFERENCES

Addonizio, M. F., & Kearney, C. P. (2012). *Education reform and the limits of policy: Lesson from Michigan.* Kalamazoo, MI: Upjohn Institute for Employment Research.

Angelova, K. (2012, October 2). Bleak photos capture the fall of Detroit. *Business Insider.* Retrieved from https://www.businessinsider.com/the-incredible-decline-of-detroit-photos-2012-10

Anyon, J. (1997). *Ghetto schooling: A political economy of urban educational reform.* New York, NY: Teachers College Press.

Apple, M.W. (2001). Comparing neoliberal projects and inequality in education. *Comparative Education, 37*(4), 409–423.

Arsen, D., Clay, T., Davis, T., Devaney, T., Fulcher-Dawson, R., & Plank, D. N. (2005). *Adequacy, equity, and capital spending in Michigan schools: The unfinished business of proposal A.* The Education Policy Center at Michigan State University.

Black, S. M. (2016). *An examination of urban school governance reform in Detroit Public Schools, 1999–2014* (Unpublished dissertation). Wayne State University, Detroit, MI.

Bowman, K. L. (2013). State takeovers of school districts and related litigation: Michigan as a case study. *The Urban Lawyer, 45*(1). Retrieved from https://

education.msu.edu/epc/library/documents/WP29Bowman2012StateTake-overs.pdf

Bukowski, D. (2008, April 6). Calloway launches restructuring plan. *Michigan Citizen.* p. A1, A4.

Bulkley, K. E. (2010). Portfolio management models in urban school reform. In K. E. Bulkley, J. R. Henig, H. M. Levin (Eds.), *Between public and private: Politics, governance, and the new portfolio models for urban school reform* (pp. 3–26). Cambridge, MA: Harvard Education Press.

Bulkley, K., & Fisler, J. (2003). A decade of charter schools: From theory to practice. *Educational Policy, 119*(17), 317–342.

Carlson, D., & Lavertu, S. (2015). *School closures and student achievement: An analysis of Ohio's urban district and charter schools.* Columbus, OH: Thomas B. Fordham Institute.

Celis, W. (1994, March 17). Michigan votes for revolution in financing its public schools. *The New York Times.* Retrieved from http://www.nytimes.com/1994/03/17/us/michigan-votes-for-revolution-in-financing-its-public-schools.html?pagewanted=all

Chandler, A. D., Jr. (1977). *The visible hand: The managerial revolution in American business.* Cambridge, MA: Harvard University Press.

Chubb, J. E., & Moe, T. M. (1988). Politics, markets, and the organization of schools. *American Political Science Review, 82* (4), 1065–1087.

Chubb, J. E., & Moe, T. M. (1990). *Politics, markets, and America's schools.* Washington, DC: Brookings Institution Press.

Dardot, P., Laval, C. (2013). *The new way of the world: On neo-liberal society.* London, England: Verso.

Data Driven Detroit. (2012). *State of the Detroit child.* Detroit, MI: Author. Retrieved from https://datadrivendetroit.org/files/SGN/D3_2012_SDCReport_Updated.pdf

Dawsey, C. P. (2012, March 14). State names Detroit schools for takeover. *Detroit Free Press,* p. A3.

Deeds, V., & Pattillo, M. (2015). Organizational "failure" and institutional pluralism: A case study of an urban school closure. Urban Education, 50(4), 474–504.

de la Torre, M., Gordon, M. F., & Cowhy, J. (2015). *School closings in Chicago: Understanding families' choices and constraints for new school enrollment.* Chicago, IL: Consortium on Chicago School Research.

de la Torre, M., & Gwynne, J. (2009). *When schools close: Effects on displaced students in Chicago public schools.* Chicago, IL: Consortium on Chicago School Research.

DeVito, L. (2015, October 29). Detroit schools lag behind national average in reading and math, report says. *Metro Times.* Retrieved form http://www.metrotimes.com/Blogs/archives/2015/10/29/detroit-schools-lag-behind-national-average-in-reading-and-math-report-says

Dolan, M. (2011, February 22). Detroit schools' cuts plan approved. *The Wall Street Journal.* Retrieved from http://www.wsj.com/articles/SB100014240527487036106045761587835134452 12

Dowdall, E. (2011). *Closing public schools in Philadelphia: Lessons from six urban districts.* Philadelphia, PA: Pew Charitable Trusts.

Duggan, L. (2003). *The twilight of equality: Neoliberalism, cultural politics, and the attack on democracy*. Boston, MA: Beacon Press.

Duncan, E. (2013). *The color of change? Race and charter schools in an age of neoliberal education reform* (Unpublished doctoral dissertation). Vanderbilt University, Nashville, TN.

Einhorn, E. (2016, April 11). *The extreme sacrifice Detroit parents make to access better schools*. Retrieved from http://www.theatlantic.com/education/archive/2016/04/the-extreme-sacrifice-detroit-parents-make-to-access-better-schools/477585/

Engberg, J., Gill, B., Zamarro, G., & Zimmer, R. (2012). Closing schools in a shrinking district: Do student outcomes depend on which schools are closed? *Journal of Urban Economics, 71*, 189–203.

Felton, R. (2016, December 11). Trump's choice for education secretary raises fears in Detroit. *The Guardian*. Retrieved from https://www.theguardian.com/us-news/2016/dec/11/betsy-devos-trump-education-secretary-michigan-charter-schools

Fine, M. (2012). Disrupting peace/provoking conflict: Stories of school closings and struggles for educational justice. *Peace and Conflict: Journal of Peace Psychology, 18*(2), 144–146.

Friedman, M. (1955). The role of government in education. *Economics and the Public Interest*. Retrieved from https://la.utexas.edu/users/hcleaver/330T/350kPEEFriedmanRoleOfGovttable.pdf

Fuller, B. (2000). The public square, big or small? Charter schools in political context. In B. Fuller, E. Wexler, K. Zernike (Eds.), *Inside charter schools: The paradox of radical decentralization* (pp. 12–65). Cambridge, MA: Harvard University Press.

Garnett, N. S. (2015). School closures as education reform: New evidence from Chicago and Ohio. *Journal of School Choice, 9*(4), 649–652.

Goenner, J. N. (2011). *The origination of Michigan's charter school policy: An historical analysis* (Dissertation). Michigan State University, Michigan.

Graham, P. A. (1995). Assimilation, adjustment, and access: An antiquarian view of American education. In D. Ravitch & M. A. Vinovskis (Eds.), *Learning from the past: What history teaches us about school reform* (pp. 3–24). Baltimore, MD: The Johns Hopkins University Press.

Gray, K. (2016, June 9). Legislature OKs $617M Detroit public schools rescue plan. *Detroit Free Press*. Retrieved from http://www.freep.com/story/news/politics/2016/06/09/dps-package-wins-gop-support-headed-gov-snyder/85630880/

Gross, A. (2014, April 2). The EAA: How a policy package created Michigan's statewide district. *Education Dive*. Retrieved from http://www.educationdive.com/news/the-eaa-how-a-policy-package-created-michigans-statewide-district/246066/

Grover, J., & van der Velde, Y. (2016). *A school district in crisis: Detroit's public schools 1842–2015. Loveland Technologies*. Retrieved from https://makeloveland.com/reports

Hammer, P. J. (2011). The fate of the Detroit public schools: Governance, finance, and competition. *The Journal of Law and Society, 13*(1), 111–153.

Hankins, K. B., & Martin, D. G. (2006). Charter schools and urban regimes in neoliberal context: Making workers and new spaces in metropolitan Atlanta. *International Journal of Urban and Regional Research, 30*(3), 528–547.

Harvey, D. (1989). From managerialism to entrepreneurialism: The transformation in urban governance in late capitalism. *Geografiska Annaler, 71*(1), 3–17.

Harvey, D. (2005). *A brief history of neoliberalism.* Oxford, England: Oxford University Press.

Hicks, M. (2016, May 11). Rhodes faces hostile crowd at DPS hearing. *Detroit News.* Retrieved from http://www.detroitnews.com/story/news/local/detroit-city/2016/05/11/rhodes-faces-hostile-crowd-dps-hearing/84217826/

Henderson, S. (2016, June 25). Language and privilege make Detroit schools debacle worse. *Detroit Free Press.* Retrieved from http://www.freep.com/story/opinion/columnists/stephen-henderson/2016/06/25/detroit-public-schools-plan/86339806/

Henig, J. (2013). *The end of exceptionalism in American education: The changing politics of school reform.* Cambridge, MA: Harvard Education Press.

Henig, J. R., Hula, R. C., Orr, M., & Pedescleaux, D. (1999). *The color of school reform: Race, politics, and the challenge of urban education.* Princeton, NJ: Princeton University Press.

Henig, J. R., & Rich, W. C. (Eds.). (2004). *Mayors in the middle: Politics, race, and mayoral control of urban schools.* Princeton, NJ: Princeton University Press.

Hursh, D.W. (2016) *The end of public schools: The corporate reform agenda to privatize education.* New York, NY: Routledge.

Izraeli, O., & Murphy, K. J. (2007). The impact of proposal a on school financing, equity, and quality of public schools in the state of Michigan. *Journal of Education Finance, 33*(2), 111–129.

Kang, L. (2015). *The dismantling of an urban school system: Detroit, 1980–2014* (Unpublished dissertation). University of Michigan, Ann Arbor.

Kang, L., & Slay, K.E. (2017). *The consequences of school governance change in Detroit: From Proposal A to the Education Achievement Authority.* American Education Research Association Annual Conference, 2017. Washington, D.C.

Kellogg, A. P. (2009, December 21). Detroit schools push for change. *Wall Street Journal,* p. A4.

Kretchmar, K. (2014). Democracy (in) action: A critical policy analysis of New York City public school closings by teachers, students, administrators, and community members. *Education and Urban Society, 46*(1), 3–29.

Lipman, P. (2011a). Contesting the city: Neoliberal urbanism and the cultural politics of education reform in Chicago. *Discourse: Studies in the Cultural Politics of Education, 32* (2), 217–234.

Lipman, P. (2011b). *The new political economy of urban education: Neoliberalism, race, and the right to the city.* New York, NY: Routledge.

Lipman, P., & Haines, N. (2007). From education accountability to privatization and African American exclusion—Chicago public schools' "Renaissance 2010." *Educational Policy, 21,* 471–502.

Lipman, P., & Hursh, D. (2007). Renaissance 2010: The reassertion of ruling-class power through neoliberal policies in Chicago. *Policy Futures in Education, 5*(2), 160–178.

Livengood, C. (2014, March 20). Michigan house narrowly passes EAA expansion bill. *Detroit News.* Retrieved from http://www.detroitnews.com/article/20140320/POLITICS02/303200131

Lubienski, C., Gulosino, C., &. Weitzel, P. (2009). School choice and competitive incentives: Mapping the distribution of educational opportunities across local education markets. *American Journal of Education, 115*(4), 601–647.

MacDonald, C. (2005, January 21). School chief wants to stay. *Detroit News,* p. 01D.

Manna, P. (2011). *Collision course: Federal education policy meet state and local realities.* Washington DC: CQ Press.

Mason, M. L., & Arsen, D. (2014). Michigan's education achievement authority and the future of public education in Detroit: The challenge of aligning policy design and policy goals. (Working Paper). College of Education Michigan State University, December 2014.

McGuinn, P., & Manna, P. (Eds.). (2013). *Education governance for the twenty-first century: Overcoming the structural barriers to school reform.* Washington DC: Brookings Institution Press.

Mirel, J. (1999). *The rise and fall of an Urban school system: Detroit, 1907–81* (2nd ed.). Ann Arbor: The University of Michigan Press.

Mirel, J. (2004). Detroit: There is still a long road to travel, and success is far from assured. In J. R. Henig & W. C. Rich (Eds.), *Mayors in the middle: Politics, race, and mayoral control of urban schools* (pp. 120–158). Princeton, NJ: Princeton University Press.

Mrozowski, J. (2009, April 9). DPS to close 23 schools, lay off 600, use $200 million for school upgrades. *Detroit News,* p. A5.

Murray, D. (2010, March 5). Michigan's loss of race to the top funding doesn't negate need for school reforms. *MLive.* Retrieved from http://www.mlive.com/news/grand-rapids/index.ssf/2010/03/michigan_loss_of_race_to_the_t.html.

Pattillo, M. (2007). *Black on the block: The politics of race and class in the city.* Chicago, IL: University of Chicago Press.

Peck, J., & Tickell, A. (2002). Neoliberalizing space. *Antipode 34*(3), 380–404.

Pedroni, T. C. (2013, May 2). Trust and transparency among EAA issues. *Detroit Free Press.* Retrieved from http://search.proquest.com.proxy.lib.umich.edu/docview/1347562523?accountid=14667

Pedroni, T. (2011). Urban shrinkage as a performance of whiteness: Neoliberal urban restructuring, education, and racial containment in the post-industrial, global niche city. *Discourse: Studies in the Cultural Politics of Education, 32*(2), 203–215.

Ravitch, D. (1974). *The great school wars: A history of the New York City public schools.* Baltimore, MD: The Johns Hopkins University Press.

Ravitch, D. (2010). *The death and life of the great American school system: How testing and choice are undermining education.* New York, NY: Basic Books.

Reckhow, S. (2010). Disseminating and legitimating a new approach: The role of foundations. In K. E. Bulkley, J. R. Henig, & H. Levin (Eds.), *Between public and private: Politics, governance, and the new portfolio models for urban school reform* (pp. 277–304). Cambridge, MA: Harvard Education Press.

Reed, D. S. (2014). *Building the federal schoolhouse: Localism and the American education state*. Oxford, England: Oxford University Press.

Rich, W. C. (2009). Who's afraid of a mayoral takeover of Detroit Public Schools? In J. P. Viteritti (Ed.), *When mayors take charge: School governance in the City* (pp. 148–170), Washington DC: The Brookings Institution.

Rizga, K. (2017, March/April). Trump's education secretary pick has spent a lifetime working to end public education as we know it. *Mother Jones*. Retrieved from https://www.motherjones.com/politics/2017/01/betsy-devos-christian-schools-vouchers-charter-education-secretary/

Saltman, K. (2000). *Collateral damage: Corporatizing public schools—a threat to democracy*. Lanham, MD: Rowman & Littlefield.

Saltman, K. (2010). *The gift of education: Public education and venture philanthropy*. New York, NY: Palgrave Macmillan.

Sands, D. (2012, November 5). Elena Herrada, Detroit school board member, defends vote to withdraw from the EAA district. *Huffington Post*. Retrieved from http://www.huffingtonpost.com/2012/11/15/elena-herrada-detroit-school-board-eaa_n_2137281.html.

Schultz, M. (2009, July 11). DPS gives control of lagging schools to private sector. *Detroit News*. Retrieved from http://search.proquest.com.ezproxy.gvsu.edu/docview/404420716?accountid=39473

Shipps, D. (2006). *School reform, corporate style: Chicago, 1880–2000*. Lawrence: University Press of Kansas.

Smith, N. (2014). *Redefining the school district in Michigan*. Columbus, OH: Thomas B. Fordham Institute.

Snyder, R. (2011). *A special message from Governor Rick Snyder: Education reform*. Retrieved from http://www.michigan.gov/documents/snyder/SpecialMessage onEducationReform_35158 6_7.pdf

Stambach, A., & Becker, N.C. (2006). Finding the old in the new: On race and class in US charter school debates. *Race, Ethnicity and Education, 9*(2), 159–182.

Stone, C. (1989). *Regime politics: Governing Atlanta, 1946–1988*. Lawrence, KS: University Press of Kansas.

Strauss, V. (2016, October 15). NAACP ratifies controversial resolution for a moratorium on charter schools. *Washington Post*. Retrieved from https://www.washingtonpost.com/news/answer-sheet/wp/2016/10/15/naacp-ratifies-controversial-resolution-for-a-moratorium-on-charter-schools/?utm_term=.34753d9fc3b5

Stuart-Wells, A., Slayton, J., & Scott, J. (2002). Defining democracy in the neoliberal age: Charter school reform and educational consumption. *American Educational Research Journal, 39*(2), 337–361.

Sugrue, T. (2005). *The origins of the urban crisis: Race and inequality in postwar Detroit*. Princeton, NJ: Princeton University Press.

Sunderman, G. L., & Payne, A. (2009). *Does closing schools cause educational harm? A review of the literature*. Bethesda, MD: Mid-Atlantic Equity Center.

Tyack, D. (1974). *The one best system: A history of American urban education*. Cambridge, MA: Harvard University Press.

Tyack, D., & Cuban, L. (1995). *Tinkering toward utopia: A century of public school reform*. Cambridge, MA: Harvard University Press.

U.S. Census Bureau. (1980). *Electronic ownership by household.* Washington DC: Government Printing Office. Retrieved from https://www2.census.gov/prod2/decennial/documents/1980/1980censusofpopu80124uns_bw.pdf.

Welch, S. (2010, March 14). Absent no more: School reform attracting once-reluctant foundations. *Crain's Detroit Business.* Retrieved from http://www.crainsdetroit.com/article/20100314/SUB01/303149954/absent-no-more-school-reform-attracting-once-reluctant

Wolch, J. (1990). *Shadow state: Government and voluntary sector in transition.* New York, NY: The Foundation Center.

Wong, K. K., Shen, F. X., Anagnostopoulos, D., & Rutledge, S. (2007). *The education mayor: Improving America's schools.* Washington DC: Georgetown University Press.

Yin, R. K. (2003). *Case study research: Design and methods* (3rd ed.). Thousand Oaks, CA: SAGE.

Zaniewski, A. (2016, November 7). EAA to pay $2.25 million to Detroit district, return schools by July. *Detroit Free Press.* Retrieved from http://www.freep.com/story/news/education/2016/11/07/eaa-schools-education-dpscd/93417992/

Zernike, K. (2016, June 28). A sea of charter schools in Detroit leaves students adrift. *New York Times.* Retrieved from http://www.nytimes.com/2016/06/29/us/for-detroits-children-more-school-choice-but-not-better-schools.html?_r=0

CHAPTER 5

AN OPEN AND SHUT CASE

Gentrification and School Closure Decisions in Washington, DC

Esa Syeed
California State University–Long Beach

ABSTRACT

Mass school closures in lower-income communities of color are now a fixture of the urban education landscape. We can also readily observe processes of gentrification that are fundamentally reshaping the demographic and spatial dimensions of cities nationwide. While researchers have begun to show that affluent and typically White families now enrolling in city schools can both foster and inhibit educational equity (Cucchiara & Horvat, 2009; Posey-Maddox, 2014), the relationship between school closures and gentrification is less clear. In this study, I look to recent events in the rapidly changing city of Washington, DC to better understand the role of gentrification in the school closure decision-making process. Focusing on the 2012–2013 school year—when district officials proposed the closure of 20 schools—I weave together discourse analysis of testimony from public hearings, interviews with parents and community members, official reports, and demographic and school-level data to demonstrate how community members and local leaders deploy gen-

Shuttered Schools, pages 125–151
Copyright © 2019 by Information Age Publishing
All rights of reproduction in any form reserved.

trification as both an asset and a threat to defending schools against potential closure. I found that those school communities undergoing the greatest demographic change were able to invoke gentrification as an asset in improving schools through increased enrollment and parental investment, and were eventually taken off the closure list. But those communities that held the school system responsible for school conditions and who saw gentrification as a threat were unsuccessful in their bids to save their schools. The chapter cautions policymakers and education leaders who view gentrification as a potential school improvement strategy by highlighting inequities in school closure decisions and outcomes.

For many years, a ghostly brick building sat vacant just a few blocks from the campus of Georgetown University in Washington, DC. Affixed to a street-facing wall, the name associated with the building for more than a century is still spelled out in block letters: "WORMLEY SCHOOL." Although undergraduates had generated their own lore about the building, the history of the Wormley School offers a vantage point into the complex issue of school closures in DC.

Local historians recount the legacy of James Wormley, the school's namesake, in the annals of DC history as a free-born Black man who became a successful hotelier and civic leader. Wormley's businesses served as a launching pad for his other career as a power-broker who kept the company of lawmakers, foreign dignitaries, and other elites who frequented his hotel. As a leader in the capital city's Black community, Wormley garnered support from his Congressional coterie in sponsoring legislation to create the city's first publicly funded schools for Black children. To ensure that his father's educational legacy would endure after his passing in 1884, Wormley's son advocated that a new school proposed for "colored children" be named in honor of his father. In 1885, the Wormley Public Elementary School for the Colored opened its doors in Georgetown, a neighborhood that had long been home to a sizable, albeit isolated, Black community (Gelderman, 2012).

But as they entered the new century, Black families found their historic place in the increasingly affluent neighborhood grow more tenuous and unsustainable. Reflecting changing residential patterns, education officials consolidated Wormley with another school serving students of color in 1930 to make up for the underutilized space. By mid-century, the confluence of several forces would come to spell the end of Black Georgetown (Lesko, Babb, & Gibbs, 1991). Underlying the seemingly laissez-faire hand of market forces driving up housing costs, civic leaders and merchants drummed up Georgetown's reputation for attracting the rich and famous that fashioned it into a "chic" destination neighborhood. These changes gained the force of law in 1950 when Congress passed the Old Georgetown Act. Written ostensibly for preservationist purposes, the mandate effectively cleared slums and pushed out Black residents (Lesko et al., 1991). Amid the sharp decline in the local Black population, the city shuttered Wormley as a neighborhood elementary school in 1952. The building, however, took on various administrative and educational incarnations before it was later condemned, sold, re-sold, and ultimately landed in the hands of a private developer in 2005 (Howard, 2005; Matthews, 2009). Today, the building is adorned with stainless steel appliances, granite countertops, white oak flooring, and despite the lettering that still remains on its walls, goes by a new name: Wormley Row (Lerner, 2012). The multi-million dollar conversion of the school into high-end townhomes and condominiums is only the latest chapter in the storied legacy of the historic school.

The life, death, and rebirth of the Wormley School is instructive for a variety of reasons. The school's history weaves together various threads that at times overlook the autopsy of a school closure: race, neighborhood change, public space, and private interests. Instead of narratives that focus on school closures as a consequence of educational failure, wherein students or teachers are blamed for the deterioration of a school, the Wormley example actually positions closures as important markers of broader changes in the landscape of urban education. The transformation of a school named for a Black education advocate into high-end housing is just one in a heap of critical ironies coming out of present patterns of neighborhood change and gentrification in DC.

Fast forwarding to the most recent round of mass DC school closures in 2012, this chapter revisits the complexity of the longstanding problem of school closures at a time when gentrification has reshaped America's urban centers. When school officials proposed the closing of 20 schools that year, two on the list were located in neighborhoods with some of the most extensive redevelopment and concentrated population growth. As a result, they also had a growing proportion of middle-class and White families enrolling their children. These schools were eventually taken off the list, with district leaders citing their superior proposals for increasing enrollment. The schools that were closed were all located in predominately Black and lower-income neighborhoods.

Drawing on testimony from public hearings, official reports, and interviews with parents and community members, I developed a qualitative case study of the 2012–2013 school closure process in DC and examine how affected communities advocated for their schools. I found that racial and socioeconomic changes driven by gentrification served divergent purposes for school communities attempting to resist closure. Newer, middle-class, and predominately White parents were able to invoke gentrification as an asset in improving schools through increased enrollment and parental investment. Furthermore, their proposals for keeping schools open relied less on the school district for support, and instead made parents primarily responsible for increasing enrollment in their schools. On the other hand, those communities in lower-income and predominately Black neighborhoods that held the school system responsible for school conditions and who generally saw gentrification as a threat were unsuccessful in their bids to save their schools. Additionally, these were school communities that had endured closure decisions in the past, as opposed to those more recently arrived middle-class families who had just begun to engage in the city's education politics.

The study's findings highlight a troubling aspect of gentrification's impact on urban public school systems. By being more responsive to the engagement efforts of middle-class parents over others, the school system appeared to relieve itself of its own responsibilities and instead supported a school improvement strategy that leaned much more on privileged parents. Such a school improvement strategy may obscure the more long-standing and perpetual inequity faced by lower-income communities of color. These findings focus primarily on how school districts design these processes, and how they can promote more equitable approaches to community engagement in cities that are becoming increasingly gentrified.

ROOTING GENTRIFICATION: TOWARDS AN EQUITABLE VISION OF URBAN CHANGE

The purpose of this chapter is to examine the ways in which gentrification plays a role in school closure decision-making processes. As a complex, global phenomenon, debates over gentrification rage in scholarly circles and in popular discourse. Within this ongoing debate, Atkinson (2003) suggests scholars must "redefine the gentrification problem as one less about theory and more about a people-relevant and communicable issue to which practical responses can be addressed" (p. 2349). I see my intervention here as one that roots gentrification in the lived realities of those affected by school closures. While acknowledging its global nature and theoretical perspectives, this chapter focuses on the very particular way in which systematic inequalities borne of gentrification manifest in school closure decisions. This framing can have several practical implications. First, I critically examine the overly optimistic tones in which gentrification is often described. Rather, I posit that massive urban change brought on by waves of gentrification must be adequately contextualized and understood in light of racial, class, and power dynamics that are relevant to urban school closures. Additionally, it is vital that we see gentrification as systematic and calculated, as opposed to an organic process driven by individual level choices. Based on this critical framing of gentrification, we can consider the possibilities for equitable urban development and its relevance to school closures decisions.

Reversing trends of White flight that followed school desegregation in the 1950s and 1960s, middle-class—and mostly White—families have been returning to cities across the country in large numbers in recent decades (Posey-Maddox, Kimelberg, & Cucchiara, 2014). Their arrival initiated gentrification processes with widespread impacts on city life. In particular, gentrification is characterized by the influx of higher income residents into lower-income areas, displacement and/or marginalization of previous residents, increased investments, and changes to the character or culture of those neighborhoods (Kennedy & Leonard, 2001).

With regards to public education, some have taken a hopeful view and suggested that this type of neighborhood change signals the best opportunity in at least a generation to engineer truly diverse schools that benefit all children (Petrilli, 2012). But gentrification is also seen as a threat to public education and its propensity to displace and marginalize minority communities has warranted harsh critique (Lipman, 2011). As newcomers increasingly enroll their children in urban schools, sometimes in response to carefully crafted plans city and education leaders develop, research has only begun to reveal the possible impact these decisions have.

The potential for gentrification to marginalize is predicated in part upon the orientation to "frontierism" inherent within it. Through rose-colored glasses, cities become new "frontiers" for "urban pioneers" who are willing to invest in what they consider formerly undesirable neighborhoods in order to suit their preferences and lifestyle (Williams & Smith, 2007). Embedded within gentrification is also an "inherent optimism" that spurs radical transformations, but meanwhile also "negates the real history of urban development and change" (Williams & Smith, 2007, p. 204). The real history of urban change must also account for institutionalized racism in the form of intense segregation and economic disinvestment, yet the ideology of post-racialism normalizes and decontextualizes processes of gentrification in the post-civil rights era (Prince, 2014). Through a "colorblind," post-racial lens, however, the racial dimensions of gentrification become obscured and racial power hierarchies flatten (Wester, 2009).

Despite evidence to the contrary, many city leaders actively promote gentrification as a form of "urban renaissance" they believe will create more integrated, liveable, and sustainable communities (Lees, 2008). Within the education sector, similar ideas abound as district leaders seek to lure new city residents as a school improvement strategy. Based on her study of a gentrifying elementary school, Posey-Maddox (2014) warns against this path to educational reform. In particular, her research demonstrates how middle-class parental activism, even when well-intentioned, can exclude or marginalize lower-income parents due to differences in the social or cultural capital needed to access power. Additionally, by encouraging middle-class parental engagement, districts are ceding their responsibilities for improving schools to more affluent parents. Posey-Maddox concludes that school districts must be primarily accountable for ensuring that lower-income families of color can also participate and benefit from school improvements rather than be shut off from them. Cucchiara (2013) similarly offers a critique of cities that welcome gentrification as a school improvement strategy, noting that reforms must also address deep-seated issues related to heightened austerity, concentrated poverty, and educational governance that contribute to persistent academic underperformance.

As a global, neoliberal project, it is important to note that gentrification is not merely a neutral process of re-urbanization based solely on the individual tastes or cosmopolitan interests of bohemians or hipsters. Rather, with global capital moving across borders to support a wide range of real estate and commercial developments in urban neighborhoods that are also home to public schools, gentrification enjoys a great deal of transnational structural support (Lipman, 2011). This unshakeable reality renders gentrification a far more complex issue that rises above the individual student, family, or school. Up to this point, most research focused on gentrification in urban schools has provided rich, detailed case studies of particular communities, areas, or schools (Cucchiara, 2013; Posey-Maddox, 2014; Stillman, 2012). To build on these valuable contributions, the present study expands the scope of investigation to the city-wide level to get a better sense of gentrification's influence on an issue that mobilized diverse communities across DC.

LITERATURE REVIEW

School closures have become a crucible for contemporary school systems. The decision-making processes behind them have led to particularly explosive bouts of community engagement in cities like New York and Chicago where scores of schools of have been shut. The processes involved in closing schools provide a window into the embattled role of communities in public education reform today. This chapter is situated in literatures that link gentrification, mass school closures, and community engagement in education decision-making.

Community Engagement in School Closures

A catch-all term used for everything from back to school nights to community organizing, it is important to note that I adopt a particular definition of community engagement in public education that makes a few important distinctions. I refer specifically here to the means by which people collectively influence decision-making processes that impact their schools and communities (Orr & Rogers, 2011). This definition captures both the efforts with which communities mobilize around particular issues, as well as the ways in which school districts attempt to engage them in decision-making. As a result, I consider both "bottom up" approaches of mobilization initiated by communities as well as "top down" approaches to deliberation initiated by city officials.

When community engagement works, it can have a significant impact on school districts. In their influential study on urban school politics, Stone, Henig, Jones, and Pierannunzi (2001) studied 11 major cities and the conditions that led to the transformation of their districts' schools. The comparative study revealed that while most cities experienced only sporadic attempts to transform their lower-performing schools, the authors found that those districts where communities came together around shared educational visions and reform agendas were able to sustain education reforms aimed at improving student achievement.

Given the explosive nature of school closures and the intense response they ignite, community engagement in these processes can have a wider impact beyond determining the fate of particular school buildings. Nationwide, closures have led to greater political instability in school systems and weakened public trust (Pew Charitable Trusts, 2011). For example, Lipman, Gutstein, Gutierrez, and Blanche (2015) detail how Chicago residents came to see the school district's closure hearings as disempowering because of their inauthentic design and noticeable absence of actual decision-makers. Citing the disproportionate impact of closures on minority communities, activist groups in various cities have attempted to frame the issue as a civil rights matter and have filed lawsuits and federal-level complaints (Sanchez, 2013). In addition to breeding resentment between system leadership and affected communities, studies have also shown that closures have the possibility of driving wedges between communities with competing interests in determining school closure decisions (Pappas, 2012).

Within community engagement processes, there are numerous narratives of school closures that emerge. Studies have centered community voices in school closure decision-making processes in order to provide a counter-narrative to what could otherwise become a technocratic discussion. Although education leaders are driven by narrowly defined logics of utilization or academic performance, affected communities have emphasized the history, symbolic value, and sense of identity tied to their schools (Ayala & Galletta, 2012; Good, 2016). While communities in this study did invoke similarly immeasurable values of their individual schools, they also attempted to re-frame school closures in terms of their lived experiences, historical inequities, and emerging demographic trends. In this study, I listen to community voices to hear the story they tell about the broader changes to the city's urban educational landscape.

Additionally, the nature of school closures themselves further present unique challenges for community engagement. Rather than bringing residents together to consider maximizing educational opportunity, school closures pit communities in an uncomfortable negotiation around the distribution of "educational harm" that can negatively impact academic outcomes (Sunderman & Payne, 2009). Engagement processes around school closure present a precarious foundation for building a common vision for school quality across an entire system, particularly when only certain groups or areas persistently endure the loss of their schools. Given the clear and disproportionate impact of closures on lower-income communities of color (de la Torre & Gwynne, 2009; Sunderman & Payne, 2009), these negotiations appear to be more like foregone conclusions. Recent experiences in DC reflect how opportunities for engagement around decisions to shutter public schools may backfire and further exacerbate distrust of the school system and create turmoil between communities.

Community Engagement and Gentrification

Mirroring the academic achievement gap, community engagement in public education remains unequal across racial and class lines. Studies have consistently demonstrated the types of cultural and institutional hurdles lower-income and minority communities must overcome to exercise their full participation in educational institutions (Chambers, 2006; Lareau & Horvat, 1999; Noguera, 2001). In school districts that have historically served these populations, education leaders must design more empowering and inclusive models of community engagement that require a greater level of prioritization and investment (Ishimaru, 2014). In the context of gentrifying cities with increasingly stark demographic disparities, educators then must contend with the critical question of which voices they respond to in shaping education decisions. Research on gentrifying schools has already demonstrated a propensity to focus on dominant perspectives of higher income and White parents (Posey-Maddox et al., 2014).

When it comes to more recently arrived families in gentrifying cities, studies have often focused on new parents' choices and anxieties of where to enroll their children (Roda & Wells, 2013; Stillman, 2012). It becomes easy to rely on a framing of educational "consumerism" in which these parents are individualized in their navigation of school choices. For example, an analysis of middle-class, White parents' choices suggests a preference for charter schools over neighborhood schools in DC (Rosenblat & Howard, 2015). But the reality is more complicated and we may overlook the nuanced role these parents play in citywide issues like school closures. In fact, some parents I interviewed suggested that city officials considered closing schools in gentrifying neighborhoods only because they assumed local residents would not care and just transfer to charters. Moving beyond a "consumer" frame, I see parents from the gentrifying schools as having a broader political role in impacting the outcomes of school closures.

One way of zeroing in on the relationship between gentrification and community engagement in public education is to look at patterns in the outcomes of decision-making processes. In a review of literature on gentrification and urban schools, Posey-Maddox (2014) and colleagues outline a few promising areas for further inquiry. In particular, they pose the question: "To what extent are decision-making processes regarding the prioritization and use of new resources open and democratic versus stratified along class or racial/ethnic lines?" Additionally, they also encourage researchers "to document the extent to which schools with a growing middle-class population experience a disproportionate share of district resources and/or attention from administrative leaders" (Posey-Maddox et al., 2014, p. 452). Applied to the present study, we can inspect what types of criteria are weighed in the closure decision-making process for evidence of the evenness of the playing field. In terms of process outcomes, we can consider the sparing of a school as an invaluable resource that district leaders must decide how to allocate between diverse communities.

Connecting School Closures and Gentrification

The decision to close or repurpose urban schools occurs at the nexus of competing interests and underlying trends that reveals a tension between school districts, charter schools, diverse public school communities, and developers. In the literature, researchers have only begun to elaborate on the relationship between gentrification and school closures. I present some broad aspects of this relationship, but acknowledge that additional investigation is needed.

In competitive urban real estate markets, closed schools become a valuable commodity. Seeking to anchor affluent urban newcomers and keep them from attending private schools or fleeing to the suburbs once they have children, cities like Philadelphia have invested in marketing and preparing schools for this emerging demographic (Cucchiara, 2013). In the case of a gentrifying Chicago neighborhood, Smith and Stovall (2008) found that closed schools once attended by lower-income families were re-opened as selective admissions schools and re-branded to cater to more affluent families. Aside from their educational repurposing, scholars have also drawn connections between closed school buildings and the drive for urban land development in gentrifying cities, particularly as closed school buildings are used for real estate or commercial purposes (Fenwick, 2013).

Moreover, as gentrification displaces communities, it is possible to conceive how heightened development pressures could reduce local school enrollments. Gordon (2008) found that attempts to create mixed-income developments in an English community actually threatened the viability of schools and extracurricular programs as families confronted their changing neighborhood. Based on the scant existing literature, further research is needed to substantiate and properly characterize the relationship between school closures and gentrification.

In the erratic landscape of urban education now awash with various school choice mechanisms, the fate of neighborhood schools remains unclear as newly arriving families may exhibit a greater sense of entitlement or demands in deciding where to enroll their children. A review of literature indicates that gentrifier parents typically opt for more selective charter or public schools (Jordan & Gallagher, 2015). These decisions may have broader, rippling effects across entire districts. Research shows that gentrification has been tied to increased presence of charter schools in some urban contexts, though it is not a consistent finding (Davis & Oakley, 2013). In the education marketplace, school choice can result in zero-sum competition with clear winners and losers between education sectors. Looking at enrollment patterns following the closure of 28 DC schools in 2008, The Urban Institute (2014a) found that affected students attended charters at more than twice the rate of those from schools that did not close. These findings echo the anecdotal evidence cited by long-term community members I interviewed who argue that school closures must be viewed in light of the city's burgeoning charter sector.

Ultimately, a complex story emerges from this study that explores the relationship between school closures and gentrification. The fact that middle-class parents in gentrifying neighborhoods decided to invest and support neighborhood schools slated for closure also subverts the notion that they see themselves strictly as individual "consumers" who prefer to shop the educational marketplace. As a result, we are able to observe the peculiar situation in which these parents are also subjected to the kinds of education policies that communities of color have grown accustomed to. The study also locates the impact of gentrification not just in the outcomes of school closures, but rather on the negotiations present in deciding which schools to close.

RESEARCH CONTEXT: SCHOOL CLOSURES IN DC

School closures have a long legacy in large urban school districts like DC. In particular, the 2008 school closures helmed by Michelle Rhee, the polarizing schools Chancellor at the time, provide an important backdrop that district officials and community members readily invoked in the 2012 process. During that time, I was a public school teacher at a school slated for closure. The meetings I recall were often hectic as participants vocalized a sense of futility in their involvement. Even the *Washington Post* editorial board, typically offering broad support to Rhee's leadership, admonished her administration for holding meetings that did not allow for authentic engagement platforms. In a 2008 editorial, they inquired, "What's the harm in going the extra mile to erase any doubt that people are getting a fair hearing?" Years later, the new Chancellor, Kaya Henderson, explained that in the 2008 closure process, "We engaged the community by telling them what we were going to do *to* them" and went on to make only what she called "token changes" to the closure plan (Martin, 2013). As a result, she assessed, "our political capital was spent, our political support was weakened, and we lost the investment of many of our community members." In fact, local analysts have tied Rhee's eventual resignation to the political fallout following the 2008 wave of hotly contested school closures (Turque & Cohen, 2010).

Four years later, DC Public Schools (DCPS) announced plans to close 20 more schools, citing underutilization as a primary criterion. When Chancellor Kaya Henderson presented the closure list, she was very explicit about it being framed as a flexible proposal rather than a final list etched in stone. At a community meeting, Henderson told the audience that she "introduced this as a proposal" and was "serious about listening to community input, about using it to amend, tweak, strengthen the set of recommendations that we made" (Brown, 2012). At the same time, she also hinted at the need for equity in the process. "I want to make sure that this is not a case of the squeaky wheel gets the grease," she assured communities early on in the process.

But Henderson offered another caveat to community engagement that speaks in part to the process' unequal outcomes. "Don't come to me with a petition with 500 signatures saying, 'Don't close my school,' she cautioned, 'come to me with 500 enrollment forms'" (Bannon, 2012, p. 32). So rather than mobilize broad support, school communities were called upon to take the lead in reversing patterns of low enrollment that could buoy underutilized schools. As this chapter demonstrates, fashioning community engagement in such a way overtly privileges some groups over others.

The months that followed were tense, full of spirited meetings and aggressive campaigning from the affected schools. Communities confronted the school system's closure decisions by publicizing their plight on social media, organizing public demonstrations and rallies, testifying before the DC Council, attending community meetings, developing counter-proposals and, in one case, taking city and school leaders to court. In addition to local newspapers and blogs, DC's school closures also received national-level media attention.

Less than two months since the list was first announced, in January 2013, DCPS released its final consolidation and reorganization plan, "Better Schools for All Students." The plan provides a rationale for the reasons why some schools stayed open and others were closed. Table 5.1 lists all schools proposed for closure and the final decisions regarding their fate. Five schools were removed from the list, two of which have been the subject of much celebration, as well as consternation, in communities across DC. Both in media accounts of the process and from interviews with community leaders, these two elementary schools, Garrison and Francis-Stevens, were identified as waging particularly effective campaigns against potential closure. The two schools have a growing proportion of newcomer families enrolling their children in them and are located in neighborhoods with some of the most extensive redevelopment and concentrated population growth. The schools that were closed were all located in predominately Black and lower-income neighborhoods. According to court documents, of the final

TABLE 5.1	**DC Public Schools Consolidation and Reorganization Plan**		
School Name	Ward	Final Decision	Rationale
Shaw Middle School	1	Closed	Consolidated into 6–12 program in modernized building
Francis-Stevens Education Campus (K–8)	2	Open	Merged with selected high school to serve Pre-K–12 students
Garrison Elementary School	2	Open	New demographic data and school's commitment to recruit students
MacFarland Middle School	4	Closed	Consolidated with nearby Pre-K–8 schools
Thurgood Marshall ES	5	Closed	Too few students living in-boundary, but building will be kept in inventory
Spingam High School	5	Closed	Planned re-opening as a vocational training center
Davis ES	7	Closed	Low-enrolled due to child population decline, in close proximity to similar schools
Kenilworth ES	7	Closed	Low numbers of school-age population
Ron Brown MS	7	Closed	Consolidated with another middle school
Smothers ES	7	Open	Has a healthy utilization rate and steady enrollment growth
Winston Education Campus (K–8)	7	Closed	Low enrollment and poorly designed facility
Ferebee-Hope ES	8	Closed	Area has excess building capacity
Johnson MS	8	Open	Safety concerns around possible consolidation
Malcolm X ES	8	Open	Serves as a site for piloting a neighborhood-based charter school
MC Terrell ES	8	Closed	Half a mile from nearby elementary school

Note: Adapted from DCPS (2013) "Better Schools for All: DCPS' Consolidation and Reorganization Plan"

15 schools that were closed, 93% of students were Black and only 0.2%—six students—were White (Boasberg, 2014).

In addition to what is stated in the plan, in a *Washington Post* article Chancellor Henderson shared some of her reasoning about how community proposals influenced her decision-making. She deflected claims that she had been unfair in responding to community ideas across the city by noting, "Lots of folks came up with plans. Some we were able to move with, others we were not able to" (Brown, 2013b). Proposals they were not able to "move with," she further explained, included those that called for millions of dollars in additional investments. In the winning proposals, she found they demonstrated a community's willingness to help recruit new students and also cited demographic data showing neighborhood growth. It should be noted that some of the schools in predominately Black and lower-income neighborhoods were spared. However, the reasons behind these decisions did not appear to be clearly linked to community proposals, but rather more urgent concerns with safety.

The outcomes of the closure process have served as a reckoning for school communities across the rapidly changing city. It is particularly important to consider these developments in the context of DC's historical identity as "Chocolate City," so-called in recognition of the city's majority Black population. Beyond just an indicator of the city's demographic composition, Hopkinson (2012) argues that as "Chocolate City," DC offered "a unique angle of vision, an alternate lens to see world power" (p. x) that had become an integral part of the identity of Washingtonians for generations. But the city's Black majority dropped steeply from 70% in 1980 to 49% in 2013 (Urban Institute, 2014b). These racial changes are also attended by a significant and growing income gap between the richest and poorest residents, cited as being one of the largest among the nation's biggest cities (Biegler, 2012). Analysis of racial and class migration into and out of DC reveals patterns consistent with displacement and gentrification, as lower-income and Black residents left and White and higher-income residents moved in during the first decade of the new millennium (Sturtevant, 2013).

The changing racial and socioeconomic tides of the city have caused local residents to question whether the sparing of these schools is in some way a fulfillment of "The Plan"—a conspiracy first put forth in the 1970s that alleged that Whites intended to take back the Black-led city (Prince, 2014). In the city's construction boom, the dwindling stock of affordable housing, upgraded public amenities, or even school closures, residents observe the manifestations of "The Plan" in their everyday life. For example, a popular, nationally broadcasted radio show ran a story about gentrification that opened with the curious case of a DC school slated for closure in 2008. In an interview, a parent characterized the potential closure as a "land grab," and citing evidence of the school's success and valued role in the predominantly African American community, asked, "What else can it be?" (Jeter, 2008). Whether there is an articulated "plan" or not, we can acknowledge both the symbolic and very real implications of school closure decisions in a city that has seen its legacy as "Chocolate City" steadily fade.

METHODS AND DATA

This chapter relies on a variety of interview, documentary, and media sources to reconstruct the events surrounding the school closure process that took place between November 2012 and January 2013. I first analyzed testimony from recordings of the two DC Council hearings that took place right after the list was publicized in late November 2012. In these official accounts, I noted which communities were represented and how they discussed the proposed closure of their schools. The online platform, engagedcps.org, houses public input data that is open access and available to the public. Uploaded on the site are proposals and information created by various school communities. Additionally, one can find notes taken from nearly 40 different table discussions held across all four community meetings to gather input on the district's closure proposal. Though often written in shorthand, the notes do incorporate a wide range of opinions that help supplement other data or evidence.

The study also draws from a series of semi-structured interviews that add nuance to the narrative of how different school communities strategized and responded to the potential closing of their schools. I conducted 15 interviews with community members from across the city who were directly involved in the school closure process. Interviewees reflected the diverse array of actors involved in the coordinated responses to school closures, including parents or family members, church leaders, community organizers, homeowners, neighborhood representatives. Pseudonyms are used for interviewees, though the names of schools remain unchanged. Additionally, I interviewed 10 public officials across various agencies and offices overseeing public education with firsthand experience with the school closure decisions. Interviewees were identified based on their presence in official and media records, as well as through snowball sampling.

Across all these data sources, I generated themes relating to issues of neighborhood change and gentrification. In particular, I was interested in examining how participants saw attributes related to changing demographics—namely race, class, and geography—as well as historical developments in public education play out in school closure decision-making. Rather than focus on a single community, I explore the similarities and differences between how Garrison and Francis-Stevens went about their advocacy with other school communities that were not successful. Table 5.2 provides a brief demographic and educational profile of each ward in the city during

TABLE 5.2   SY 2012–13 Ward Profiles: Demographic and Education Data

Ward	Race/Ethnicity of Selected Groups[a]	Median Income of Families with Children[a]	Total Student Enrollment[b]	% Charter Enrollment[b]	% Free/ Reduced Price Meal[c]
1	33.3% Black 39.4% White 22.0% Hispanic 4.5% Asian	$58,827	11,342	52.3%	73.7%
2	9.2% Black 69.5% White 9.4% Hispanic 9.1% Asian	$173,250	3,472	21.6%	52.6%
3	5.2% Black 77.1% White 7.9% Hispanic 6.2% Asian	$217,404	6,144	0.0%	18.0%
4	60.5% Black 18.4% White 18.3%Hispanic 1.5% Asian	$67,224	11,991	40.6%	80.2%
5	77.4% Black 12.7% White 7.2% Hispanic 1.3% Asian	$45,096	11,540	55.0%	87.3%
6	40.6% Black 47.6% White 5.4% Hispanic 4.4% Asian	$97,431	9,894	37.9%	74.5%
7	95.9% Black 1.5% White 2.0% Hispanic 0.3% Asian	$35,351	11,950	53.0%	94.2%
8	94.1% Black 3.7% White 1.5% Hispanic 0.3% Asian	$26,709	14,052	45.4%	95.3%

Compiled From:
[a] DC Kids Count Data Center (http://datacenter.kidscount.org/)
[b] DC Neighborhood Info Ward Profiles (http://www.neighborhoodinfodc.org/wards/wards.html)
[c] Office of the State Superintendent, as reported by 21st Century Schools Fund (http://www.21csf.org/csf-home/DocUploads/DataShop/DS–355.pdf)

the 2012–2013 school year when this process took place. In the sections that follow, I report on the findings that reflect the most significant areas for divergence and convergence between affected communities.

FINDINGS

In this section I focus on some of the key themes that emerged from the 2012–2013 school closure process, with an eye toward the role of gentrification. In the following two sections, I recount how communities discussed the reasons why their schools should stay open and who would be responsible for making needed improvements. In the final section, I elaborate on the lived experience of closures and how they compared between the diverse communities involved.

"Don't Get in the Way!": Parent-Driven School Improvement

An important line of argument for communities was communicating why their schools were essential to the future of a rapidly changing city. While all communities alluded to demographic changes, the Ward 2 schools most forcefully made the case that changes in their neighborhoods would bolster support for currently underutilized schools.

The narrative of neighborhood change crafted by Ward 2 schools took on an optimistic tone. According to city planning documents, Wards 1 and 2, located in the heart of the city, are poised to experience the greatest growth in the student population (DC Public Schools, 2013). To demonstrate their demographic advantage, Francis-Stevens strategically assembled a group to attend a private presentation their school would give before the Chancellor. Among those who attended, interviewees recall, was a pregnant mother who could represent the commitment and growth the school was expected to see in coming years. DC City Councilmember Catania, who lives only a few blocks from Francis-Stevens, shared his own anecdotal observation at a hearing. He recalled, "It's not scientific, but I see a lot of kids trick or treating [in the neighborhood] ... lot of infants and toddlers" (D.C. Council, 2012a). Dima, a Garrison parent, testified that since DCPS appeared to be "run like a business" she drew a telling analogy: "Starbucks or Walmart ... they would never look at the demographics and walk away" (D.C. Council, 2012b). These parents made clear that the school system stood to benefit from an emerging market of young families.

Parents from these schools also spoke of their own value as active parents whose investments would show returns for their individual schools. In her testimony, Dima further pleaded that keeping the school open would guarantee her commitment as an invested parent: "Work with me, use me, keep me in the trenches ... I will stay, I will fight." A common flourish in hearing testimony or meeting notes was the ominous threat that parents would leave DC if their schools were closed. For example, when wrapping up her testimony at a hearing, Ann did not mince her words with her warning: "You will lose me if you close Garrison" (D.C. Council, 2012a). As self-proclaimed drivers of school improvement, they hoped to ensure that school officials would recognize the value they bring to the table.

Beyond the immediate role in their own schools, these parents also spoke of their impact on the city at large and claimed responsibility for reversing the trend of young couples moving out to the suburbs when their children reached school age. In table notes, Francis-Stevens families claimed that their presence would "encourage the investment of parents and families on [*sic*] the DCPS schools" at the system-level and that shutting down schools with strong parent involvement otherwise "sends a terrible message to parents in DCPS that are looking to enroll their students in the community." New, middle-class parents who had recently invested in schools attempted to position themselves as standard-bearers for beleaguered neighborhood schools that similar families may otherwise dismiss.

When identifying key aspects of their campaigns that contributed to reversing the closing decision, Garrison and Francis-Stevens' supporters referred specifically to the fact that they enjoyed a very public outpouring of support. According to Kim, elected officials confided their surprise at the support the Francis-Stevens group was able to garner. "Wow, we never knew that [there was support] within Francis-Stevens," she recalls being told by Councilmembers, "We thought that you would close and we'd never hear anything." Comments like these also seem to indicate that officials may have underestimated just how invested new parents were in their local schools.

Although parents and community members did reference the school system's shortcomings at various points through the process, Ward 2 schools also presented themselves as fairly independent in their ability to improve their schools. In their public commentary, parents and community members claimed that improvements to their schools had been largely the product of their own efforts and investments—not those of the school system. Speaking for the Garrison PTA, Ann confidently stated, "We have made Garrison into a viable option" for neighborhood families. Similarly, in table notes, a group of Francis-Stevens supporters claimed that the school community had "unlimited resources and relationships to strengthen" the school.

At times, these schools framed the involvement of the school system as an impediment to their progress rather than a key partner. In one meeting, a member of the Garrison community demanded that system leadership "[r]espect the community work, funds, and development" that residents had invested into the school by allowing it to stay open. He went on to say that if the school district would not support them, "[a]t the very least, don't get in the way!" These comments indicate that these parents saw themselves as a semi-autonomous force capable of improving schools on their own without significant support from—and indeed in spite of—DCPS.

The Ward 2 groups also proposed to shoulder most of the burden for retaining their schools. Similar to schools in other parts of the city, for example, Garrison did partially tie its hopes in remaining open to a long-sought after facility improvement that the community argued would draw in more families. But in its PowerPoint presentation to system leaders, they emphasized that the modernization would not require allocating additional money and that the community had already accessed other funds. Similarly, in their strategic plans and presentations, the Francis-Stevens community went out of its way to emphasize that no additional costs would be necessary to improve enrollment. At first glance, Francis-Stevens' four-page "Growth and Retention Plan" looks like something taken directly from the desk of a corporate strategy consultant. Tables and flowcharts indicate the various measures to enhance school climate, programmatic, and recruitment measures the school community would undertake to double the student population within five years. Moreover, they even proposed downsizing the school staff and having parent or community groups sponsor any needed additional positions. According to parents from Francis-Stevens, they were told by officials that their specific proposal was the most effective and unique of all those submitted.

Broken Promises: Addressing Systemic Causes

Rather than be constrained by making the case to save individual schools, communities in other wards of the city sought to focus on the underlying causes of school closures. Their approach required a contextualized view that explained how the city arrived at another wave of mass closures within just 4 years. First and foremost, they held the system responsible for short-changing their schools of the needed investments to sustain enrollments. These parents and community members also focused on the sizeable charter sector that had greatly expanded over the prior decade. The fact that charter schools enrolled 44% of DC's public school students during this time—the third highest percentage of charter students in any school district in the nation—was not lost on these residents (National Alliance for Public Charter Schools, 2014). They were intent on decrying the deleterious impacts of systemic disinvestment and the growing educational marketplace on schools in lower-income neighborhoods.

In the wards where schools would eventually be closed, school communities undertook a delicate balancing act of simultaneously detailing what they had been denied by the school system, while also discussing what made their schools worth sparing. Donna, the PTA president at Terrell-McGogney, mentioned the system's numerous "broken promises" that had led to diminished programming that would attract families to her school. Similarly, in a community meeting, members of the Spingarn community drew the connection between the school's withering size by pointing to the "historically deprived" and decrepit state of the large building, further asserting that "it's just as much the system's fault that its low enrolled." A local organizing group also posted signs along streets in affected communities with a clear message to district leadership: "Fix Schools, Don't Close Them!" These sentiments underscore a narrative of schools that have not received equitable investments that could support their longer-term viability.

Consequently, these communities did not adopt a similarly independent tone heard by Ward 2 groups, choosing instead to hold DCPS accountable for the state of their schools. Despite identifying potential partnerships to push for improvements, their proposals clearly held DCPS primarily responsible for taking the lead on these changes and would further require setting aside millions of dollars to see them through. But as participants found themselves shuttling between meetings, writing up their hearing testimony, and preparing PowerPoint presentations, it appeared that their explanations for why closures occurred often fell on the deaf ears of system leaders. According to Jacqueline, a community member, "there was not a lot of curiosity about the why's" among system leadership regarding the causes of closures. City and school district leaders ultimately dismissed these proposals, implying that their implementation would be impractical (Brown, 2013b).

In community engagement forums, frustrations with charter schools bubbled up frequently. In the table notes, the preponderance of critical comments about charters were clumped in the areas of the city that also have the highest concentration of charter schools. Notes from community meetings in Wards 5, 7, and 8, corroborate a pointed critique of the sector. Participants in those meetings made numerous claims about the adverse effects of charter school expansion or the quality of education they provide. Some expressed a desire for a moratorium or a "freeze" on charters. In the eyes of many participants, the closures appeared to be part of a broader city agenda to tip the scales towards a fully chartered school district. In table notes from these wards, participants repeatedly made the specific request that their schools not be turned over to charters. Additionally, participants speculated that families from closing schools would exit to charters, further depleting the system's student population. Many school communities came to see charters as a cause for closures that would further erode neighborhood schools.

Despite the connections they drew between charters and school closures, some participants strategically distanced themselves from being labeled as charter antagonists because they saw it as detrimental to their advocacy. Because of the nature of the process and knowing that their group may be discredited for holding the charter sector accountable for closures, Amber felt that it was best to focus more specifically on DCPS. Acknowledging the community's aggressive stance towards charters, Amber said,

[I] get it, completely get it. [But] I didn't want that to be part of the conversation for a very specific reason. It's because I think that DCPS has some ownership, and I wanted to talk about DCPS, and DCPS's decisions, DCPS's issues. And when you start, this, to get a conversation talking about charters, then it's a distraction.

So, even as stakeholders connected the school closure decisions to charter schools, it was seen as an issue that could delegitimize their advocacy before key decision-makers.

Although charter critiques were concentrated in the city's eastern wards, where charters are heavily concentrated, Ward 2 stakeholders did discuss the role of the charter sector in their advocacy as well. Most of their language around charters was far more innocuous and played into the notion of school competition. Kim noted that due to Francis-Stevens' location in an area projected to see increases in school-age children in coming years, that it presented a "competitive advantage" over charters if it were to remain open. Echoing the statement, Garrison's proposal also suggested that physical improvements would provide a "competitive edge over charter schools in the area." These statements, along with others noted in community meetings, suggest that participants representing Ward 2 schools did not publicly adopt a similarly hardline against charters. Their arguments also reflect the relatively lower concentration of charters in the center of the city where these schools are located.

Burn Out: Surviving School Closure

Although they always manage to spark a fierce community outcry, school closures have actually been a common fixture of urban school politics for decades. Given this history, we can observe how the level of experience communities had with school closures impacted their advocacy. While deciding whether to hold the school system accountable for school closures can be viewed as a function of class privilege, this can also be situated in the lived experience of fighting for school improvements over a longer period of time.

Longer-term residents often hearkened back to their involvement in earlier closing struggles. Amber, herself a product of the school system and now a community leader, prefaced her hearing testimony with a little history: "Actually, the first time I testified about school closures, it was about 20 years ago, and I was 5 years old and they wanted to close my school..." (D.C. Council, 2012a). This individual experience reflected the fact that many of the schools on the 2013 list were already the products of previous consolidations (Levy, 2012). Daniel, a community organizer, also related that his group's unsuccessful attempt to obtain a legal injunction against the closures was "demoralizing" for parents who were involved. "That's always the risk, you know," he went on to say, "and it did take a toll on folks." Due to the constant threat and long history of closures in DC, we should consider the capacity and energies of some schools to continually advocate for themselves.

Communities that mobilized successfully to retain their schools were celebrated in media and in comments from public officials. For example, the Garrison community's ability to mobilize its neighbors was highlighted by a local real estate blog that gushed about the activism of a "new generation" of parents arising out of the city's "baby boom" (Paul, 2012). Underlying the experiences of these parents and community members was evidence of an extensive level of involvement spurred by their flexibility and newness to schooling issues. For a number of these parents and community members, they identified the closures as their first true foray into public school activism. For example, Nate, a Francis-Stevens parent, talked about his evolution from a more distant PTA supporter to a campaign leader who—once the proposed closure was announced—took on the specific task of media outreach. Similarly, Ann from Garrison described their school's campaign as her "second full-time job" (Brown, 2013a). Kim, also a Francis-Stevens parent, shared that she was able to take a temporary leave from her own job to devote herself to the campaign to save their school. She recalls an "all-consuming" schedule that included hours-long strategy sessions and regular meetings with officials. But even in their victory, these newer, middle-class families reported the toll the process took on them. The school closure process, Kim recounted, "burned you so bad" in the end. Starting out with a core group of five families, she reported, her cadre was left with only one family that she says is still working "full steam" in advocating for the school.

If closures or similarly devastating policies continue to be implemented, we may question what costs they incur for maintaining the involvement of active and engaged parents and community members. Taking the discouraging experiences of recently involved Ward 2 parents as a starting point, we may begin to grasp the long-term impact closures have had for those communities that have repeatedly faced these challenges over the preceding decades. While the activism and engagement of new parents may make headlines as a gentrifying city broadcasts its hopes of a promising educational future, the legacy of overcoming dispossession in communities of color becomes an uncomfortable historical footnote.

IMPLICATIONS AND CONCLUSIONS

To truly appreciate the significance of closed schools as artifacts that attest to the changes in urban education, we can compare them with those schools that have managed to survive through challenging times. The difference between these open and shut schools reflects a persistent power dynamic in community engagement that is rooted deeply in the social contexts of education and forces us to confront the various racial, socioeconomic, and educational implications of school closures. In those areas and communities hardest hit, the closures appeared to have fulfilled a "politics as usual" narrative. During an interview with Christina, a community leader who took part in the process, she voiced her dismay at the results:

> During the consolidations we mobilized several groups of families and the Chancellor sat there and said, "We're not going to just listen to the people with the loudest voices or the people with the most money." But if you look at the round of closings, that's exactly what they did...It looks fishy. It's a lot of White faces, it's a lot of people who are of higher socioeconomic status...

Moreover, for these communities, the process did not adequately address long-standing inequality or the causes of school closures. Without acknowledging systemic issues in the city's schools, residents are left to wonder whether future waves of closures should be anticipated and in what ways gentrification may shape future educational decisions.

While their efforts appeared to have paid off, Ward 2 interviewees were left with a degree of uncertainty and discomfort in their relationship with the school system. Emily, a former Garrison parent who still avidly supports the school, emphasized that the school remained open because it had "very real reasons, data-based reasons." However, she was quick to acknowledge that "it was also because it could pull together its community and because it had maybe the time or the energy" to mount an effective campaign. Reflecting on the challenges inherent to the process, she went on to explain that closure decisions should be more data-driven and fit within long-term plans in the future, "so it shouldn't be about who shows their face in front of such and such committee the most or who manages to get more people down to the Wilson Building [DC's city hall] on a Council day. It really shouldn't be." Even in their victory, Ward 2 parents recognized how forms of privilege can operate in shaping these types of decisions and expressed wariness around working with district officials in the future.

This chapter should not be misread as either a vilification of outspoken middle-class parents or a celebration of their efforts. Their involvement is complicated and the fact remains that in the schools that were spared, lower-income students still comprise the majority population. I also do not want to suggest that shuttering schools attended by more privileged families would somehow better serve the cause of equity. Finally, I do not intend to recommend any "best practices" in how to more effectively close schools.

Rather, as gentrification deepens sources of inequality, what this chapter should bring to light is the need for equitable processes of community engagement that provide authentic platforms for parents and community members to participate in shaping public education decisions. In this case, the criteria set out by school system leaders for effective school improvement proposals explicitly privileged middle-class parent engagement. Furthermore, the city's approach erased disadvantaged communities' historical struggles with school improvement efforts, dismissed their legitimate concerns with underlying systemic causes, and absolved the educational establishment of responsibility. Finally, the design of school closure processes can position communities to be defensive or even antagonistic towards one another. School closure processes can also erode relationships between increasingly diverse public school constituencies. Across the board, whether in communities where schools stayed open or were shut, the school closure process did little to support a unified vision of school improvement that DCPS had hoped to inculcate. Instead, it put on display how inequality is embedded not only in school closure outcomes, but even in the seemingly democratic and "fair" decision-making processes behind them.

In the future, engagement may position communities to deliberate on longer-term planning that includes developing more transparent criteria used to determine when or how to consolidate schools. Without developing engagement platforms that work towards preventative measures or safeguards against future closures, system leaders will focus on achieving only marginal improvements in the public acceptance of them. Several prior closure episodes prove that grasping at such straws will do little to bolster systemic reforms.

Looking ahead, broader demographic and political forces spell an uncertain future for the city's public schools. Even after DC's student population has slowly rebounded and grown after several decades, long-standing inequalities in specialized programming and the continued expansion of school choice may mean that future closures are still imminent. Many long-term residents who have witnessed successive waves of closures expressed a deep skepticism about DC's plan to retain its public schools, speculating that the school system's leadership is inclined to further charter expansion. At the same time, new parents are actively enrolling in gentrifying neighborhood schools. The implications for maintaining diversity and equity into the future are unclear. Long-term DC residents are slowly coming to terms with the fact that the sun is setting on their once "Chocolate City." While the investments and engagement of affluent families may be alluring to city leaders, decision-makers must ensure that educational equity concerns do not become overshadowed.

REFERENCES

Atkinson, R. (2003). Introduction: Misunderstood saviour or vengeful wrecker? The many meanings and problems of gentrification. *Urban Studies, 40*(12), 2343–2350.

Ayala, J., & Galletta, A. (2012). Documenting disappearing spaces: Erasure and remembrance in two high school closures. *Peace and Conflict: Journal of Peace Psychology, 18*(2), 149–155.

Bannon, D. (2012, December 12). Parents prod Henderson for specifics. *The Northwest Current*. Retrieved from https://issuu.com/currentnewspapers/docs/ch_12-12-12_1

Boasberg, J. (2014). Memorandum Opinion: *Shannon Marie Smith et al. v. Kaya Henderson, Chancellor of the District of Columbia Public Schools et al.* United States District Court for the District of Columbia. Civil Action No. 13-420 (JEB). Retrieved from https://www.courtlistener.com/opinion/2684837/smith-v-henderson/

Biegler, C. (2012). A big gap: Income inequality in the district remains one of the highest in the nation. Washington, DC: DC Fiscal Policy Institute. Retrieved from http://www.dcfpi.org/wp-content/uploads/2012/03/03-08- 12incomeinequality1.pdf

Brown, E. (2012, November 30). At D.C. school-closure forums, parents urge Henderson to consider alternatives. *The Washington Post*. Retrieved from https://www.washingtonpost.com/local/education/at-dc-school-closure-forums-parents-urge-henderson-to-consider-alternatives/2012/11/30/62fe83ee-3b08-11e2-8a97-363b0f9a0ab3_story.html

Brown, E. (2013a, January 1). D.C. parents develop alternatives to chancellor's school-closure plan. *The Washington Post*. Retrieved from http://www.washingtonpost.com/local/education/dc-parents-develop-alternatives-to-chancellors-school-closure-plan/2013/01/01/3e58f9e4-4b92-11e2-b709-667035ff9029_story.html

Brown, E. (2013b, January 17). D.C. to close 15 under-enrolled schools. *The Washington Post*. Retrieved from http://www.washingtonpost.com/local/education/chancellor-kaya-henderson-names-15-dc-schools-on-closure-list/2013/01/17/e04202fa-6023-11e2-9940-6fc488f3fecd_story.html

Chambers, S. (2006). *Mayors and schools: Minority voices and democratic tensions in urban education*. Philadelphia, PA: Temple University Press.

Cucchiara, M. B. (2013). *Marketing schools, marketing cities: Who wins and who loses when schools become urban amenities*. Chicago, IL: University of Chicago Press.

Cucchiara, M. B., & Horvat, E. M. (2009). Perils and promises: Middle-class parental involvement in urban schools. *American Educational Research Journal, 46*(4), 974–1004.

D.C. Council. (2012a). Review of school closures within the District of Columbia public schools, Committee of the whole. November 15. [Video]. Retrieved from http://dc.granicus.com/MediaPlayer.php?view_id=4&clip_id=1497

D.C. Council. (2012b). Review of school closures within the District of Columbia public schools, Committee of the whole. November 19. [Video]. Retrieved from http://dc.granicus.com/MediaPlayer.php?view_id=4&clip_id=1502

D.C. Public Schools. (2013). Better schools for all students: DCPS' consolidation and reorganization plan. Retrieved from http://dcps.dc.gov/DCPS/Files/downloads/COMMUNITY/CR/Consolidation percent20Plan.pdf

Davis, T., & Oakley, D. (2013). Linking charter school emergence to urban revitalization and gentrification: A socio-spatial analysis of three cities. *Journal of Urban Affairs, 35*(1), 81–102.

de la Torre, M., & Gwynne, J. (2009). *When schools close: Effects on displaced students in Chicago public schools.* Chicago, IL: Consortium on Chicago School Research.

Fenwick, L. (2013, May 28). Urban school reform is really about land development (not kids). *The Washington Post.* Retrieved from https://www.washingtonpost.com/news/answer-sheet/wp/2013/05/28/ed-school-dean-urban-school-reform-is-really-about-land-development-not-kids/

Gelderman, C. (2012). *A free man of color and his hotel: Race, reconstruction, and the role of the federal government.* Washington, DC: Potomac Books.

Good, R. (2016). Histories that root us: Neighborhood, place, and the protest of school closures in Philadelphia. *Urban Geography,* doi:10.1080/02723638.2016.1182286.

Gordon, J. A. (2008). Community responsive schools, mixed housing, and community regeneration. *Journal of Education Policy, 23*(2), 181–192.

Hopkinson, N. (2012). *Go-go live: The musical life and death of a chocolate city.* Durham, NC: Duke University Press.

Howard, E. (2005, March 1). University to sell Wormley property. *The Hoya.* Retrieved from http://www.thehoya.com/university-to-sell-wormley-property

Ishimaru, A. (2014). Rewriting the rules of engagement: elaborating a model of district community collaboration. *Harvard Educational Review 84*(2), 188–216.

Jeter, J. (2008, February 29). Human Resources (No. 350) [Audio podcast]. *This American Life.* Retrieved from https://www.thisamericanlife.org/350/human-resources/act-two-0

Jordan, R., & Gallagher, M. (2015). Does school choice affect gentrification? Washington, DC: Urban Institute.

Kennedy, M., & Leonard, P. (2001). *Dealing with neighborhood change: A primer on gentrification and policy choices.* Washington, DC: The Brookings Institution.

Lareau, A., & Horvat, E. (1999). Moments of social inclusion and exclusion race, class, and cultural capital in family-school relationships. *Sociology of Education, 72*(1), 37–53.

Lees, L. (2008). Gentrification and social mixing: Towards an inclusive urban renaissance? *Urban Studies, 45*(12), 2449–2470.

Lerner, M. (2012, September 6). Luxury home: Georgetown's Wormley row fits right in. *The Washington Times.* Retrieved from http://www.washingtontimes.com/news/2012/sep/6/luxury-home-georgetowns-wormley-row-fits-right-in/

Lesko, K., Babb, V., & Gibbs, C. (1991). *Black Georgetown remembered: A history of its black community from the founding of "The Town of George" in 1751 to the present day.* Washington, DC: Georgetown University.

Levy, M. (2012). DCPS schools closed 1976–2012. DC SHAPPE. Retrieved from https://sites.google.com/site/shappesite

Lipman, P. (2011). *The new political economy of urban education: Neoliberalism, race, and the right to the city.* New York, NY: Routledge.

Lipman, P., Gutstein, E., Gutierrez, R. R., & Blanche, T. (2015). *Should Chicago have an elected representative school board? A new review of the evidence.* Chicago, IL: Collaborative for Equity and Justice In Education, University of Illinois at Chicago. Retrieved from http://ceje.uic.edu/wp- content/uploads/2013/11/CEJE-ERSB-Report-2-16-15.pdf

Martin, M. (2013). School closings: How administrations decide. *NPR.* Retrieved from http://www.npr.org/2013/03/21/174943853/-school- closings-how-administrations-decide

Matthews, T. (2009, October 8). Survey of historic buildings in Georgetown: The Wormley School. *The Georgetown Metropolitan.* Retrieved from http://georgetownmetropolitan.com/2009/10/08/survey-of-historic-school -buildings-in-georgetown-the-wormley-school/

Letting Everyone Be Heard. (2008, January 13). *The Washington Post.* Retrieved from http://www.washingtonpost.com/wp-dyn/content/article/2008/01/12/AR2008011202344.html

National Alliance for Public Charter Schools. (2014). *A growing movement: America's largest charter school communities* (9th ed.) Washington, DC: National Alliance for Public Charter Schools.

Noguera, P. (2001). Transforming urban schools through investments in the social capital of parents. In S. Saegert, J. P. Thompson, & M. Warren (Eds.), *Social Capital and Poor Communities* (pp. 189–212). New York, NY: Russell Sage.

Orr, M., & Rogers, J. (2011). Unequal schools, unequal voice: The need for public engagement for public education. In M. Orr & J. Rogers (Eds.), *Public engagement for public education: Joining forces to revitalize democracy and equalize schools* (pp. 1–26). Palo Alto, CA: Stanford University Press.

Pappas, L. (2012). School closings and parent engagement. *Peace and Conflict: Journal of Peace Psychology, 18,* 165–172.

Paul, S. (2012, August 22). Activist moms: School reform through listservs, Facebook and action. *UrbanTurf.* Retrieved from http://dc.urbanturf.com/articles/blog/activist_moms_listservs_prompt_school_reform/5921

Petrilli, M. (2012). *The diverse schools dilemma: A parent's guide to socioeconomically mixed public schools.* Washington, DC: Thomas B. Fordham Institute.

Pew Charitable Trusts. (2011). *Closing schools in Philadelphia: Lessons from six urban districts.* Philadelphia, PA: Pew Charitable Trusts, Philadelphia Research Initiative. Retrieved from http://www.pewtrusts.org/~/media/Assets/2011/10/19/ClosingPublicSchoolsPhiladelphia.pdf

Posey-Maddox, L. (2014). *When middle-class parents choose urban schools: Class, race, and the challenge of equity in public education.* Chicago, IL: University of Chicago Press.

Posey-Maddox, L., Kimelberg, S. M., & Cucchiara, M. (2014). Middle-class parents and urban public schools: Current research and future directions. *Sociology Compass, 8*(4), 446–456.

Prince, S. (2014). *African Americans and gentrification in Washington, D.C. Race, class and social justice in the nation's capital.* Burlington, VT: Ashgate.

Roda, A., & Wells, A. S. (2013). School choice policies and racial segregation: Where White parents' good intentions, anxiety, and privilege collide. *American Journal of Education, 119*(2), 261–293.

Rosenblat, J., & Howard, T. (2015, February 20). How gentrification is leaving public schools behind. *U.S. News and World Report*. Retrieved from http://www.usnews.com/news/articles/2015/02/20/how-gentrification-is-leaving-publicschools-behind

Sanchez, C. (2013, March 23). School closures pit race and poverty against budgets. *NPR*. Retrieved from http://www.npr.org/2013/03/23/175104850/race-poverty-central-to-national-school-closure-debate

Smith, J., & Stovall, D. (2008). Coming home to new homes and new schools: Critical race theory and the new politics of containment. *Journal of Education Policy*, *23*(2), 135–152.

Stillman, J. B. (2012). *Gentrification and schools: The process of integration when whites reverse flight.* New York, NY: Palgrave MacMillan.

Stone, C., Henig, J., Jones, B., & Pierannunzi, C. (2001). *Building civic capacity: The politics of reforming urban public schools.* Lawrence: University Press of Kansas.

Sturtevant, L. (2013). The New District of Columbia: What Population Growth and Demographic Change Mean for the City. *Journal of Urban Affairs, 36*(2), 276–299.

Sunderman, G., & Payne, A. (2009). Does closing schools cause educational harm? A review of the research. Mid-Atlantic Equity Center. Retrieved from http://files.eric.ed.gov/fulltext/ED543514.pdf

Turque, B., & Cohen, J. (2010, February 1). D.C. schools chancellor rhee's approval rating in deep slide. *The Washington Post*. Retrieved from http://www.washingtonpost.com/wp-dyn/content/article/2010/01/31/AR2010013102757.html

Urban Institute. (2014a). *Chapter 1: Demographics.* Washington, DC: Our changing city. Washington, DC: Author. Retrieved from http://datatools.urban.org/features/OurChangingCity/ demographics

Urban Institute. (2014b). *Chapter 2: Schools.* Washington, DC: Our changing city. Washington, DC: Author. Retrieved from http://datatools.urban.org/features/OurChangingCity/schools/index.html

Wester, M. (2009). Forgetting to re-member: "Post-racial" amnesia and racial history. *Reconstruction*. 9(3). Retrieved from http://reconstruction.eserver.org/Issues/093/wester.shtml

Williams, P., & Smith, N. (2007). From "renaissance" to restructuring: The dynamics of contemporary urban development. In N. Smith & P. Williams (Eds.), *Gentrification of the City* (pp. 204–224). Boston, MA: Allen & Unwin.

CHAPTER 6

COMPLICATING "SECTOR" AGNOSTICISM

Relational and Spatial Displacement and Dispossession Through School Closure in Cleveland

Anne Galletta
Cleveland State University

When East High closed down, it was hard for me to get to Glenville High School, now that I go to Glenville. And this is a map of my route, how I've got to travel. I live right here on Hough Avenue, on [East] 89th . . . I got to catch the 38 [bus] right here from

my house, and then from the 38 right here take me to 105 [street]. Then from 105 I got to catch the 10 [bus] all the way down to 105 and St. Clair. And from St. Clair I got to catch the 1 [bus] on 105 and St. Clair . . . and from the 1, it take me all the way to 113th. This is 3 buses I have to catch to get to this one location.

—Liana, youth researcher and former East High student, displaced by school closure (Jones & Schilling, 2011)[1]

In January 2010, the chief executive officer of the Cleveland Metropolitan School District (CMSD) announced the Cleveland Transformation Plan, which called for "fundamental changes in . . . how schools are designed and how they operate" (Cleveland Metropolitan School District, 2010, p. 2). The plan categorized schools in the district for one of four key actions: maintain as "growth schools"; intensively support as "refocus schools"; replace leadership or require teachers to reapply for their positions, redesign the school or convert it to a charter for "repurpose schools"; or close the school and reassign students to other schools (p. 25). East High School, which Liana attended, was listed for closure. The morning after the announcement, students at East expressed disbelief at the news. Uncertainty persisted until the school board approved the Transformation Plan on March 9, 2010 (Ott, 2010b). Within three months of the approval, fourteen elementary schools and two high schools were closed in the district, nearly all of which were located on the east side of Cleveland serving mostly poor and working class African American students. The district closed seven additional east side schools the following year (Ott, 2011b).

In a film documenting the 2010 closure of East High School in Cleveland, youth researcher and former East High student Liana narrates her extensive route to her receiving school, Glenville High School (Jones & Schilling, 2011). Tapping the point of origin, her home in Cleveland's Hough neighborhood, her finger traces her route through city streets and bus stops. At the close of her description, Liana's arm reaches back to her home on the map, follows the distance travelled, and critiques the trip she took daily not of her volition or that of her family. The distance evident in Liana's narrative is not only in terms of mileage but also reflects the Duboisian veil between the lives of poor and working class students of color and urban educational policy (Du Bois, 1995, p. 45). Liana conveys with some irony three bus rides to "get to this *one* location." Also suggested is a resistance to the imposition of relational and spatial displacement. Inclusion of Liana's story in the documentary film, *Lives in Transition: Eviction Notice*, takes to task the discourse of school closure as benefiting students (Jones & Schilling, 2011).[2] In Liana's map and narrative, displacement as a consequence of school closure is rendered visible. To grasp the full import of her experience, this chapter considers Liana's relationship to the Hough neighborhood of Cleveland, itself a receiving site for Black families displaced during the 1950s through urban renewal, and a site of significant racial unrest in 1966 due to accumulating racial discrimination in employment, housing, policing, and education. Though Liana's school closed in 2010, this trajectory of spatial and relational displacement and dispossession can be traced back historically. Further, it can be mapped beyond 2010 to current permutations of school closure as school replacement. The task, then, is to locate the traces of this history, to connect the past to the present, and to employ those connections as a source of critique and a humanizing restoration (Martín-Baró, 1994). In a related manner, historian and Haitian scholar Michel-Rolph Trouillot (1995) equates historical erasure with the power of elites to silence aspects of the past that destabilize the balance of power in the present. Trouillot cautions, "Effective silencing does not require a conspiracy, not even a political consensus. Its roots are structural" (p. 196).

The purpose of this chapter is to examine the experience of school closure among Cleveland students living on the city's predominantly African American east side. This research focuses on both the lived experience of students and families and to historical and current policy contexts. In doing so, the study notes redrawn spatial and relational boundaries, particularly as public assets have shifted in terms of space, material resources, and governance. In doing so, this study offers a counterstory to race-neutral ahistorical ways of viewing school closure. While attending to the costs and consequences of school closure, this chapter also explores the underdeveloped topic of benefits—for whom, by whom, and toward what purpose?

THEORETICAL FRAMEWORK

This chapter explores the production of racialized educational experiences resulting from a view of racial inequality that is "curious and compassionately" misframed (Du Bois 1995, p. 44). This research argues that the discourse of "sector agnosticism," interrogated below, underscores how an ideology of race-neutrality absent historical analysis in school closure maintains the Duboisian veil (Du Bois, 1995, p. 45). In investigating the relationship between school closure and sector agnosticism, this study relies upon the work of critical race theorists Kimberle Crenshaw, Neil Gotanda, Gary Peller, and Kendall Thomas (1995). In the mid-1980s, Crenshaw et al. developed critical race theory (CRT) in critique of legal studies for its failure to disentangle relations of power accorded to race, often embedded in seemingly mundane and unrelated structures. Within the shift of the courts away from race conscious legal analysis and remedies of the 1960s and early 1970s and toward race neutrality, most salient in the 1990s and the first two decades of 2000, the aversion to race-consciousness shaped the norms and expectations of district officials and a majority of elected officials. The legal context and cultural accompaniment of race neutrality reconfigured normative understandings, precluding alternate ways of seeing the entanglement of privilege and exclusion. Without a counterstory, the narrative in educational reform has been historically thin and colorblind, ideologically tilling the soil for policy enactments and legislation converging liberal interests in educational equity with the full currency of profit management.

Race is understood here as a social construction with material consequences, "a materiality that in significant ways has been produced and sustained by law" and by educational policy (Crenshaw et al., 1995, p. xxvi). Crenshaw et al. (1995) wrote of how they envisioned their work as in CRT:

> Laws produced racial power not simply through narrowing the scope of, say, of anti-discrimination remedies, nor through racially-biased decision-making, but instead through myriad legal rules, many of them having nothing to do with rules against discrimination, that continued to reproduce the structures and practice of racial domination. In short, we accepted the crit emphasis on how law produces and is the product of social power and we cross-cut this theme with an effort to understand this dynamic in the context of race and racism. With such an analysis in hand, critical race theory allows us to better understand how racial power can be produced even from within a liberal discourse that is relatively autonomous from organized vectors of racial power. (p. xxv)

This research conceptualizes school closure as central to the racialized processes of relational and spatial displacement and dispossession. In the dispossession of public services and assets, and their accumulation within the private sphere, there is evident what social psychologists Michelle Fine and Jessica Ruglis (2009) refer to as accumulation by dispossession, drawing on the work of economist David Harvey (2004) who developed the concept. Accumulation through dispossession occurs when resources once accessible publicly, such as clean water, Internet speed, green spaces, parks, and school buildings, are contracted out or sold to private entities. In the realm of racial justice, Derrick Bell (1995) underscores how some degree of privilege is more likely to yield its location of power and structural assets when there are benefits to be accrued in other forums or venues. In this manner, the unraveling of racial justice occurs at the same time racial justice is set in place. Through the analysis of history and the lived experience of youth of color in Cleveland poor and working class neighborhoods, the racialization of privilege and exclusion surfaces with greater clarity.

Attending to students' lived experience of school closure in the city of Cleveland, within its history of racial privilege and exclusion, is the aim of this chapter. To carry out this task conceptually, this study draws upon the work of clinical psychiatrist and public health advocate and scholar Mindy

Fullilove, particularly her study of urban renewal in Pittsburgh's Hill District. In an interview with Charles Meadows, an elder member of the Roanoke, Virginia, Black community, Fullilove notes Mr. Meadow's deep cynicism toward stated goals and intentions within his city. Fullilove follows the cadence and rhythm of this elder's story through poetic phrasing:

> They cut everything through the black section,
> They can use it at any time.
> And they hold meetings,
> And they all have a big political talk,
> "continued good things are gonna happen to you out of this
>   movement,
> and this is progress."
> And who—what the good things,
> Who they gonna benefit?
> (Fullilove, 2004, p. 106)

Mr. Meadows situates "progress" as outside the Black community, while the Black community bears the costs and consequences of urban renewal. In Pittsburgh, as in Cleveland and across the United States, there was no one-for-one replacement of the housing that was destroyed. Moreover, eligibility requirements were put in place for families wishing to rent or buy new properties. Families from intact neighborhoods were dispersed. The land on which thousands of Black families lived was purchased at low cost and transferred into sources of high profit. Fullilove's (2004) poetic phrasing reveals Mr. Meadow's compelling analysis of the dispossession of the Black community as within an interdependent set of relations with the gains among elites who benefitted from public policy toward the accumulation of private wealth.

Fullilove (2004) lays out several mechanisms of displacement, including an evolving articulation of space as "distressed" that often misdiagnosed the causes of distress. Once applied, however, the label not only reinforced community stigma but further veiled the factors contributing to its level of stress. This is the process of dispossession, as the meaning given to space by those most closely associated with it is diminished. The labels of "distressed" or "blighted" or "failing" take hold among those largely at a distance from the daily lives of people living in the designated space. The assignment of the label sets the stage for disinvestment. Well before any such action is taken, the psychological impact of the label acts as a force field enveloping the space in fear, uncertainty, stasis, and deterioration. Dispossession, then, had transpired before urban renewal was effectuated. At the same time, the assets and resources from which individuals and groups were dispossessed become available to those within long and/or recently established public–private networks through ease of purchase, lease, or annexation.

Displacement and accumulation through dispossession are evident in the zealous takeover of urban school districts by the state, mayoral control, and public–private partnerships. Governance structures are weakened and new structural arrangements shift the relationship between families and schools. Central urban districts often employ a philosophy of individual social mobility whereby the nature of the school–community relationship is one of consumption, and institutions are created, sustained, or extinguished through supply and demand. Schools are assigned themes that attract culturally-informed views of schooling, and the school brands set the social stratification in motion. Family choice of particular schools results in oversubscribed schools with waiting lists, triggering dwindling enrollments in other schools. These stark differences are frequently related to the particular neighborhood location of schools, the extent to which their programs are bolstered by private partnerships or middle class family volunteering and material resources as well as their racial, ethnic and/or social class demographics (Cucchiara, 2013; Kimelberg, 2014; Posey-Maddox, 2014, 2016).

To advance this school choice landscape, under-enrolled, underperforming, and under-resourced district schools are closed, opening up the educational market for new models. As noted by Andy Smarick (2012), a senior policy fellow at the Thomas B. Fordham Institute, which is a sponsor of a number of Ohio charter schools, "Closing schools isn't just a way to right-size a district that's lost enrollment; it's the way to continuously shed failing programs" (p. 3).

Citing Foster and Kaplan (2004), Smarick (2012) refers to this process as "creative destruction," which allows for a "healthy churn" of school options. Unsuccessful schools, whether district or charter, are closed, and new schools replace them. Achieving the school choice imaginary requires what Smarick refers to as "sector agnosticism." This stance constitutes "complete ambivalence" toward the types of schools located in a school district, reflecting an "ecumenical" approach toward traditional district schools and charter schools as choice options (p. 3). In his discussion, agnosticism presumes a dispassionate stance and a deliberate setting aside of preference toward any particular "sector" within the matrix of schooling options. A portfolio system relies on this concept of sector agnosticism in arguing for private entities' access within the public sector to contract for educational services and establishing schools. Alternatively, Milward (1994) refers to these processes as the hollowing out of the state.

Portfolio systems exist in Chicago, Denver, New Orleans, New York City, and Philadelphia, among other cities. Employing investment discourse, portfolio systems offer school options, developing niche areas of focus and branding to distinguish schools. These systems assume parental access to resources and social networks to inform their choice of a school that is the "best fit" for their child. Portfolio systems aim for a single enrollment system that does not distinguish between district schools and charter schools, increasingly restructuring resource distribution with fewer sector distinctions. Unlike controlled choice programs, the portfolio system is entirely deregulated in terms of attention to proportional representation of students by race, ethnicity, poverty, English language learners, students with disabilities, and students who are homeless.

School closure and replacement are well positioned in the discourse of "sector agnosticism" through which capitalist notions of efficiency, competition, and the free market converge with liberal aspirations and desire for racial equality. However, the agnosticism sought in school closure demands a subtraction of the central struggle as to how to analytically frame racial inequality as a social problem. Like urban renewal, school closure and replacement in the context of competitive, deregulated school choice assigns labels of educational "blightedness" to schools, based on metrics that occlude the sources of their malaise. Well before a school's closure or redesign, the mechanics of dispossession are at work. Like the displacement process in urban renewal, the closing or replacement of one's schools provides no guarantees that the benefits of this wide scale policy initiative will serve one's family well.

The production of stigma—of identifying schools by high-stakes standardized measures presumed objective—and diminishing the subjective meanings among those associated with a school—assigns the label of blight, justifying displacement and dispossession. While these processes are portrayed as a necessary change serving the interest of all students, an analysis of who carries the costs and who realizes the benefits is needed to recast this story of school reform.

In the following literature review, key issues related to the use of school closure in urban school districts are addressed, providing the backdrop within education contributing to displacement and disinvestment.

REVIEW OF THE LITERATURE

School closures have been prominent in federal accountability legislation through No Child Left Behind and in educational reform free market school choice options at the state level. In 2009, the federal government provided additional educational funding during grave economic conditions. The American Recovery and Reinvestment Act (ARRA) reflected a new twist in school improvement through the competitive structuring of access to resources as evident in the Race to the Top Fund and the investment in four forms of "intervention," including school closure (Trujillo &

Renée, 2012). The School Improvement Grant program, authorized by the Elementary and Secondary Education Act (ESEA), included school closure as an intervention, representing what Mead (2012) refers to as "the first federalized school choice program" (p. 57). State legislation and local policy enactments have accelerated school choice options. Private foundations and corporations often provide additional support for school choice (Au & Ferrare, 2015; Fabricant & Fine, 2012; Kumashiro, 2012; Picower & Mayorga, 2015). The Every Student Succeeds Act (ESSA), reauthorizing ESEA and signed into law in 2015, reduced federal involvement and placed the onus on states for accountability. There is a direct connection between school closure, redesign, and replacement as it relates to the prevailing ideology within school choice of parents as individual consumers in an unregulated market of school options. Under the leadership of Betsy DeVos as U.S. Secretary of Education, this ideology of reform is expected to accelerate.

Academic Impact

There is little research illustrating increased academic proficiency resulting from school closure. What is evident is that school closure disproportionately impacts students of color, poor and working class students, immigrant students, and students with disabilities (Brummet 2014; de la Torre & Gwynne, 2009; Engberg, Gill, Zamarro, & Zimmer, 2012; Hernandez & Galletta, 2016). The announcement of school closure is typically followed by a drop in achievement. Research indicates variation in academic success in the years following school closure, including sustained depressed performance (Kirshner, Gaertner, and Pozzoboni, 2010; Steggert & Galletta, 2013), as well as a return to a similar trajectory, or trend, of performance for most students (Brummet 2014; de la Torre & Gwynne, 2009; Engberg et al., 2012); other studies point to improvement following school closure but note the achievement level remains below proficiency (Carlson & Lavertu, 2015; Kemple, 2015). Social and academic progress, already vulnerable due to high rates of student mobility, may be negatively affected as school closure may exacerbate mobility rates, impeding academic progress (Rumberger & Lim, 2008).

Relational Impact

Important social ties anchor children and youth to community institutions, including their schools. A study of relational impact attends to resources available through social support, reciprocity, sense of belonging, and the social capital generated from strong relational ties (Coleman, 1988;

Putnam, 2000; Stanton-Salazar, 2001). These are critical ingredients within the educational setting.

The desire to sustain relationships with teachers and adults in the school building is a key concern of families experiencing closure (Deeds & Pattillo, 2015; de la Torre, Gordon, Moore, & Cowhy, 2015; Kirshner et al., 2010; Valencia, 1984). At the elementary level, an ethnographic study by Deeds and Pattillo (2015) reported that the closure of the study focus, an elementary school in Newark, New Jersey, reflected a disjuncture between the district's view of the school and that of parents and students, who did not perceive the school as having failed them and saw the closure as illegitimate. At the high school level, Kirshner et al. (2010) found students displaced by school closure narrated the loss of relationships among peers and between students and teachers.

Alternatively, de la Torre and Gwynne (2009) in their study of 44 Chicago school closings between 2001 and 2006, reported differences in teacher support as critical in explaining variation in displaced elementary school students' achievement (p. 26), with gains in learning evident in schools in which high levels of positive interaction between students and teachers were reported by students. Kirshner et al. (2010) note that in their study of a high school closure in western U.S. roughly half of the survey and interview respondents reported the presence of a caring adult in the receiving school. For students experiencing school closure, the loss of relationships may be lessened when resources and educational structures in the receiving school address this loss.

In a later study, de la Torre et al. (2015) found that following the 2013 Chicago school closures, families were more likely to select the district welcoming school (DWS) when it sustained relational ties from the closed school, among other criteria. One parent's story illustrates the degree to which sustained relationships were important to families and parents' dual role as citizen and caretaker for one's children. The parent expressed her opposition to her child's school closure through participation in a protest. At the same time, in investigating her options, she selected a school that employed a staff member from the closed school whom she trusted and viewed as providing some level of continuity (p. 27).

Students and their families have engaged in parallel work as they raise questions about the utility of school closure at the same time they navigate their options. Allweis, Grant, and Manning (2015) studied over 500 images posted on various media sources related to the shuttering of 54 Chicago school buildings in 2013. Among these, they categorized 80 images as focused on students and revealing relationally-based activities, with the majority of images showing protests of the closures.

Spatial Impact

The loss of a neighborhood school produces stress for the families, particularly as it relates to the spatial arrangement of neighborhoods and receiving schools. De la Torre et al. (2015) note that Chicago families affected by the 2013 closures were more likely to send their children to the designated welcoming school if they lived in close proximity to it, with 75% of students enrolled when the designated school was 0.5 miles or less from students' residence and 83% if it was relocated to the site of the closed school (p. 18). Transportation was available when distance was involved, but the transportation left from and returned to the closed school site, not the students' homes. The authors note that many families did not view the options available as choice options because their lack of transportation foreclosed traveling to a school other than the welcoming school. When parents did not choose, they were assigned to the designated welcoming school (p. 9).

When schools are closed through a phase out process, students experience an interruption in access to the school building and in their sense of identity as associated with the school. This sense of exclusion is evident in the writing of Melissa Kissoon (2012), who narrated being perceived as a "trespasser" in her Brooklyn New York City high school, which served low-income students of color. While four new schools were being phased into her school building, Kissoon and her peers found the spatial boundaries narrowing and their sense of exclusion quite salient. The phasing out of large comprehensive high schools is a common strategy employed in school replacement, an increasing variation of school closure.

Understanding the depth of relational and spatial attachments is brought into full relief with a metaphor that effectively humanizes the impact of school closure. In their study of 2010 school closure experiences, Cleveland youth researchers suggested the theme of eviction to reflect their experience of an imposed action on the part of the an outside entity, indifferent to the consequences of displacement and dispossession (Jones & Schilling, 2011). In the film conveying their experiences, students expressed: loss of access to their high school building and resources such as after-school programs; academic interruptions; separation from teachers and staff; and the disruption of peer networks. On a sheet of paper posted in Liana's high school hallway during the last week of school in June 2010, one student wrote: "RIP East" (Jones & Schilling, 2011).

Summing Up

Evident in a review of the literature on school closure is the pattern in urban settings revealing its disproportionate impact on students of color, poor and working class students, English language learners, and students with disabilities. Also evident is the accumulation of dispossession (Fine & Ruglis, 2009; Harvey, 2004; Hernandez & Galletta, 2016) as cities implement waves of closures, redesigns, and school replacements. Whether the theory of action is based on accountability through efforts to attain outcome equity related to anti-poverty legislation such as the ESSA, or an economic theory of free market school choice made possible through access to capital from closed schools, or the convergence of both persuasions, the consequences of these policies reveal little advancement in academic proficiency and much by way of relational and spatial displacement and disruption. The experience of being removed from a space viewed as "home" in a broader context of displacement and frequent unpredictable loss was evident in student survey findings, as discussed later in this chapter.

METHODS

The chapter draws from a case study of Cleveland using primary and secondary sources as well as observational data. As a faculty member in a college of education who collaborated with teachers and administrators in nearby schools, the author observed school, district, and community meetings during the school closures in 2010 and 2011 and studied archival documents associated with House Bill 525, the state legislation through which displacement and dispossession were codified. Board meetings were observed and documents analyzed of the Cleveland Transformation Alliance, charged with monitoring the Cleveland Plan and assessing the quality of district and charter schools within the city. The author also attended and participated in the role of a university critical friend in an open and informal gathering of community members through the Cleveland Education Committee, an inclusive gathering of individuals from the east and west sides of Cleveland who met monthly at a local eatery in the St. Clair-Superior neighborhood on the east side to discuss ideas and issues related to education in the city of Cleveland.[3] In addition to working with educators and students in East High School when it was designated for closure in 2010, the author also was involved in project work when the district designated eight schools in the district for redesign in the Spring of 2017.

The case study includes data from a survey administered in the Fall of 2012. The survey questions relate to ninth grade students' experience of frequently changing schools, having one's school closed, and securing transportation to and from school. (The focal survey questions are included in Appendix A.) Survey results reported for this chapter include the responses of students in three eastside comprehensive high schools, which served as receiving schools when East High and South High closed in 2010, as well as one small theme-based school that opened the school year following the June 2010 closures. Nearly all of the school closures in 2010

TABLE 6.1   Racial and Ethnic Data on Survey Participants with District Demographic Data for School Year Survey Administered

Race or Ethnicity	Percentage of Students Identifying by Race/ Ethnicity	District Demographics in 2012–2013
American India/Alaskan Native	2.42%	0.2%
Asian American or Pacific Islander	0.81%	0.9%
Black/African American	87.90%	66.9%
Latino/Hispanic	1.61%	14.4%
Multiracial	7.26%	2.9%
White/European American	0%	14.7%

and 2011 occurred in these Cleveland eastside neighborhoods, which are predominantly African American, poor and working class. The sample is small at 126 students, and as such, it falls short of a broader representative sampling and engagement of students within and across all of the district's eastside high schools, a key limitation. Nonetheless, these data are included since they offer a counterstory to the sector agnosticism made possible through race-neutral ahistorical ways of viewing school closure.

Among the 126 ninth grade students from the four eastside high schools who responded to the survey, 87.90% identified as Black/African American. The demographic data for race and ethnicity are detailed in Table 6.1, including the data for the district the year the survey was administered. Among the students, 52.8% identified as male and 47.2% were female, with one student skipping the question, perhaps due to its limited construction of gender identities. A discussion of the full survey results, part of a multimethod study, is available in Cooke et al. (2015).

FINDINGS

This first section of findings traces the processes of displacement and dispossession through the city and state's history. The second section reports Cleveland students' experiences of challenges in school transportation, frequently changing schools, and transition due to school closure as reported in the Fall of 2012.

Contextualizing Spatial and Relational Dimensions as Structural Entanglement Evident in the City's History

Not intending to be exhaustive, the history discussed here is organized to highlight six junctures of relational and spatial displacement and dispossession from the mid-20th century to the current period. These include the following: (a) urban renewal in Black neighborhoods; (b) relay classes, intact busing, and accelerated school construction of Black schools; (c) desegregation and increased poverty concentration in the city; (d) state involvement and accumulation by dispossession through fundamental shifts toward school choice; (e) closing schools argued as district transformation; and (f) legislating the Cleveland Plan and deepening structural entanglement of privilege and exclusion.

Urban Renewal in Black Neighborhoods

Historically, Cleveland drew European immigrants and African Americans moving north, and its current neighborhoods carry reminders of this history as do its schools. The city reflects a history of tension concerning segregation within and beyond its borders. In the years following the 1949 federal housing act, the city designated one-eighth of its land for urban renewal, optimistic for downtown revitalization and a way to slow the exit of residents and businesses to the suburbs (Keating, Krumholz, & Perry 1995, p. 333; Swanstrom, 1985, pp. 92–100). The 1960 census showed a loss of 39,000 residents from the city (Miller & Wheeler, 1995).

In this city of great ethnic diversity, urban renewal efforts in the 1950s focused largely on Black neighborhoods, particularly in the near eastside downtown area where housing of 1,780 African American families from poor neighborhoods was demolished and not replaced (Keating, Krumholz, & Perry, 1995). Relocation assistance was not provided. Testimony before the U.S. Civil Rights Commission in Cleveland includes statements by city officials that in areas designated for urban renewal, housing codes were not enforced and police and fire protection cut back, allowing for deterioration and cheaper costs in buying and clearing the land (Swanstrom, 1985, p. 97). Evidence suggests that 1200 families moved before renewal began, relocating in the Hough neighborhood where housing enforcement was lax and conditions overcrowded. Cleveland's urban renewal in the 1950s took place in the location of what is now St. Vincent's Hospital and the original Cuyahoga Community College campus, as well as other civic institutions, many of which are tax-exempt (Swanstrom, 1985, p. 98).

Relay Classes, Intact Busing, and Accelerated School Construction of Black Schools

In the 1950s, segregated Black schools became overcrowded while White schools were increasingly under enrolled. To address overcrowding, the district used relay classes, approved by the state of Ohio, which maintained half-day schooling in some eastside Black neighborhoods between 1957 and 1962. Beginning in 1962, two additional strategies were employed: (a) intact busing of Black students in White schools, which maintained racial segregation within the building, and (b) accelerated school construction deep within Black neighborhoods (Carl, 2011; Moore, 2002; Whyte, 2003). The United Freedom Movement, the Hazeldell Parents Association, the NAACP, and the Cleveland Congress of Racial Equality (CORE) protested the district policies through picketing, sit-ins, and a major school boycott (Carl, 2011; Moore, 2002; Whyte, 2003). In 1964, *Craggett v. Cleveland BOE*, a suit against the district's segregative practices, lost in the courts. The late 1950s through the 1970s, particularly the 1960s, represented a vibrant period of collective resistance to racial exclusion (Dunn, Whyte, Hardiman, Hatten, & Jones, 2016; Moore, 2002; Whyte, 2003), reflecting the diversity of the Black community in Cleveland through differing tactics and levels of political involvement, including the 1967 mayoral election of Carl B. Stokes.

Desegregation Amid Increased Poverty Concentration in the City

Overcrowding in Black schools continued, and the district failed to address the issue through desegregation of its schools. Instead, Superintendent Paul W. Briggs instituted a rapid program of school construction. Between 1964 and 1972, the district built 33 new schools (Whyte, 2003). Responding to concerns expressed about educational inequality, the district established new programs and new schools while retaining racial segregation. The NAACP continued to prepare evidence of persistent segregation in Cleveland schools, later used in the *Reed v. Rhodes* decision, which ruled in its favor in 1976. The accelerated school building that further segregated students, among other liabilities, was noted by Judge Battisti in his 1976 *Reed v. Rhodes* ruling, which led to a program of busing from the late 1970s to mid 1990s. Other system improvements were required by the consent decree, addressing the quality of instruction in the schools and availability of resources.

At the same time, the city was experiencing considerable population loss with a decrease of 24% in the 1970s (Keating, Krumholz, & Metzger, 1995, p. 334) and a higher concentration in poverty. While the probability of the poor interacting with the poor in isolation was .27 in 1970, it increased to .32 in 1980, and .40 in 1990, in contrast with .04, .05, and .07 in 1970, 1980, and 1990 in the western suburbs (Coulton & Chow, 1995, p. 218).

As noted earlier, the financial stress of the Cleveland district continued to be exacerbated by policies of tax abatement, which were used alongside federal funding for urban development to attract downtown growth. Through the urban development action grant (UDAG) program, the city drew on 70% of this program's dollars for downtown commercial-office projects between 1981 and 1988 (Keating et al., 1995, p. 340). Tax abatements were used as an instrument of economic development, favoring downtown revitalization. Tax abatements impacted public education in the city. In 1978, the Cleveland district could not meet its financial obligations, turning over its financial responsibility to a state controlling board to address a $20.7 million deficit (Swanstrom, 1985, p. 141). Public opposition to tax abatement included the United AutoWorkers, United Steelworkers, the Ohio Public Interest Campaign (OPIC), Active Clevelanders Together (ACT), and the Commission of Catholic Community Action (p. 138). Dennis Kucinich, who was elected in 1978, interrupted this form of corporate subsidization during his brief term as mayor. Tax abatements returned in the 1980s, initially focused on market-rate residential development and later to support low- and moderate-income housing (Keating et al., 1995). Through city legislation passed in 1991, all areas of the city, with the exception of the downtown area, were designated as eligible for community reinvestment, including residential and industrial areas. However, major projects, such as a stadium, arena, and Rock 'n Roll Hall of Fame were granted tax abatements in the 1990s, amid challenges from the Cleveland board of education (Keating et al., 1995).

State Involvement and Accumulation by Dispossession Through Fundamental Shifts Toward School Choice

As early as 1989, there was discussion of a state takeover of the school district, due to conflict between the board and the superintendent. In 1995, the state declared the district to be in a "state of crisis" due to its debt and low student achievement (White, 1998). The judge overseeing the Cleveland desegregation case ordered the state education department to assume direct control over the district and relegated the local school board to an advisory role (Bradley, 1995). Subsequent district action involved its restructuring of debt and securing its first levy since 1983 (Reinhard, 1997). In 1998, a shift from state to mayoral control of the school board was secured, as well as the declaration of "unitary status" and the district's release from its desegregation consent decree. However, the discourse of crisis persisted, setting the stage for a series of legislative decisions, which resulted in substantive change in current school governance conditions. In 2002, despite considerable debate, the city approved continued mayoral control.

Efforts by the Governor's Commission on Educational Choice, founded by Governor George Voinovich in 1992, had been underway to provide state funding for private school vouchers. The commission was led by businessman and later online charter school entrepreneur David Brennan. The Cleveland voucher program began in the 1996–1997 school year. Carl (2011) notes that state assemblyman and voucher advocate Michael Fox viewed the underperformance of students in Cleveland and the recent state takeover as conducive for piloting a voucher program, with Fox stating, "The school district was a mess, it was impossible to defend it" (Carl, 2011, p. 170). Also in 1997, House Bill 55 allowed for the establishment of charter schools when they were serving a challenged district, such as any of the Ohio "Big Eight" districts. Both the voucher and charter movements were argued as a solution for academic failure on the part of the district. Chief Justice Rehnquist reflected this argument in his 2002 *Zelman v. Simmons-Harris* majority opinion, ruling vouchers as constitutionally permissible: "There is no dispute that the program was enacted for the valid nonreligious purpose of providing educational assistance to poor children in a demonstrably failing public school system ... The Ohio program is entirely neutral with respect to religion" (Oyez, 2001).

District reform efforts paralleled an increase in legislative and judicial support for privatized alternatives, viewed as a solution to the failure of a high-poverty urban district. Additionally, the city's long history of private–public partnerships was sustained, largely directed to commercial development, with a particular focus on the downtown area. Tax abatement continued to be used as a tool for development, shortchanging the funding of the district schools (Keating et al., 1995). Efforts at educational reform were compromised by a 2004 budget deficit, leading to budget cuts, teacher layoffs, and reconfiguration of the district from middle schools to K–8 schools. In the interim, the state formula for school funding, largely dependent on property taxes and ruled unconstitutional by the state Supreme Court in 1997, remained unaddressed by the state legislature despite requirements for remedy by the *DeRolph v. State of Ohio* I–IV rulings.

While concentrated poverty and racial isolation increased, neighborhoods retained a sense of identity and history, and schools reflected these characteristics. Although accelerated school construction in the eastside was seen as problematic in the 1950s, the schools that were built became an integral part of the infrastructure of Black collective life. The crucial association of neighborhoods and school buildings was evident as a central theme among parents and students who opposed eastside school closures in 2010 and 2011.

Closing Schools Argued as District Transformation

In January 2010, the CMSD announced the implementation of its Academic Transformation Plan. With considerable detail, the district laid out a design for addressing instruction and improving achievement as well as offering wraparound services in some schools. The plan aimed to "right-size the district by eliminating excess capacity, addressing overcrowding and ensuring effective use of resources" (CMSD Academic Transformation Plan, slide 6). In June of 2010, 14 elementary schools and two high schools were closed in the district, nearly all of which were located on the eastside of Cleveland, serving mostly poor and working class African American students. The following year, the district closed seven additional schools, all of which were on the eastside (Ott, 2011b).

While the district had held community feedback sessions in Fall 2009 as the plan was being developed (Ott, 2009), the reaction to the announcement of school closures in the following spring suggests parents, students, and educators' concerns persisted. District officials argued the school closures were necessary due to three key challenges the district faced: an ongoing drop in enrollment, leading to the underutilization of school buildings; low performance on standardized measures collected at the state level as part of federal funding requirements through No Child Left Behind; and a substantial district budget deficit.

Clearly resources were necessary for the high rate of child poverty in the city and its impact on the needs of students within city schools. A portion of the district's funding gap would be addressed partially through backing of local foundations, which promised the district support contingent upon the board of education's approval of the Academic Transformation Plan (Ott, 2010a). Additional funding was anticipated at the federal level. The district subsequently participated in the state's proposal for Race to the Top, which awarded Ohio $400 million, of which Cleveland was to receive $29.5 million over 4 years. It also was awarded a School Improvement Grant with the potential to draw on $36.7 million over 4 years (Ott, 2011a). Both of these funding sources included an emphasis on "turning around" schools, and they relied on school closure as one form of "intervention."

Following the 2010 implementation of the Academic Transformation Plan, public–private partnerships increased, some resulting in the establishment of theme-based district high schools offering specialized programing and considerable resources. Although few were competitively selective schools, the students drawn to enroll may bring parental support and resources unlike their peers in the comprehensive high schools. As enrollment shifted from comprehensive high schools to newly created theme-based high schools with corporate or philanthropic partners, the neighborhood based comprehensive high schools experienced shifts in the level of support these schools needed to provide their students.

For example, the proportion of students with disabilities within comprehensive high schools exceeded the district average. This was actually evident before the 2010 Academic Transformation Plan. High levels of students with disabilities existed in the two high schools closed at the end of the 2009–2010 school year. In 2009–2010, East High School's final year, the school reported enrollment of 717 students, 37.1% of whom were students with disabilities (Ohio Department of Education School Report Card, n.d.). South High School, also closed at the end of that year, reported of its 896 students that 38.3% had disabilities. The year following high school closure, East Technical High School, a receiving school rated as "academic emergency," reported an enrollment of 822, of which 37.1% were students with disabilities, an increase of 10% from the year before.

The variation in student characteristics between theme-based high schools and comprehensive high schools continued to be stark in the enrollment of students with disabilities. In the 2013–2014 school year, the district-wide average enrollment of students with disabilities was 23.9% (Ohio Department of Education School Report Card, n.d.). The four comprehensive eastside high schools in particular that received students displaced by school closure reflected percentages that ranged from a high of 40.7 to a low of 31%. Specialized theme high schools on the eastside reported lower percentages in 2013–2014 of enrollment of students with disabilities, ranging from a high of 11.5 to a low of 0% (Ohio Department of Education School Report Card, n.d.).

Legislating the Cleveland Plan and Deepening Structural Entanglement of Privilege and Exclusion

In June of 2012, the state legislature approved and the governor signed into law House Bill 525 in support of the Cleveland Plan for Transforming Schools (O'Donnell, 2012). The Cleveland Plan of 2012 distinguished itself from the district's 2010 Academic Transformation Plan in that it opened lines of shared authority and school financing with private entities. The mayor of Cleveland, district CEO, the business community, and a network of charter schools partnering with the school district were key actors in the planning. The teachers union was included later, after its absence was underscored publicly. The first among the Cleveland Plan's four goals was to "grow the number of high-performing district and charter schools in Cleveland and close and replace failing schools" (Jackson, 2012, p. 6). The plan also established a public–private organization, the Cleveland Transformation Alliance, with authority to carry out aspects of the Cleveland Plan, including assessing the quality of all public schools, which would be reviewed annually. As the plan authorized the district to share a portion of local school levy proceeds with high-performing charter schools that partner with the district, a first in the state of Ohio, and involved changes in employment practices and district autonomy and flexibility, it required state approval (Jackson, 2012, p. 13).

The Cleveland Transformation Alliance wielded considerable social and political influence as it drew on the city and county business leadership, influential private foundations, a charter organization supported by wealthy donors, higher education leadership, and local religious, community, and parent leaders. The chief executive officer of the Ohio Alliance for Public Charter Schools, before becoming senior vice president of the National Charter Schools Institute, was an original member of the Alliance board. The president of the Greater Cleveland Partnership, the regional chamber of commerce with a membership of 8,000, also played an early active role in securing support for HB 525 and subsequent interaction at the state and city level. Along with Cleveland's mayor in the position of Alliance chair, board memberships included the chief executive officer of the district and well-established social networks in the city and the region. The networking reach of the Alliance's members, its dissemination of the progress of the Cleveland Plan and its campaign of support, along with its close work with the district, secured a tax levy increase in 2012 and a renewal of the same tax in 2016.

The support for the Cleveland Plan among members of the Cleveland Teachers Union (CTU) waned in the years following the legislation. It was viewed initially as a survival tactic to ward off a state takeover similar to that of Recovery School District in New Orleans (Hoven, 2015). The CTU voted to strike in August 2016, identifying demands in the following areas: increasing availability of music, art, and gym classes; reducing excessive testing of students in the district; changing the teacher evaluation system; and better compensating teacher aides (O'Donnell, 2017). While the strike was averted, the tentative agreement between the district and the union was rejected several weeks later as concerns about excessive testing and teacher evaluations remained. In March of 2017, the district and union agreed to a 3-year contract. The contract eliminated a key strategy in the Cleveland Plan that tied school improvement to merit-based pay raises. All but those teachers with the lowest evaluation rating of "ineffective" would receive pay raises (O'Donnell, 2017).

There remained frustration among teachers over the district's shifts in programmatic focus without teacher input, particularly in the 23 schools designated for closure or redesign, the "investment schools." Teachers in these schools, often serving the most academically vulnerable students in economically stressed neighborhoods, experience "investment" more as surveillance than support. Teachers reported frequent unannounced classroom visits by consultants hired by the district to provide training through various school improvement programs (Cleveland Education Committee Meeting, April 24, 2017). While the portfolio system emphasizes school autonomy, the legislation places the final decision making authority for corrective action plans in the hands of the chief executive officer (O'Donnell, 2015).

At the high school level, comprehensive schools long established and rooted in Cleveland neighborhoods were phased out. In their place, high school buildings each opened 2–3 small schools with a particular programmatic focus. The district's website describes its schools as offering career and technical academies, arts and performance-oriented schools, and STEM-focused schools. This reconfiguration of schools and school programs is reflected in the 2012 Cleveland Plan, which indicates the following: "closure and reassignment of students to better schools, closure and start-up of a new school, phase in of a new program and phase out of the old, or turning the school over to a capable charter operator" (Jackson, 2012, p. 7).

The push for school closure and replacement has garnered private funding supportive of the district achieving "sector agnosticism" while charter schools have gained possession of former publicly owned facilities. These schools may or may not enroll students from the neighborhood once served by the closed school as Cleveland's portfolio system draws across the city and outside the district. Recognized for its cultivation of a portfolio system, the district received a $100,000 planning grant in 2014 from the National Association of Charter School Authorizers, supported by Bill and Melinda Gates Foundation, which recognized Cleveland as a "Gates Compact City." The grant was awarded for the purpose of supporting joint district–charter strategies to improve low-performing schools, strengthen special education services, and increase charter school access to district facilities. From the Laura and John Arnold Foundation, the Cleveland Transformation Alliance received $1,375,000 to provide parents with information on school choices, and the district received $1.5 million to establish an enrollment computer system inclusive of district and charter school choices for families.

District enrollment halted its downward trend in the 2014–2015 school year. In 2016–2017, the district enrollment of 38,949 included those who lived in Cleveland. It also included 2,886 students who lived in nearby suburbs but commute to district sponsored charters and specialized Cleveland schools. This out-of-district students enrollment has increased since 2013–2014 and appears to be contributing to economic and racial diversity in some of the district's high-performing citywide schools and charter schools. Charter school enrollment was 16,651 in 2016–2017 (Cleveland Transformation Alliance, 2017, p. 23). In the 2016–2017 school year, the district partnered with 19 charter schools, numbering 5,857 students in CMSD partnering charters (p. 23).

In its role of assessing district and charter schools in the district, the Cleveland Transformation Alliance has found its tracking of student achievement challenged by changing measures used at the state level over several years. During its board meetings in 2017, the Alliance reviewed its reporting documents on the progress of the Cleveland Plan and devoted considerable time to discussing the presentation of data. In the high-stakes environment of reporting academic performance, some fracturing of cross-sector unity was evident. For example, a board member representing a partnering charter recommended the partnering charters' achievement data not be folded into an aggregate of district data. Another board member noted that if partnering charters were part of the district, why would the Alliance report their scores separately? In later meetings, concerns were expressed about how much space a sector received in the progress report and where language may have been more positive or negative toward a particular sector.[4]

In the 2016–2017 school year, academic proficiency as measured by state tests indicated that the downward trend in the district and across the state had halted. For the first time, the state employed the same set of standards and testing measures as the year before. District schools averaged 56.2 out of a possible 120 in their performance index (PI), a measure of how students perform on state tests. Charter schools not in partnership with the district averaged 67.1, and district-partnering charters averaged 73.8 in their respective PI measures (Cleveland Transformation Alliance, 2017, p. 27). The performance index for the state of Ohio that same year was 84.1%. The Alliance's progress report indicates that Cleveland ranks sixth among Ohio's eight urban districts in terms of it performance index (Cleveland Transformation Alliance, 2017, p. 27).

At a national level, the National Assessment of Educational Progress (NAEP) reports that in Grade 4 reading the percentage of students in Cleveland who performed at or above the NAEP proficient level was 11% in 2015. This percentage was smaller than NAEP's comparison of large cities, which had 27% of their students at or above the NAEP proficient level. In Grade 8 reading, the percentage of students in Cleveland who performed at or above the NAEP proficient level was also 11% in 2015. This percentage was smaller than large cities (25%).[5]

In terms of measures of Value-Added (VA) Student Growth, schools across the state and the district have not recovered from a steep drop in growth measures occurring in 2016. The growth measure for the district, district-partnering charters, and non-partnering charters requires a more detailed discussion than can be provided here. The Alliance's progress report indicates that Cleveland ranks seventh among Ohio's eight urban districts in terms of its value-added measure (Cleveland Transformation Alliance, 2017, p. 29).

A positive development in the high school graduation rate is the increase from 52% in 2010 to 72% in 2016. However, the high schools are stratified in the degree to which students experience neighborhood and family stress in terms of high levels of poverty, health issues, and substandard and lead-exposed housing. Schools are also stratified to the extent to which they are located in historically economically and racially segregated neighborhoods. For example, in the 2016 report from the Alliance, two high schools were reported to have a waiting list (Cleveland Transformation Alliance, 2016, p. 26). One of these high schools is a specialized district school located on Cleveland State University campus in downtown Cleveland to which students commuted by the public bus and rail system or by family car. The 4-year graduation rate of this downtown high school in the university setting was 92.3% in 2015–2016. An under-enrolled high school serving the high-poverty Central neighborhood area south of the Euclid Avenue corridor and the university reported a considerably lower graduation rate. The graduate rate in this racially and economically isolated neighborhood was 60.3% in 2015–2016.

A review of this phase of the district's history illustrates the high-stakes nature of a school reform culture reliant on state standardized tests. These scores and their interpretation determine crucial decisions regarding closure of schools, graduation of students, and evaluation of teachers and principals. Smarick's (2012) notion of "continuously shed[ding] failing programs" of schools (p. 3) based on high-stakes standardized measures is problematic when these measures are subject to changes at the state level. Moreover, this account-ability logic is substantially flawed due to broader contextual factors, such as the disproportionality of student characteristics, particularly in terms of what buildings absorb the most academically vulnerable students and students with disabilities. There is also much unevenness in access to resources external to the school and internal to the school's parent population. Without an analysis of how school choice has exacerbated race and class stratification within the portfolio system, the entanglement of privilege and exclusion is sustained.

The chapter now moves from findings from this analysis of district his-tory and current context to the perspectives of students who attended the district as ninth grade students in 2012. The survey data contextualize at the student level the conditions on the ground as the district moved more aggressively into its stance of sector agnosticism.

Survey Data Results

In this section, data from a survey of ninth grade students are reported, looking specifically at students attending three comprehensive high schools and a small, theme-based district school on Cleveland's eastside. The data capture students' experiences in the first year of the Cleveland Transforma-tion Plan of 2012, and 2 years after the first wave of school closures. The survey questions for the data reported here are in Appendix A.

Although other schools were included in the survey, this chapter focuses only on the responses from eastside schools that agreed to participate. The focus on the responses of a subset of the data is intended to understand the experience of school closure as situated in the history and current context of Cleveland's eastside neighborhoods. The findings below, not exhaustive to the survey, include the following: questions concerning transportation, changing schools, school closure transition, and school closure impact.

Getting to and From School

The policy in the 3 years following the 2010 school closures required high school students to live three or more miles away from their school in order to be eligible for transportation. Access to school transportation for high school students was provided through tickets for the RTA. For students experienc-ing school closure, their travel to the receiving school may have resulted in a distance close to, but still below, the 3-mile requirement. Liana's narrative, which opens this chapter, illustrates the circuitous route she had to take to her receiving school. Just under the 3-mile limit, Liana relied on several teachers who picked her up when she could not cover the cost of the RTA ticket. Liana's story reflects a central concern in the school closure literature, which involves securing safe, accessible, reliable, and low-cost transportation.

Upon the opening of the 2012–2013 school year, 3 years after the first wave of school closures, transportation to school remained an issue, as evident in responses to the 2012 ninth grade student survey. Slightly over one-third of the respondents reported taking the RTA. When asked how they paid for their bus ticket, 26%[6] said their families gave them money; 35% responded that the school provided the ticket; and 14% reported that they bought their ticket from another student. Students noted other ways of getting to school, with 35% reporting that they walked to school; 22% saying someone drives them to school; and 6% reporting being transported by the school district's shuttle system. The shuttle system was put in place in the 2012–2013 year with stops at designated locations to which students walked and were then transported by bus to school. Use of the shuttle was uneven. Open-ended survey data indicated that the cost of the RTA ticket for those ineligible for transportation was a burden on families, as noted by a survey respondent: "I think the school should provide ... RTA tickets because I have a long way to go [a]nd my parents can't really afford it."

A year and a half after the survey was administered, the district changed its transportation policy, increasing access to public transportation for high school students in January 2014. More recently, for the 2017–2018 school year 7th–12th grade students who lived at least a mile from their neighborhood school were eligible for a RTA swipe card. Students in kindergarten through sixth grade who lived one mile or more from school were eligible for "some form of transportation service."[7]

Transportation was available to students enrolling in charter schools according the district website. Charter school students in Grades 7–12 living one mile or more from the school were eligible for an RTA swipe card. Those students in K–6 living one mile or over from their charter school were also eligible for bus transportation. If none were available, parents were provided reimbursement for the cost of transportation, with some limitations. However, the website notes for special transfer (voluntary assignment), "Parents waive transportation when enrolling their student in a non-neighborhood school" and encourages those with transportation concerns to contact Student Assignments "to see if a closer school is available." Although the district portfolio system encourages parents to select "the right school for your child," there appear to be limitations to enrolling one's child in a district school outside of one's neighborhood.

Frequency of Changing Schools

Among students from the eastside of Cleveland whose survey data are reported here, half reported having attended five or more schools since kindergarten, and 7% reported attending more than nine schools before completing their K–8 schooling. In one eastside comprehensive high school, 35% of the respondents cited school closure as a reason they had to leave one school for another. This reason was nearly as common as a family move to a different neighborhood.[8]

At a public meeting during which youth researchers presented a summary of the survey data, the following narrative was shared by a youth researcher:

> As a CMSD student, I changed schools a whole lot. It affected a lot of areas in my life that I feel I cannot get back. My academics suffered, my social relationships suffered, and my overall sense of belonging . . .

In her narrative, the young woman spoke of her years in East High School, as "the only school that I had spent more than one year attending." In January of her senior year, the district announced the closure of her high school. As a senior, she was a member of the last senior class to graduate from the high school.

Transitioning and Impact

Ninth grade students were asked if they attended a school that closed, how was their experience transitioning into a new school. Because they took the survey in the fall of their first year in high school, their experience of school closure would draw from their K–8 years. Responses from students in the eastside neighborhoods indicated the following: 9% reported the transition was very hard; 29% indicated it was hard; 53% reported the transition was easy; and 8% said it was very easy. These responses suggest for more than half the students the transition following was not difficult. This is in contrast to the narrative of hardship at this chapter's opening by Liana, a high school student. However, the ease suggested in the ninth grade responses is complicated in the open-ended question that follows in the survey, "If you attended a school that closed, how did it impact your life?"

Table 6.2 provides the themes and percentages (rounded) of responses reflecting each theme. As indicated in Table 6.2, 10% of the responses were not applicable and 4% were not clear.[9]

Coding of the remaining open-ended data yielded the following key themes: (a) constraints, struggle, and loss; (b) no impact; (c) conditions improved after the transition, or some event or condition buffered the transition; (d) opportunities for new friends and positive changes in self and school; and (e) adjustments and adaptation. These are discussed below.

Constraints, Struggle, and Loss

Students reported that the school closure experience represented some form of loss, particularly loss of relationships with friends or adults in their

TABLE 6.2 Thematic Categories for Open-Ended Responses on Impact of School Closure	
Thematic Categories	**Percentage of Responses Coded in This Category**
Constraints, struggle, and loss	26%
Reported no impact	23%
Initial constraints followed by opportunities or conditions improved after transition/something buffered transition	15%
Opportunities for new friends and positive changes in self and school	13%
Adjustments and adaptation	10%
Not applicable	10%
Not clear	4%

closed school. For example, a student noted, "It was hard because everyone I knew was getting split up into diff[erent] schools and I had to say bye to some of my friends." Some of the responses indicated a relational unmooring with people or space, and a loss of memories, as in the following, "It didn't change my life that much but I did feel like I lost a part of me because I miss and love a lot of my old teachers and just walking past the place make[s] me think of all the good and bad times I had there in my childhood." Most frequent within this theme was an expression of anger, sadness, or confusion. A student responded, "It did not impact my life in a good way because I loved that school and the fact that it closed down well that made me very sad," and another stated, "Not that much but I was mad cause I really like that school." In the case of the latter response, there is evident nonchalance coupled with anger. Sentiments such as these were the most frequent, representing 26% of the responses. The statement below reflects multiple dimensions of loss and constraints, revealing also the strain on the receiving school:

> All my friends were gone[.] I was expecting to graduate from my school. It also hurt me when I went to another school because we were all packed in the class room. It was very hard to learn something because there were people from different gangs that often fought. My eight[h] grade year was terrible I was packed in the class with at least 40 other kids. [T]here was not enough books to go around [and] people were stealing books out of lockers. It was not easy switching schools

Reported No Impact

Twenty-three percent of the students responded an absence of impact from the closing of their school. These responses tended to be brief statements, such as "it really didn't impact my life" or "nothing." This response may relate to the finding that more than half of the students reported an ease in transitioning schools during the experience of school closure. It may also suggest that there was little change in the experience of school characteristics and programming for the students in the move from the closed school to the receiving school.

Initial Constraints Followed by Opportunities or Conditions Improved After Transition or Specific Conditions Buffered Transition

Students narrated difficulties and adjustments but followed that statement with an indication that, after some time, they viewed their experience as positive. For example, a student responded, "It impacted my life because I loved my friends and fellow teachers. It was very hard getting used to a new school but after a while I started loving it." These responses represented 3% of the coded data. Additionally, there was evidence in some of these responses that an event or condition softened negative school closure impact. In these responses, students indicated that something occurred to reduce negative impact of the closure, such as moving at the same time the school closed, only attending the receiving school for a year, or simply, "I didn't care." These responses reflected 12% of the coded open-ended data.

Opportunities for New Friends and Positive Changes in Self and School

Students reported that school closure had resulted in a positive experience. Students reported that closure had "change[d] my ways of being a better person ... and a new me." There was anticipation of a new school. Also noted was access to new friends, as in the following, "It impacted my life by helping me get to know other students because the school I went to it was just my friends, and ... so it was good to make new friends and get to know different people." These responses reflected 13% of the coded responses.

Adjustment and Adaptation

These responses began in a similar manner as the responses coded "initial constraints followed by opportunities." However, they did not include a statement of eventually viewing the experience as one of opportunity. These statements typically used the language of "had to" or "just had to" and they narrated changes in relationships with teachers and students and adjusting to the facility itself. For example, "I had to meet new teachers and friends and get used to how teachers teach and how others act." There is a sense in these statements of coping, and perhaps successfully doing so, but there is no indication of a benefit for doing so. These responses represented 10% of the coded data.

DISCUSSION

The chapter opened with youth researcher Liana mapping her route and narrating the multiple buses she needed to take to arrive at her receiving school. In a testimony to her resilience and to the support provided by teachers who themselves were displaced by school closures, Liana got to school through an informal network of support. In a portfolio school district, the problem of distance and travel costs reveal the Duboisian veil between the lives of students of color in poor and working class neighborhoods and the social and political forces at work in producing urban educational policy (Du Bois, 1995, p. 45). Moving across levels of analysis to provide a fully textured study of who bears the costs and who shares in the benefits of school closure, the study examined history and the current policy context, and then situated student perspectives through survey data in this deeply contextualized study.

In the Academic Transformation Plan of 2010, the closing of 23 schools over 2 years altered social and spatial relations. The shuttering of a neighborhood school, and the displacement of students, often placing the burden of transportation costs and logistics on families struggling economically, revealed distinct and salient changes for students sometimes embedded in a narrative of nonchalance or new understandings of self. Families within and outside the district with transportation resources were able to transport their children to charters that performed academically higher than neighborhood schools or theme-based district schools with considerable university, corporate, or philanthropic support.

Actualization of Sector Agnosticism Through Displacement and Erasure

In these forms of relational and spatial displacement, the sector agnosticism of portfolio school systems is actualized (Smarick, 2012). As evident in Fullilove's study of urban renewal, this strategy of educational reform renders silent a history of human relationships and leads to the disappearance of artifacts revealing such relations (Fullilove, 2004). To "continuously shed failing programs" (Smarick, 2012, p. 3) is to employ erasure as a district reform strategy (Ayala & Galletta, 2012). This approach disproportionately impacts students of color, poor and working class students, English language learners, and students with disabilities. Buildings are shuttered or neighborhood schools are phased out and replaced by new educational entities, often overseen by privatized or nonprofit organizations without accountability to the public. Objects and spaces of historical importance and cultural markings are painted over, discarded, or stored somewhere—essentially erased from facilities significant to the lived experience of students.

Collective memory is diminished over time due to the lack of access to a facility that once offered relational space. What is valued by students is dismissed as less important by those distant from the closure experience. Meaningful spatial context is simply not addressed in theories of action for improving public education (Deeds & Pattillo, 2015). The angle of vision of those who "have been removed," as noted by poet and youth researcher Eddie Ashford (Jones, Stewart, Ayala, & Galletta, 2015), crucial to understanding the full continuum of the school closure experience, is omitted, absent attention to the contexts and processes experienced by students, families, and educators.

Tracing Accumulation by Dispossession Enabled by "Sector Agnosticism"

School closure dispossesses urban communities from three important public assets: facilities, public participation, and relational networks. When districts close or phase out a school and replace it with a new district school or a charter school, one community's dispossession may become another's source of accumulation. This may occur in a charter school conversion; it may also occur when a district theme school attracts students with more resources and fewer needs for services. It may draw more economically diverse families and pull in middle class parents, whose support for the school, as welcoming as this may be, may yield reduced access to the school building by those once affiliated with it (Posey-Maddox, 2016).

Spatial displacement is related to the agnostic stance with regard to public or private sectors of schooling as evident in the portfolio system. This displacement and accumulation by dispossession connects the past to the present. For example, Citizen's Academy, a K–5 charter school operated by Breakthrough Schools and sponsored by Cleveland Metropolitan School District, is housed in what used to be Joseph F. Landis Elementary School, which was closed as part of the Academic Transformation Plan in 2010 (see Figure 6.1). This building was constructed in 1963 during the district's accelerated construction of schools in racially isolated predominantly Black neighborhoods. In the 2009–2010 school year, the year it closed, Joseph F. Landis had an enrollment of 360 students, 94.9% of whom were Black and 33.9% of whom had disabilities (Ohio Department of Education School Report Card, n.d). This proportion of students with disabilities is considerably different from that of the charter school now residing in Landis' closed facility. According to the 2015 Cleveland Transformation Alliance *School Quality Guide* on Cleveland charter and district schools, the enrollment of students with disabilities at Citizen's Academy was 10.6%. While the enrollment of 443 students is over 95% African American, there is little way of knowing if the same community

Figure 6.1 Citizen's Academy, a K–5 charter, formerly Joseph F. Landis Elementary School, built in 1963 and closed in 2010 as part of the Academic Transformation Plan.

of children once served by Landis was attending Citizen's Academy (Cleveland Transformation Alliance, 2015).

In the closing of Joseph F. Landis Elementary School and its acquisition by Breakthrough Schools, we see evidence of Smarick's notion of "creative destruction" (Smarick, 2012). Landis, a district school with a long history in an economically distressed neighborhood, was made available to the charter organization. Although charter schools are funded by the state for each student enrolled, they are sponsored and managed by private entities, and their policies and practices are determined by those entities. In the process of portfolio "churn," children with disabilities were displaced as evident in the decrease in percentage of children with disabilities at Citizen's Academy. These differences in who bears the costs and who benefits from the closure trouble the sector agnosticism advocated by Smarick (2012).

Privatized Capital Through Gentrification in Waitlisted Downtown Schools

Within the portfolio system emphasis on agnosticism, parents are expected to assess schools and in their selection (or exit) they are informed by the quality of the school itself and not its sector affiliation. Sociologist Shelley Kimelberg (2014) studied the experience of middle class and upper middle class mostly White Boston parents whose children attended city schools. Parents narrated the type of strategy in school choice they had the resources to exercise. As one parent noted, "If it doesn't work, we're out of here" (p. 217). Kimelberg refers to this approach as reflecting a privilege of risk among middle class parents who bring "a safety net of financial, human, and cultural capital that emboldened them to consider a choice—urban public schooling" (p. 230).

Downtown areas in Philadelphia (Cucchiara, 2013), Chicago (Lipman & Haines, 2007; Posey-Maddox, 2014, 2016), and Boston (Kimelberg, 2014), among other cities, are seeing increases in the enrollment of children from middle and upper middle class families in urban public schools in gentrifying neighborhoods or in open-district transfer programs. This has generated excitement among district officials and city planners. Resources associated with middle class parents include social networking, volunteering, and contributions of materials to fill substantive budgetary gaps in programming, particularly in the cocurricular classes (art, music, library). Schools seeing middle class enrollment are likely to also experience an increase in enrichment activities, higher adult to child ratio in the classroom, and improved conditions in staffing. At the same time, Kimelberg (2014) notes that the impact of middle class enrollment may be with particular schools, not the entire district. An outcome of the influx of middle class parents in a deregulated and free market-oriented portfolio system has the potential to fill up popular niche schools with branding that attracts middle class parents, leaving fewer available seats to students from poor and working class neighborhoods. Kimelberg notes that some elementary schools in Boston "witnessed significant drops in their proportions of low-income students, in some cases by more than 30 percentage points" (p. 230)

Gentrifying neighborhoods offer schools and cities increased racial and economic diversity and have the potential to desegregate schools. Middle class parents preferring to remain in urban settings with access to cultural institutions, the arts, and diverse spaces for gathering have invested in residential areas within neighborhoods undergoing considerable socioeconomic and racial change. White middle class parents report the benefits to their children in being in a more diverse school setting than the suburban schools to which they might have relocated.

However, in Posey-Maddox's study of the middle class involvement in urban school choice, she cautions that the improvements in neighborhood schools in downtown areas is unstable in its reliance on this "infusion of private capital" (Posey-Maddox, 2016, p. 186). She warns that this private capital of individual parent and/or community volunteerism is unsustainable because it relies on the commitments of private donors: "Cuts to traditional public school budgets, for example, create the conditions for parents with the economic, cultural, and social means to do so to take up economic matters formerly managed and supported by the state" (Posey-Maddox, 2016, p. 194). A similar case might be made concerning charter school reliance on private donors.

In this manner, portfolio systems sustain the interdependent entanglement of state dispossession of public funds and assets along with the investment of private sources in terms of middle class family resources, individual donor contributions, corporate support, and philanthropic programs. Dispossession, then, is accompanied by capital accumulation through privatized interests—whether this be the investment of middle class parents whose children attend specialized district schools or the involvement of wealthy donors eager to support the revitalization of their cities while benefiting from tax deductions for their contributions. Tax abatements to industry and new residents also reflect enactments of privatized investment. Through private investment at these complex levels, the state of Ohio is relieved of its fiscal and regulatory role.

CONCLUSION

Study findings suggest that the intentional "disruption" on the part of state and local actors toward altering the status quo reveals broad trends in replicating inequality. Instead of meaningful change providing students of color, poor students, and students with disabilities a qualitatively different educational experience, there is evidence of greater stress for students and families and the normalization of displacement and dispossession within the agnostic stance and discourse toward school choice and school closure. These patterns point to the racialization of educational policies as evident in dimensions of relational and spatial reconfiguration and shifts in assets from the public to the private.

In the case of urban renewal, accelerated school construction, tax abatement, state legislation for school choice, school closure and replacement, and the implementation of a portfolio system of school choice, a pattern of costs and benefits are evident. Policies not explicitly driven by racially discriminatory intent, perhaps even developed as ameliorative for the poor, serve to reproduce racial and social class inequalities. These policies displace those historically and currently marginalized by race, class, disability, and language use. Such shifts in relational and spatial capital have their roots in earlier legislative, policy, and political change, where private interests and agents have influenced past decisions and subsequent directions.

As evident in the local Cleveland economy and education in the late 20th century, and reflecting Derrick Bell's theory of convergence (Bell, 1995), private interests converged with moral pressures to address poverty and school inequities, yielding policy and legislation aimed at economic growth and educational opportunity. However, these efforts also included assurances to power brokers that deep-seated traditions of privilege would be sustained, as evident in the favoring of individual social mobility, deregulation, and unconstrained freedom of choice. Accompanying these traditions was the relinquishing public assets and services to unregulated private entities. As a result, benefits related to private accumulation of space, relationships, and capital that were once part of the social contract and role of the state have been displaced, acquired through the state's dispossession of these public assets. Parallel efforts in the development of theme-based district schools occur along with the redesign, replacement, or closure of schools in high poverty neighborhoods rated by the state as failing—the educational label of "blight."

Such structural entanglement of privilege and exclusion has produced "circuits of dispossession" and the loss of relational and spatial capital among students of color and their families (Fine & Ruglis, 2009; Harvey, 2004). In this manner, the social contract between citizen and the state is obstructed as families navigate school choices that include considerable variation in the characteristics of students enrolled, access to enrollment, and distance traveled from home to school sites (Hernandez & Galletta, 2016).

The question addressed in this chapter is what are the costs and consequences of school closure and who benefits from school closure and its permutations as school redesign, phase-out, and replacement? Contextualizing the historical and the lived experience of students reveals the costs of what is often hidden from view. Surfacing displacement and accumulation by dispossession in the privatization and gentrification processes uncovers how the focus on individualized social mobility evident in the phrase "the right school for your child" benefits those already equipped with economic and social resources to exercise school choice.

This chapter examined the experience of school closure among Cleveland students living on the city's predominantly African American eastside. It attended to both the lived experience of students and families as well as historical and current policy contexts. In doing so, the study noted redrawn spatial and relational boundaries, particularly as public assets have shifted in terms of space, material resources, and governance. As noted in the opening of the chapter, Liana's story interrupts the smoothness of the school transformation motif. Forms of school shuttering and extinction in terms of school legacies have occurred as well as the disappearance of neighborhood schools through "phasing out" and "replacement."

When asked what happened to those displaced by urban renewal in the 1950s, the city of Cleveland had no record of the relocation of 60% of those displaced (Swanstrom, 1985, footnote 28, p. 271). What assurances are there that this more recent iteration of structural entanglement is not contributing to the uprooting and disappearance of working class and poor students of color as well as students with disabilities? Absent a critical examination of displacement and dispossession, "sector" agnosticism is sustained and racial inequality replicated.

NOTES

1. The student's name is a pseudonym.
2. The film noted in the beginning of this chapter, *Lives in Transition: Eviction Notice* (Jones & Schilling, 2011), documents the experience of 10 students impacted by the 2010 high school closures, either as students displaced or as students already enrolled in the schools receiving displaced students. Through participatory action research, these students took on the role of youth researchers and studied state and local policy, history, and current experiences of students as it related to school closure. Findings from that study produced four key themes: concerns about depressed achievement during the year of and the year following the closure announcement; transportation challenges getting to the receiving school; loss of student and teacher relationships when the school closed; and questions about the future use of the high school buildings. Liana (pseudonym) was a youth researcher on the project. For background on the study and the use of participatory action research, see Jones et al. (2015).
3. My role as a university critical friend involved sharing research on issues of concern for the Cleveland Education Committee and engaging in dialogue on the educational policy at the district, state, and federal level.
4. Cleveland Transformation Alliance Board Meetings, 1/23/17; 9/25/17. Notes from Board discussion.
5. See District Profile on the website of the National Assessment of Educational Progress (NAEP), retrieved from https://www.nationsreportcard.gov/profiles/districtprofile?chort=1&sub=MAT&sj=XQ&sfj=NL&st=MN&year=2015R3
6. Percentages for reporting survey data provide rounded numbers.
7. For those not eligible for district transportation, the district website indicates that purchase of one-way tickets at a discounted price of $1.65 and two-ride tickets at $3.30 at the district's transportation office. The district's policy differs from the state in that the district offers greater access to transportation. The state requirement is over two miles for K–8, with no requirement to transport students in Grades 9–12. See http://www.clevelandmetroschools.org/Page/596
8. Because the district's grade configuration is K–8 and 9–12, the ninth grade students would experience one school change that was promotional: completion of eighth grade. Eighth grade graduation was listed as one of the survey items available as reasons for changing schools.
9. An example of an unclear response is the following: "It affected my life because all the teachers cared." Because it was not clear if the teachers were from the closed school or the receiving school, or both, the response was coded as "not clear."

APPENDIX: SURVEY QUESTIONS REFLECTING
DIMENSIONS OF SCHOOL CLOSURE

4. Since Kindergarten, how many schools have you attended?

    ☐ 1–2   ☐ 3–4   ☐ 5–6   ☐ 7–9   ☐ More than 9

7. If you attended a school that was closed, how was your experience transitioning to a new school?

    ☐ Very hard   ☐ Hard   ☐ Easy   ☐ Very easy
    ☐ I did not attend a school that was closed

8. If you attended a school that closed, how did it impact your life? [open-ended question]

9. How do you most often get to school?

    ☐ I ride a high school shuttle bus   ☐ Drive myself
    ☐ Someone else drives me   ☐ Bike   ☐ Walk
    ☐ I ride the RTA bus.   ☐ Other (please specify)

11. If you take the RTA, how do you pay for your ticket? (Check all that apply)

    ☐ I use my own money.   ☐ My parents/family give me money.
    ☐ The school provides the ticket.   ☐ I buy my bus ticket from another student.   ☐ I do not take the RTA.

13. What other thoughts do you have about your experience getting an RTA ticket or riding the high school shuttle bus? [open-ended question]

REFERENCES

Allweis, A., Grant, C. A., & Manning, K. (2015) Behind the photos and the tears: Media images, neoliberal discourses, racialized constructions of space and school closings in Chicago. *Race Ethnicity and Education, 18*(5), 611–631. Retrieved from http://dx.doi.org/10.1080/13613324.2014.969223

Au, W., & Ferrare, J. J. (Eds.). (2015). *Mapping corporate education reform: Power and policy networks in the neoliberal state.* New York, NY: Routledge.

Ayala, J., & Galletta, A. (2012). Documenting disappearing spaces: Erasure and remembrance in two high school closures. *Peace and Conflict: Journal of Peace Psychology, 18*(2), 149–155.

Bell, D. A. (1995). Brown v Board of Education and the interest convergence. In K. Crenshaw, N. Gotanda, G. Peller, & K. Thomas (Eds.), *Critical race theory: The key writings from the movement* (pp. 20–29). New York, NY: The New Press.

Bradley, A. (1995, March 15). 'Crisis' spurs state takeover. *Education Week.* Retrieved from http://www.edweek.org/ew/articles/1995/03/15/25cleve.h14.html?qs=crisis+spurs+takeover+in+cleveland

Brummet, Q. (2014). The effect of school closings on student achievement. *Journal of Public Economics, 119*, 108–124.

Carl, J. (2011). *Freedom of choice: Vouchers in American education.* Santa Barbara, CA: Praeger.

Carlson, D., & Lavertu, S. (2015). *School closures and student achievement: An analysis of Ohio's urban district and charter schools.* Columbus, OH: Thomas B. Fordham Institute.

Cleveland Metropolitan School District. (2010) *CMSD academic transformation plan. A strategic development initiative.* Cleveland, OH: Author. Retrieved from http://media.cleveland.com/metro/other/transformation-media-kit.pdf

Cleveland Transformation Alliance. (2015). *Choose your school! Cleveland school selection guide.* Cleveland, OH: Author.

Cleveland Transformation Alliance. (2016). *A report to the community on the implementation and impact of Cleveland's plan for transforming schools.* Cleveland, OH: Author..

Cleveland Transformation Alliance. (Fall, 2017). *A report to the community on the implementation and impact of Cleveland's plan for transforming schools.* Cleveland, OH: Author. Retrieved from https://mycleschool.org/wp-content/uploads/2018/05/Alliance-Report-Design_FINAL.compressed_0-2.pdf

Coleman, J. S. (1988). Social capital in the creation of human capital. *American Journal of Sociology.* 94, S95–S120.

Cooke, R., Evans, C., Galletta, A., Gullatt, L., Johnson, M., Kaufman, A., . . . Whitmore, S. (2015, April). *Educational policy—It's personal!* Paper presented at the American Educational Research Association annual meeting. Chicago, IL.

Coulton, C. J., & Chow, J. (1995). The impact of poverty on Cleveland neighborhoods. In W. D. Keating, N. Krumholz, & D. C. Perry (Eds.), *Cleveland: A metropolitan reader* (pp. 202–227). Kent, OH: Kent State University Press.

Craggett v. Board of Education of Cleveland City School District, 234 F. Supp. 381 (1964).

Crenshaw, K., Gotanda, N., Peller, G., & Thomas, K. (1995). *Critical race theory: The key writings that informed the movement.* New York, NY: The New Press.

Cucchiara, M. B. (2013). *Marketing schools, marketing cities: Who wins and who loses when schools become urban amenities.* Chicago, IL: University of Chicago Press.

Deeds, V., & Pattillo, M. (2015). Organizational "failure" and institutional pluralism: A case study of an urban school closure. *Urban Education, 50*(4), 474–504.

de la Torre, M., & Gwynne, J. (2009, October). *When schools close: Effects on displaced students in Chicago public schools.* Chicago, IL: Consortium on Chicago School Research. Retrieved from http://ccsr.uchicago.edu/publications/when-schools-close-effects-displaced-students-chicago-public-schools

de la Torre, M., Gordon, M. F., Moore, P., & Cowhy, J. (2015). *School closings in Chicago: Understanding families' choices and constraints for new school enrollment.* Chicago, IL: The University of Chicago Consortium on Chicago School Research.

Du Bois, W. E. B. (1995). *The souls of Black folk.* New York, NY: Penguin Books. (Originally published in 1903)

Dunn, R. A., Hardiman, J., Hattie, A., Jones, M. D., & Whyte, D. (2016). *Boycott, busing, & beyond: The history and implications of school desegregation in the urban north.* Dubuque, IA: Kendall Hunt.

Engberg, J., Gill, B., Zamarro, G., & Zimmer, R. (2012). Closing schools in a shrinking district: Do student outcomes depend on which schools are closed? *Journal of Urban Economics, 71*(2), 189–203.

Fabricant, M., & Fine, M. (2012). *Charter schools and the corporate makeover of public education: What's at stake?* New York, NY: Teachers College Press.

Fine, M., & Ruglis, J. (2009). Circuits and consequences of dispossession: The racialized realignment of the public youth for U.S. youth. *Transforming Anthropology, 17*(1), 20–33.

Foster, R., & Kaplan, S. (2004). *Creative destruction: Why companies that are built to last underperform the market—and how to successfully transform them.* New York, NY: Broadway Business.

Fullilove, M. T. (2004). *Root schock: How tearing up city neighborhoods hurts America, and what we can do about it.* New York, NY: One World Ballantine Books.

Harvey, D. (2004). The new imperialism: Accumulation by dispossession. *Socialist Register, 40,* 63–87.

Hernandez, J., & Galletta, A. (2016). The continuum of structural violence: Sustaining exclusion through school closures. *Community Psychology in Global Perspective, 2*(2), 21–39.

Hoven, C. (2015). Coalition forms to seek plans, tools and resources necessary for success at 23 Investment Schools. *Plain Press, 42*(7), p. 1, 5, 8.

Jackson, F. G. (2012). Cleveland's plan for transforming schools: Reinventing public education in our city and serving as a model of innovation for the state of Ohio. Retrieved from http://www.clevelandmetroschools.org/cms/lib05/OH01915844/Centricity/Domain/98/ClevelandPlanandLegislation.pdf

Jones, V., & Schilling, E. (2011). *Lives in transition: Eviction notice* [Video]. Retrieved from https://vimeo.com/27023571

Jones, V., Stewart, C., Ayala, J., & Galletta, A. (2015). Expressions of agency: Contemplating youth voice and adult roles in participatory action research. In J. Conner, R. Ebby-Rosin, & A. Slattery (Eds.), *National Society for the Study of Education Yearbook: Student Voice in American Educational Policy* (pp. 135–152). New York, NY: Teachers College Press.

Keating, W. D., Krumholz, N., & Perry, D. C. (Eds.). (1995). *Cleveland: A metropolitan reader.* Kent, OH: Kent State University Press.

Kemple, J. J. (2015). *High school closures in New York City: Impacts on students' academic outcomes, attendance, and mobility.* New York, NY: Research Alliance for New York City Schools.

Kimelberg, S. M. (2014). Middle-class parents, risk, and urban schools. In A. Lareau & K. Goyette (Eds.), *Choosing homes, choosing schools* (pp. 207–236). New York, NY: Russell Sage.

Kirshner, B., Gaertner, M., & Pozzoboni, K. (2010). Tracing transitions: The effects of high school closure on displaced students. *Educational Evaluation and Policy Analysis, 32*(3), 407–429.

Kissoon, M. (2012). The urban youth collaborative speech: An alternative to school closing. *Peace and Conflict: Journal of Peace Psychology, 18*(2), 147–148.

Kumashiro, K. K. (2012). When billionaires become educational experts. *Academe, 98*(3). Retrieved from http://www.aaup.org/article/when-billionaires-become-educational-experts#.UV7eHaWrjww

Lipman, P., & Haines, N. (2007). From accountability to privatization and African American exclusion: Chicago's "Renaissance 2010." *Educational Policy, 21*(3), 471–502.

Martín-Baró, I. (1994). *Writings for a liberation psychology.* Cambridge, MA: Harvard University Press.

Mead, J. H. (2012). How legislation and litigation shape school choice. In G. Miron, K. G. Welner, P. H. Hinchey, & W. J. Mathis (Eds.), *Exploring the school choice universe: Evidence and recommendations.* Boulder, CO: National Education Policy Center.

Miller, C. P., & Wheeler, R. A. (1995). Cleveland: The making and remaking of an American city. In W. D. Keating, N. Krumholz, & D. C. Perry (Eds.), *Cleveland: A Metropolitan Reader* (pp. 31–48). Kent, OH: Kent State University Press.

Milward, H. B. (1994). Implications of contracting out: The new role for the hollow state. In P. W. Ingraham & B. S. Romsek (Eds.), *New Paradigms for Government: Issues for the Changing Public Service* (pp. 41–62). San Francisco, CA: Jossey-Bass.

Moore, L. N. (2002). The school desegregation crisis of Cleveland, Ohio, 1963–1964: The catalyst for black political power in a Northern city. *Journal of Urban History, 28*(2), 135–157.

O'Donnell, P. (2012, July 2). Governor John Kasich to sign Cleveland schools bill built through coalition. *The Plain Dealer.* Retrieved from http://www.cleveland.com/metro/index.ssf/2012/07/gov_john_kasich_signing_clevel.html

O'Donnell, P. (2015, April 27). Peace between Cleveland schools and teachers over? Union shoots for 1,500 member protest at school board Tuesday. *The Plain Dealer.* Retrieved from http://www.cleveland.com/metro/index.ssf/2015/04/peace_between_cleveland_school.html

O'Donnell, P. (2017, February 16). What's in the new tentative Cleveland teacher contract? Details and full contract here. *The Plain Dealer.* Retrieved from http://www.cleveland.com/metro/index.ssf/2017/02/whats_in_the_new_tentative_cle.html

Ohio Department of Education School Report Card. (n.d.). Retrieved from https://reportcardstorage.education.ohio.gov/archives-2010/2010-018556.pdf

Ott, T. (2009, October 5). Cleveland schools' transformation plan draws comments, but not all on the mark. *The Plain Dealer.* Retrieved from http://blog.cleveland.com/metro/2009/10/cleveland_schools_transformati.html

Ott, T. (2010a, February 28). George Gund Foundation approves 2.5 million to support first year of Cleveland schools transformation plan; $4 million more could follow. *The Plain Dealer.* Retrieved from http://blog.cleveland.com/metro/2010/02/gund_foundation_gives_25_milli.html

Ott, T. (2010b, March 9). Cleveland school approves board plan. *The Plain Dealer.* Retrieved from http://blog.cleveland.com/metro/2010/03/cleveland_school_board_approve.html

Ott, T. (2011a, February 13). School Improvement Grant Program has positive impact on Cleveland. *The Plain Dealer.* Retrieved from http://blog.cleveland.com/metro/2011/02/school_improvement_grant_progr.html

Ott, T. (2011b, April 5). Cleveland school board lays off 643 teachers, closes 7 schools. *The Plain Dealer.* Retrieved from http://blog.cleveland.com/metro/2011/04/cleveland_schools_lay_off_xx_c.html

Oyez. (2001). *Zelman v. Simmons-Harris.* Opinion announcement June 27, 2002. Retrieved from https://www.oyez.org/cases/2001/00-1751

Picower, B., & Mayorga, E. (2015). *What race got to do with it? How current school reform policy maintains racial and economic inequality.* New York, NY: Peter Lang.

Posey-Maddox, L. (2014). *When middle-class parents choose urban schools: Class, race and the challenge of equity in public education.* Chicago, IL: University of Chicago Press.

Posey-Maddox, L. (2016). Beyond the consumer: Parents, privatization, and fundraising in US urban public schooling. *Journal of Educational Policy, 31*(2), 178–197. doi:10.1080/02680939.2015.1065345

Putnam, R. D. (2000). *The collapse and revival of American community.* New York, NY: Simon & Schuster.

Reed v. Rhodes, 455 F. Supp. 569 (N.D. Ohio 1978).

Reinhard, B. (1997, May 21). Bill to give Cleveland mayor school control advances. *Education Week.* Retrieved from http://www.edweek.org/ew/articles/1997/05/21/34ohio.h16.html?qs=beth+reinhard+and+may+1997

Rumberger, R., & Lim, S. (2008). *Why students drop out of school: A review of 25 years of research.* Santa Barbara, CA: California Dropout Research Project.

Smarick, A. (2012). *The urban school system of the future: Applying the principles and lessons of chartering.* Lanham, MI: Rowman & Littlefield.

Stanton-Salazar, R. D. (2001). *Manufacturing hope and despair: The school and kin support networks of U.S.-Mexican youth.* New York, NY: Teachers College Press.

Steggert, S., & Galletta, A. (2013, April). *The Press of school accountability: A close look at school closure.* Paper presentation at the Annual Meeting of the American Educational Research Association, San Francisco, CA.

Swanstrom, T. (1985). *The crisis of growth politics: Cleveland, Kusinich, and the challenge of urban populism.* Philadelphia, PA: Temple University Press.

Trouillot, M.-R. (1995). *Silencing the past: Power and production of history.* Boston, MA: Beacon Press.

Trujillo, T., & Renée, M. (2012). *Democratic school turnarounds: Pursuing equity and learning from evidence.* Boulder, CO: National Educational Policy Center. Retrieved from http://nepc.colorado.edu/files/pb-turnaroundequity_0.pdf

Valencia, R. R. (1984). The school closure issue and the Chicano community: A follow-up study of the Angeles case. *The Urban Review, 16*(3), 145–163.

White, K. (1998, September 16). In Cleveland, Mayor White takes control. *Education Week.* Retrieved from https://www.edweek.org/ew/articles/1998/09/16/02cleve.h18.html?qs=White+1998

Whyte, D. M. (2003). *African-American community politics and racial equality in Cleveland public schools: 1933–1973* (Doctoral dissertation). Case Western Reserve University, Cleveland, Ohio.

Zelman v. Simmons-Harris. (2001). Oyez. Retrieved from https://www.oyez.org/cases/2001/00-1751

CHAPTER 7

THE IMPLICATIONS OF COLORBLIND DECISION-MAKING ABOUT THE CLOSURE, RENOVATION OR REBUILD OF (ALMOST) EVERY SCHOOL IN NORTH LITTLE ROCK, ARKANSAS

Kendra Lowery
Ball State University

Scholarship on contemporary school closures suggests that conceptions of school failure, market-based competition and school choice, and fiscal concerns in urban and rural communities appear to be driving the upward trend of public school closure (Andrews, Duncombe, & Yinger, 2002; Deeds & Pattillo, 2015; Finnigan & Lavner, 2012; Post & Stambach, 1999; Siegel-Hawley, Bridges, & Shields, 2017). Leaders in the North Little Rock School District (NLRSD) did not create a plan to close schools in the context of school

Shuttered Schools, pages 193–228
Copyright © 2019 by Information Age Publishing
All rights of reproduction in any form reserved.

failure and fiscal crisis (i.e., because of low-performing schools or a state takeover) as was the case with prominent school closings in Philadelphia, Detroit, New York, and Chicago (Finnigan & Lavner, 2012; Kretchmar, 2014). However, budget concerns regarding the cost of maintaining old buildings that were not technology-ready—another reason for school closings nationally—led district leaders to create a plan for a rebirth of the district. Out of everything old, there would be something new, in the form of completely new or renovated buildings for nearly every school in the district. The new buildings would be built for the future—able to handle the technology and community space needs for teaching 21st century learners. The appearance, technology, access, and physical plant of each building would be equally advanced regardless of the neighborhood in which it was located.

Despite this increased focus on school closure, few studies explain the actual process of closing schools or the decision-making processes at the center of school closures (Deeds & Pattillo 2015). This chapter contributes to scholarship on school closure in three ways. First, it examines a unique case of school closure in North Little Rock, Arkansas. This case is unique because 17/18 schools in the district were closed, rebuilt or renovated between 2012 and 2017.[1] Second, in contrast to the extant literature about the reason for school closures, district officials committed to the plan in order to prepare students for 21st century learning, rather than in response to school failure or financial crisis. In other words, the impetus for the reallocation of resources was not in response to school failure, but in the pursuit of equity. Third, using the theoretical frame of colorblind ideology (Bonilla-Silva & Forman, 2000; Choi, 2008; Lewis, 2001), the implications of colorblindness on district decision-making about the school closure process, allocation of school resources and resulting school demographics are analyzed. Critical race theorists confront colorblind ideology as problematic (Crenshaw, 1988; Lopez, 2003). Given the substantial amount of literature on the pitfalls of colorblind ideology, this adds to the complexities of claims in extant literature.

This chapter is a case study of the school closings and rebuilds in North Little Rock. In particular, it focuses on the district's decision-making process in order to analyze the contributing factors that created the "need" for rebuilding the district, and its impact on schools, family, and community. District leaders stated several times that the decision-making was based on what was best for all students, without concern for racial equity. The school superintendent and consultants made claims about focusing on all children as a conscious alternative to discussing race. That is, they invoked colorblind strategies as an explicit attempt to advocate for equity. Through the lens of contemporary racial theory, two questions guide this analysis: How did district leaders and consultants engage race in decision-making processes? What are the implications of colorblind decision-making about resource allocation, school closure and rebuilding on the demographic composition of schools? Findings indicate that district decision-making about school closures and resource allocations that eliminated race as a factor created surface-level parity in school resources and access to those resources, and did not address underlying issues of racism that are ever-present due to the legacy of racism in the city. Choosing not to view the impact of educational resources through a racial lens, while creating surface-level equity, does not eliminate racial inequity.

FRAMEWORK

Colorblind Ideology

Colorblind ideology, also characterized as race neutrality, is an ideology espoused by people who articulate a desire to function in a world in which they either believe or desire race-based inequities—racism—to be over. In their analysis of college students' discourse and beliefs about race, Bonilla-Silva and Forman (2000) articulated this relationship between a person's language and beliefs: "In our analysis we assume, as discourse analysts do, that people use talk (language) to construct versions of the social world" (p. 69). The authors asserted that colorblind ideology is the dominant racial framework in our society and that it is characterized by six habits of mind borne out through people's language: decontextualized notions of liberalism; cultural explanations, deficit-based explanations as the root of inequity; avoidance of overt racial language and use of subtle or racially coded language; the explanation of racial inequity as a natural outcome; discrimination is decreasingly significant and pervasive; and belief in the free market ideology justifies continuing racism (as people should not be forced to desegregate).

Critical Race Theory

Colorblind ideology is the antithesis of critical race theory (CRT). CRT examines the ways in which race and racism function in the law and in society (Delgado & Stefancic, 2017). Rather than the researcher or actor turning a blind eye to race (or color), critical race theorists identify, name, and explore the role of race in society. CRT began as an outgrowth of critical legal studies by legal scholars seeking to identify and transform racialized power dynamics (Crenshaw, 1988; Delgado & Stefancic, 2017).

A review of the many complex tenets of CRT and the ever-growing application of CRT in education (Howard & Navarro, 2016; Ladson-Billings & Tate, 1995) is outside of the scope of this chapter. However, a core principle of CRT is the assertion that colorblind notions of equality are problematic.

For example, Crenshaw (1988) described Reagan's neoconservative agenda as "profoundly hostile to the civil rights policies of the previous two decades" (p. 1337) because it

> singles out race-specific civil rights policies as one of the most significant threats to the democratic political system. Emphasizing the need for strictly colorblind policies, this view calls for the repeal of affirmative action and other race-specific remedial policies, urges an end to class-based remedies, and calls for the Administration to limit remedies to what it calls "actual victims" of discrimination. (p. 1337)

Related to the core belief that race is endemic to the United States, is the assertion that CRT analysts must not subscribe to a colorblind philosophy (Ledesma & Calderón, 2015). Proponents of colorblindness "often fail to recognize connections between the race of an individual and the real social conditions underlying litigation or other constitutional dispute" (Gotanda, 1991, p. 7). CRT theorists believe that because people of color experience racism, their stories "must be heard as a means of uncovering a racialized social reality" (Evans, 2007, p. 166).

Ladson-Billings and Tate (1995) explored the relationship between CRT and education as a lens for understanding educational inequity. They argued that racial inequity in education should be seen as "a logical and predictable result of a racialized society in which discussions of race and racism continue to be muted and marginalized" (p. 47). CRT in education scholars continue to analyze how race: intersects with multiple identities to create unique marginalizing experiences; is operationalized socially and materially; and how the relationship between racism and inequitable material conditions contributes to racial inequity in schools (Howard & Navarro, 2016; Lynn & Adams, 2002). In the case of North Little Rock, a colorblind logic emphasizing the pursuit of educational equity for all informed many justifications for school closures and rebuilds. In the balance of the chapter, the implications of this colorblind decision-making process for student outcomes are examined.

SCHOOL AND COMMUNITY CONTEXT

North Little Rock is a city of 62,304 (U.S. Census, 2010). The largest racial groups are White and African American, which represent 54% and 39.7% of the city's population, respectively (U.S. Census, 2010). The city's history includes racial segregation and discrimination brought about by the legacy of slavery and Jim Crow laws in existence before and after the landmark *Plessy v Ferguson* (1896) United States Supreme Court decision which established that separate facilities for Black people were constitutional. This history provides the context for an examination of the implications of contemporary colorblind decision-making in a district that is steeped in racial history, on the allocation of resources and schools.

Schools are certainly part of North Little Rock's legacy of racial segregation. In 1913, White students could attend a 4-year high school, while African Americans could attend a segregated school through the 10th grade. Curriculum for African American students was not extended to the 12th grade until 1928. The school remained the city's only Black secondary school campus for over 40 years (Bradburn, 2004). The city's high school, referred to as "Old Main," was built in 1929 and was designed by the same architectural firm that designed Little Rock Central High School (see Photo 7.1). North Little Rock High was the secondary school for White students until desegregation in 1966 (Cope, 2015), after a failed attempt to integrate in September 1957. Six African American male students, including Richard Lindsey, walked up the steps past a throng of jeering White students and adults hurling racial slurs at them, in order to integrate the school. (R. Lindsey, personal communication, March 22, 2016). They were denied entry, and were not recognized for their courage until decades later. "Ole Main" remained the city's high school until the 2015-2016 school year when a new building was opened.

School Closings Prior to 2012

The closing or repurposing of schools was not a new concept by 2012. North Little Rock's schools went through many name changes, closings and rebuilds prior to 2012. In order to comply with desegregation, the district

Photo 7.1   North Little Rock HIgh School. It has been replaced by the creation of a brand new state of the art high school that opened in 2015. This building is on the national historic register and was being used as administrative offices in 2016.

created a plan that closed Black schools, reassigned Black students to previously White schools, and introduced busing to the city. Racially identifiable names of schools were also abolished (Bradburn, 2004). During the 1966–1967 school year, the board integrated all 12 grades and integrated school faculties by assigning White teachers at previously all-Black schools and Black teachers at previously all-White schools. Rev. Angelo Johnson, president of the North Little Rock branch of the NAACP lamented the impact of school desegregation on African Americans: "In every situation the black community has to bear the brunt of [desegregation], and this is where the resentment is. The one who is least able to pay is the one who does pay and bears the burden" (Bradburn, 2004, p. 207).

DATA AND METHODS

This chapter is based on data from a qualitative case study. Stake (1995) described this type of research as, "the study of the particularity and complexity of a single case, coming to understand its activity within important circumstances" (p. xi). The author began collecting data on the school closure and rebuilding process in North Little Rock in 2015, 3 years into the district's process. As a result, the author was unable to conduct observations or collect participant data as the process was being developed on and implemented in its earliest stages. Data collection included interviews with community members, administration, and staff; content analysis of school district documents and newspaper articles; and observations on a 5 hour guided tour of the city that included a visit to each school. The author started by reading articles in the *North Little Rock Times* and the *Arkansas Democrat-Gazette* ($n = 32$) that addressed the referendum and Capital Improvement Plan (CIP), dating back to February 2012 when voters passed the plan. District documents that were circulated about the process, and a book and several maps that were created by a consulting firm (ABC & Associates) were analyzed. Some of the maps are reproduced in this chapter. District documents and pamphlets that were circulated about the process were analyzed, and a document created by ABC & Associates for the district that included the maps, some of which are reproduced in this chapter.

After obtaining IRB approval to conduct the study, the author recruited and contacted the participants and conducted five semi-structured interviews. Seidman (2006) explained the importance of interviews to understand processes: "The primary way a researcher can investigate an educational organization, institution, or process is through the experience of the individual people, the 'others' who make up the organization or carry out the process" (p. 10). Two of the participants—the current superintendent and the consultant—were purposefully selected because of their roles. The remaining three participants were referred by another district staff member. The interviews lasted between 45 minutes and 1 hour and were audio-recorded. The guided tour of the city lasted 5 hours. The interviews were transcribed then coded manually (Saldaña, 2016). Because participants did not share the same roles, transcripts were coded to understand each participant's unique perspective. Given the small number of participants, triangulation between interview data, relevant documents, and newspaper articles was done to increase trustworthiness.[2]

Participants

All participants are assigned pseudonyms, except for Superintendent Rodgers and Principal Charles Jones. Due to their roles, they were easily identifiable on the North Little Rock school district website at the time of this study.

Superintendent Kelly Rodgers
Rodgers is a White Arkansas native. He grew up in Little Rock, moved to Texas and had a 34-year career in education including superintendent. When Rodgers was hired as superintendent in North Little Rock, the CIP was already in motion.

David Kennedy
Kennedy is a White consultant who is the CEO of the consulting firm that specializes in using GIS software for helping school districts identify and gather information necessary for enrollment projections.

Charles Jones
Jones is the African American principal of North Little Rock Academy—the alternative school for Grades 6–12. He is a lifelong resident of North Little Rock and is a community leader and advocate for underserved students and families.

Henry Anderson
Anderson is an African American community member who is very active in the neighborhood where the North Little Rock Academy is located.

Evelyn Marks
Marks is an African American community member. She is a lifelong resident and educator in the school district.

* * *

Charles Jones and Evelyn Marks led the author on a guided tour of North Little Rock, which included a visit to each school. The author took pictures of each school building. The next section includes pictures of the buildings that were closed, the vacant lots, and the new buildings. Insight into the importance of using photographs to document aspects of school closings was gained from viewing pictures from the Philadelphia School Closing Photo Collective (urbanedjournal.org).[3] Pictures were not taken inside of the buildings, but as in Philadelphia, pictures of the building exteriors, vacant lots, and new buildings provide documentation and enhance the discussion of the nature and meaning of school closings. In several cases, pictures include the school building and either the vacant lot next to it, where the former building stood.

FINDINGS: THE DECISION-MAKING PROCESS FOR SCHOOL CLOSURES AND REBUILDING

On February 14, 2012, the North Little Rock community passed a millage increase to fund a major construction plan of its schools (Rayburn, 2012d). The CIP included a closing, rebuilding, and remodeling of nearly all North Little Rock School District (NLRSD) schools. The plan would ultimately reduce the number of schools from 21 to 13.

In 2011, district officials began talks of increasing the millage rate, which determines the amount of property tax paid, in order to fund its plans.[4] In September of that year, the school board approved a $265.6 million plan to improve district facilities over the next 5 years. The plan included "constructing and equipping news [*sic*] schools and additions to existing schools and overhauling other school facilities" (Rayburn, 2012a, p. A1) in three phases. First, a 7.4 millage increase levied to property taxes. Second, the consolidation of schools to reduce operational costs. Third, the application for state partnership funds that would contribute up to 25% (or $66 million) of the plan's $265 million dollar budget (Blad, 2012, p. B1).

Whenever a millage increase is discussed, school districts typically engage in a massive public relations effort to justify and clearly explain the tax increase. The requirements for millage increases as set forth by the Arkansas State Constitution highlight why it is important for school districts to fully inform the public about the process and rationale for a millage increase. In short, a millage increase means citizens will have to pay more property taxes. First, school districts must levy a minimum 25-mill tax rate. Second, there is no maximum limit on how many mills can be levied by school districts. Third, any changes in a school district millage must obtain voter approval (Miller, Karov, & McCullough, n.d.). District leaders pitched the millage increase to stakeholders by emphasizing the need to update facilities to create space for "21st century" technology (Rayburn, 2012b, p. A5). They asserted the changes would "improve the learning environment" (Rayburn, 2012c, p. A8), citing that the schools were not equipped with the latest technology, and did not meet state requirements for size and space. Data used to support this assessment was a 2004 state report that "identified $199.6 million in state-mandated improvements to be completed over the next several years" (Rayburn, 2012a, p. A1). Superintendent Kelly Rodgers, who was hired after the millage election in 2013, described the purpose of the plan as one which created "schools for the future...so when you walk into the schools, they won't look like normal schools." Rodgers explained that there are a lot of open areas where students can come in groups, there are courtyards, and all of the elementary schools have gyms and art classrooms, which they previously did not.

In addition, district leaders assured their stakeholders that the new and extensively renovated buildings would be safer facilities for protecting students against natural disasters, such as tornadoes (Howell, 2013a).

The North Little Rock Times characterized the district's process as a "community-led process" during which it utilized professional consultants who evaluated current facilities and projected future space requirements, and met with "thousands of parents, community members, students, teachers, administrators, staff and board members" (Rayburn, 2012a, p. A9) to develop a 5-year strategic plan that required the increased levy. The phrase "closing schools" was not used. Instead, the district's messaging was reported in the paper as "offering [schools] to the community for other use" (Rayburn, 2012c, p. A1).

Consultants and ABC & Associates

To develop its 5-year plan, the district consulted with two different architectural firms and various stakeholders (Rayburn, 2012b). Spokeswoman Brazear stated, "[The plan] provides the district with a basis for rational decision-making relative to future physical plant issues" (Rayburn, 2012b, p. A5). Once the decision was made to reduce the number of elementary schools from 13 to 9, the district contracted with ABC & Associates, a consulting firm that projects enrollment for school districts contemplating school closings. David Kennedy, the CEO of ABC & Associates, stated that his involvement began after the architectural firm that was hired by the district started looking closely at building plans and realized that in order to make "sound decisions, they needed to know what was going to happen with enrollment."

The firm, in collaboration with the district, formed a demography committee whose purpose was to redraw school boundaries. Because the firm was not associated with either the school district or the architect firm, it was able to provide an independent enrollment analysis. Kennedy explained why this was a benefit: "comprised of patrons, principals, parents and business leaders and charged with redrawing the boundaries" (Rayburn, 2014, n.p.). The firm provided an independent enrollment analysis and were not associated with either the school district or the architect firm. Kennedy elaborated:

> We know that when we are set to provide a data analysis, the first thing people may ask is, "Well, who is the contract with? Is it with the architecture firm?" So, with it being a separate contract, it got into one of our strengths, which is we're an unbiased company. The data suggests what direction you should go.

Kennedy further explained that the core element of his firm's work is their enrollment analysis, which requires understanding where students are and what enrollment will be like in the future. The company performs services ranging from enrollment analysis, demographic analysis, analysis of the instructional capacity of buildings, facilitation of a facility master plan to a realignment of a district's attendance areas, as it did in North Little Rock.

The Enrollment Projection Process

The firm gathered data from the county, city, and U.S. Census, and used GIS software to track demographics, development, and enrollment trends within very small planning areas (see Map 7.1).

According to Kennedy,

> It's all based on geography, the school district boundary, then elementary, middle and school boundaries, and further broken down by the type of development that was proposed to be built. That's a key thing as to why the projections tend to be so accurate, because it is based on all of that data.

Information about any future housing developments was integrated into their model by answering the following questions: "How many units? How many bedrooms are for each unit? Is it similar in market rate? and Is it affordable?" They also considered how demographic shifts, or a change in home values might relate to student enrollment.

Once the data was gathered and analyzed, ABC & Associates provided an enrollment forecast for each school building for the next 5 years (see Map 7.2). Kennedy attributed the accuracy of his projection model to the fact that he sought input from the city about planned or potential commercial and housing development projects that will impact enrollment patterns in the district: "That's a cornerstone of our model—being able to accurately forecast."

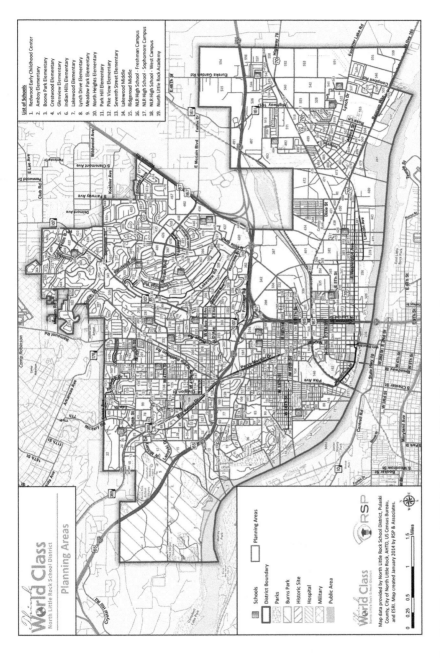

Map 7.1 Planning areas (ABC & Associates, LLC). Used with permission.

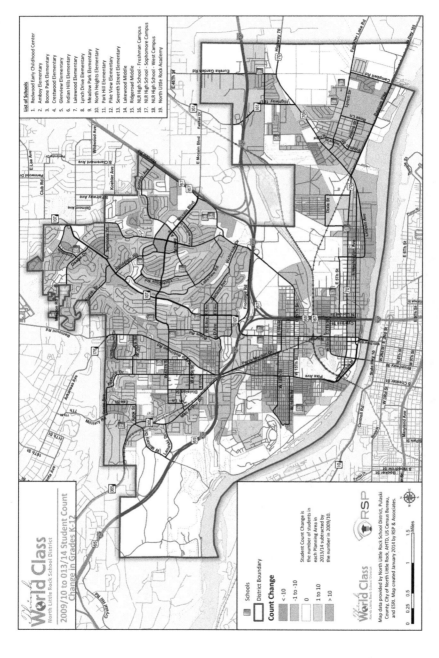

Map 7.2 Student Count Change 2009/10 to 2013/14. (ABC & Associates, LLC). Used with permission.

The maps provided valuable data for the consideration of options for closed or repurposed buildings (see Map 7.3). Those decisions were linked to the future number of students. According to Kennedy, the architects and administration also examined what the instructional programming was to be in the facilities, and how to create equal access to positive resources in buildings across the entire district. He elaborated,

> The data became the cornerstone of how many buildings do we really need. And are we seeing students in one particular area turn over versus another? How does that relate to the values that the board felt were important to the community in developing a plan . . . We ended up initiating and creating what that looked like.

ABC & Associates met with the board in 2014 to begin school boundary adjustments. Five groups were included in the process: (a) the board of education, (b) the public, (c) committees, (d) consultants, and (e) school administrators. The firm helped the board establish its vision statement or parameters for the committee's work. This included adjustments to the facility master plan, school closures and openings, grade configuration changes, student assignment, student option considerations, and other training ideas. The firm then presented the board with 10 criteria from which they selected the following four priorities: (a) contiguous planning areas, (b) balancing uneven demographic trends, (c) match between projected enrollment and building capacity, and (d) transportation efficiency.

Later that spring, the school board announced that it was moving forward with its plans for Phase I and would close Belwood Elementary, repurpose Poplar Street from a sixth grade school to the tenth grade school, close Rose City Middle School and repurpose it as the alternative secondary school (see Table 7.1). The board also indicated that during the 2014–2015 school year Lynch Drive Elementary School would close and students would be reassigned to Meadow Park and Glenview Elementary schools.

In keeping with the superintendent's commitment to involve and inform community residents about the plan's progress, the district hosted open houses, tours and orientations at North Little Rock Academy which was moved to the former Rose City Middle School, Lakewood and Ridgeroad, the two middle schools that would be options for students for the upcoming academic year, and the three high school campuses—one for ninth, one for tenth, and one for eleventh and twelfth grades. The community hosted forums, such as one in May 31, 2013 to update the community about progress on the building plan and to address concerns. On that particular day, the concerns were about the district's commitment to building a new Glenview Elementary school as previously promised for Phase II. Glenview residents had been vocal about their concerns for their neighborhood schools. Community member Evelyn Marks remembers that early on when the district

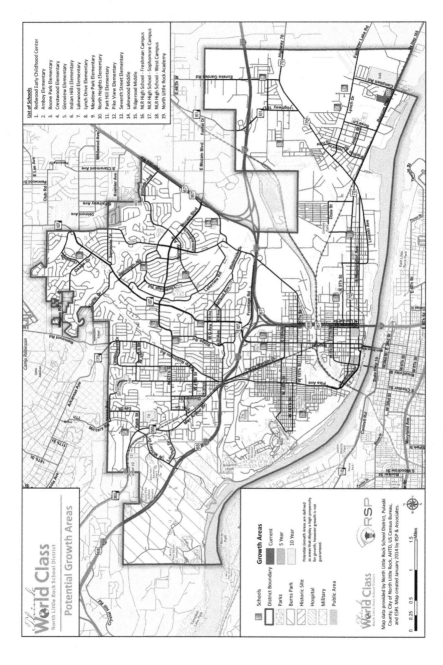

Map 7.3 Potential Growth Area. ABC & Associates. Used with permission.

TABLE 7.1 North Little Rock School District Schools Five Year Plan Phases I, II, & III		
School Name	**Status (2012–2013)**	**Status (2016–2017)**
Elementary		
Amboy	Construction for new building to begin Phase I	New building opened 2014
Belwood*	*Closed*; Students sent to Amboy Elementary	*Closed*; Sold
Boone Park	Construction for new building to begin Phase I	New building opened 2014
Crestwood	Changed from new building to renovations Phase II	Renovations complete
Glenview	Construction for new building to begin Phase II	Renovations complete
Indian Hills	Renovations to begin Phase II	Renovations complete
Lakewood	Construction for new building to begin Phase I	New building opened 2014
Lynch Drive	Scheduled to close June 2015	*Closed* earlier than planned (June 2014); Students moved to Meadow Park
Meadow Park	Construction for new building to begin Phase I	New building opened 2014
North Heights	Scheduled to close Phase II	*Closed*
Park Hill	Scheduled to close Phase II	*Closed*
Pike View	Scheduled to be renovated and *repurposed* as Early Childhood Center Phase II	Opened mid 2015–2016 year; *Repurposed* as Pike View Preschool
Redwood Early Childhood Center	*Closed*; Students moved to Pike View	*Closed*; Sold
Ridgeroad Elementary (See Ridgeroad Middle below)		Opened 2015
Seventh Street	Renovations begin Phase II	Renovations complete
Total # Elementary Schools	12	10
Middle		
Lakewood Middle	Serves grades 6 & 7; Plans to build new middle school delayed due to budget constraints; 8th graders moved to Freshman campus	Renamed North Little Rock Middle School; Renovations needed

(continued)

TABLE 7.1 North Little Rock School District Schools Five Year Plan Phases I, II, & III (continued)

School Name	Status (2012–2013)	Status (2016–2017)
Poplar Street	*Closed* as a middle school; Students moved to Lakewood and Ridgeroad; *Repurposed* as the 10th grade campus	District offices
Ridgeroad Middle	Serves grads 6, 7, & 8; Scheduled to be renovated and *repurposed* as elementary school Phase II	*Repurposed* as Ridgeroad Elementary
Rose City Middle	*Closed* as a middle school; *Repurposed* as the alternative school for grades 6–12; Students moved to Lakewood, Ridgeroad; 8th graders moved to High School East Campus	*Repurposed* as North Little Rock Academy; No improvements
Total # Middle Schools	2	1
6–12 Alternative		
Argenta Academy	Building *closed*; Academy moves to the former Rose City Middle School; renamed North Little Rock Academy	*Closed* in former building; School *moved* to former Rose City Middle and renamed North Little Rock Academy
Total # Alternative School	1	1
High (1 school, 3 different campuses)		
North Little Rock High–East Campus (Freshman Campus)	Serves Grade 9 & 8th graders that were moved from Rose City & Lakewood Middle	All grades 9–12 attend newly constructed North Little Rock High School; opened Fall 2015; Completed 2016
North Little Rock High–Poplar Street (Sophomore Campus)	Repurposed from Middle School for Phases I and II	District offices
North Little Rock High (Ole Main)	Serves Grades 11 & 12	District offices
Total # High School Campuses	3	1
Total Number of Schools	18[a]	13

Data Source: The North Little Rock Times (Howell, May 31, 2016; North Little Rock school projects, August 16, 2015; Rayburn, January 26, 2012; Rayburn, February 2, 2012; Rayburn, March 22, 2012)

[a] District accounts typically describe the consolidation from 19 to 13 buildings. This accounting includes Belwood Elementary which closed in 2012, prior to the 2012–13 school year.

discussed closing Glenview, the residents of the historically African American community spoke up. "The community did stand up. I know in the Glenview area they said, no, you're not going to close our school." At the meeting in 2013, the district's facilities construction manager confirmed that the plan was still intact (Howell, 2013a).

In July 2012, the district approved designs for the first new elementary school buildings and agreed that the same design would be used for the other new buildings to be built, reducing the fee of the architectural firm (Boulden, 2012). The district received $26 million from the state to finance its plan—considerably less than the $66 maximum allowed. The state also denied the district the funds to build the middle school. Construction began on the high school and the board chose its new superintendent, Kelly Rodgers (Rayburn, 2012f; School Board chooses Rodgers as new superintendent, 2013). In June 2013 the board approved $125 million in construction bonds to help fund the CIP (Howell, 2013b), and eventually sold $65 million in bonds in January, 2015 (Howell, 2015). The district also agreed to cut $8.3 million in operating costs by the 2016–2017 school year in order to adjust for the decreased budget (Howell, 2014c).

Budget constraints delayed completion of the CIP for more than a year. The start of new construction of four elementary schools was delayed in Phase I because "costs for the schools would exceed the projects' budgets" (Blad, 2013a, p. B1). A revised plan was approved in August 2013, a year after the original start date of Phase I. The high school was also projected to be $4 million over budget. The district created savings through "value engineering" or by saving costs on finishes and materials (Blad, 2013a, p. B1, Blad, 2013b). During his first 3 months on the job, Superintendent Rodgers worked on significant changes to the building plans related to these cuts. "I call it cutting, but we didn't cut the size of buildings. What we did, we looked at finishes, and terrazzo floors, we came in with vinyl floors. But all the schools, when you walk into them they're very similar—similar finishes. A lot of the same features."

Additional changes to the plan became necessary when the state denied funds in the CIP designated for remodeling Pike View Elementary as a Pre-K school. State aid was not available for preschools (Howell, 2013c). As a result, the new plan was to continue to educate preschool students in schools throughout the district. Keeping the original CIP within budget required the school district to continually evaluate current and projected enrollment, as well as consider the educational needs of all students.

Glenview Elementary (Photo 7.2), which is in the heart of a historically Black community, was one of the four schools that was rebuilt during Phase I. It is across the street from a community center, which provides programming in collaboration with the school. According to Principal Jones,

Photo 7.2 Glenview Elementary. The school is brand new construction.

students from the school go to the community center for physical education and other services.

Table 7.1 summarizes the district's initial plans and results, after budget and timeline changes impacted progression of the plan. Phase I involved construction of four elementary schools, repurposing of buildings and moving schools to begin the 2012–2013 school year. It was projected to last 12 to 18 months. During Phase I, Belwood Elementary was slotted for closure and students would be sent to Amboy Elementary. Other school closures, rebuilding, and renovations occurred for the following 5 years. Some aspects of Phases II and III were delayed due to budget constraints. As of January 2017, the new middle school has not been built. Otherwise, all other buildings, except the alternative secondary school have been newly built or remodeled.

The Argenta Academy building was closed after the alternative school that was operating there was moved to the former Rose City Middle School. The alternative school was renamed North Little Rock Academy. The middle school students were distributed among Lakewood and Ridgeroad Middle Schools and the High School's East Campus with the freshmen.

After a review of the context of North Little Rock and an overview of the CIP, this chapter turns to an analysis of the district's decision-making processes through an examination of the first research question: How did district leaders and consultants engage in colorblind decision-making processes?

Photo 7.3 Argenta Academy. The original site of the alternative learning high school. The building was McClendin elementary school before that was closed. The alternative education program was moved to the Rose City Middle School building and renamed North Little Rock Academy for grades 6 through 12 in 2012.

Colorblind Decision-Making Processes

Kennedy recollected that, "demographic considerations to the committee took on a very different meaning" as his firm collaborated with the community to develop new school boundaries. This new meaning was a shift from thinking about race to thinking about class and what is best for all students. He described dialogue that took place at one meeting when two women suggested that multiple low-income apartments within the same attendance area be redistributed:

> Because the way they explained it was, "There's poor but then there's *different* poor (speaker's emphasis)." I asked them to explain to me what does "different poor" mean? They said, "They just have less support than other areas in the community where they're poor, but there may be a neighbor, or there may be an uncle, or maybe a family member that can assist. But some of these other areas there is just—it's different."

> And so that kind of became one of the things as we were assembling this plan of how the boundaries would look, is knowing where those particular developments were, could it actually be accommodated where we would be able to have the same resources in multiple buildings to assist with the different student

needs. And so, that became the mantra, if we're talking about, "Well, here's where the African American kids are, here's where the Hispanic kids are," it now became more of a conversation of the entire community and the community is one North Little Rock. And we gotta take care of *all* (speaker's emphasis) of our kids . . . and with them all becoming Title I schools, they would then have access to all the same resources . . . we're eliminating things where "that building's better than this building." So we had a plan where Title I [is] in all of the schools, we've balanced the enrollment with what the capacity is, and then we've aligned some of the programming—specifically with the early childhood in closer proximity to where the students were in need of that service.

Furthermore, Kennedy stated that the committee did not discuss race in relation to the impact of school closings because at the beginning of the process, the board identified its priorities for the outcomes. None of those priorities included an examination of the issues by race:

We're improving all of the schools, the curriculum whether you go to one school or another, it's gonna be the same. As we looked at the maps, there are clear areas in the community where you'll see a clustering of where African American students are, and Hispanic students or White students, so if there was going to be a break, or a division made for demographics, it would go against the criteria that the board had asked for. That's why I say [the term] demographic took on a different meaning, in that it became more socioeconomic.

Ultimately, the board used some demographic data by focusing on socioeconomic class and making sure that the group of students classified as "different poor," were not overrepresented in certain schools. Kennedy's example illustrates that the "different poor" are poor students in under-resourced neighborhoods who were perceived to lack familial or other adult support in the community by the decision-makers. This begs the question if any representatives from the "different poor" demographic were present at any of the meetings, and whether they would identify with this constructed meaning.

The North Little Rock School District was declared unitary in May 2012. The declaration confirmed that the district satisfied all of the federal desegregation requirements placed upon it as a result of a lawsuit that began in 1982. Federal oversight of the district involved court monitors, paperwork, and required state funds to pay for "magnet schools, transfers between districts and other programs to support desegregation and keep a racial balance" (Lawson, 2012a, p. A1). The declaration of unitary status meant that district officials and the board were no longer accountable to federal oversight of its operations. However, unitary status also meant that the district lost its $7.6 million in annual state desegregation aid after the 2017–2018 school year (Howell, 2014c). This was relevant to the CIP for two reasons. First, the decrease in funds meant that the district would have to reallocate funding for the CIP into other district initiatives. Second, being released from federal oversight for racial desegregation meant that a focus on racial outcomes was no longer a required lens through which district leaders had to view educational outcomes.

Superintendent Rodgers pointed out that although the district is no longer under federal oversight for desegregation, the district's capital improvement plan addresses one of the goals of the desegregation plan:

> One of the things in the deseg [*sic*] was the parity or equity in equal facilities. Even the schools that are in high minority areas—they're exactly the same. Now, something we did, Glenview is in an area where we have a high percentage of pre-K students. We put seven pre-K classrooms there [and some campuses] have no pre-K campuses ... and then we took the old Pikeview Elementary school and did not put a gym on it, did not put an art room and remodeled it into a pre-K facility. A high percentage of our pre-K students attend Pikeview and then the rest of the pre-K classrooms are spread throughout the district based on neighborhoods and where the needs are. And that was all part of our demographer and looking at facilities ... and so we made some adjustments in the plan to meet the needs of kindergarten and pre-K students.

Lynch Drive Elementary, in the Rose City neighborhood was originally scheduled to close in June 2015. However, the district announced it would close a year earlier (in June 2014). The students were reassigned to Meadow Park Elementary (Photo 7.4). The decision to close early despite academic gains, was based on the need to save operating costs and to fill the newly constructed

Photo 7.4   Meadow Park Elementary. The school is an entirely new building. The old building was torn down.

Photo 7.5   The empty lot behind the new Meadow Park Elementary school is where the former school was before it was torn down.

Meadow Park Elementary which was slated to open in July but would not have been at capacity without the students from Lynch Drive (Howell, 2014a).

Boone Park Elementary is in the Boone Park neighborhood that was predominately White. It is now primarily composed of African Americans who are loosely described as low-income. The school is one of four that were torn down and rebuilt as brand new buildings.

All of the new buildings were constructed to look almost identical. Superintendent Rodgers reiterated that point: "When you go to our campuses you're going to see very similar finishes, very similar learning areas, open areas, lots of technology, smart TVs that are smart board interactive. Safety was considered." It supports the district's vision that all schools would receive the same resources.

In the final analysis, it is inaccurate to say that characteristics of low income and race determined which schools were closed and which neighborhoods were denied access to a neighborhood school. Not all of the schools that were closed were in poor, African American neighborhoods. However, it is more likely that poor, African American neighborhoods were impacted because two of the three neighborhoods that last schools consisted of primarily Black residents.

The new high school opened in 2015 after some delays, budget issues, community input, and potential eminent domain issues (Photo 7.7). When

Photo 7.6   View of Boone Park Elementary across the street from the empty lot where the former building existed before it was torn down.

Photo 7.7   The newly constructed North Little Rock High School. Construction was ongoing in November 2015. Two of the four towers are visible.

Photo 7.8   The football stadium in November 2015. Grade level towers which are built around the stadium are visible on the left. The back of the old high school is visible in the left background.

it opened, construction was still going on around the students. The new building is drastically different from the old one. It is gray and yellow with a modular appearance. It is divided into four towers where instruction for each grade level will occur—smaller learning communities divided by grade level. The football stadium is built directly adjacent to the back of each tower (Photo 7.8).

The second research question is addressed in the next section: What are the implications of colorblind decision-making about resource allocation and school rebuilding for the demographic composition of schools?

FINDINGS: SCHOOL DEMOGRAPHICS AFTER THE CIP

An Alternative Racialized Perspective

The school district made the decision to avoid establishing race-conscious criteria for school closings and rebuilding in North Little Rock. However, one African American community member, Henry Anderson, did not see the decisions as separate from race. He lived in the area close to North Little Rock Academy and had a racial perspective on the closing of Rose

City Middle School and the move of the alternative school to that building. An examination of the district map indicates that the southeast corner of the district was impacted significantly with the closing of Lynch Drive Elementary and Rose City Middle schools.

When asked about the consequence of there being no school for elementary or non-alternative secondary students in the southeast corner of the district, Kennedy acknowledged that there had been some discussions about that, but his firm was involved after the decisions about the facility master plan had been made.

While Anderson confirmed that the closing of Rose City was because of declining enrollment, he saw an additional layer of race in the decision-making about the school:

> So this building, which is Rose City—and this is the far east part of North Little Rock—was a middle school...Years and years ago, this community was predominately White, and then as African-Americans started moving in, you had White flight. White people started moving out. It became more of a rental property community, more African-Americans started moving in, property values went down. Again, I'm not saying African Americans bring property values down, but that's what happened, because they became more rental properties, and so what happened is that this particular school, more and more low income housing, a lot of affluent African Americans started moving out as well.

> I'm going to tell you another thing that happened is that district people—district people began to encourage high achieving African-American students to transfer out of the school, and not to go to Ridgeroad, which was predominately African American, but to go to Lakewood.

There is no formal documentation that the district engaged in these practices. However, Mr. Anderson is a lifelong resident of the city and felt that while perhaps not formal, the district engaged in race-based decision-making as described. He saw a connection between past practices to encourage the closure of schools in the African American community and the current state of schools in the city.

Charles Jones, the principal of North Little Rock Academy before and after the move to the former Rose City Middle School, lamented the closing of Lynch Drive Elementary (Photo 7.9), which is in the same area of town as the alternative school. Additionally, he identified ways in which the alternative school was not given the same educational resources as other schools. He noted that before the move, the school was in an old elementary building, designed for younger and smaller students: "The chalkboards are lower...so of course, when you're dealing with alternative schools, they make them fit other buildings." He also stated that he is aware that the

Photo 7.9   Lynch Drive Elementary. The building is vacant but was sold in December 2015.

alternative school is somehow considered inferior to the other traditional schools in the district:

> On this side of Broadway [a major street in North Little Rock], you're going to see there's no school in this area other than the alternative school, and the real kind of perception is that the alternative school is really not a real school. That's the perception... They think in terms of bad kids. And we say there's no such thing as a bad kid. There's only bad choices, situations, circumstances."

As part of the guided city tour, the author drove from Meadow Park Elementary to Glenview Elementary. The distance between the two schools was 1.2 miles. This means that the district totally rebuilt two elementary schools very close together, while closing traditional elementary and middle schools in the southeast corner of the district, or on the south side of Broadway Drive.

Another example of this intersection between race and class is in the southeastern neighborhood called Dixie. This neighborhood is historically African American and poor. Redwood Elementary was converted to Redwood Early Learning Center for pre-K students but was sold (Photo 7.10). Consequently, students cannot attend a neighborhood school.

Photo 7.10 The former Redwood Elementary School. It was supposed to become Redwood Early Learning Center, but was sold.

Tables 7.2 and 7.3 show the demographic composition of the district as a whole and by individual school for the 2012–2013 (the year construction started) and 2014–2015 school year (the most recent school data available). All data were retrieved from the Arkansas Department of Education's School Accountability website (https://adesrc.arkansas.gov/). District leaders were clear that the goal of the CIP was to create equal facilities. Students in neighborhoods with different racial demographics would have access to quality buildings no matter where they reside. In other words, the goal was to focus on the physical quality of the buildings, not demographic balance. This was important, particularly given that unitary status was declared in 2012. The district's efforts to focus on facilities rather than race is evidenced in the data.

An analysis of the data reveals that most of the changes in percentage of subgroups in a school are generally within a decrease of 1.5% to an increase of 3%. The total enrollment of Meadow Park Elementary increased by 247 students, yet the overall percent of students in subgroups did not change drastically. The largest percent change was a 3% decrease of low-income students. The biggest percent change in student subgroups was at Crestwood Elementary. African American students increased by 8.2% while White students decreased by 9%.

TABLE 7.2 North Little Rock School District Student Demographics, 2012–2013

School	Total Enrollment	Percentage									
		American Indian/ Alaskan	Asian	Black/ African American	Hawaiian/ Pacific Islander	Hispanic/ Latino	White	2 or More Races	Lmtd. English Prof.	Low Income	Eligible for Special Education
District	8,610	0.3	1.5	58.2	0.0*	6.7	33.1	0.2	5.0	70.0	9.0
Elementary School (P–5)											
Amboy	371	0.5	0.3	71.2	0.0	12.1	15.6	0.3	9.0	97.0	9.0
Boone Park	359	0.0	1.1	90.3	0.0	2.2	6.4	0.0	2.0	97.0	16.0
Crestwood	463	0.9	3.7	23.5	0.0	2.4	69.1	0.4	2.0	42.0	10.0
Glenview	170	0.0	0.0	81.8	0.6	3.5	14.1	0.0	3.0	96.0	18.0
Indian Hills	612	0.5	3.1	23.9	0.3	1.8	70.1	0.3	1.0	35.0	8.0
Lakewood	437	0.2	2.5	28.4	0.0	3.7	64.8	0.5	3.0	44.0	6.0
Lynch Drive	242	0.0	0.0	86.8	0.0	1.2	12.0	0.0	1.0	99.0	12.0
Meadow Park	183	0.5	0.0	90.2	0.0	3.3	4.4	1.6	2.0	99.0	13.0
North Heights	411	0.0	0.2	60.3	0.0	27.0	12.4	0.0	20.0	97.0	5.0
Park Hill	311	0.6	1.0	55.3	0.0	12.9	29.6	0.6	10.0	86.0	11.0
Pikeview	343	0.0	2.6	73.5	0.0	10.8	13.1	0.0	11.0	92.0	9.0
Seventh Street	254	0.0	0.8	94.1	0.0	1.6	2.4	1.2	1.0	98.0	15.0
Middle School (6–8)											
Lakewood	1,141	0.4	1.8	50.9	0.1	3.2	43.4	0.3	2.0	61.0	8.0
Ridgeroad	693	0.1	0.7	75.2	0.0	12.0	11.8	0.1	9.0	91.0	13.0
High School (9–12) & Alternative School (6–12)											
NLR Academy	164	0.0	0.0	89.6	0.0	3.0	7.3	0.0	2.0	96.0	18.0
NLR High School	2,456	0.2	1.6	55.6	0.0	6.2	36.4	0.0	3.0	59.0	7.0

TABLE 7.3 North Little Rock School District Student Demographics, 2014–2015

School	Total Enrollment	American Indian/ Alaskan	Asian	Black/ African American	Hawaiian/ Pacific Islander	Hispanic/ Latino	White	2 or More Races	Lmtd. English Prof.	Low Income	Eligible for Special Education
		Percentage									
District	8,576	0.3	1.2	59.0	0.0	7.9	31.1	0.4	5.0	71.0	10.0
Elementary Schools (P–5)											
Amboy	377	0.3	0.0	68.4	0.0	12.2	18.0	1.1	6.0	93.0	8.0
Boone Park	340	0.3	0.6	86.5	0.0	4.1	8.5	0.0	2.0	99.0	14.0
Crestwood	499	0.8	3.4	31.7	0.0	3.4	60.1	0.6	2.0	44.0	12.0
Glenview	164	0.0	0.0	76.8	0.6	6.7	15.2	0.6	5.0	99.0	13.0
Indian Hills	575	0.2	2.3	27.3	0.3	2.1	67.8	0.0	1.0	37.0	9.0
Lakewood	423	0.5	0.9	25.5	0.0	5.0	67.6	0.5	3.0	38.0	9.0
Lynch Drive	Closed										
Meadow Park	430	0.0	0.2	88.8	0.0	4.4	5.8	0.7	3.0	96.0	12.0
North Heights	415	0.5	0.0	55.2	0.0	30.1	14.0	0.2	24.0	97.0	6.0
Park Hill	324	0.0	2.2	75.7	0.0	9.6	11.0	0.8	9.0	93.0	11.0
Pikeview	354	0.6	2.3	75.7	0.0	9.6	11.0	0.8	9.0	93.0	11.0
Seventh Street	286	0.7	0.0	95.1	0.0	0.3	3.1	0.7	N/D	99.0	16.0
Middle Schools (6–8)											
Lakewood	1,149	0.3	1.4	51.7	0.0	3.4	42.6	0.5	1.0	58.0	9.0
Rideroad	618	0.2	0.0	73.0	0.0	15.2	11.5	0.2	10.0	91.0	11.0
High School (9–12) & Alternative School (6–12)											
NLR Academy	154	0.0	0.0	89.0	0.0	4.5	6.5	0.0	4.0	91.0	19.0
NLR High School	2,468	0.2	1.3	59.0	0.0	7.4	31.7	0.4	4.0	62.0	8.0

Many of the schools were largely single-race majority schools, meaning that White or African American students were highly over-represented in a single building, compared to the subgroup's representation within the entire district. In 2014–2015, while African American students comprised 59% of the district population, the subgroup constituted 68.4% of Amboy elementary students, 86.5% of Crestwood elementary, 76.8% of Glenview elementary, 88.8% of Meadow Park elementary, 75.7% of Pikeview elementary, 95.1% of Seventh Street elementary, 73.0% of Ridgeroad Middle School and 89.0% of North Little Rock Academy (the alternative school). White students comprised 31.1% of the district, yet made up 60.1% of the student population at Crestwood Elementary, 67.8% of students at Indian Hills Elementary, 67.6% of students at Lakewood Elementary, and 42.6% of students at Lakewood Middle School.

The percent of students classified as low-income was 71%. Several schools in the district had a higher percent of students in that subgroup in their schools. Students classified as low-income made up 93% of the students at Amboy elementary, 99% of students at Boone Park, Glenview, and Seventh Street Elementary schools, and 97% of North Heights Elementary. The middle schools had drastically different representations of low-income students. The total population of Lakewood Middle was almost double that of Ridgeroad Middle yet the percent of low-income students at Lakewood was 58% compared to 91% at Ridgeroad.

All of the schools with over 71% students who are low-income also had an overrepresentation of African American students, except for North Heights and Park Hill elementary schools. Both had an overrepresentation of Latino students, at 30.1% and 17.6% respectively, compared to 7.9% representation of Latino students in the district as a whole.

Demographic data in the district mirrors national data about race and schools. Schools that are majority African American and Latino are also majority low-income. Majority White schools that are not rural (as is the case in North Little Rock), are also not majority low-income. Crestwood, Indian Hills, and Lakewood Elementary schools which were at least 60% White, and between 37% and 44% of students were low-income.

Data regarding the overrepresentation of race and low-income subgroups in certain schools is relevant to an analysis of the significance of the CIP. In one respect, this work offers evidence consistent with the narrative of closing majority-African American schools and thus creating a burden on families to relocate to different schools. African American, Latino and poor students were overrepresented in Lynch Drive, North Heights, and Park Hill (i.e., the schools that closed).

However, that is not the only narrative to come out of the district's plan. The five elementary schools were completely rebuilt with brand-new buildings. Of the five, four of them had majority-African American and low-income student populations: Amboy (68.4% and 93%); Boone Park (86.5% and 99%); Glenview (76.8% and 99%), and Meadow Park (88.8% and 96%). Even though there was a redrawing of school zone boundaries along with the new schools, the fact that the district invested in new buildings and equitable resources for all of the schools disrupts, or at minimum, complicates the narrative regarding inequitable resource allocation for Black and Brown students. On one level, the outcomes of the CIP challenge Jim Crow realities of separate and unequal neighborhood schools based on race. It begs the question, what does it mean to support a plan that does not manage, or seek to mitigate racial segregation as a result of neighborhood demographics, but focuses on capital investments in all of its schools?

Additional questions remain unanswered. In the coming years, as additional supplies, new technologies, or building upkeep are needed, it is possible that donations from parent organizations in schools with fewer students characterized as low-income will be greater than in the schools with higher numbers of students characterized as low-income. It remains to be seen how the social capital of middle-class and White parents is used to leverage community resources and donations and collaborations that overshadow those of poor, Black and Brown families. These unknowns have the potential to reinscribe inequities in the buildings.

DISCUSSION

Although many schools in our nation are racially segregated (Orfield, Ee, Frankenberg, & Siegel-Hawley, 2016), the case of the CIP in North Little Rock defies the assumed narrative that the "poor, Black schools" would get closed and those students would not have access to top-notch educational resources. In other words, the district turned the separate but (un)equal narrative of disservice to Black, Brown and poor students on its head in one aspect, by investing in equal facilities for all students throughout the district, within the reality of racially unbalanced schools. This financial investment is a statement of support for all students. It supports the old adage, "Put your money where your mouth is." The district did that in meaningful ways by investing in new schools towards its mission of creating world class schools.

The Entire District: All in and Equal?

In July, 2012 when the district decided to reduce its middle schools from three to two (and ultimately one), its leaders emphasized that each school would receive the same quality of equipment and resources so there would not be unequal distribution of resources or perceived unequal distribution.

The district spokesperson stated that both middle schools had been equipped similarly "so that students will receive the same educational experience if they attend either building" (Rayburn, 2012e, p. A6).

David Kennedy stated that the focus on the entire district as opposed to individual subgroups was a surprise and welcome change to district planning:

> It became more "we're North Little Rock." I think that had such a positive influence on the process that when the board made their recommendation to approve the boundaries, all of the board members—it didn't matter what their background was—were like, "Wow, we didn't imagine that it would go this way," . . . And so, this was probably by far one of the best experiences that we've ever had facilitating the process.

Kennedy also thought the fact that every school except for the alternative school was upgraded in some fashion, contributed to the successful community collaboration towards the plan and eliminated possible feelings of marginalization. He noted, "I can't think of really any district that's been able to do that. It eliminated the perceptions [about] conditions and made excellent places for students to have a learning environment."

However, issues of class and race remain visible. For instance, schools that were originally set to close remained open due to the community's agency. However, the southeast section of North Little Rock lost its schools. Evelyn Marks saw this through the lens of class: "You know, in the Rose City area . . . there's a lot of rental properties. People are—socioeconomically they are—They don't have the funding."

Race was a salient issue with African Americans in the community. White participants did not see anything significant about race and celebrated the removal of race as an issue in the district's plan. This suggests that there is, in fact, much work to do. Although the planning and enrollment projection data was objectively gathered with the intention of not making race-based decisions, it is clear that there is a different impact on communities based on the intersection of race and class—those being African American and lower middle class to poor.

When discussing the closing of Lynch Drive and Redwood Elementary/Early Learning Center, Principal Jones's reflection was reminiscent of earlier comments about the burden on Blacks:

> I think you'll see the issues are with the kids in the African-American neighborhoods, they're going to be bussed out. The kids in some of the White neighborhoods, there's a possibility that you might be bussed out. Not necessarily that you would be, but there's a possibility, but if there's no school in your neighborhood, you're going to be bussed out.

Leaders in the North Little Rock School District set out to challenge the discriminatory practices of separate and unequal funding and resource allocation based on race and income in the development and execution of the CIP. Hence, discussions about its goals centered on equitable resource allocation. One might claim that the plan was a success when viewed through the lens of financial and building resources. A more significant assessment of the extent to which world class schools (as stated in the district's vision statement) are achieved, is whether all student subgroups are provided equitable access to high-quality instruction and achievement.

NOTES

1. The one exception was an alternative learning school, which would eventually move into a repurposed middle school building.
2. The author transcribed three of the interviews. The remaining interviews were professionally transcribed (the contractor signed confidentiality agreements).
3. The collective described its history and purpose: Wanting to capture the last moments of these public spaces—some of which had served generations of students and their families for nearly 100 years and all of which were important community cornerstones... The Philadelphia School Closing Photo Collective was born and grew to include not only amateur, hobby, and professional photographers, but other artists and concerned citizens using poetry and other formats to document and reflect on the meanings of these closings to the individuals committed to working there, as well as the students, families, and communities these schools served. (Bach, Finkel, Holman, Saul, & Smith, 2014, p. 8).
4. One mill equals one thousandth, or .001 of one dollar (Miller, Karov, & McCullough, n.d.). "Local millage rates determine the amount you pay per $1,000 of assessed value" (p. 2). An owner of a property with a taxable value by the county assessor of $100,000, and is assessed a 1 mill tax rate, owes $100 in taxes. Property with a tax value assessed at $200,000 yields $200 in taxes. At the time of the discussion about the special election, the millage rate was 40.9 mills (Rayburn, 2012a), resulting in a $4,090 tax bill for a property owner whose property was valued at $100,000. The district's proposal of a 7.4 millage increase to 48.3 mills would result in the property owner mentioned above paying an increase of $740 a year, for a total of $4,830.

REFERENCES

Andrews, M., Duncombe, W., & Yinger, J. (2002). Revisiting economies of size in American education: Are we any closer to a consensus? *Economics of Education Review, 21*(3), 245–262.

Arkansas School Report Cards. (2016–2017). Arkansas Department of Education. North Little Rock School District. Retrieved from https://adesrc.arkansas .gov/

Bach, A., Finkel, H., Holman, M., Saul, J., & Smith, T. (2014). Philadelphia school closings photo collective statement. *Perspectives on Urban Education, 11*(2), 8–9.

Blad, E. (2012, February 14). Tax vote in NLR is today. *Arkansas Democrat-Gazette,* p. B1.

Blad, E. (2013a, August, 27). NLR board approves revised school projects. *Arkansas Democrat-Gazette,* pp. B1, B8.

Blad, E. (2013b, September 13). NLR high school renovation changes OK'd. *Arkansas Democrat-Gazette,* p. B3.

Bonilla-Silva, E., & Forman, T. A. (2000). "I am not a racist but…": Mapping White college students' racial ideology in the USA. *Discourse & Society, 11*(1), 50–85.

Boulden, B. (2012, July 26). School board OKs design for new schools. *The North Little Rock Times,* p. B4.

Bradburn, C. (2004). *On the opposite shore: The making of North Little Rock.* North Little Rock, AR: City of North Little Rock.

Choi, J. (2008). Unlearning colorblind ideologies in education class. *Educational Foundations, Summer-Fall,* 53–71.

Cope, G. (2015). "Something would develop to prevent it": North Little Rock and school desegregation, 1954–1957. *The Arkansas Historical Quarterly, 74*(2), 109–129.

Crenshaw, K. W. (1988). Race, reform, and retrenchment: Transformation and legitimation in antidiscrimination law. *Harvard Law Review, 101*(7), 1331–1387.

Delgado, R., & Stefancic, J. (2017). *Critical race theory: An introduction.* (3rd ed). New York, NY: New York University Press.

Deeds, V., & Pattillo, M. (2015). Organizational "failure" and institutional pluralism: A case study of an urban school closure. *Urban Education, 50*(4), 474–504. doi:10.1177/0042085913519337

Evans, A. E. (2007). School leaders and their sensemaking about race and demographic change. *Educational Administration Quarterly, 43*(2), 159–188. doi:10.1177/0013151X06294575

Finnigan, K. S., & Lavner, M. (2012). A political analysis of community influence over school closure. *Urban Review, 44*(1), 133–151. doi:10.1007/s11256-001-0179-9

Gotanda, N. (1991). A critique of "our constitution is colorblind." *Stanford Law Review, 44*(1), 1–68.

Howard, T. C., & Navarro, O. (2016). Critical race theory 20 years later: Where do we go from here? *Urban Education, 51*(3), 253–273. doi:10.1177/0042085915622541

Howell, C. (2013a, May 31). 2 school projects in NLR a go, forum is assured. *Arkansas Democrat-Gazette,* p. B4.

Howell, C. (2013b, June 21). Bond Sale OK'd for NLR schools. *Arkansas Democrat-Gazette,* pp. B1, B8.

Howell, C. (2013c, May 7). NLR district wants $9.25 million more in state school aid. *Arkansas Democrat-Gazette,* pp. B1, B2.

Howell, C. (2014a, April 18). Lynch Drive Elementary approved to close in June. *Arkansas Democrat-Gazette,* pp. B1, B5.

Howell, C. (2014b, December 17). NLR board backs $20M in school upgrades. *Arkansas Democrat-Gazette*, p. B6.

Howell, C. (2015a, January 22). NLR School Board OKs sale of $65.5M in bonds. *Arkansas Democrat-Gazette*, p. B2.

Kretchmar, K. (2014). Democracy (In)action: A critical policy analysis of New York school closings by teachers, students, administrators, and community members. *Education and Urban Society, 46*(1), 3–29. doi:10.1177/0013124511424108

Ladson-Billings, G., & Tate, W. F., IV. (1995). Toward a critical race theory of education. *Teachers College Record, 97*(1), 47–68.

Lawson, B. (2012a, May 31). NLR schools declared unitary. *The North Little Rock Times*, p. A1, A5.

Ledesma, M. C., & Calderón, D. (2015). Critical race theory in education: A review of past literature and a look to the future. *Qualitative Inquiry, 21*(3), 206–222. doi:10.1177/1077800414557825

Lewis, A. E. (2001). There is no "race" in the schoolyard: Colorblind ideology in an (almost) all-White school. *American Educational Research Journal, 38*(4), 781–811.

Lopez, G. R. (2003). The (racially neutral) politics of education: A critical race theory perspective. *Educational Administration Quarterly, 39*(1), 68–94.

Lynn, M., & Adams, M. (2002). Introductory overview to the special issue critical race theory and education: Recent developments in the field. *Equity & Excellence in Education, 35*(2), 87–92.

Miller, W., Karov, V., & McCullough, S. (n.d.). Administration of Arkansas' Property Tax (FSPPC114). Fayetteville: The University of Arkansas Division of Agriculture's Public Policy Center. Retrieved from https://www.arcountydata.com/docs/UofA_ADMIN_OF_ARK_PROPERTY_TAX.pdf

North Little Rock School Projects. (2015, August 16). *Arkansas Democrat-Gazette*. Retrieved from https://www.arkansasonline.com/news/2015/aug/16/north-little-rock-school-projects/

Orfield, G., Ee., J., Frankenberg, E., & Siegel-Hawley, G. (2016). *Brown at 62: School segregation by race, poverty, and state*. Civil Rights Project/Proyecto Derechos Civiles. Retrieved from https://files.eric.ed.gov/fulltext/ED565900.pdf

Parker, L., & Lynn, M. (2002). What's race got to do with it? Critical race theory's conflicts with and connections to qualitative research methodology and epistemology. *Qualitative Inquiry, 8*(1), 7–22.

Philadelphia School Closings Photo Collective Statement. (n.d.). Retrieved from http://urbanedjournal.org/archive/volume-11-issue-2-summer-2014/philadelphia-school-closings-photo-collective-statement

Post, D., & Stambach, A. (1999). District consolidation and rural school closure: E pluribus unum? *Journal of Research in Rural Education, 15*(2), 106–117.

Rayburn, G. (2012a, January 19). NLRSD hopes voters approve proposed 7.4 millage increase. *The North Little Rock Times*, pp. A1, A9.

Rayburn, G. (2012b, January 26). NLR schools want more funds for five-year plan. *The North Little Rock Times*, p. A5.

Rayburn, G. (2012c, February 2). Early voting nears for millage. *The North Little Rock Times*, pp. A1, A8.

Rayburn, G. (2012d, February 16). NLR millage increase passes. *The North Little Rock Times*, pp. A1, A7.

Rayburn, G. (2012e, July 5). Changes planned for upcoming school year at NLRSD. *The North Little Rock Times*, p. A6.

Rayburn, G. (2012f, May 9). State allots $26 million for NLR school plan. *The North Little Rock Times*, p. A1, A3.

Saldaña, J. (2016). *The coding manual for qualitative researchers*. (3rd ed.). Thousand Oaks, CA: SAGE.

School Board chooses Rodgers as new superintendent. (2013, February 7). *The North Little Rock* Times, p. A1.

Seidman, I. (2006). *Interviewing as qualitative research: A guide for researchers in education and the social sciences* (3rd ed.). New York, NY: Teachers College Press.

Siegel-Hawley, G., Bridges, K., & Shields, T. J. (2017). Solidifying segregation or promoting diversity? School closure and rezoning in an urban district. *Educational Administration Quarterly, 53*(1), 107–141. doi:10.1177/0013161X16659346

Stake, R. E. (1995). *The art of case study research*. Thousand Oaks, CA: SAGE.

The Encyclopedia of Arkansas History and Culture. (n.d.). North Little Rock (Pulaski County). Retrieved from http://www.encyclopediaofarkansas.net/encyclopedia/entry-detail.aspx?entryID=973

U.S. Census. (2010). Quick Facts. North Little Rock city Arkansas. Retrieved from http://www.census.gov/quickfacts/table/PST045215/0550450

SECTION II

IMPLICATIONS

CHAPTER 8

THE EFFECTS OF PUBLIC ELEMENTARY SCHOOLS CLOSURES ON NEIGHBORHOOD HOUSING VALUES IN U.S. METROPOLITAN AREAS, 2000–2010

Noli Brazil
University of California, Davis

ABSTRACT

Public school closures have become increasingly common in the United States, particularly in urban areas. Public reaction to the recent rash of school closures has been contentious and largely negative. A key component to the argument against school closures is that they negatively affect the economic health and well-being of local neighborhoods, which they might do in a number of ways including signaling neighborhood disinvestment and

Shuttered Schools, pages 231–257
Copyright © 2019 by Information Age Publishing
231

introducing physical blight when school buildings remain vacant. Combining 2000–2010 school-level data from the National Center for Education Statistics Common Core of Data with neighborhood-level data from the Census, the current study examines the effects of public elementary school closures in metropolitan areas on an important indicator of neighborhood economic health—housing values. I found a statistically significant negative association between the neighborhood elementary school closure rate and median housing values. This negative impact is greater in neighborhoods with larger proportions of African-Americans. However, I found no moderating effect for neighborhood percent Hispanic, and a positive effect for percent White. I found that elementary school open rates were positively associated with housing values, indicating a possible counterbalancing or replacement effect to a school closure.

Public school closures have become increasingly common in the United States. In the 2013–2014 school year, 1,785 public schools closed, up 43% from 1,248 in 1998–1999 (National Center for Education Statistics [NCES], 2013). Urban areas, in particular, have witnessed the largest increases. The percent of school closures in central cities with populations greater than or equal to 250,000 increased from 11.6% in 1998–1999 to 21.3% in 2013–2014 (NCES, 2013). The largest mass public school closing in U.S. history occurred in 2013, when 49 elementary schools closed in Chicago. Once a largely rural phenomenon, public school closures have become an increasingly popular strategy in urban school reform.

The increase in public school closures in urban areas has been met with strong opposition. A key component to the argument against school closures is that they negatively impact local neighborhoods (Anderson, 2015). In particular, claims often allude to the potential negative effects of school closures on the economic health of local communities (Cohen, 2016). Since Tiebout's (1956) seminal piece, arguing that households "vote with their feet" in response to preferences over packages of local public goods, a large body of literature has documented strong associations between local schools and various indicators of neighborhood economic well-being, in particular housing prices, supply of housing, unemployment rates, and capital investments in the housing stock (Hilber & Mayer, 2009; Horn, 2015; Nguyen-Hoang & Yinger, 2011; Oates, 1969). Public school closures might negatively impact the economic health of local neighborhoods by signaling disinvestment in already declining communities, eliminating schools as community resources, and introducing blight if they remain vacant after closure. Opponents further argue that because school closures are typically located in low-income and majority-Black neighborhoods, whose residents often rely on local schools for resources beyond those provided to resident youth, it is these neighborhoods that bear the brunt of the impact, making it "all the more likely that these neighborhoods will deteriorate further" (Strauss, 2013, n.p.).

Although the effects of school closures on neighborhoods have received significant attention from public school advocates and the media, they have been largely neglected in the academic literature. Combining 2000–2010 school-level data from the NCES Common Core of Data with neighborhood-level data from the Census, the current chapter fills this gap by examining the effects of metropolitan public elementary school closures on an important indicator of neighborhood economic health—housing values. I examine the effects of school closures on all metropolitan neighborhoods, and examine any differential effects based on neighborhood racial composition. In the following sections, I delineate the various hypotheses regarding the effects of school closures on neighborhood housing values, first examining their potential positive effects and then outlining their negative consequences. I then describe the data and methods for the analyses, followed by an outline of the results. I conclude the chapter with a discussion of the main findings and implications for policy and future scholarly research.

LINKING PUBLIC SCHOOL CLOSURES WITH NEIGHBORHOOD HOUSING VALUES

Housing values provide a window into household demand for public services, including the quality and health of the local public school. Tiebout sorting theory, which asserts that households make residential decisions in response to local differences in public services, forms the theoretical framework linking public schools to neighborhood housing values (Tiebout, 1956). According to this theory, a residential location is a collection of desirable characteristics such as shelter, local amenities, and comfort. By treating a residential location as a sum of its parts, a hedonic model generates estimates of a household's willingness to pay for each component characteristic. Homeownership is a form of investment in a neighborhood, as it is highly correlated with neighborhood tenure, attachment, and satisfaction (Rohe, McCarthy, & Van Zandt, 2000). Therefore, the amount a household is willing to pay for a house is a measure of their initial investment in the neighborhood. At an aggregate level, higher homeownership rates and property values proxy greater resident investment.

In a simplified hedonic model, households derive satisfaction from consuming a set of residential characteristics. They earn an income y and can only consume combinations of Z that are affordable to that income. Preferences for different combinations of Z vary according to a set of socioeconomic characteristics X such as household size and race/ethnicity. The amount a household with income y and characteristics X is willing to pay to live in a location with characteristics Z is derived from the following equation

$$R = R(z_1, z_2, \ldots, z_n, X, y)$$

The actual price must account for the local tax rate and discounted for present value

$$P = \frac{R(z_1, z_2, \ldots, z_n, X, y)}{\theta + \tau_R}$$

The hedonic price function describes the highest price offered for a residential location as a function of its characteristics, which include neighborhood characteristics as well as local school characteristics.

A long line of literature has shown that school characteristics play an integral role in determining P (Nguyen-Hoang & Yinger, 2011). In general, households are willing to pay higher housing prices in neighborhoods with quality schools (Oates, 1969). Many families use school quality as the sole or primary factor for choosing a neighborhood (Lareau, 2014). In the words of one prospective buyer evaluating a neighborhood, "we didn't even look [there] because the schools . . . they're just bad" (Holme, 2002, p. 193). Although much of the literature has focused on families with school-aged children, there is evidence that local schools influence the residential selection of households without children (Hilber & Mayer, 2009). Because school quality is capitalized into house prices, childless households may choose neighborhoods with good schools to maximize home values. In this context, households pay for housing based not only on their own preferences, but also those of eventual buyers (Brueckner & Joo, 1991).

From the theoretical framework established in this section, we can generate hypotheses regarding the positive and negative effects of school closures on housing values. A school's quality is often measured by its academic performance, with many empirical studies finding strong positive associations between school academic achievement and local housing values. According to Tiebout sorting theory, if closed schools are generally lower performing, closures should curb declining home values, and potentially increase them if higher quality schools replace closed schools. However, academic performance may not be the only school characteristic capitalized into local home values. Schools often provide local neighborhoods, particularly disadvantaged and predominantly Black communities, with resources beyond those provided to resident youth. Closures take these resources away from local neighborhoods, thus leading to a decrease in housing values, which may have been already declining in historically disinvested communities. The following sections further outline these and other countervailing effects.

POSITIVE EFFECTS OF SCHOOL CLOSURES
ON NEIGHBORHOOD ECONOMIC WELL-BEING

Closures might lead to greater neighborhood economic health if they remove public schools with characteristics that pull down housing values. Poor academic performance is a commonly cited reason for closing a school (De la Torre & Gwynne, 2009). Driven by the No Child Left Behind Act (NCLB), federal and state education laws have encouraged the closure of chronically low performing schools. NCLB requires districts to divide schools into academic tiers based on performance on state standardized tests, and provides funding for interventions in the lowest performing schools, many of which might arguably be considered near or complete closure. As such, NCLB established school closure as a convenient remedy for low academic performance. NCLB sanctions may lower housing values for neighborhoods attached to failing schools, as Bogin and Ngyuen-Hoang (2014) found in their study of housing sale transactions in Charlotte. In this case, neighborhoods may be better off closing their failing schools in order to curb the negative cascading effects of NCLB sanctions on housing values. In general, several studies have found a strong positive association between school standardized test scores and local housing values. In a comprehensive review of these studies, Nguyen-Hoang and Yinger (2011) found that on average a one standard deviation improvement in school test scores is associated with a 1 to 4% increase in nearby housing values.

Declining student enrollment, budget constraints, and substandard building conditions are other common reasons for closing schools in urban neighborhoods (De la Torre, Gordon, Moore, & Cowhy, 2015). In turn, these characteristics may be depressing local neighborhood housing values. Using data from Florida, Figlio and Lucas (2004) find that state assigned school grades, which combine standardized test scores with other school characteristics such as suspension and absenteeism rates, were strongly associated with housing sale prices. Brasington (1999) found that expenditures per pupil and pupil–teacher ratios are capitalized into housing prices. Underfunded schools with declining enrollment, high mobility rates, and poor academic performance may compel wealthier residents to move out of their neighborhoods. In turn, these residents are either not replaced or substituted by lower income residents who provide a lower tax base for the community, which then compels businesses to move out.

School closures may not only curb declining home values, but also increase them if closed schools are replaced by higher quality schools. Burdick-Will, Keels, and Schuble (2013) found neighborhoods in Chicago that lost schools were also the neighborhoods most likely to receive new schools. They hypothesized that "to the extent that Chicago's new schools do indeed provide enhanced academic opportunities, one could take the view that those who most need new schools are receiving them" (p. 78).

The communitarian argument against school closures offers an opposing view—school closures "disrupt," "destabilize," and "devastate" communities. Opponents of school closures argue that these effects are particularly true in disadvantaged, minority neighborhoods that rely on schools for a wide variety of community resources. The next section addresses these claims by describing the reasons why school closures may negatively impact the economic health of local neighborhoods.

NEGATIVE EFFECTS OF SCHOOL CLOSURES ON NEIGHBORHOOD ECONOMIC WELL-BEING

There are at least three possible ways in which public school closures might negatively impact neighborhood housing values. First, schools provide non-education specific resources that are capitalized into local housing values. Closing schools takes these resources away from the neighborhood and thus reduces its housing values. Second, school closures introduce physical blight if school buildings remain vacant. Third, closures signal disinvestment in the neighborhood.

Public schools can provide two types of noneducation specific resources to the local neighborhood—physical infrastructure (school buildings and grounds) and community services. Schools have an incentive for opening their buildings to the community given that community use often helps secure support for the tax increases required to pay for school construction bonds (Filardo, Vincent, Allen, & Franklin, 2010). Similarly, school facilities benefit community organizations because of their size, scale, affordability, proximity, and specialized spaces (Vincent, 2014). Most school districts currently have obligations, in law or in practice, to allow some levels of general public use of grounds for recreation and to support civic uses, such as voting, community meetings, and special events (Filardo et al., 2010). For example, churches regularly use school auditoriums for services and government agencies often locate offices in underutilized schools. Schools also offer large open spaces that are tailored for youth activities (e.g., playgrounds, open fields, basketball courts), which are especially important in urban areas where publicly accessible and safe spaces for physical activity and recreation are limited (Vincent, 2014). Several studies have found that an increased shared use of facilities outside of school hours is associated with greater youth physical activity and lower rates of juvenile delinquency (Eccles & Templeton, 2002; Kanters et al., 2014).

Once a public school is closed, its facilities are often no longer available for public use. Figure 8.1 shows the percentage of school buildings by use

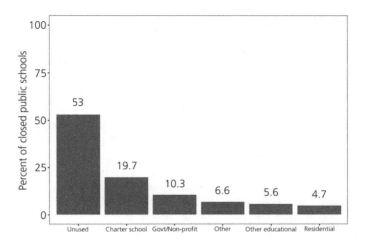

Figure 8.1 Percent of closed public school buildings by purpose after closure, 12 cities, 2005–2012. *Source:* Adapted from (Dowdall & Warner, 2013)

after school closure between 2005 and 2012 in 12 large cities in the United States (Dowdall & Warner, 2013). About a quarter of school buildings were repurposed for educational uses, such as conversion into charter and private schools. The rest, however, were either still on the market or sold to government and private organizations for residential and office space.

In addition to their buildings, public schools can offer noneducation specific services to local residents (Brazil, 2016). Schools often collaborate with community organizations to sponsor community interventions and offer educational, health, economic, and social services. For example, the San Francisco Unified School District has more than 400 nonprofit organizations operating programs in one or more of the city's nearly 97 public schools (Filardo et al., 2010). More than two-thirds of school-based health centers nationwide, which is a collaboration of public health departments, local hospitals, nonprofit organizations, and school systems offering medical services, such as immunizations and illness prevention care, within public schools, reported providing services to individuals beyond the student population (Keeton, Soleimanpour, & Brindis, 2012). Schools can also empower local residents by acting as important sources of local employment and offering leadership opportunities within the school to parents and other community members (Chung, 2002; Warren, Hong, Rubin, & Uy, 2009). For example, the Los Angeles Unified School District is the third largest employer in Los Angeles County, which has a population of approximately 10 million (Chung, 2002).

Poor, Black inner-city neighborhoods in particular rely on local schools as vital sources for community services. Wilson (1987) argues that macro-social and economic trends beginning in the 1970s including middle-class Black suburbanization and the deindustrialization of cities led to the ecological concentration of poor Blacks in the inner city. Because of private and government institutional disinvestment, low levels of political capital, and severe isolation from the mainstream, poor Black inner-city neighborhoods lack access to basic resources including healthy food, medical services, educational support, skills training, and employment opportunities (Squires & Kubrin, 2005; Massey & Denton, 1993; Wilson, 1987). This also includes safe areas for after school play, which are in short supply in inner city neighborhoods that lack open space and are often unsafe during after school hours (Gallimore, Brown, & Werner, 2011). Residents in disadvantaged and isolated communities often rely on public neighborhood institutions such as local schools for these resources. Schools can also act as resource brokers that connect socially isolated residents to businesses, nonprofits, and government agencies (Small, 2006). This is the perspective of the community schools movement, which promotes collaboration between community-based organizations and public schools. Proponents of this movement often frame community schools as equalizers of neighborhood racial and socioeconomic inequality because they can offer the health and social services that are severely lacking in minority neighborhoods (Dryfoos, 1994; Warren, 2005).

Figure 8.1 also shows that more than half of school properties are unsold (Dowdall & Warner, 2013). The typical urban school for sale is old, large, and located in a residential area, limiting its resale ability (Dowdall & Warner, 2013). Demolition is often more expensive than keeping buildings up and not maintaining them (Dowdall & Warner, 2013). By remaining unsold, closed schools prevent the land from being used in a productive manner, particularly as a tax-generating vehicle for the local community, which then depresses nearby housing values.

The negative effects of abandoned school buildings are magnified if they deteriorate, becoming magnets for illicit activities. The association between abandoned buildings and crime is rooted in theories of neighborhood disorder, specifically the broken windows theory. According to this theory, visual cues of disorder attract crime because offenders assume from these cues that residents are indifferent to what goes on in the neighborhood (Wilson & Kelling, 1982). Anecdotal evidence shows that residents often associate local criminal activity with abandoned school buildings. For example, after a murder that took place in an abandoned school building in Decatur, GA, residents observed that the building was "a bed of bad activity" and complained that by leaving the school abandoned, the district was "sticking a dagger in [their] neighborhood" (Harding, 2016). Studies have found positive associations between vacancy rates and criminal activity (Cui & Walsh, 2015; Raleigh & Galster, 2015). For example, Spelman (1993) found that crimes such as drug dealing and prostitution were found to take place within the confines of over 80% of abandoned buildings surveyed in certain areas.

Abandoned buildings also introduce health and environmental hazards into the neighborhood. Abandoned buildings are more susceptible to fires caused by accident or arson, which can also damage neighboring property, including residential units. Other hazards include rodent infestation, toxic waste proliferation, and general waste disposal (Anderson, 2015). Skogan (1992) argues that increased hazards associated with neighborhood physical disorder discourage commercial and residential investment. One study estimates that local governments lose up to $6 billion in revenue from abandoned buildings due to lost property taxes (Bass et al., 2005). Other studies have linked physical disorder to decreased neighborhood satisfaction and increased residential mobility (Sampson, 2012). Several studies have found that vacant buildings decrease local property values (Han, 2014; Mikelbank, 2008; Shlay & Whitman, 2006), which in turn reduces the likelihood of further investment in the area, creating a cascading downward cycle of diminished housing values.

The third way school closures affect neighborhood economic health is by signaling disinvestment in the neighborhood. Homebuyers and current residents often use the health of local public schools as a barometer for neighborhood quality. Public school closures signal complete school failure, which in turn represent a symptom of neighborhood decline for prospective and current residents. The signal is magnified if school buildings remain vacant. Abandonment has been viewed as an indicator of market failure, a symptom of disinvestment, or the result of a neighborhood's life cycle, instead of being viewed as a problem itself (Accordino & Johnson, 2000).

The image of a neighborhood's public school has many implications, including how it can be used as a strategy to retain urban working- and middle-class families who may otherwise leave in search of better public schools for their children (Lyson, 2002). As unambiguous measures of school failure, school closures can represent a clear signal of neighborhood decline. A national survey of adults revealed that 84% of respondents believed that even when a public school is failing for several years, the best response is to keep the school open and try to improve it rather than shut it down (Phi Delta Kappa & Gallup, 2016). This result indicates that the presence of a neighborhood school offers psychic benefits to residents above and beyond the education it provides to local youth, particularly in declining neighborhoods where the school represents one of the few local institutions unscathed by surrounding blight. As one resident of a neighborhood losing its local school puts it, "people watched out for the neighborhood because they were watching the kids. [With the school closure] the neighborhood is basically gone now, and I don't think there is any survival in this neighborhood" (Associated Press, 2010). School closures may trigger the out-migration of families seeking to live closer to a school, institutional and residential disinvestment, and a general malaise among residents, which the preceding quote conveys (Ding & Knaap, 2002; Perkins & Taylor, 2002; Ross, 2000; Sampson & Raudenbush, 1999).

The role of the local school as a symbol of neighborhood pride and stability may have greater importance in poor, Black communities. Schools in such communities not only provide health, financial and educational resources, but also social resources that help bind the community together. In this case, resident interactions will stem not only from the formal or deliberate actions of the school, but also from informal encounters that are central to the formation of social capital (Sampson, 2012). Consequently, schools become key brokers of within neighborhood resident relationships, forging it as a central institution for formal and informal attachment to the neighborhood community (Cohen-Vogel, Goldring, & Smrekar, 2010). Schools can also help mobilize residents under community wide objectives and initiatives. When financial and other resources are in short supply, as they typically are in poor, inner city communities, residents can mobilize the built-in social relationships within local schools to lobby for greater resources (Warren et al., 2009). The school becomes a platform for the community's voice, and a representation of neighborhood goals. These contributions raise the status of the school in the Black neighborhood on par with other historically Black institutions. As one teacher in a historically Black elementary school puts it,

> A community is only as good as the school that is in it. The basis of the Black community used to be the Black Church. [The local elementary school] has served an essential role, just as the Black Church has played in the African American community. (Morris, 1999, p. 584)

DATA AND METHODS

For this study, I conduct a national-level analysis examining the effects of metropolitan school closures on neighborhood housing values. I used census-defined tracts as the measure of neighborhoods. Census tracts are compact and homogenous territorial units with relatively permanent boundaries and a population of about 4,000 people. I included tracts located in metropolitan areas in the contiguous United States, thus capturing 84% of the total U.S. population in 2010. To ensure that results are based on a consistent set of boundaries, I standardized census tracts to 2010 boundaries. I excluded tracts where more than 25% of the residents lived in group quarters (e.g., prisons) yielding a final analytic sample of 45,916 metropolitan neighborhoods.

The main independent variable in the analysis is the neighborhood elementary school closure rate between 2000 and 2010, which was calculated using yearly public school-level data from the NCES Common Core of Data. For each school year, the sample contains all elementary schools open in the current school year or closed since the last school year. I excluded non-regular schools (special education, vocational, and alternative), schools missing longitude and latitude data for all years, and charter and magnet schools. The analysis focuses on elementary schools because school attendance boundaries for middle and high schools are often quite large or non-existent (i.e., open enrollment; Saporito & Van Riper, 2016).

Using GIS software, I geolocated schools using their longitude and latitude values. I then constructed circular buffers around the centroids of each census tract. Schools belonging to a neighborhood are located within the boundaries of the census tract or the area between the buffer and the border of the tract. Buffer areas provide a more realistic representation of the spatial reach of a neighborhood because students from different tracts often attend the same nearby schools, especially in more compact tracts in dense urban areas. To determine the size of the buffer radius, I used the following formula adapted from Burdick-Will et al. (2013):

$$\sqrt{\frac{\sqrt{(2 * \text{Area}) / n}}{\pi}},$$

where *Area* and *n* are the area and the total number of public schools in the metropolitan area, respectively. The buffer radius ranges from a low of 0.8 miles for several metropolitan areas, including New York, NY and San Francisco, CA to a high of 2.9 in Flagstaff, AZ. Figure 8.2 shows an example buffer for a census tract in Chicago. The radius is 0.9 miles, black points represent elementary schools that were open at the end of the observation period, and red points represent elementary schools closed during the period. The school closure rate represents the percentage of public elementary schools within the circular buffer that were ever open between the 2001–2002 and 2008–2009 school years that permanently closed during this period. The school closure rate for the shaded census tract shown in Figure 8.2 is one-third. If a buffer does not capture a school within its boundaries, its radius is extended until a school is captured.

The main dependent variable is the log median value of owner occupied housing units in a census tract in 2010. In all models, I controlled for the 2000 log median value of housing units in 2010 dollars and the change in log median values from 1990 to 2000. I also controlled for neighborhood-level

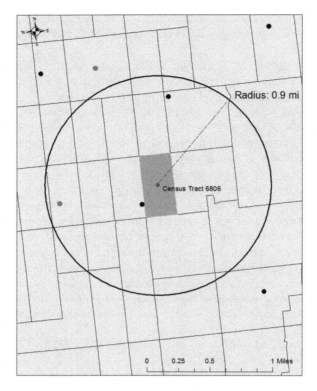

Figure 8.2 Example tract circular buffer area, Chicago. Note: Black circles represent schools open at the end of 2010. Red circles represent schools closed between 2000 and 2010. Blue circle represents census tract centroid.

structural characteristics measured in 2000 that may be correlated with local school closure rates and housing values. I included a measure of concentrated disadvantage, which is an index composed of the percent of households on government assistance, the household poverty rate, percent of female-headed families, and the unemployment rate. Following the methods used by Morenoff, Sampson, and Raudenbush's (2001, p. 527), I standardized each of the indicators, summed the resulting z-scores, and then divided by the number of indicators in order to construct the scale. This produced a composite measure that evenly weighs each of the original variables. I accounted for the neighborhood's school-aged population by controlling for the percentage of residents under the age of 18. I also included the percentage of residents with a college degree and log population size. Given that trends in neighborhood characteristics have been associated with school closure (Burdick-Will et al., 2013), I controlled for changes in concentrated disadvantage and percentage of residents under the age of 18 from 1990 to 2000. All tract-level data came from the Geolytics Neighborhood Change Database. I also controlled for the number of elementary schools ever open in the neighborhood between the 2001–2002 and 2008–2009 school years. Lastly, I included the 2008 county foreclosure rate, obtained from the United States Department of Housing and Urban Development, to control for the effects of the Great Recession.

Figure 8.3 shows census tracts in Chicago shaded by (a) 2000 percentage of Black residents, (b) 2000 poverty rate, and (c) 2010 log median values. The red points represent all elementary schools closed in Chicago between 2000 and 2010. The maps illustrate three sources of bias that need to be addressed in the modelling process. First, school closures are commonly found in neighborhoods with certain characteristics. Figures 8.3a and 8.3b show that closed schools in Chicago reside in poor, predominantly Black census tracts. Second, school closures are clustered together. This clustering indicates a spatial correlation in the school closure rate, which is partially built in through the construction of the neighborhood buffers because they often overlap, particularly in dense areas. As a result of the spatial correlation in the school closure rate (and other independent variables), an exogenous interactive relationship between nearby neighborhoods are formed such that the median housing values of a spatial unit is associated with the determinants of housing values in other, nearby spatial units. Third, neighborhood median housing values are also spatially clustered, leading to an endogenous interactive relationship, which indicates that the outcome of a neighborhood is dependent on the outcome of other, nearby neighborhoods.

In order to address these issues, I ran a Spatial Durbin model, which takes on the following form

$$\log(Y_{2010}) = \beta^0 + \beta^1 SchClose_{2001-09} + \beta^2 X + \rho W \log(Y_{2010})$$
$$+ \alpha W SchClose_{2001-09} + \theta WX + \varepsilon$$

where Y_{2010} is the median housing value in 2010, $SchClose_{2001-09}$ is the neighborhood elementary school closure rate and X is a set of neighborhood characteristics including $\log(Y_{2000})$ which controls for omitted variables that are correlated with property values and remained constant during the decade. The parameters ρ, α, and θ represent the spatial lag effects of nearby values of the outcome, school closure rate, and control variables, respectively. Not only does the model control for a set of neighborhood explanatory variables, but also nearby housing values, school closure rates, and explanatory variables.

The term W in the above equation refers to the spatial weights matrix, which determines neighborhood connectivity, or how nearby neighborhoods

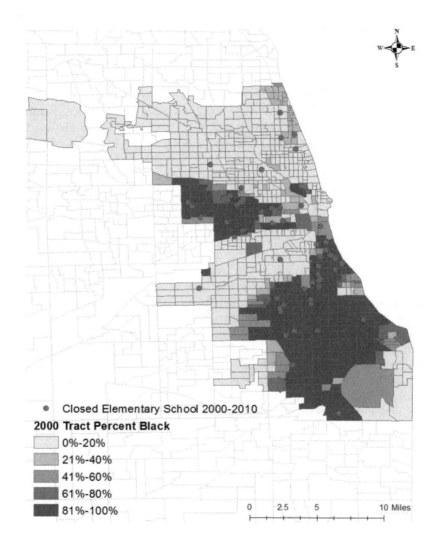

Figure 8.3 Maps of tract characteristics and closed schools, Chicago. (a) 2000 percent Black. *(continued)*

are related to the focal neighborhood. Each nearby census tract is given a row-standardized weight using the following criteria

$$w_{ij} \begin{cases} 1, & \text{if within radius } r \\ d_{ij}^{-1}, & \text{otherwise} \end{cases}$$

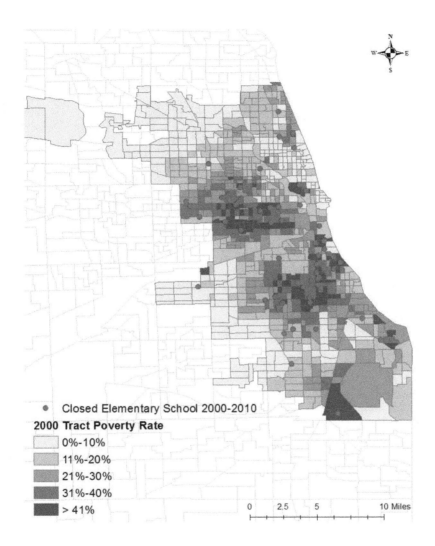

Figure 8.3 Maps of tract characteristics and closed schools, Chicago. (b) 2000 poverty rate. *(continued)*

which gives a weight of 1 to nearby neighborhoods *j* entirely or partially within the circular buffer and a weight of 1 over the distance of the neighborhood *j* centroid to the focal neighborhood *i* centroid for all neighborhoods outside the buffer.

I first ran a basic linear regression model including the elementary school closure rate and basic control variables. Next, I controlled for the percent

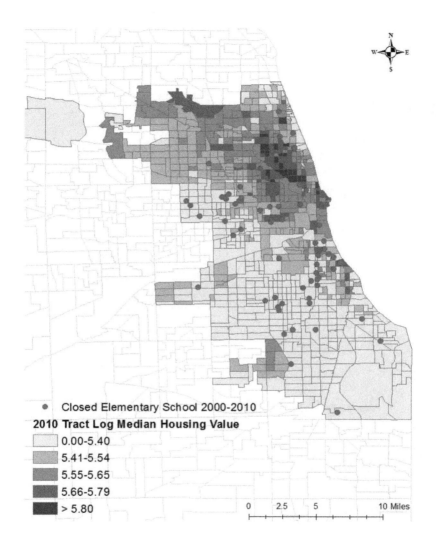

Figure 8.3 Maps of tract characteristics and closed schools, Chicago. (c) 2010 log median housing value.

of public elementary schools opening in a neighborhood during the period. The inclusion of the school open rate accounted for a counteractive replacement effect whereby new schools simply replaced the closed schools. In this case, we might find that the negative effects of school closures will disappear. Second, I controlled for the percentage of charter schools that opened in a neighborhood. For this measure, the denominator is the total number of ever opened schools and the numerator is the total number of charter schools opened during the observation period. Charter schools play a prominent role in debates surrounding public school closures. Opponents of charter schools argue that charter schools are driving school closures because they siphon student enrollment from regular public schools and district officials consider them as quick replacements for underperforming schools (Garnett, 2014). Third, I included 2000 tract percent non-Hispanic Black and its interaction with the school closure rate. I ran similar models including percentage non-Hispanic White and percentage Hispanic, separately. These models test for the moderating effects of neighborhood racial composition. In other words, they test whether school closures have a greater (lesser) effect in neighborhoods with greater percentages of Black, White, or Hispanic residents.

RESULTS

Table 8.1 displays descriptive statistics of the variables used in the analysis for the entire sample and disaggregated by tracts with and without a school closure between 2000 and 2010. Neighborhoods overall experienced a mean closure rate of 6%, with an overwhelming majority of neighborhoods not experiencing a single closure (87%). Of the neighborhoods that did experience a closure, the closure rate was 43%. These tracts had a greater percentage of Black and concentrated disadvantage, but lower percentage White and percentage with a college degree relative to tracts not experiencing a school closure. Both sets of tracts had similar percent Hispanic and percent of residents under 18 years of age.

Neighborhood school closure rates vary geographically. At the state level, Washington, DC (20.9%), Michigan (18.3%), and Ohio (15.8%) have the highest neighborhood school closure rates. On the opposite end of the spectrum, New Hampshire, Nevada, and Vermont have closure rates below 1%. At the regional level, neighborhoods in the Midwest had the highest average neighborhood-level closure rates (9.5%), followed by the Northeast (5.3%), South (4.2%), and West (3.9%).

Table 8.2 displays results from models examining the association between elementary school closure rates and median housing values. For each model, I present estimates of the main and spatial lag effects. The first column shows results for a model including the school closure rate and the full set of control variables. The included covariates show expected associations. Whereas log population size, concentrated disadvantage, an increase in concentrated disadvantage from 1990 to 2000, urban compared to suburban tracts, and the county foreclosure rate are associated with lower housing values, the percentage of residents with a college degree, the percentage of residents under the age of 18, log housing values in 2000, and the increase in these three variables from 1990 to 2000 are associated with higher housing values. Most importantly, I found a statistically significant

TABLE 8.1 Descriptive Characteristics of Neighborhood Sample

Variable	Total	Tracts With a Closed Elementary School	Tracts Without a Closed Elementary School
2010 log median value	12.23	11.98	12.27
Elementary school closure rate	0.06	0.43	0.00
Elementary non charter school closure rate	0.07	0.10	0.07
Elementary charter school closure rate	0.02	0.04	0.02
Number of ever open elementary schools	2.64	4.48	2.37
2008 county foreclosure rate	4.92	5.20	4.88
2000 Tract Characteristics			
Log population	8.17	8.12	8.18
Percent Black	0.15	0.28	0.13
Percent White	0.65	0.53	0.67
Percent Hispanic	0.14	0.14	0.15
Percent under 18 years old	0.26	0.26	0.26
Concentrated disadvantage	−0.01	0.56	−0.10
Percent with college degree	0.25	0.20	0.26
Log median value	11.96	11.71	12.00
1990–2000 Tract Characteristics			
Percent Black	0.02	0.02	0.02
Percent White	−0.08	−0.07	−0.08
Percent Hispanic	0.04	0.03	0.04
Percent under 18 years old	0.00	0.00	0.00
Concentrated disadvantage	0.00	−0.07	0.01
Log median value	0.57	0.62	0.56
N	45,916	5,891	40,025

negative association between the neighborhood elementary school closure rate and log median housing values: for every one percentage point increase in the school closure rate, median housing values decreased by 4.59% ($e^{-0.047} - 1$). I also found a statistically significant negative effect for the school closure rates in nearby neighborhoods: for every one percentage point increase in the school closure rate of nearby neighborhoods, median housing values decreased by 11.31% ($e^{-0.120} - 1$) in the focal neighborhood.

The next two columns show results from models including the regular and charter elementary public school open rates. The results for the school closure rate from column 1 did not change after including the school open rates. I also found that a one-percentage point increase in the school open rate is associated with a 1.92% increase ($e^{0.019} - 1$) in median housing values. I

TABLE 8.2 Regression of Log Median Housing Values in 2010 on Elementary School Closure Rates Between 2000 and 2010, U.S. Metropolitan Neighborhoods

Variable	Estimate	Lag Estimate	Estimate	Lag Estimate	Estimate	Lag Estimate
Elementary school closure rate	−0.047*** (0.008)	−0.120*** (0.013)	−0.048*** (0.008)	−0.117*** (0.013)	−0.048*** (0.009)	−0.122*** (0.014)
Elementary school open rate			0.019** (0.007)	−0.049*** (0.009)		
Elementary charter school open rate					0.092*** (0.019)	0.060 (0.035)
Number of ever opened schools	0.015*** (0.001)	0.005*** (0.001)	0.015*** (0.001)	0.005*** (0.001)	0.015*** (0.001)	0.005*** (0.001)
Log population	−0.006** (0.002)	−0.079*** (0.004)	−0.005*** (0.001)	−0.082*** (0.004)	−0.006*** (0.002)	−0.079*** (0.004)
Percent 18 years old and under	0.371*** (0.024)	−0.567*** (0.038)	0.363*** (0.023)	−0.540*** (0.038)	0.375*** (0.026)	−0.566*** (0.040)
Concentrated disadvantage	−0.053*** (0.002)	−0.014*** (0.004)	−0.053*** (0.002)	−0.013*** (0.002)	−0.052*** (0.002)	−0.014*** (0.004)
Percent of 25+ year olds with a college degree	0.069*** (0.009)	−0.125*** (0.016)	0.071*** (0.008)	−0.127*** (0.018)	0.068*** (0.014)	−0.128*** (0.019)
Log median housing value, 2000	1.018*** (0.002)	0.185*** (0.007)	1.017*** (0.002)	0.183*** (0.007)	1.018*** (0.002)	0.184*** (0.007)
County foreclosure rate, 2008	−0.002*** (0.000)	0.004*** (0.001)	−0.002*** (0.000)	0.004*** (0.001)	−0.002* (0.001)	0.003 (0.003)
Urban tract	−0.018*** (0.003)	−0.036*** (0.005)	−0.018*** (0.003)	−0.035*** (0.004)	−0.019*** (0.004)	−0.036*** (0.005)
Change 1990–2000						
Percent 18 years old and under	0.224*** (0.047)	0.354*** (0.092)	0.227*** (0.031)	0.355*** (0.069)	0.227** (0.069)	0.353 (0.185)
Concentrated disadvantage	−0.073*** (0.004)	0.071*** (0.007)	−0.073*** (0.004)	0.072*** (0.006)	−0.073*** (0.004)	0.071*** (0.006)
Log median housing value	0.309*** (0.005)	−0.052*** (0.007)	0.310*** (0.005)	−0.051*** (0.006)	0.310*** (0.005)	−0.053*** (0.007)
Intercept	−0.024*** (0.007)		−0.017*** (0.005)		−0.024*** (0.006)	

* $p \leq 0.05$; ** $p \leq 0.01$; *** $p \leq 0.001$
Note: Standard errors are in parentheses

found an even larger increase ($e^{0.092} − 1 = 9.64\%$) for the charter school open rate. These results suggest counterbalancing or replacement effects—the negative effect of a school closure on neighborhood housing values may be offset by the positive effect of a school opening in the local neighborhood.

Table 8.3 presents results for models including racial composition and its interaction with the school closure rate. The models without interactions

TABLE 8.3 Regression of Log Median Housing Values in 2010 on Elementary School Closure Rates Interacted With Percent Non-Hispanic Black, Percent Hispanic, and Percent Non-Hispanic White

Variable	Estimate	Lag Estimate	Estimate	Lag Estimate	Estimate	Lag Estimate	Estimate	Lag Estimate	Estimate	Lag Estimate	Estimate	Lag Estimate
Elementary school closure rate	-0.039*** (0.008)	-0.116*** (0.014)	-0.007 (0.007)	-0.106*** (0.018)	-0.035*** (0.007)	-0.102*** (0.013)	-0.042*** (0.009)	-0.091*** (0.003)	-0.041*** (0.008)	-0.090*** (0.014)	-0.117*** (0.026)	-0.130 (0.069)
% Non-Hispanic Black, 2000	-0.017*** (0.004)	0.049*** (0.007)	-0.002*** (0.000)	0.053*** (0.014)								
% Non-Hispanic Black, 1990–2000	-0.375*** (0.023)	-0.144* (0.068)	-0.379*** (0.021)	-0.146* (0.048)								
Elementary school closure rate × % Non-Hispanic Black, 2000			-0.143*** (0.022)	-0.032*** (0.004)								
% Hispanic, 2000					0.166*** (0.011)	-0.037 (0.026)	0.163*** (0.015)	-0.033* (0.013)				
% Hispanic, 1990–2000					-0.154*** (0.026)	0.159* (0.066)	-0.154*** (0.032)	0.160*** (0.035)				
Elementary school closure rate × % Hispanic, 2000							0.071 (0.065)	-0.119 (0.089)				
% Non-Hispanic White, 2000									-0.081*** (0.008)	-0.129*** (0.009)	-0.089*** (0.010)	-0.130*** (0.025)
% Non-Hispanic White, 1990–2000									0.167*** (0.015)	-0.008*** (0.001)	0.171*** (0.019)	-0.007*** (0.001)
Elementary school closure rate × % Non-Hispanic White, 2000											0.119*** (0.034)	0.066 (0.045)
Intercept	0.108*** (0.017)	0.113 (0.086)	0.163*** (0.027)		0.163*** (0.058)		0.163*** (0.058)		0.284*** (0.049)		0.304* (0.121)	

* $p \le 0.05$; ** $p \le 0.01$; *** $p \le 0.001$

Note: Standard errors are in parentheses. All models include control variables listed in Table 8.1

reveal that the negative main and lag effects of the elementary school closure rate are robust to the inclusion of neighborhood racial composition. The main estimate for the coefficient of the interaction of percentage Black and the closure rate is negative and statistically significant, indicating that the negative effect of school closures on housing values is greater in neighborhoods with a larger percentage of Blacks. In contrast, I found a statistically significant positive coefficient for the percentage of White interaction, which indicates that school closures have a weaker if not a positive effect on housing values in neighborhoods with a higher percentage of Whites. These results indicate differential school closure effects depending on the racial composition of the neighborhood—stronger negative effects in Black neighborhoods and weaker, potentially positive effects in White neighborhoods. I found no statistically significant effect on the interaction between neighborhood percentage of Hispanics and the school closure rate.

DISCUSSION

Results from this study provide empirical support for the argument that public school closures negatively affect the economic health of local neighborhoods. The study found a statistically significant association between the neighborhood elementary school closure rate and median housing values. These results are robust to the inclusion of a wide set of neighborhood control variables, spatial dependency in the outcome and independent variables, and open rates of regular public elementary schools and charter elementary schools.

The results also indicate that school openings may offset the independent negative effects of school closures. A neighborhood experiencing a decline in median housing values after an elementary school closure will experience an increase if either a regular or charter elementary school is opened within the neighborhood's buffer area. Burdick-Will et al. (2013) found in their analysis of Chicago school closures that the odds a neighborhood opens at least one new school are 6.6 times greater if there is also at least one closed school in the neighborhood. In this case, the neighborhoods that need new schools are receiving them.

The results also show that school closures have greater negative effects in neighborhoods with larger percentages of Black residents. This result may be explained by the greater dependency of Black neighborhoods on local schools for community services. Moreover, neighborhoods with larger percentages of Black residents tend to be more disadvantaged and segregated, and experienced declining socioeconomic status between 2000 and 2010 (Intrator, Tannen, & Massey, 2016). Given this compounding effect of baseline disadvantage and trending decline, a school closure may act as a tipping point for these neighborhoods such that the preceding decline may accelerate and be difficult to reverse. This is especially the case if school districts have a difficult time selling abandoned school buildings, which is likely the case in already declining and disinvested communities that have trouble attracting new businesses and residents. Moreover, poor, Black neighborhoods may either not receive a new higher quality school or not open a school at all. Although new schools tend to open in neighborhoods that are not necessarily affluent, these neighborhoods have experienced recent revitalization, gentrification, and neighborhood ascent (Burdick-Will et al., 2013; Owens, 2012). An expansion of attendance boundaries to a nearby school may not counterbalance any negative effects because distance to the nearest school is often quite far (Lee & Lubienski, 2017) and proximity to the school is itself likely capitalized into local housing values, particularly for disadvantaged residents. Moreover, majority black neighborhoods are not only disadvantaged but are also surrounded by spatial disadvantage in the extralocal residential environment, which suggests that an expansion of school attendance boundaries will capture not only a school that is geographically distant, but one that may be equally or more disadvantaged (Sharkey, 2014).

School closures have the opposite effect on White neighborhoods—they increase median housing values in tracts with larger percentages of White residents. This result may indicate the important differences between the role of school closures in White and Black neighborhoods, with school closures representing the removal of low quality schools depressing local housing values in White neighborhoods and the removal of important sources of community pride and investment above and beyond school performance in Black neighborhoods. Moreover, White neighborhoods may be able to recover more quickly after a school closure, which includes the institutional investment to effectively repurpose closed schools, the ability to attract new, potentially higher quality new schools, and expand school boundaries to include nearby higher quality schools.

There are several limitations of this study that might serve as avenues of future research. First, this study has assumed that the census tract represents a reasonable choice for measuring neighborhoods. Although the use of census-defined geographies to measure neighborhoods is common, future studies relying on other measures of neighborhood are needed. Second, future research should examine the effects of school closures on other neighborhood outcomes, including the mechanisms outlined in the background section of this chapter. Understanding the specific pathways through which school closures harm neighborhoods will better inform strategies for lessening their impact on the local community. For example, if the abandonment of closed school buildings is the primary mechanism driving lower neighborhood housing values, district and city officials should prioritize the timely reoccupation and maintenance of abandoned schools. Third, given the presence of unobserved endogeneity and potential measurement error in the timing and location of school closures, the current study cannot make causal claims regarding the effects of school closures. To address this issue, future research should rely on more spatio-temporally refined data. Lastly, future research should explore school heterogeneity in closure effects, specifically by type and quality of the school. In particular, the effects of school closure likely vary by school academic performance, with higher achieving schools that are closed due to nonperformance related reasons having greater negative effects (Rosburg, Isakson, Ecker, & Strauss, 2017).

The major contribution of this study is to show empirically that school closures impact neighborhoods through their negative association with median housing values. This finding should compel city and district officials to factor in the school–neighborhood relationship in the closure decision making process, which includes the front-end of this process when deciding whether or not to close a school as well as the back end when formulating ways to mitigate the effects of closures. In both cases, the input of community based organizations and local community leaders are needed. This is particularly important in poor, Black neighborhoods that rely on schools above and beyond the education they provide to local youth. In this case, in addition to school performance, under-enrollment, building conditions, and funding constraints, the socioeconomic decline in the local neighborhood and the reliance of the neighborhood on the local school for social services are additional factors that need to be considered in the closure decision process. The results also indicate that school openings may counter the independent negative effects of school closures and thus school district officials should attempt to replace closed schools in a timely fashion.

In assessing the overall impact of school closures, the study's findings should be viewed in conjunction with the current literature on school closure effects on displaced students and other impacted populations. Moreover, the study's findings should be placed in the context of other emergent neighborhood and school issues that complicate the relationship between neighborhoods and local schools, including the rising presence of school choice initiatives, local housing policies that influence where families decide to live, and larger social forces changing the demographic composition of neighborhoods, including gentrification and segregation. School closures in districts with an increasing presence of school choice have different implications for neighborhoods than closures in districts where school choice is absent. In the former, the effects of school closures are complicated by the presence of charter schools and enrollment out of attendance boundaries. In the latter, the effects may be more of an issue of building abandonment and disinvestment.

The impact of school closures is complicated by a myriad of factors that may help or disadvantage stakeholders under certain conditions. As urban school districts continue to rely on school closures to address poor academic performance and diminishing financial resources, more research is needed in order to understand under what conditions this increasingly popular strategy of reform may be effective. Previous research has largely focused on the effects of school closure rates on displaced students. In order for further clarity to emerge on such a complicated, hotly debated, and emotionally charged issue, studies examining the effects of school closures, both empirical and qualitative, on other outcomes, at different contextual levels, and for different socioeconomic and racial groups are needed.

REFERENCES

Accordino, J., & Johnson, G. T. (2000). Addressing the vacant and abandoned property problem. Journal of Urban Affairs, 22(3), 301–315.

Anderson, C. L. (2015) *The disparate impact of shuttered schools, Journal of Gender Social Policy and Law, 23*(2), 319–351.

Associated Press. (2010, March 23). Closing schools affects communities as well as kids. *USA Today. Retrieved from* http://usatoday30.usatoday.com/news/education/2010-03-23-school-closings_N.htm

Bass, M., Chen, D., Leonard, J., Leonard, J., Mueller, L., Cheryl, L., . . . Snyder, K. (2005). *Vacant properties: The true costs to communities.* National Vacant Properties Campaign. Retrieved from http://www.smartgrowthamerica.org/documents/true-costs.pdf

Brasington, D. (1999). Which measures of school quality does the housing market value? *Journal of Real Estate Research, 18*(3), 395–413.

Brazil, N. (2016). The effects of social context on youth outcomes: Studying neighborhoods and schools simultaneously. *Teachers College Record, 118*(7), 1–30.

Brueckner, J. K., & Joo, M. S. (1991). Voting with capitalization. *Regional Science and Urban Economics, 21*(3), 453–467.

Burdick-Will, J., Keels, M., & Schuble, T. (2013). Closing and opening schools: The association between neighborhood characteristics and the location of new educational opportunities in a large urban district. *Journal of Urban Affairs, 35*(1), 59–80.

Chung, C. (2002). *Using public schools as community-development tools: Strategies for community based developers.* Cambridge, MA: Joint Center for Housing Studies of Harvard University and Neighborhood Reinvestment Corporation.

Cohen, R. (2016, April 11). School closures: A blunt instrument. *The American Prospect.* http://prospect.org/article/school-closures-blunt-instrument-0

Cohen-Vogel, L., Goldring, E., & Smrekar, C. (2010). The influence of local conditions on social service partnerships, parent involvement, and community engagement in neighborhood schools. *American Journal of Education, 117*(1), 51–78.

Cui, L., & Walsh, R. (2015). Foreclosure, vacancy and crime. *Journal of Urban Economics, 87*, 72–84.

De la Torre, M., & Gwynne, J. (2009). *When schools close: Effects on displaced students in Chicago public schools. Research Report.* Chicago, IL: University of Chicago Consortium on Chicago School Research.

De la Torre, M., Gordon, M. F., Moore, P., & Cowhy, J. (2015). *School closings in Chicago: Understanding families' choices and constraints for new school enrollment.* Chicago, IL: University of Chicago Consortium on Chicago School Research.

Ding, C., & Knaap, G. J. (2002). Property values in inner-city neighborhoods: The effects of homeownership, housing investment, and economic development. *Housing Policy Debate, 13*(4), 701–727.

Dowdall, E., & Warner, S. (2013). Shuttered public schools: The struggle to bring old buildings new life. *The Pew Charitable Trusts.* Retrieved from http://www. pewtrusts.org/uploadedFiles/wwwpewtrustsorg/Reports/Philadelphia_Research_Initiative/Philadelphia-School-Closings.pdf

Dryfoos, J. G. (1994). Full-service schools. San Francisco, CA: Jossey-Bass.

Eccles, J. S., & Templeton, J. (2002). Extracurricular and other after-school activities for youth. *Review of research in education, 26*, 113–180.

Figlio, D. N., & Lucas, M. E. (2004). What's in a grade? School report cards and the housing market. *American Economic Review, 94*(3), 591–604.

Filardo, M., Vincent, J. M., Allen, M., & Franklin, J., (2010). Joint use of public schools: A framework for a new social contract. Washington, DC: 21st Century School Fund and Center for Cities and Schools.

Gallimore, J. M., Brown, B. B., & Werner, C. M. (2011). Walking routes to school in new urban and suburban neighborhoods: An environmental walkability analysis of blocks and routes. *Journal of Environmental Psychology, 31*(2), 184–191.

Garnett, N. S. (2014). Disparate impact, public-school closures and parental choice, *Chicago Legal Forum, 2014*(1), Article 5. https://chicagounbound.uchicago.edu/uclf/vol2014/iss1/5

Han, H. S. (2014). The impact of abandoned properties on nearby property values. *Housing Policy Debate, 24*(2), 311–334.

Harding, A. (2016). *Arrest made after teen found dead near abandoned school.* Retrieved from http://meredithaz.worldnow.com/story/30356020/neighbors-speak-out-after-body-found-near-abandoned-school

Hilber, C. A., & Mayer, C. (2009). Why do households without children support local public schools? Linking house price capitalization to school spending. *Journal of Urban Economics, 65*(1), 74–90.

Holme, J. J. (2002). Buying homes, buying schools: School choice and the social construction of school quality. *Harvard Educational Review, 72*(2), 177–206.

Horn, K. M. (2015). Can improvements in schools spur neighborhood revitalization? Evidence from building investments. *Regional Science and Urban Economics, 52*, 108–118.

Intrator, J., Tannen, J., & Massey, D. S. (2016). Segregation by race and income in the United States 1970–2010. *Social Science Research.* https://doi.org/10.1016/j.ssresearch.2016.08.003

Kanters, M. A., Bocarro, J. N., Filardo, M., Edwards, M. B., McKenzie, T. L., & Floyd, M. F. (2014). Shared use of school facilities with community organizations and afterschool physical activity program participation: A cost–benefit assessment. *Journal of School Health, 84*(5), 302–309.

Keeton, V., Soleimanpour, S., & Brindis, C. D. (2012). School-based health centers in an era of health care reform: Building on history. *Current problems in pediatric and adolescent health care, 42*(6), 132–156.

Lareau, A. (2014). Schools, Housing, and the Reproduction of Inequality. In A. Lareau & K. Goyette (Eds.), *Choosing homes, choosing schools* (pp. 268–294). New York, NY: Russell Sage.

Lee, J., & Lubienski, C. (2017). The impact of school closures on equity of access in Chicago. *Education and Urban Society, 49*(1), 53–80.

Lyson, T. A. (2002). What does a school mean to a community? Assessing the social and economic benefits of schools to rural villages in New York. *Journal of Research in Rural Education, 17*(3), 131–137.

Massey, D. S., & Denton, N. A. (1993). *American apartheid: Segregation and the making of the underclass.* Cambridge, MA: Harvard University Press.

Mikelbank, B. A. (2008). Spatial analysis of the impact of vacant, abandoned and foreclosed properties. Working paper submitted to Office of Community Affairs Federal Reserve Bank of Cleveland.

Morenoff, J. D., Sampson, R. J., & Raudenbush, S. W. (2001). Neighborhood inequality, collective efficacy, and the spatial dynamics of urban violence. *Criminology, 39*(3), 517–558.

Morris, J. E. (1999). A pillar of strength an African American school's communal bonds with families and community since Brown. *Urban Education, 33*(5), 584–605.

National Center for Education Statistics. (2013). Common core of data: School years 1998–99 through 2013–14. Washington, DC: Author.

Nguyen-Hoang, P., & Yinger, J. (2011). The capitalization of school quality into house values: A review. *Journal of Housing Economics, 20*(1), 30–48.

Oates, W. E., (1969). The effects of property taxes and local public spending on property values: An empirical study of tax capitalization and the Tiebout hypothesis. *Journal of Political Economy, 77*(6), 957–971.

Owens, A. (2012). Neighborhoods on the rise: A typology of neighborhoods experiencing socioeconomic ascent. *City & Community, 11*(4), 345–369.

Perkins, D. D., & Taylor, R. B. (2002). Ecological assessments of community disorder: Their relationship to fear of crime and theoretical implications. In *Ecological research to promote social change* (pp. 127–170). New York, NY: Springer.

Phi Delta Kappa & Gallup. (2016). The 48th PDK/gallup poll of the public's attitudes toward the public schools. *Phi Delta Kappan, 98*(1). Retrieved from http://pdkpoll2015.pdkintl.org/wp-content/uploads/2016/08/pdk-poll48_2016.pdf

Raleigh, E., & Galster, G. (2015). Neighborhood disinvestment, abandonment, and crime dynamics. *Journal of Urban Affairs, 37*(4), 367–396.

Rohe, W. M., McCarthy, G., & Van Zandt, S. (2000). The social benefits and costs of homeownership: A critical assessment of the research. Washington, DC: Research Institute for Housing America.

Rosburg, A., Isakson, H., Ecker, M., & Strauss, T. (2017). Beyond standardized test scores: The impact of a public school closure on house prices. *Journal of Housing Research, 26*(2), 119–135.

Ross, C. E. (2000). Neighborhood disadvantage and adult depression. *Health and Social Behavior, 41*, 177–187.

Sampson, R. J. (2012). *Great American city: Chicago and the enduring neighborhood effect.* Chicago: IL: University of Chicago Press.

Sampson, R. J., & Raudenbush, S. W. (1999). Systematic social observation of public spaces: A new look at disorder in urban Neighborhoods. *American journal of sociology, 105*(3), 603–651.

Saporito, S., & Van Riper, D. (2016). Do irregularly shaped school attendance zones contribute to racial segregation or integration? *Social Currents, 3*(1), 64–83.

Sharkey, P. (2014). Spatial Segmentation and the Black Middle Class. *American Journal of Sociology, 119*(4), 903–954.

Shlay, A. B., & Whitman, G. (2006). Research for democracy: Linking community organizing and research to leverage blight policy. *City & Community, 5*(2), 153–171.

Skogan, W. G. (1992). *Disorder and decline: Crime and the spiral of decay in American neighborhoods.* Oakland, CA: University of California Press.

Small, M. L. (2006). Neighborhood institutions as resource brokers: Childcare centers, interorganizational ties, and resource access among the poor. *Social Problems, 53*(2), 274–292.

Spelman, W. (1993). Abandoned buildings: Magnets for crime? *Journal of Criminal Justice, 21*(5), 481–495.

Squires, G. D., & Kubrin, C. E. (2005). Privileged places: Race, uneven development and the geography of opportunity in urban America. *Urban Studies, 42*(1), 47–68.

Strauss, V. (2013, March 6). How closing schools hurts neighborhoods. *Washington Post.* Retrieved from https://www.washingtonpost.com/news/answer-sheet/wp/2013/03/06/how-closing-schools-hurts-neighborhoods/?noredirect=on&utm_term=.ae6ad669157d

Tiebout, C. M. (1956). A pure theory of local expenditures. *The Journal of Political Economy*, 416–424.

Vincent, J. M. (2014). Joint use of public schools a framework for promoting healthy communities. *Journal of Planning Education and Research, 34*(2), 153–168.

Warren, M. (2005). Communities and schools: A new view of urban education reform. *Harvard Educational Review, 75*(2), 133–173.

Warren, M., Hong, S., Rubin, C., & Uy, P. (2009). Beyond the bake sale: A community-based relational approach to parent engagement in schools. *The Teachers College Record, 111*(9), 2209–2254.

Wilson, W. J. (1987). *The truly disadvantaged: The inner city, the underclass, and public policy.* Chicago, IL: University of Chicago Press.

Wilson, J. Q., & Kelling, G. L. (1982). Broken windows. *Atlantic Monthly, 249*(3), 29–38.

CHAPTER 9

"A SPOKE IN A WHEEL"

School Closures and the Continued Violation of Public Trust

Sally A. Nuamah
Princeton University

ABSTRACT

Since 2001, more than 100 traditional public schools have been closed across the Chicagoland area. Most recently, in 2013, 54 public schools were closed—the most schools closed in a single year in U.S history. Nearly 90% of those affected were either Black or Latino. Despite the large number of school closures and its targeted nature, there exist very few investigations on how those affected by closures think about them. This chapter investigates the relationship between education reform policy and public attitudes. Utilizing qualitative data from community meeting transcripts, ethnographic observations, and interviews, this chapter argues that community members' encounters with the varied and multiple manifestations of education policy implemented by Chicago Public Schools (CPS) over the past decade are inconsistent with the stated objectives of the school closure policy. The inconsistencies experienced by citizens contribute to general

Shuttered Schools, pages 259–285

suspicion and distrust of the real objectives behind the 2013 school closing policy, its implementers, and politics, at large.

Public schools have long acted as anchors of the community and cradles of democracy. Indeed, the relative size of the public school system as compared to any other institution of government is unmatched, nor is its normative value in the everyday lives of citizens (Hochschild & Scovronick, 2003). Yet, in part as a result of government efforts to "turn around"[1] public schools in order resolve issues of economic crises, low performance, and under-enrollment, public schools have been closed at increasing rate in recent years (see U.S Department of Education—Blueprint for Reform, 2010; National Council for Education Statistics, n.d.).

While schools are being closed across the United States, the CPS system made history in 2013 when it closed the most schools in a single year. Nearly 90% of the schools targeted for closure were attended by large majorities of low-income African-American students. Yet, in these same communities' public school systems have become central to community empowerment, employment, and stability (Henig, Hula, Orr, & Pedescleaux, 2001). The targeted nature of school closure raises important questions about the fairness of how the American government distributes public goods among its citizenry, and the impact that these decisions have on the political beliefs of Americans most directly affected by them.

Literature on policy feedback, provides a useful approach for examining the relationship between policy experience and political behavior, more generally. These works identify the ways in which consistent interactions with the design, framing, and discourse around policies can structure individuals' experiences with the political process. Citizens' use their encounters with policy as a lens for understanding their juxtaposition to the State at large. Thus, these experiences thus teach citizens important political lessons about government and democracy (i.e., Pierson, 1993; Soss, 1999; Mettler, 2005; Burch, 2013).

In the case of Chicago, a group of people have been consistently affected by changes in the historical role and function of public schools—institutions through which citizens are most likely to experience government and acquire civic skills (Hochschild & Scovronick, 2003). Thus, one would expect citizens' experiences with school closings to influence their political attitudes and reveal much about the state of American democracy today. Yet, despite the importance and direct consequence of the policy of public school closure on the lives of residents, these questions are yet to be taken on by policy feedback or even public opinion scholars. This chapter addresses these shortcomings through an analysis of attitudes toward school closures compiled from interview data, community meeting observations and transcripts on Chicago. This chapter analyzes how experiences with education shape public attitudes towards the school closure policy and its broader consequences for public trust.

The analysis reveals that community members' encounters with the *various and multiple* manifestations of education policy implemented by CPS contribute to general suspicion, and ultimately distrust, of the real objectives behind the current closing policy. In particular, this study demonstrates how citizens' experiences with closure are inconsistent with the stated objectives of the policy. These inconsistencies have negative feedback effects on public attitudes as they appear reflective of the continued violation of public trust by CPS. Accordingly, citizens' express oppositional attitudes towards the closure policy, as well as towards those policy actors involved in crafting and implementing it.

The remainder of the chapter is divided into the following sections: The first section reviews the literature on attitudes toward education with a particular focus on school closure. This section is followed by a review of policy feedback literature and its relationship to education attitudes. The section that follows addresses theories of policy feedback in relation to public trust. The chapter then provides a brief overview of school closures in one case, Chicago, before delving into the data, methods, and strategies for analyzing the case. The next section describes the findings in relationship to the argument. The final section addresses alternative explanations and limitations and concludes with the implications of the findings on democratic society.

PUBLIC ATTITUDES TOWARD EDUCATION

Public opinion on education yields important insights on the state of democracy. As stated by Hochschild & Scovronick (2003), "most parents have experienced public schools themselves and hold stronger more fully developed views about education than about most other policy arenas" (p. 80). They go on to state that, "public education uses more resources and involves more people than any other government program for social welfare. It is the main activity of local governments and the largest single expenditure of almost all state governments" (p. 8). The persistent encounters with education that citizens are exposed to, in addition to the sheer size of the educational system relative to other forms of social welfare typically studied such as AFDC/TANF, Medicare, or Social Security justifies the need to examine the potential consequences for education policies on public attitudes. Yet, there exist very few investigations of attitudes towards public schools, specifically, and education, generally. Additionally, even in the instances when questions have been asked on surveys, very few investigations of these attitudes have been conducted (Hochschild & Scott, 1998).

Instead, the majority of studies in public opinion include education as an independent variable in the analysis. In particular, these works demonstrate the multiple ways in which educational attainment is linked to increased levels of political engagement and interest through voting, donating, and participating in an array of civic activities (Converse, 1972; Wolfinger & Rosenstone, 1980; Rosenstone & Hansen, 1993; Verba, Schlozman, Brady, & Brady 1995; Sondheimer & Green, 2010). Thus, while education is included as an independent variable, we know very little about attitudes towards education, as a dependent variable.

The few studies that collect attitudes towards school closures, in particular, report generally negative feelings towards these policy decisions among parents (even when confronted with evidence of budget and performance crises facing the school). In a survey conducted by Phi Delta Kappa in 2010, for example, when parents were asked, "What should be done about low performing schools?" more than half (54%) said the best solution was to "keep the school open with existing teachers and principals and provide comprehensive outside support (Bushaw & Lopez, 2010, p. 10)." Only 11% of those surveyed supported "closing schools and sending the students to other higher performing schools nearby" (Bushaw & Lopez, 2010, p. 11). These same questions were asked again in the 2013 survey conducted by Phi Delta Kappa, and 47% of White parents supported public school closings compared to 33% of non-White parents. While a majority of those surveyed expressed opposition to closure, the findings raised questions about exactly who was opposed and for what reasons.

In 2010, the Public Agenda conducted a qualitative study on school closures that included 40 focus group interviews with parents and local school district leaders. During the focus groups, parents were given a hypothetical school closing scenario that mimicked the conditions of a real one. The case study and the prompts were varied to suit the different focus groups. Ultimately, the results reveal that from the onset parents reject all of the options that involved closing the school even when confronted with compelling data (Public Agenda, 2012, p. 12). The 2012 Public Agenda reports describes citizens' opposition to closure as related to fears that "school closings make a community look bad and send a message that schools can't function in that community" (p. 49). While the study finds that when provided with more information some parents were willing to reconsider their position, both reports provide evidence of general opposition to school closures by parents.

As it relates specifically to Chicago, the particular focus of this chapter, the only representative survey that asks questions about school closings was jointly led by the *Chicago Tribune*, The University of Chicago's National Opinion Research Center (NORC), and the Joyce Foundation before the announcement of closure in February 2013 (NORC, 2013). A little over

1,000 persons were surveyed with about half of the sample including parents with children in CPS. The survey reveals that while only 6% of respondents selected closing a school as a solution for removing low quality schools, in another question that asked about supporting school closure as a solution for resolving issues of under-enrollment, a majority of respondents somewhat or mostly agreed with the proposal (NORC, 2013).

The above data demonstrates how it is difficult to tease out attitudes towards school closure as few studies exist on the topic. Most challenging for parsing out opinion on these issues is the fact that scholars of public opinion study these factors in isolation from the broad policy environment in which they are constituted. In other words, public opinion scholars primarily examine attitudes as shaping policies and exclude the reverse ways in which policies themselves shape attitudes. As a result, these studies fail to account for the ways in which one's actual experience with the policy he or she is responding to may play a proactive role in influencing his or her attitude towards it. This calls for a more targeted analysis of public attitudes towards closure and education broadly.

POLICY FEEDBACK AND EDUCATION ATTITUDES

An emerging literature within political science titled, policy feedback, addresses this gap in the current way opinion is studied by emphasizing the multiple ways in which citizens' experiences with policies can shape political behavior and politics, at large. As stated by Soss and Schram (2007), policies

> can set political agendas and shape identities and interests. They can influence beliefs about what is possible, desirable, and normal. They can alter conceptions of citizenship and status. They can channel or constrain agency, define incentives, and redistribute resources. They can convey cues that define, arouse, or pacify constituencies. (p. 113)

By defining membership—determining who counts; framing agendas—shaping the meaning of a problem; administering practices—through design and implementation, policies can have specific feedback effects that convey to citizens their rights, privileges, duties and obligations, and place and value as members of the community. Citizens' experiences with public policies and politics, then, can shape their life circumstances, the state, and world around them (Campbell, 2002; Mettler & Soss, 2004; Pierson, 1993; Pierson & Skocpol, 2002; Thelen, 1999).

The policy feedback literature pays special attention to two mechanisms by which feedback effects are translated onto citizens: resources and interpretive. Resource effects refer to the spoils and material incentives that a policy can provide to citizens. Interpretive effects refer to the impact of policies on the cognitive processes of citizens (for full review see Pierson, 1993). For example, Mettler's (2005) work on the GI bill finds that the WWII veterans who took advantage of the benefits of the bill engaged in higher levels of civic participation thereafter. She explains their increased participation levels as an *interpretive effect* that resulted in part from the recipients' desire to reciprocate for the *resources* that they received from the government. In addition, Andrea Campbell's (2003) work on social security demonstrates how recipients of the program, especially those of lower income, benefit from resources of free time and money (retirement). Social security recipients then utilized their increased capacity to participate to combat future threats to their benefits. Each of the above examples highlight the specific ways in which resource and interpretive effects can positively shape political engagement among recipients of government programs.

Yet, policy feedback effects can also be negative. For example, Soss's (1999) study of welfare recipients illustrates how their negative interactions with welfare bureaucrats contributed to stigmatized characterizations of themselves as "undeserving" of the assistance provided through the program. These negative social constructions contribute to negative views of the policy actors providing the service and consequently spillover to perceptions of the government at large. One particularly relevant feature of policy feedback for this work is the ways in which the *administration* of a program, or the policy *design* shape feedback effects. Indeed, Soss (1999) attributes the negative interpretive effects found among AFDC/TANF recipients to the arbitrary and unprofessional design of the welfare program itself. This is in direct contrast to the inclusive design of the Head Start and/or the social security program, where recipients are made to feel entitled to their benefits through a more efficient and responsive system. By examining the specific design of public policy programs, policy feedback literature is able to locate *how* policies directly impact citizens' perception of themselves, policy and politics.

It remains the case, however, that a majority of these works focus on issues such as welfare at the exclusion of educational policy issues. Yet, education directly affects most people's daily life over time, with a majority of American citizens' directly acquiring civic skills through public schools (Hochschild & Scovronick, 2003). Thus, one would expect experiences with education to shape citizens' political attitudes. And certainly proponents of feedback have acknowledged the importance of examining education and its potential political consequences. Mettler and Soss's (2004) piece pose the specific question of how educational policies influence patterns of political opinion. Nonetheless, this has yet to be taken on.

POLICY FEEDBACK, EDUCATION POLICY, AND PUBLIC TRUST

This chapter takes on this question of how citizens' education experiences teach them about policy and politics with a particular focus on public trust. Established works in political science demonstrate how trust often acts as a determinant of policy attitude (see e.g., Hetherington 1998, 2005). Trust is typically measured by the extent to which citizens' feel that policy makers will do what they say or rather what citizens expect them to do. Therefore, inconsistent behavior by policy makers will lead to perceptions of government as untrustworthy. Distrust is defined as long held grievances accumulated over time and are thus not easily reversible (Levi & Stoker, 2000). Public trust is necessary to garner support for government programs that may require sacrifice for some groups for the benefit of everyone. Thus, trust is an important factor in public policy because citizens have to believe that policy makers will put their sacrifices to good use. Otherwise, citizens will not support them (Hetherington, 2005; Hetherington & Globetti, 2002).

Public school closure, in large cities like Chicago, acts as an especially important policy by which to explore the feedback effects of education experiences on public attitudes and public trust. The policy is nominally nonracial and yet requires sacrifice on behalf of primarily African Americans, theoretically for their own benefit. Therefore, unlike affirmative action, busing or even welfare, other more privileged groups are not asked to sacrifice anything, nor will they directly benefit. This raises important questions as to how theories of trust operate in contexts where those affected are the exclusive winners and losers of the policy. More generally, the targeted nature of the policy should contribute to negative attitudes toward the policy and policy makers as citizens come to view themselves as taking on costs—loss of school, participation in meetings, and protest—borne by no other groups, even if only temporary.

This chapter focuses on the case of Chicago, where the school closure policy has been instituted for over a decade, as an important case for exploring these issues. Since school closures in Chicago have affected similar communities repeatedly over time, those affected by the recent round of school closures have education experiences by which to draw from in the development of their opinion. More specifically, if they view their experiences as inconsistent with the objective of the policy then this should affect trust for decision-makers that are implementing the policy. The next section provides a focused review of the school closure history in Chicago—the case for which this analysis is based.

CONTEMPORARY PUBLIC SCHOOL CLOSURE IN CHICAGO

Beginning in 2001, under the leadership of CEO of CPS, Arne Duncan, federal legislation of No Child Left Behind encouraged the use of straightforward accountability measures within CPS by awarding federal funding based on achievement thresholds (NCLB, 2001).[2] A year later, in 2002, it was under Duncan's leadership that the first round of schools (3) were closed for not meeting performance standards.[3] Framed largely as an issue of low performance, Arne Duncan stated, "We don't believe these schools, as they currently exist, will ever measure up."[4] The decision to close the schools was followed by the establishment of the Renaissance 2010 policy in 2004—a policy that sought to produce 100 new high performing schools in disadvantaged communities by 2010 (Bulkley, Henig & Levin, 2010). Renaissance 2010, in addition to the Illinois State Charter Law, incentivized the development of independent school operators—charter, contract, and performance—in hope to create a more competitive educational environment that would hold schools accountable and thus enhance performance (Lipman & Hursh, 2007). School closures and charter schools occurred in tandem with the establishment of the turnaround policy in 2006—a model that maintains the school building and students but replaces the teachers and staff. By 2011, over 100 schools were closed and/or turned around as a result of these policies (Chicago Public Schools, 2012b).

In March 2012, the CPS board decided unanimously to close and/or turn around 17 public schools for low performance. While there was widespread outrage by parents and community members for the decision, it was not until November 2012, when CPS announced that it would be undergoing its largest number of school closures to date that thousands of parents and community members began to organize against the decision. Yet, this time, CPS framed school closings as a response to "underutilization." CPS described the underutilization issue in the following way:

> Chicago has experienced a significant population decline—it has 145,000 fewer school-age children today than it did in 2000, centered primarily on the south and west sides. This population decline has been the primary driver of underutilized schools in our District—CPS has space for 511,000 students but only 403,000 are enrolled.[5]

The decline in population, according to CPS, left a number of schools, primarily on Chicago's south and west sides, under-enrolled.[6] Accordingly, in November 2012, CPS proposed a list of over 330 schools that could potentially be closed. By June 2013, 49 of the original 330 schools were closed affecting over 12,000 students across the Chicagoland area (see Ahmed-Allah, Chase, & Secter, 2013). African Americans made up 88% of those affected, despite only representing about 47% of the public school population.[7] The large-scale, and targeted, nature of school closures in Chicago meant that specific communities experienced the policy process in ways that could impact their perceptions of the policy.

How Policy Experience Shape Public Attitudes Toward School Closure and Violate Public Trust

This chapter focuses on the role of the school closing policy design to first define membership, which makes certain populations more eligible for school closings than others. Those deemed as eligible are then subjected to the policy in practice—attending meetings, followed by the actual closing of schools. These practices serve as a form of political learning for those persons that have encountered them, whether directly or indirectly, as they reflect the interpretation of citizens' experiences with the closure process, in particular, and education policy encounters, generally. Citizens' interpretations of their experiences, and thus the lessons learned, particularly when compared to CPS objectives, likely shape their attitudes toward the policy and politics.

Policy feedback provides a comprehensive approach by which to examine the political attitudes of those targeted. Specifically, the negative educational feedback effects of a policy relates to the *resources* that are being taken away—the public school—and the *interpretive* effects that result, specifically as it relates to political trust. In this study, political trust is the key outcome of citizens' policy experience largely because the closure policy requires citizens to believe that the closure of their school will in fact benefit them in the long-term through the consolidation of resources. Yet, if citizens do not see evidence of these benefits then this should shape their trust in the policy, decision makers, and thus, government.[8]

DATA, METHODS, AND STRATEGIES FOR ANALYSIS

Data Collection

The data for this investigation consists of meeting transcripts, field notes (participant observation) taken at community meeting sites, in addition to semi-structured follow-up on interviews with parents, and in-depth interviews with elites—CPS officials, alderman, and organizational leaders. As Mettler and Soss (2004) state, "Public opinion tends to rely on surveys such as ANES, which collect little data about experiences with public programs" (p. 66). By contrast, community meetings provide important access to a wide array of attitudes in a concentrated environment over a short period of time.

A typical meeting was held at a church or a school after work hours, around 7 p.m., and lasted between two to three hours. Each school on the closing list was given 6 minutes total to provide commentary; 2 minutes each for three people total. The meetings were held in two rounds; with the first round including an initial list of 330 schools, and the second round including a reduced list of 129 schools. The number of schools facing closure per network varied, with some networks like Wood as low as one school, versus networks such as Park with up to 19 schools.

Each of the meetings were run by either the chief network officer and/ or the Family and Community Engagement officer (FACE) of that network. A group of about five to seven CPS officials' generally sat at a table located at the front center of the room, while the person tasked with running the meeting called up community members' who had signed up to participate on behalf of their school. Each person called upon would then come up to the microphone that stood across from the CPS officials. For the duration of the meeting, CPS, in addition to everyone in the audience would sit, stand, and/or cheer, as each speaker would speak into the microphone and list several reasons why his/her school should not be closed. The meetings were attended by on average 800 people per meeting, majority of which were parents across networks. Parents spoke the most at the meetings, followed by teachers. Several CPS officials were in attendance, but only one to two spoke per meeting. At the of the end of the 7-week period, over 5,000 people attended at least one of the 28 meetings held across 14 communities, or "networks"—CPS grouped schools by networks (see Table 9A.1 in Appendices).

Selecting Cases Within Chicago

Of the 14 networks, six were selected, which account for about 40% of the closures but vary in terms of race and experience, to follow closely over a 3-month period. Of the networks selected as focus areas, two of the neighborhoods/networks' were historically Black, one historically Hispanic, a majority of which were from Mexican descent, and one mixed, between Puerto Ricans, Mexicans, and Blacks. The other two were majority White. At these six networks, the author conducted ethnographic observations across 12 of the 28 meetings, although transcripts were collected and analyzed across all 28 meetings.

In the networks of focus, the author attended at least two meetings and stayed the entire time. In the first half of a meeting, the author spent a majority of time observing the speakers and members of the audience. At one meeting, public commentary was observed, and at the second meeting smaller break-out sessions were observed. The author also observed both the small and large meetings to gauge concerns raised against school closings not only when presented in a formal public setting, but also in the more tight-knit small group setting. The different meeting types enable an investigation that accounts for context and consistency in the responses of meeting attendees. Furthermore, by observing different types of meetings, this analysis distinguishes between those who attended the meeting as an activist versus general members of the community. This distinction ensures that a variety of voices were represented in the research. In total, the author observed 4 breakout groups and 8 large meetings directly, totaling 36 hours of observation.[9]

The ethnographic observations and meeting transcripts are combined with 25 short follow-up parent interviews of 20 minutes or less conducted before, during, and after each community meeting. The interviews were conducted to collect data on how parents responded to questions about their opinion when asked directly rather than just observed in a meeting. Finally, since CPS did not respond to the concerns raised at these meetings, 10 hour long in-depth elite interviews with CPS officials and Aldermen were conducted to get official responses on closure decisions.

Altogether, data collection included 28 meeting transcripts, nearly half (12) of which are supplemented by ethnographic observations, follow-up on interviews of parents (25) and in-depth interviews of elites (10), thereby ensuring triangulation of the data. Fortunately, as a native Chicagoan, a person of color and a woman, the author matched the characteristics of many of the people affected. These shared characteristics had a positive impact on getting people to participate in the interview.[10]

ANALYSIS

Coding for Policy Attitudes

The analysis involved an iterative coding process (see Skogan & Hartnett, 1997, p. 120 for similar process). The first set of codes were developed after attending the first set of community meetings and then recoded and finalized at the second set of meetings attended. The coding was based on the key concerns citizens' raised for their position on school closure and were counted and categorized by the number of mentions per issue. For example, violence and gangs were both issues that were included under the crime category. Therefore, if violence was mentioned 100 times and gangs mentioned 200 times, each of these issues were added together, thereby resulting in a total of 300 mentions for the crime category (see "Coding" in Appendices). The purpose of counting issue mentions is to gauge which concerns were most commonly raised in relationship to one's policy attitude, in this case, opposition to school closure, before determining how citizens came to hold these attitudes.

This type of coding was applied to transcripts across all 14 networks (28 meetings) in order to develop a fairly exhaustive set of coding categories. These categories include crime, family, fairness, politics, mistrust, charter, safe havens, resources, stability, race/race coded, listen, community, special needs, and overcrowding. Categories were then grouped into which issues were raised the most by those against school closings in order to shorten the list. Final codes included: crime, community, charter, trust/politics, and race/race coded. These codes/categories reflect the issues that were most salient across all networks.[11] The codes were then triangulated through additional interviews, described below, and local media sources. Most important, all of the transcripts are publicly available on the CPS website and thus can be used to verify the coding scheme.

Coding for Experience

After coding for the issues raised, rationales expressed in the interviews were examined in order to determine how citizens came to raise the issues mentioned above. This exercise is most crucial for the analysis. More specifically, the ways that interviewees discussed their experiences was coded for how it related to their policy attitude. In this case, experience is defined as any instance in which a person has encountered actions associated with an education reform policy. These encounters can range from an actual experience with a closure to simply being a resident in a community that has experienced targeted education reform policies. Special attention is paid to how experiences were discussed particularly as they relate to perspectives on school closure. The full list of rationales related to experience comprises the bulk of the analysis. Below are typical examples of how experiences were being used in the discussion of school closure attitudes:

> Every year, they ignore. How many of us here actually think they really care? Year after year after year, and they ignore. So, here is an idea for CPS, hold the community forum where they say, "Hey, community members, what do you need? . . . Have they done that?" (Lincoln, 02/06/2013)

> So, this year [Rose] received an influx of students from the [Lea] and [Washington] because of the closing last year school. Every day our students are suffering because our students' safety has been jeopardized. By adding students to our school, they have been in consistent, physical and verbal altercations with other students. We experience several gang fights, bullying, issues because of different territories, and that's the problem we're here for, territory. If our school closes, we are going to have a territory problem, territory representative. (Rose, 02/13/2013)

The above quotes highlight the continual nature of residents' experiences with different iterations of similar types of educational policies. In particular, they highlight how they come to associate the closure policy with largely negative outcomes related to increased crime and general lack of "care" for the growth and development of the communities affected. Ultimately, these concerns are embedded in general feelings of frustration and disbelief that the current round of closure will have positive impacts on their respective communities.

Comparing Citizens and CPS

Accordingly, analysis included in-depth interviews conducted with CPS school officials and their elite counterparts in reactions to opposition by the public of school closures. Below are typical examples of the explanations used in response to decisions to close down schools.

> By law you cannot borrow for your operating budget but you can for your capital budget which is much smaller, up to 800 to 900 million, but we had to slash it—it's about 300 million or something like that. Under law we have to fund our pension—400 to 500 million is used on pension—the school system did not have to pay into pension for a few years and it just kicks the can down the road and as Rahm said we no longer have any more road left...we can't just say we have a budget problem, we need to fix this...One of the tough decision was to close these 49 elementary schools.

> I don't expect teachers to fix social ills, poverty, housing, racial discrimination. We can't expect our schools to fix everything that is wrong but we can expect them to do better than they do...But we do not see increases in college readiness—we need not only to graduate but ready to go to college and if not then prepare them for this modern labor force and more credits that can be acquired for post college work while in H.S.

Each of the above statements demonstrate how closure is justified by CPS elites, and other sympathetic officials, on the premise that the closure of the school will result in positive outcomes whether related to resolving the "budget problem," enabling students to be "ready to go to college" and/or providing accountability in order to accelerate student achievement. Theoretically, then, school closures should contribute to positive outcomes for citizens. Yet, comparing the statements made between affected residents and CPS officials, findings indicate that community residents experiences with, and understanding of, school closures are inconsistent with CPS stated objectives—leading to mistrust and suspicion of state agencies and officials. The remainder of the chapter utilizes the data to demonstrate how experiences with education policies have negative feedback effects on attitudes towards the closure policy and ultimately have consequences for public trust.

THE FEEDBACK EFFECTS OF EDUCATION POLICY:
HOW EXPERIENCES WITH SCHOOL CLOSURE SHAPE
PUBLIC ATTITUDES

Policy experiences can have negative or positive feedback effects on public opinion. As mentioned above, much of these effects are explained as a consequence of the policy design and the particular ways in which it is administered. Similarly, community members affected by closure develop attitudes toward the policy and government based on their various educational experiences with the design and administration of educational policies by the school district.

Indeed, when public school officials in Chicago place particular schools on the recommended closure list, those who would be potentially affected by the decision are required to participate in a series of organized meetings—two community meetings and a public hearing. Their participation in the meetings are supposed to ensure that they have an opportunity to defend against the closure and/or contribute to the way in which the closure process occurs. And indeed from their participation at these meetings, in the context of their encounters with the school district at large, there are specific educational feedback effects that they take away from their experiences.

It is important to note that according to CPS, the school closure policy was developed as mechanism to:

> Remove underutilized facilities that spread...limited resources too thin... then redirect those dollars to ALL schools, then...make investments that support student growth through new technology, AC, libraries, art/music, more counselors and nurses, and others. (CPS Presentation—Belmont, 3)

In short, school closures were meant to contribute to positive outcomes for students. Yet, citizens' described their experiences with the school closure process in ways that appear inconsistent with what is being expressed as an objective of the policy by its perpetrators, CPS. Indeed, while a number of persons affected by the current round of school closure had particularly high levels of experience with the school closure process, they also experienced increased exposure to negative education experiences, despite CPS claims of the benefits. Below are examples of statements made at community meetings by parents who had multiple experiences attending meetings on school closure:

> We have been in this school action—we have been on this school action list before. What do you think it does to a child who has to every year fight for their school to stay open? (Rose, 02/27/2013)

The problem we see at our school is that these schools are definitely on the hit list to be closed each and every year. If these schools are continuing to be on the hit list each and every year as a potential of being closed, how is it that we can attract the top talent to come to our schools to teach, to lead us, to be the principals...? (Park, 02/27/2013)

The above statements demonstrate the ways in which community members' express feelings toward their repeated experiences with the policy process. In the particular cases described, school closures appear to have negative cognitive implications on the child and the ability for the school to "attract the top talent." Because these negative outcomes are the opposite of what CPS claims, residents' past experiences challenge the notion that the current meeting will lead to positive or even consistent outcomes for those affected. Instead, their experiences contribute to suspicion, and thus distrust, of the policy and policy makers especially as it relates to external efficacy. As another parent stated at a community meeting in Belmont:

I already said all these things. I said all these things, and this is the third time I'm up here, and they tell me somebody is listening. I want to know who it is. If I have to keep repeating myself, over and over and over again, who is listening to me? Who? Somebody tell me who that is. I turn in all my papers the last time. Why do I need to do it again? I said this I don't know how many times... (Belmont, 04/13/2013)

In the above example, the parent is expressing her frustration with participating in meetings, and yet still being ignored "over and over again." This lack of responsiveness by decision makers contributes to a belief that no one is listening which forces her to question the purpose of participating in the process again. Thus, her experiences with the process in the past provide a basis for her distrust in the value of participating in the current process, regardless of the positive outcomes promised by CPS officials. These inconsistencies contribute to negative feedback effects, particularly as it relates to policy attitudes and government trust.

THE SHIFTING JUSTIFICATIONS OF CLOSURE AND ITS IMPACTS ON PUBLIC TRUST

A key contribution to these distrustful attitudes are the past framings of the school closure policy by CPS described earlier in the review. In the early years of closure, based on section 5/34-8.3 of the Illinois School Code, the school board described themselves as closing schools "due to chronic academic failure (see CPS Recommendation, May 22, 2002)."[12] It was not until the 2012–2013 school year that the school district reframed the policy as a solution to resolve "underutilization, [which] result[ed] in financial resources being invested in half-empty buildings that are costly to maintain and repair (see CPS Transition Plan, July, 2013)."[13] These changes in the framing of the policy by CPS did not go unnoticed by community members. Many community members expressed frustration with the lack of clarity about exactly what purpose school closings were meant to serve. Below are examples from two of the six select network meetings:

> A few years ago it was overcrowding, now it's undercrowding . . . You're just going to shut them down and pass them around and relocate them again later. (Field note, Park, 02/18/2013)

> Also, we were told that we shouldn't have to go through this again, since we went through this last year. Why are we going through this again? School utilization was not an issue two years ago when you tried to close us then. Thank you. (Rose, 02/27/2013)

In the above examples, community residents are invoking upon their experiences with school closings and CPS, and as a result, are expressing frustration, confusion, and suspicion. More specifically, both statements illustrate how the shift in the framing of the policy's purpose—from a matter of schools' "overcrowding" to a matter of "undercrowding," led affected participants to cast the issue as a revolving door policy with no clear purpose or end in sight. As a result, the community members question the policy and the motives behind it. Indeed, some expressed concerns that the policy was constructed to give away resources to charter schools. As one parent stated:

> First we're not performing right, then we didn't have enough kids, then we didn't have enough money. What is it? I'll tell you what it is, you know, it's about the $98 million that charters like UNO are getting, and our schools are not getting. We are not going to allow you keep watching while our resources are taken somewhere else. (Lincoln, 03/01/2013)

This parent's statement addresses the various ways in which school closure has been framed as a basis to build her claim that the policy is in fact not benefiting the communities it is meant to serve. Instead, she views school closures as contributing to the growth and expansion of charter schools. Her decision to attribute the school closure policy to charter schools, despite what CPS claims, is indicative of her distrust of CPS and the policy, itself.

Community members more broadly observe similar inconsistencies between their experiences and the stated objective of the policy. Thus, they too attribute school closures to other issues such as gentrification rather than what CPS states as the justification of the policy. Below are two examples of persons who fall into this category:

It's not only about closing schools, it's about the area where these schools are sitting at, plans for a city development. Think about it. Think about it. I have seen the changes. I've been in [Belmont] over 50 years. (Belmont, 04/13/2013)

When you destabilize the school system in the neighborhood, and I say follow the money and understand the history. If you look, the development has already hit us at Roosevelt and California. Whenever there is gentrification, they build a new school or increase the school or fix the school where they at. For instance, [Lea], if they found that much money for capital funds for a private school, how come they couldn't find it for a public school? (Belmont, 04/13/2013)

In each of the examples, community members discuss experiences with the "changes" in their neighborhood and how these changes are related to the closure of public schools. In particular, citizens are connecting their encounters with, or understandings of, school closure to other issues they deem as unfair, in this case the gentrification of neighborhoods and the lack of funding for public schools. By making this connection, it is clear that citizens have not experienced positive effects of the policy, and thus do not trust that the current school closures will have positive impacts on their communities. Their experiences, therefore, contribute to negative feedback effects as it relates to the policy attitudes and public trust.

POLICY MISMATCH: THE ROLE OF SCHOOL CLOSURE IMPLEMENTATION AND OUTCOMES ON PUBLIC ATTITUDES

Citizens feelings of suspicion and distrust are further exacerbated by their understandings of the policy's purpose based on the specific way it was implemented and its actual impacts. While one might expect a school closing to literally mean the shutting down of a school building, school closings actually took on various forms. School actions taken by CPS during this period include co-location—two schools sharing one space; consolidation—combining two schools into one school; closure—the shutting down of a building; phase out—no new entering classes; and reassignment of boundary changes—changing neighborhood district lines for who can go to which schools in a single area.[14] Thus, interpretations of school closings by citizens were also based on their experience with one or more of these practices respectively. A typical example of a parent-teacher that experienced more than one type of school closure in the Park network is stated below:

I have been a victim of four school actions during the course of my career between school closings, turnarounds, whatever else you want, reconstruction . . . Each time I had to get adjusted to a new group of students and figure

> out my goals for these students, and when I have gotten to become a com-
> munity with students in schools, then CPS comes in and disrupts everything,
> including jobs and personal community relationships ... So, you know, I do
> not know if these hearings are a sham, or whether you are really listening to
> what these people in this community said. (Park, 02/18/2013)

In this statement the parent-teacher has had multiple and different experiences with school closings. It appears that her experiences with these different forms serve to reinforce doubts about the policy's purpose. Each time a
school closing occurred for her, she not only had to adjust to a new community of students but manage to reorient her teachings goals after CPS (via
the school closing policy) "comes in and disrupts everything." The teacher'
experiences with the different faces of school closings' as one marked by
disruption is certainly not representative of the intended goal of the policy
indicating the significance of policy implementation to her understanding.
Thus, the apparent inconsistency between the policy on the ground and
the policy as abstraction makes her question not only the policy, but also
the whole process of policy development. This is illustrated in her belief
that the most recent hearings "are a sham" and further demonstrates the
ways in which community members' experiences with closings make them
suspicious towards the school closure policy and the policy process, at large.

Perhaps unsurprisingly, the consequences of school closings were as varied
as their practices. While CPS framed school closings as enabling students to
attend/be placed in more competitive schools, one of the only assessments
on the impacts of school closures in Chicago revealed that 40% of displaced
students were sent to schools on probation. In fact, the report finds that displaced students were likely to change schools a second time after their initial
displacement (see De la Torre & Gwynne, 2009). Thus, there exists no evidence, at the time of the current closing policy, to suggest that this iteration
of the policy would be better for students. Additionally, despite the policy's
continued usage over the past decade, it was not clear the school district ben-
efited from a leaner budget as promised by the district. This precise concern
was expressed by a parent from the Belmont network:

> These schools have been closed for years, and the deficit still goes up hun-
> dreds of thousands of dollars a year, and you know why? It's because you
> keep giving charter schools a dollar to open up a school and give them all
> of our dollars, so stop being confused, and stop trying to confuse us. (Chess,
> 02/19/2013)

The above quote demonstrates how the use of the school closing policy
as a solution for reducing the budget deficit is read by some community
members with suspicion. This is because when the policy was enacted in the
past it did not lead to a reduction in the deficit. Thus, residents' question

the policy's ability to achieve the outcomes it claims, based on their understanding of previous iterations of the policy and its failure to achieve those same goals in the past. Given that it does not appear that the policy has had the positive outcomes CPS intends, community members' experiences with these unclear outcomes—in terms of recurring student displacement and school closings, as well as higher, rather than lower, deficits—seems inconsistent with the solution CPS is putting forth. These inconsistencies between policy goal and policy outcome contribute to their suspicious interpretations of, and ultimately negative attitudes towards, the closure policy.

CONCLUSION AND ADDITIONAL CONSIDERATIONS

Altogether, this study demonstrates that community members' experiences with actions associated with education generally have shaped more recent attitudes towards the closure policy. By focusing on negative feedback effects of the policy as it relates to the resources that are being taken away— the public school—and the interpretive effects that result, specifically as it relates to public trust, findings show that experiences have often been inconsistent with the stated objectives of the policy. Community members' experiences with these inconsistencies contribute to their suspicion surrounding the real objectives behind the closing policy. These suspicious interpretations directly shape parents' oppositional attitudes towards school closures and public distrust for the policy makers, more generally.

In the future, it would be useful to both expand the sample and also consider how attitudes towards school closing can change to the point of outright reversal. While most of the persons in the sample attended meetings, an account of responses from those not in attendance would also be useful for a closer investigation of the various ways in which experience plays out in the selected networks differently and why. Nonetheless, the meetings attracted persons that typically do not participate but were essentially forced to defend against the closing of their school.

Additionally, it could be argued that attitudes revealed in this analysis have more to do with what elites from groups like the CTU or CPS convey to citizens rather than actual experiences with education policy. However, this possibility does not negate the role of experience in itself. While attitudes towards policy issues are influenced by a diverse array of competing organized interests (i.e., elites), and the information they make available, it is important not to neglect the role of experience in this process. As one community leader stated,

> I have to object to the idea that people do not have agency or that unions are manipulating people . . . that goes for the youth and same with parents. It's

like they don't have their own experiences. I think they are extremely important but I don't think that people can't think for themselves... they use their
own understanding... but just to assume they are brainwashed? Why can't
Black and Brown people have their own ideas?

The statement further emphasizes the broader point that because these
parents have real experiences even if they are learning from elites, this
learning happens within experiential parameters. Personal experiences
with school closings may constrain the ability of elites to frame them in
whatever ways they choose.

Finally, it is also important to note that many of the targeted communities
are simultaneously experiencing the effects of other policies (i.e., large-scale
plans for transformation), which are likely reinforcing attitudes towards the
school closing policy as well. Future analysis should consider how to account
for different experiences with interrelated policies. More generally, serious
consideration of the situated nature of interpretation is advisable (Spillane,
2000). A situated approach takes into account the ways in which context, and
the particular, matter for how experience and knowledge is used to interpret
policy meanings. Being more explicit about the role of context and prior
knowledge for attitudes towards the policy of school closings will enable a
more comprehensive and nuanced analysis of the topic.

Nonetheless, the chapter finds that community members' encounters
with the various and multiple manifestations of education policy over the
past decade (as implemented by CPS) are inconsistent with the stated objectives of the policy. These inconsistencies contribute to general suspicion
of the real objectives behind the 2013 school closing policy and thus shape
oppositional attitudes towards the policy, its implementers, and politics, at
large. The chapter contributes to our understanding of the development
and implementation of education policy by constructing one of the only
academic investigations of how citizens think about school closings and why.
Furthermore, by comparing policy objectives to citizens' interpretation of
their experiences with those policies on the ground, the analysis provides a
systematic approach to the investigation of educational feedback effects that
can be utilized to examine other policies as well—not just school closures.

Beyond the literature, this work has serious implications on understanding how citizens' everyday policy experiences shape their broader political
attitudes. Citizens have some of their most intimate experiences with politics within education. Yet, by focusing on school closure, we learn about
the specific ways citizens trust in public institutions such as education is
violated routinely. This violation of trust over time plays a critical role in
how new policies are interpreted and thus attitudes are shaped. These attitudes can directly shape citizens' propensity to engage in formal political
spaces where their voices are too often marginalized from the democratic

process. By understanding public attitudes towards closure, then, we gain valuable insights for citizens' relationship to democracy and the tools needed to improve it.

NOTES

1. Turn around in this case includes four potential reforms to an educational institution:
   (a) students stay in same school and the staff are replaced with new public school staff, (b) students stay and staff are replaced with charter operators, (c) new standards and strategies are developed to better tailor the needs of students, or (d) the school is permanently shut down. See U.S Department of Education. (2010). Blueprint for Reform Report (for more information see https://www2.ed.gov/policy/elsec/leg/blueprint/blueprint.pdf).
2. For details related to No Child Left Behind (2001; see http://www2.ed.gov/nclb/landing.jhtml.
3. This refers to the official policy of school closings. Schools had been closed on a circumstantial basis before it was introduced as an official policy.
4. See Lenz, Linda. (2004). "Lessons from Chicago." Catalyst Chicago. June 15, 2004 (retrieved from http://www.catalyst-chicago.org/news/2011/11/07/lessons-from-chicago).
5. See CPS Presentation, Austin-North Lawndale Network Meeting, January 31, 2013, p. 1
6. This decline can also be explained by the growth of the Charter school movement. According to the Illinois Charter School Network homepage in May 2013, "Illinois charter schools comprise 55 schools over 124 campuses, 39 of which fill 110 campuses in Chicago, serving nearly 50,000 students" (retrieved from https://www.incschools.org/). These students are likely coming from the traditional public school system. In addition, and perhaps most important, the closure of public housing projects and the economic crises in 2008 in these same neighborhoods contributed directly to the population loss.
7. Calculated using CPS—data and statistics (retrieved from http://cps.edu/SchoolData/Pages/SchoolData.aspx).
8. It is important to note that the limitation of political learning to notions of trust does not mean that other lessons are not being learned. Limiting the concept of political learning to government trust enables me to minimize the lessons learned to those most relevant to the outcome of interest.
9. In some cases, break-out sessions were ineffective as community members expressed that they did not want to be "divided." In these instances, break-out sessions were not conducted at all.
10. The author learned that community participants were often looking for ways to share their stories in order to save their schools and thus saw me as someone they could trust to help and/or that they wanted to help. For elites, it was clearly communicated that the author was not a reporter.

11. Certainly, decisions had to be made, as often one comment can include references to three different issues. In this case, judgment calls were made based on how much of the comment referenced one issue over another

12. The specific recommendations of closure due to academic performance can be retrieved from https://www.cpsboe.org/content/actions/2002_05/02-0522-EX04.pdf

13. The specific transition plan referenced above can be retrieved from http://schoolinfo.cps.edu/SchoolActions/Download.aspx?fid=3058

14. See for example, Chicago Public Schools Consolidation Press Release. December 1, 2015 retrieved from http://cps.edu/News/Press_releases/Pages/PR1_12_01_15.aspx

APPENDIX A

TABLE 9A.1   Average Attendance Across Two Meetings

Total		Belmont	Lincoln	Chester	Rose	Park	Wood
Total Attendance	5,150	1,000	1,200	800	800	850	500
Total Speakers	327	52	72	59	49	58	37
Parents	148	26	30	30	16	28	18
CPS Officials	37	9	5	8	10	6	9
Teachers	118	12	30	18	30	20	8
Politicians	24	5	7	3	3	4	2

As illustrated in the table, parents spoke the most at the meetings, followed by teachers. Several members of CPS were in attendance, but only 1–2 spoke. The politician's category includes alderman, state representatives, and committeeman. However, mostly alderman spoke. It is important to note that these numbers reflect averages across two meetings. In Pilsen, for example, the number of schools on the list diminished drastically (from 10 to 3) between the first and second meeting, thus the numbers in each of the above categories declined. It is also important to mention that there were a substantial number of CPS officials at the second meeting than the first across all meetings. Moreover, official numbers of people in attendance have not yet been made officially available so these are reported averages.

APPENDIX B
Coding

Categories

Crime

The *crime* category received one of the highest percentage of mentions of any other category—26%. Crime mentions included any reference to gangs, violence, guns, safety, and similarly related themes. A typical example of what would go into the crime frame includes statements' such as the following:

> You are talking about sending those kids from this side of Austin, I mean, we got to admit, we got wars in the community, we got gangs in our community. They don't become gang bangers in high school. They start from somewhere else. So, these kids are about to go from here to here. So, we're talking about tearing our kids' life. We have the big thing about them being senselessly murdered. So, why we're going to add fuel to the fire and put our kids in harm's way?

> (Man stands up and shows gang map) If you send kids from one side of the community to another—you will put our kids in harm's way. Our kids safety and education . . .

> It is the safety of our children. The safety of our children is a primary concern. Barbara Byrd-Bennett said this during a conference call with reporters, according to the Sun Times. She also said for children to travel farther, or to put children in the danger of crossing a gang barrier, does not make sense to me.

> I'll give you an example. We just had an incident where a young man was killed on . . . Street, and he was killed by somebody from the . . . side of the community, and he killed somebody on the [other] side of the community, and these kind of tensions are going on. So, I'm saying that to say if you put these two schools together, it's not going to work. It won't work in our community. You give us some years to work on it, it will work, but it won't work.

In this statement it is clear that the person is arguing that because of the safety concerns that could result related to gangs, the school should not be closed down.

Community

The *community* category tied with crime at 26% and included referrals to schools as safe havens, or places of stability, family, and overall pillars of the community. Yet, this category also included references to special needs students. This is because many of the schools spoke of how closing the school would affect their special needs populations by disrupting the relationship built with these students thereby stagnating progress. A few typical examples of sentiments that were placed in the community category, including one specific to special need students,' are below:

> Goodlow is not just a school, it's a family, it's a home, it's an environment, it's a community. Their passion just runs deep, and I really, really wish that I could say something that would help you truly understand that you can't close this school.

> . . . My daughter is safe, this school is a safe haven, if I'm late, I can call the parents. This impacts the whole community . . .

> . . . You need to realize, one out of every three kids in the schools at North Lawndale are special ed children. They are special ed children. So, we have created public schools that are really therapeutic schools. We have to realize that before we make our decisions.

As we can see, particularly in the latter statement, even if the word community was not used, the overall statement is expressing a concern for the impact closings will have on an established community at that school.

Charter

The *charter* category was the second most popular category and included any references to the term "charter" and any general mentions of charter school operators such as UNO, Noble, and KIPP. An example of comments made against school closings using the charter issues include:

> I'm here today to bring you a message. Stop our school closings. Stop the proliferation of charter schools. You cannot say you are going to close even one of our public schools; and in the same breath, say you're going to use our resources that belong to our schools to fund privatized schools. Private schools that will be funded with public monies, our money.

> 120 new schools many of which are charter were open while 100 CPs schools were closed. Why are we here?

> This is about destabilizing communities. This is about failed charter schools. Charter schools are failing, but they want to sell Black people and Latino people a dream that charter schools are doing better than the neighborhood schools.

> We are here to say "no" to school closings, not in [Ches], not anywhere. We are here to say "no" to charters, turnarounds, and military schools where they are not wanted.

In this statement, the speaker is associating the closing of public school with the funding of charter schools, and privatized schooling more generally. The participant is thus using Charter schools' to explain opposition toward school closings.

Trust/Politics

The *trust/politics* category received 15% of all mentions and included any referrals to suspicion, transparency and accountability, and politics. A few examples of the various statements that were included in this category are below:

> ... we don't trust you. If you're going to try to start building trust, you got to tell us the truth.

> ... It's amazing to me how you can find a billion dollars, I don't know if you heard about that, to refurbish Grant Park, but we can't find money to better our schools. It's amazing to me how you can find money to get all these raises to all the politicians, but we can't find money to better our schools."

In both of the above statements, the speakers are expressing their suspicion of the reasons put forth by CPS for closing schools—to reduce the budget, and general mistrust for CPS more generally.

Race/Race Coded

The *race/race coded* category received 7% of all mentions and included any direct references to *race*, such as racism," in addition to *race-coded* sentiments, which instead used non-explicit referrals to race such as apartheid, and genocide, and comparisons to non-majority Black/Hispanic neighborhoods like Lincoln Park, or the suburbs. An example of the latter concern includes:

> ... In reading through the history of the schools that you guys want to close, why is it that there's a disproportionate amount of schools that is on the south side and the west side that are closing, and then there are not that many schools in, if any, on the north side that's closing? This is hitting the south side and the west side the hardest of anybody.

> This is about the decline of Black and Latino teachers. Black children—Black teachers teach Black children. When you close schools that are 99% Black, you are saying, "Black teachers, we don't want you. You are not good enough."

In this typical example, though the term race was not used, the concern has racial undertones given its implicit comparison between the south and west sides, which are majority Black, and the north side, which is not.

REFERENCES

Bulkley, K. E., Henig, J. R., & Levin, H. M. (2010). *Between public and private: Politics, governance, and the new portfolio models for urban school reform.* Cambridge, MA: Harvard Education Press.

Burch, T. (2013). *Trading democracy for justice: Criminal convictions and the decline of neighborhood political participation.* Chicago, IL: University of Chicago Press.

Bushaw, W. J., & Lopez, S. J. (2010). A time for change: The 42nd annual Phi Delta Kappa/Gallup Poll of the public's attitudes toward the public schools. *Phi Delta Kappan, 92*(1), 8–26.

Campbell, A. L. (2002). Self-interest, social security, and the distinctive participation patterns of senior citizens. *American Political Science Review, 96*(03), 565–574.

Campbell, A. L. (2003). Participatory reactions to policy threats: Senior citizens and the defense of social security and medicare. *Political Behavior, 25*(1), 29–49.

Chicago Tribune (2013). *Crime in Chicago. Crimes reported by community area.* Retrieved from http://crime.chicagotribune.com/

Chicago Public Schools. (2012b). *School action guidelines 2012–2013, definition of underutilization,* p. 3. Retrieved from http://www.cps.edu/About_CPS/Policies _and_guidelines/Documents/SpaceUtilizationSt andards.pdf

Converse, P. E. (1972). Change in the American electorate. In A. Campbell & P. E. Converse (Eds.), *The Human Meaning of Social Change* (pp. 263–337). New York, NY: Russell Sage Foundation.

De la Torre, M., & Gwynne, J. (2009). *When schools close: Effects on displaced students in Chicago public schools* [Research Report]. Chicago, IL: Consortium on Chicago School Research. Retrieved from https://eric.ed.gov/?id=ED510792

Henig, J. R., Hula, R. C., Orr, M., & Pedescleaux, D. S. (2001). *The color of school reform: Race, politics, and the challenge of urban education.* Princeton, NJ: Princeton University Press.

Hetherington, M. J. (2005). *Why trust matters: Declining political trust and the demise of American liberalism.* Princeton, NJ: Princeton University Press.

Hetherington, M. J. (1998). The political relevance of political trust. *American Political Science Review, 92*(04), 791–808.

Hetherington, M. J., & Globetti, S. (2002). Political trust and racial policy preferences. *American Journal of Political Science, 46*(2), 253–275.

Hochschild, J., & Scott, B. (1998). Trends: Governance and reform of public education in the United States. *The Public Opinion Quarterly, 62*(1), 79–120.

Hochschild, J. L., & Scovronick, N. (2003). *The American dream and the public schools.* New York, NY: Oxford University Press.

Levi, M., & Stoker, L. (2000). Political trust and trustworthiness. *Annual Review of Political Science, 3*(1), 475–507.

Lipman, P., & Hursh, D. (2007). Renaissance 2010: The reassertion of ruling-class power through neoliberal policies in Chicago. *Policy futures in education, 5*(2), 160–178.

Mettler, S. (2005). The only good thing was the GI bill: Effects of the education and training provisions on African-American veterans' political participation. *Studies in American Political Development, 19*(01), 31–52.

Mettler, S., & Soss, J. (2004). The consequences of public policy for democratic citizenship: Bridging policy studies and mass politics. *Perspectives on Politics, 2*(01), 55–73.

Miles, M. B., & Huberman, A. M. (1994). *Qualitative data analysis: A sourcebook of new methods.* Thousand Oaks, CA: SAGE.

NORC. (2013). Joyce foundation–Chicago tribune survey. Chicago, IL: University of Chicago. Retrieved from http://s3.documentcloud.org/documents/627036/joyce-foundation-chicago-tribune-public.pdf

Pierson, P. (1993). When effect becomes cause: Policy feedback and political change. *World politics, 45*(04), 595–628.

Pierson, P., & Skocpol, T. (2002). Historical institutionalism in contemporary political science. *Political Science: The State of the Discipline, 3,* 693–721.

Public Agenda. (2012). Community responses to school reform in Chicago: Opportunities for local stakeholder engagement. New York, NY: Public Agenda.

Rosenstone, S., & Hansen, J. M. (1993). *Mobilization, participation, and democracy in America.* Boston, MA: Pearson.

Skogan, W. G., & Hartnett, S. M. (1997). *Community policing, Chicago style* (pp. 8–55). New York, NY: Oxford University Press.

Sondheimer, R. M., & Green, D. P. (2010). Using experiments to estimate the effects of education on voter turnout. *American Journal of Political Science, 54*(1), 174–189.

Soss, J. (1999). Lessons of welfare: Policy design, political learning, and political action. *American Political Science Review, 93*(02), 363–380.

Soss, J., & Schram, S. F. (2007). A public transformed? Welfare reform as policy feedback. *American Political Science Review, 101*(1), 111–127.

Thelen, K. (1999). Historical institutionalism in comparative politics. *Annual review of political science, 2*(1), 369–404.

United States Department of Education. (2010). A blueprint for reform: The reauthorization of the elementary and secondary education act. U.S. Department of Education, Office of Planning, Evaluation and Policy Development.

Verba, S., Schlozman, K. L., Brady, H. E., & Brady, H. E. (1995). *Voice and equality: Civic voluntarism in American politics* (Vol. 4). Cambridge, MA: Harvard University Press.

Wolfinger, R. E., & Rosenstone, S. J. (1980). *Who votes?* (Vol. 22). New Haven, CT: Yale University Press.

CHAPTER 10

SCHOOL CLOSURES AND THE POLITICAL EDUCATION OF U.S. TEACHERS

Lauren Ware Stark
University of Virginia

Rhiannon M. Maton
State University of New York College at Cortland

In the years following the passage of No Child Left Behind in 2001, urban school districts across the United States experimented with new models of market-based school reform with the stated purpose of decreasing educational costs and improving student performance. Operating alternately under mayoral or gubernatorial control, districts in cities such as Chicago, New Orleans, New York, Philadelphia, and Washington DC engaged in a "portfolio district" model that prioritizes decentralization, school evaluation using standardized test scores, charter school development, and school closures or turnarounds (e.g., Bulkley, Henig, & Levin, 2010). Using the metaphor of the stock portfolio, the portfolio district model recasts district superintendents as CEOs investing and disinvesting in schools based on

Shuttered Schools, pages 287–324
Copyright © 2019 by Information Age Publishing
All rights of reproduction in any form reserved.

their performance (Saltman, 2010). The portfolio model gained national significance with the implementation of the federal reform initiative Race to the Top (de la Torre & Gwynne, 2009). Under Race to the Top, states receiving competitive federal grant money must select from four options to reform "priority schools" identified as failing based on standardized test scores: turnarounds, restarts, transformations, or school closures (U.S. Department of Education, 2009). This reform strategy remained popular in the years following the implementation of Race to the Top, especially in grant-recipient states such as Delaware, Illinois, New York, and Pennsylvania. School districts in cities such as Chicago and Philadelphia have been particularly focused on market-based school "renaissance" models, gaining national media attention for their use of market-based school reforms such as school closures (e.g., Rich & Hurdle, 2013).

In the face of such closures, community organizers and teachers have developed powerful networks for challenging systems of oppression both locally and nationally. Grassroots organizations have contested school closures in their local contexts and have collaborated in developing national research and action campaigns. Working in solidarity with these organizations, teachers have likewise developed a growing movement of rank-and-file educators who engage in a new form of union organizing that they conceptualize as social justice unionism (SJU). Working both within and outside of their local unions, teachers' social justice caucuses use grassroots organizing strategies, partner with community organizations, and advocate for the needs of students, families, and communities alongside traditional bread-and-butter issues like income and benefits (Peterson, 1997; Weiner, 2012). While educators increasingly face poor working conditions (Johnson, Kraft, & Papay, 2012) and decreasing labor rights (Robertson, 2008) in their cities and schools, closures arguably represent a moment where teachers' material interests are inextricably linked with those of their students and communities. In this way, resisting closures presents an opportunity for enhanced political engagement among both teachers and the communities they serve, pointing toward the possibility of collective organizing against austerity and broader systems of oppression.

In this chapter, we investigate the relationship between school closures and the political education of U.S. teachers. Drawing on two qualitative studies, one by each author, this chapter asks: How do teachers in social justice unions perceive and respond to school closures? What cultural processes characterize political education about school closures within social justice caucuses? In order to answer these questions, we first review the literature on school closures and political education, building on these literatures to develop a conceptual framework that identifies five cultural processes of political education within social justice caucuses: situational, relational, structured, mobilized, and networked political education. We apply this framework to analyzing teacher organizing in social justice caucuses in Chicago and Philadelphia. We further argue that school closures support the development of political education efforts within social justice caucuses of teachers' unions.

CONCEPTUALIZING POLITICAL EDUCATION IN RESPONSE TO SCHOOL CLOSURES

This chapter builds on research on both school closures and political education. As a qualitative study of teacher responses to school closures and other turnaround policies, it contributes to the policy literature on school closures (de la Torre & Gwynne, 2009; Larsen, 2014; Valencia, 1984), detailing how education organizers conceptualize and respond to school closures. Moreover, in documenting the cultural processes of political education within social justice caucuses responding to school closures, it contributes to the interdisciplinary literature on political education within social movements (Choudry & Kapoor, 2013; Diani, 1996; Foley, 1999; Hall, Clover, Crowther, & Scandrett, 2012).

Policy Perspectives on School Closures

While policy groups, think tanks, and local and federal governments have conceptualized school closures as an efficient solution to cut education costs and boost student performance (Research for Action, 2013), other researchers have highlighted the cost of school closures. Critical scholars have analyzed the effects of school closures on communities in major cities such as Chicago and Philadelphia, noting that the closure process has destabilized low-income communities, displacing students and teachers while offering no measurable academic benefits (de la Torre & Gwynne, 2009; Larsen, 2014; Valencia, 1984). Likewise, union and grassroots researchers have offered public scholarship on the impact of closings in cities across the country, noting the disproportionate impact of school closings on students of color (Opportunity to Learn Campaign, 2013) and the subsequent destabilization of schools and communities (Journey for Justice Alliance, 2014). Union researchers have further noted the disproportionate impact of school closures on teachers of color (Caref, Hainds, Hilgendorf, Jankov, & Russell, 2012).

Critical and public scholars have also provided useful theoretical frameworks for conceptualizing school closures within broader sociopolitical processes, including neoliberalism and systemic racism. Neoliberalism can be understood as a "complex, often incoherent, unstable and even contradictory set of practices that are organized around a certain imagination of the 'market'" (Shamir, 2008, p. 3). Some critical scholars point to the relationship between neoliberalism and racism in school closings, conceptualizing school closures as part of a racialized system of "educational apartheid" (Caref et al., 2012, p. 9)—a school system with high degrees of racial segregation within and between schools (Street, 2005). Other scholars connect closures with neoliberalism, racism, and capitalism, stating that school closures might be understood as part of a broader social and political process of neoliberalism and systemic racism (see Buras, 2014; Lipman, 2011; Picower & Mayorga, 2015). With these frameworks in mind, critical scholars understand school closures as part of a broader system of interrelated oppressions in the U.S. education system and society as a whole, symptomatic of both macro-political trends such as neoliberalism and racism and micro-political trends such as gentrification and undemocratic educational governance.

Political Education within Social Movements, Labor Unions, and Grassroots Organizations

In conceptualizing the role of school closures and social justice caucuses in the political development of rank-and-file teachers, this study contributes to the developing literature on political education in social movements, labor unions, and grassroots organizations. This literature draws on a number of disciplinary traditions, including the sociology of knowledge, social movement studies, and informal and adult education. Within these interrelated literatures, scholars have offered conceptual and empirical research documenting the nature and practice of political education in social movements. Most recently, scholars have contributed to a growing tradition of research on education, tracing cultural processes within social movements and adult education.

Our study builds on scholarship examining the political education of adult learners in informal settings (Choudry, 2015; Chovanec, 2009; Foley, 1999; Hall & Clover, 2005; Freire, 1970), interrogating the political education of activists and teachers engaged in social movements. We do so by integrating frameworks that understand social movements as spaces of collective learning (Choudry, 2015; Foley, 1999) through specific cultural processes (Johnston, 1995). The study of informal political education has its roots in the traditions of popular education and critical pedagogy (Horton & Freire, 1990; Freire, 1970). In his work as an organizer, educator, and social theorist, Freire (1970) conceptualized political education as the process of supporting "oppressed" peoples' development of "critical consciousness" through an iterative process of "praxis," defined as "reflection and action directed at the structures to be transformed" (p. 126). For Horton and

Freire (1990), political education within social movements is an ongoing process: "When we're in the process of mobilizing or organizing [...] Education is before, is during, and is after. It's a process, a permanent process" (p. 117). Horton and Freire therefore see political education as rooted in an iterative process through which people work together to think through sociopolitical processes and collectively develop new critical frames.

Social movements have been conceptualized as spaces of ongoing collective learning within both the social movement literature and the adult education literature. McAdam (1982) identifies "cognitive liberation" as one of the three central dimensions of social movement organizing, arguing that organizers must work collectively to analyze and respond to their social conditions (p. 51). Foley (1999) similarly argues that social movements are spaces of critical research and theory production, suggesting that political education plays a central role in contemporary social struggles (Foley, 2001).

Building on these frameworks, several scholars conceptualize social movements as sites of the creation, development, and enactment of knowledge (Casas-Cortés, Osterweil, & Powell, 2008; Chabot, 2010; Choudry, 2015; Choudry & Kapoor, 2013; Conway, 2011; Cox, 2014; Holst, 2002; Hosseini, 2010). By conceptualizing social movements as spaces of collective learning, these scholars build on the tradition of researchers focusing on cognitive (Eyerman & Jamison, 1991) and cultural processes (Johnston, 1995) within social movements including the use of shared interpretive frames (Diani, 1996; della Porta & Diani, 1999). Other social movement and adult education scholars have focused on distinct cultural processes of political education. For example, scholars have traced emotional (Goodwin, Jasper, & Polletta, 2001), narrative (Davis, 2002; Polletta, 2006), political (Barker & Krinsky, 2009), and ethical (Hall et al., 2012; Stark, 2016b) processes of political education within social movements.

In this chapter, we conceptualize political education as a series of interconnected cultural processes, many of which are inquiry-based. Our work builds on that of scholars within the fields of adult education, popular education, and the sociology of social movements. By focusing on cultural processes within social movements, scholars draw attention to the "intersubjective frameworks or cultural structures [that] connect the cognitive to the macro-social," tracing how communities learn and change through "individual cognition but also inter-subjectively, through shared scripts and cultural structures, such as 'frames', 'narratives' and 'cultural repertoires'" (Lamont, Beljean, & Clair, 2014, p. 573). Using this conceptual lens, scholars note not only the individual, cognitive dimensions of political education within a social movement but also the collective, cultural dimensions.

While scholars of adult education, popular education, and sociology do not widely discuss political education in social movements as a series of cultural processes, we can recognize examples of cultural processes within their work.

Within his praxis of critical pedagogy, Freire (1970) argues that structured political education through literacy circles and problem-posing are able to strengthen social movements advancing the interests of adult learners. Likewise, Horton and Freire (1990) and Cochran-Smith and Lytle (1999) highlight the importance of structured political education through collective inquiry. McAdam (1982) suggests that political education can be supported through a range of cultural processes such as participation in movement actions, one-on-one conversations, and structured discussion groups (see Tarlau, 2014).

Within the growing body of research conceptualizing social movements as spaces of collective learning, there are few empirical studies that develop a conceptual framework for political education in social movements "from the ground up" (Choudry & Kapoor, 2013). Likewise, few studies have outlined the complex range of cultural processes that characterize political education within social movements (Bevington & Dixon, 2005; Tarlau, 2014), instead focusing on discrete cognitive or cultural processes within a social movement, such as the use of ethical frameworks (Hall et al., 2012) or narratives (Davis, 2002). There are furthermore few studies outlining cultural processes of political education within social justice caucuses in teachers' unions, particularly as they relate to school closures. With these gaps in mind, we offer a framework for understanding the nature of political education within movements that are responding to market-based reforms such as school closures. More specifically, we trace the complex cultural processes of political education within social justice caucus organizing. In this framework, we conceptualize learning and knowledge production within social movements as a complex series of cultural processes of political education. Drawing on the work of popular educators (Horton & Freire, 1990), social movement scholars (Chabot, 2010; Diani, 1996; Eyerman & Jamison, 1991; Tarrow, 2010), and informal education researchers (Choudry, 2015; Chovanec, 2009; Foley, 1999; Hall & Clover, 2005), we note that social justice caucus members learn collectively through a complex range of cultural processes. These processes include: situational, relational, structured, mobilized, and networked political education.

In outlining the cultural processes that characterize political education within social justice caucuses, this study aims to build on research on political education within social movements. Likewise, in its discussion of political education in response to closures, this study aims to contribute to the research on school closures.

CONTEXTS, METHODOLOGY, AND METHODS

This chapter develops a framework for understanding political education by examining cultural processes in the political education of teachers organizing in response to school closures in Chicago and Philadelphia. In so doing, it brings together data from two studies, one conducted by each author. The first study was conducted by Stark and is an ethnography documenting the work of teacher organizers within a national network of social justice caucuses. The second study was conducted by Maton and employs participatory action research (PAR) to examine the role of learning in Philadelphia's Caucus of Working Educators. Together, these studies provide substantial insight into how teachers experience and understand the effects of school closures and how they adapt their political outlooks and behavior through these experiences.

Contexts

While school closures can be linked to teacher organizing across the United States, this study focuses on social justice caucuses in Philadelphia and Chicago. The cities each have distinct urban political economy and history, but also share important characteristics. In each city, schools have been governed by an unelected school board which prioritizes efficiency and accountability. School boards in both cities have closed significant portions of their public schools over the past 20 years, following market-based portfolio models of school reform. Considerable community and teacher resistance has ensued in response to closures in both cities, and social justice caucuses have developed in both Chicago and Philadelphia in response to market-based education reforms such as school closures.

Chicago

Chicago has been a laboratory for market-based education reform for the past 2 decades, as well as a site of considerable community and teacher resistance. Closures continued following Arne Duncan's tenure as CEO of Chicago Public Schools. Following a portfolio district model, Duncan closed a total of 38 schools between 2001–2006 (de la Torre & Gwynne, 2009). Later, in 2013, the mayor-designated Chicago Board of Education voted to close a record 49 schools, the largest single round of closures in U.S. history (Cohen, 2016). These closures disproportionately affected students of color, with the majority of closed schools serving predominately African American and Latinx students (Caref et al., 2012). They also disproportionately affected teachers of color, with African American teachers representing 65% of the teaching force in schools slated for closure in 2011 and only 26% of the Chicago Public Schools teaching force as a whole (Caref et al., 2012).

As public schools were closed in Chicago, charter schools developed across the city, with charter enrollment increasing ninefold between 2000 and 2013, from 5,400 to 48,700 students (Institute on Metropolitan Opportunity, 2014). These new charter schools have served predominately Black and Latinx students, who made up 96% of charter school enrollment in both 2000 and 2013, while only making up 84–85% of non-charter enrollment in the same years (Institute on Metropolitan Opportunity, 2014). These demographic differences exacerbate the "diversity gap" between teachers and students in Chicago schools, with a diversity gap of 43% between teachers and students in non-charter public schools and a diversity gap of 65% between teachers and students in charter schools (Caref et al., 2012).

Community members have organized to challenge school closures throughout the past 2 decades through organizations such as the Kenwood-Oakland Community Organization. Teachers have consistently organized in solidarity with these community organizations. As part of this organizing, a group of Chicago teachers developed the Caucus of Rank-and-File Educators (CORE), arguably the most well-known social justice caucus in the United States.

The Caucus of Rank-and-File Educators, Chicago. The CORE grew out of teachers' efforts to fight against school closures. The group that would become CORE held its first planning meeting in a union hall in early 2008, bringing together educators with a range of experiences: organizers who had challenged school closures; "lefties" who had led previous progressive caucuses; progressives who had worked on campaigns such as the fight against school militarization; and new teachers who were eager to find ways to organize against the closures and layoffs that had affected their students and colleagues (Stark, interview, August 4, 2015).

After formally developing their caucus, CORE organizers continued organizing in solidarity with community groups and grassroots networks to advocate for equitable public schools and organize against school closures. CORE teachers collaborated with community organizations such as the Kenwood-Oakland Community Organization (KOCO) and activist networks such as Teachers for Social Justice (TSJ). Through this work, CORE ultimately went on to win leadership positions within the Chicago Teachers Union (CTU), where they continued organizing against closures and used research, forums, and mass demonstrations to argue that there were links between closures and systemic racism (Bradbury, Brenner, Brown, Slaughter, & Winslow, 2014). Through a newly-established research department, CTU researchers developed reports on racial inequalities in school closures, teacher layoffs, and charter expansion (Caref et al., 2012). They further developed campaigns that centered educational and social justice within union organizing, including the campaign for the Schools Chicago Students Deserve and the campaign for a Just Chicago (Chicago Teachers Union Foundation Library, 2016). They also notably led the 2012 teacher strike, which presented a nationwide example of the potential of broad coalition-building in labor organizing for social and educational justice (Weiner, 2012; Uetricht, 2014).

Philadelphia

Like Chicago, Philadelphia has operated under an unelected governing body, the School Reform Commission, which since 2001 has focused on decreasing costs and improving performance through closures and charter school expansion. Charter schools in the city have rapidly expanded over time since the first charter school opened in 1997 (Welk, 2010). In 2007 Philadelphia charter schools served 32,000 students and have expanded to serve over 62,000 students, or 30% of the public school district's students (Kelley, 2015; National Alliance for Public Charter Schools, 2019). State law dictates that there is no cap on charter school expansion (National Alliance for Public Charter Schools, 2016), although the district enforces limits on new school growth, and these vary year by year.

Meanwhile, there are ongoing closures of neighborhood schools, with the now-disbanded School Reform Commission voting to close 6 schools in 2012, and 24 schools in 2013 alone (DeJarnatt, 2014). Of the schools closed in 2013, 81% of the students were African American, 11% were Latino, and only 4% were White. Overall, 93% of the students affected by the 2013 closures were low-income (The Schott Foundation for Public Education, 2013). The district has also enforced strict budget cuts in Philadelphia, leading to the 2013–2014 complete elimination of nurses, guidance counselors, teacher aides, and vice principals (see DeJarnatt, 2014), some positions of which were restored in the following school year. As is the case in other cities, the School Reform Commission's mass closure plans failed to live up to their stated goals, gaining very little cost savings and displacing thousands of students (Jack & Sludden, 2013).

Like Chicago, Philadelphia has seen mass community actions and organizing against school closures, with at least 1,000 students, parents, and teachers speaking out against closures at planning meetings (Jack & Sludden, 2013). Alongside students, parents and community members and their organizations, educators have established a number of teacher-led grassroots and union organizations, including the Caucus of Working Educators, that directly challenge school closings and engage in political education to build an organized resistance.

The Caucus of Working Educators, Philadelphia. Philadelphia's Caucus of Working Educators (WE) was founded in March 2014 and emerged as a result of ongoing work by activist educators in Philadelphia. Many of the original founders of WE were members of Teacher Action Group Philadelphia (TAG), which formed in 2009 and has sponsored a range of critical education workshops, conferences, reading groups, and campaigns of protest and resistance since its inception. WE built on this work and continues to partner with TAG and overlap in some of its membership. WE members assert that they would like to transform their union, the Philadelphia Federation of Teachers (PFT), into a "fighting union" that actively resists and counters school closures while supporting the development of healthy and vibrant local public schooling.

Active WE members include a range of leftist constituents: district educators including teachers, nurses, and counselors; local charter school educators; community members and parents; and university and post-secondary educators (Maton, 2016a). WE agitates for policy change at the school, district, state, and national levels. Active campaigns and committees have included: union election; Opt Out campaign against standardized testing; local and state political and electoral campaigns; a teacher professional development campaign; a campaign to educate preservice teachers about unions and union renewal; and an active racial justice committee. WE also continues to collaborate with TAG to create spaces to theorize and resist school closures and related systems of oppression, including through the annual summer reading series and ongoing reading groups (Riley, 2015). WE regularly partners with area organizations on mutually-sponsored campaigns, such as "Fight for $15" campaign, the Philly Socialists, and other area groups and events. WE also partners with local parents and community members to actively resist and protest local school closures and turnarounds. WE organizers and members tend to frame school closures as part of an intertwined process of market-driven reform and systemic racism (Maton, 2016a, 2016c; Khalek, 2013) and see their activism as a way of fostering critical hope in the face of ongoing school closures and district privatization (Stern & Brown, 2016).

Methodology and Methods

The authors bring together two studies in this chapter. The studies were conducted separately but hold in common that they engaged qualitative research techniques in order to build a deep view of teachers' development of political consciousness through political action in the wake of school closures. Stark's research primarily draws upon ethnographic methodology and methods, while Maton draws upon PAR traditions. Both studies draw on the methodological tradition of critical constructivism, which centers the social construction of knowledge within the context of complex power structures (Kincheloe, 2005; Kincheloe, McLaren, Steinberg, & Monzó, 2017).

Ethnographic Research

Ethnographic research endeavors to offer detailed descriptions and interpretations of social structures, connecting the researcher's analyses to those of participants (Wolcott, 1987; Wolcott, 1999). Ethnographers draw on a range of predominately qualitative methods to offer a "thick" description of cultural processes (Geertz, 1973), which can be understood as the ways that participants operationalize their own cultural knowledge (Spindler & Spindler, 1997). Most ethnographic research includes participant observation: describing cultural processes in naturalistic settings and crafting ethnographic field notes that capture salient dialogue and vibrant descriptions from the observed experiences (Emerson, Fretz, & Shaw, 1995). Ethnographic research often also includes in-depth, open-ended ethnographic interviews (Spradley, 1979) as well as the collection and analysis of documents and artifacts (Spindler & Spindler, 1997).

Stark has employed ethnographic research methods throughout her research on teacher organizing in social justice caucuses in the social justice unionist UCORE network, including CORE and WE. More specifically, she engaged in a variation of ethnography conceptualized as "network ethnography," in which researchers use ethnographic methods to trace cultural processes across multiple sites, identifying key sites using social network analysis (Howard, 2002). Stark has used participant observation, ethnographic interviewing, and document analysis throughout her research on the UCORE network. In this research, Stark is interested in the movement of policies across social justice caucuses, as well as the cultural processes that characterize caucus organizing across the UCORE network. As a teacher organizer and supporting member of several network caucuses, Stark takes an activist stance in her research.

Participatory Action Research

Participatory action research brings together action research traditions with emancipatory theory and practice (Marshall & Rossman, 2011). Building on action research traditions, PAR tends to seek tangible and useful results that directly benefit participants (Stringer, 2007). PAR strives for emancipatory purposes, goals, and outcomes (see Freire, 1970) that emphasize the "full collaboration between researcher and participants in positing the questions to be pursued and in gathering data to respond to them" (Marshall & Rossman, 2011, p. 23).

Maton has employed PAR methodology throughout her research partnership with the Caucus of WE. Maton's research is primarily concerned with the form and function of activist teacher learning individually and in groups, and she facilitated an inquiry group that brought together a small group of participants to consider the nature and consequences of structural racism within schools and WE. A number of tangible organizational actions resulted from Maton's study, including: the formation of a caucus racial justice committee; the writing and release of organizational statements about racial justice; and, a series of professional development workshops led and designed by and for teachers. In line with PAR, Maton's partnership with WE members emphasized collaboration, democratic decision-making and dynamics, critical reflection, and action-focused outcomes.

Data Collection and Analysis

This chapter primarily focuses on oral history interviews with teacher organizers who faced closures of their own school or others in their community, fieldwork from teachers organizing in Chicago and Philadelphia, and documents from both contexts. Stark's study includes over 150 hours of fieldwork in spaces that bring caucus organizers together from across the country, as well as individual caucus meetings and actions. It also includes 29 oral history interviews with teachers engaged in caucus organizing in cities including Chicago, Philadelphia, Los Angeles, and Seattle, as well as document analysis of caucus newsletters, platforms, and social media posts. Maton's project includes over 170 hours of participant observation in organizational meetings and events, 35 semi-structured interviews with caucus members, and analysis of documents produced and published by organizational members on websites and social media.

Data analysis in both projects occurred in three iterative phases. Phase one involved triangulation of data sources, continuously analyzing and relating field notes, interviews, and documents (LeCompte & Schensul, 1999; Prior, 2002). Through this process, we sought to "discover, identify and ask questions about" patterns in the data (Charmaz, 1983, p. 112). Phase two involved three parts: developing a coding key that emerged directly from both sets of data, integrating our separate codes to develop a single set of codes, and then re-coding the data accordingly (Marshall & Rossman, 2011). Phase three involved two parts. First, we engaged in member-checking (Bernal, 1998) the initial findings of our independent studies through informal conversations with participants; this ongoing and iterative process aims to support participant critical engagement and feedback on research findings. Second, we continued to review data in light of the main identified themes and findings, and engaged in inductive analysis (Patton, 1980) and axial coding (Marshall & Rossman, 2011).

While our data analysis generally followed these stages, it was conducted iteratively throughout the research process. Credibility was determined using the guidelines of critical constructivist research. These criteria include providing rich analyses of complex social phenomena, integrating multiple perspectives, building on previous theoretical constructs, offering a cohesive portrayal of interrelated social processes, developing a novel analysis that is relevant to both researchers and participants, acknowledging the significance of context and culture, tracing the dialectical relationship between individual experiences and social structures, and supporting just social action by marginalized groups (Kincheloe, 2005, pp. 43–45).

Building on the data analysis methods described above, this chapter asks: How do teachers in social justice unions perceive and respond to school closures? What cultural processes characterize political education about school closures within social justice caucuses?

FINDINGS

Our findings indicate that there is a relationship between school closures and the perspectives and actions of social justice unionist teachers. We find that closures can support the political education of teachers and the development of grassroots activist organizations, including social justice unionist caucuses. Teacher political education was a pattern that emerged for teachers who had had little prior involvement in political resistance, protest, activism, or unions; teachers who had previously been engaged in personal political learning and stances but not directly involved in activist organizing; as well as teachers who had some organizing experience. Across teachers with these different extents of prior knowledge and involvement in leftist analysis and movements, we find that there was growth in teachers' critical political perspectives and analysis as a result of their observations and experiences with school closures. Generally speaking, we find that market-based reforms such as closures support the political education of teachers and communities. This political education can be seen immediately following the implementation of reform policies as well as in the ongoing work of social justice caucuses.

Our findings show that there were five main cultural processes through which teacher political education took place in connection with school closures. These cultural processes of political education are: situational, relational, structured, mobilized, and networked political education (see Figure 10.1).

Each of these cultural processes of political education act as processes of perspectival change and learning. *Situational political education* can be understood as context-dependent political development in response to a specific policy or experience. *Relational political education* can be understood as political development through relationships that support the growth of a particular political viewpoint, including a relationships with a friend or colleague who has experienced or organized against market-based reforms such as school closures. *Structured political education* can be understood as political development through participation in activities with an explicit agenda to educate rank-and-file members, potential members, or allies. *Mobilized political education* can be understood as political development through engagement in a political action, such as a strike or rally. And, *networked political education* can be understood as sustained political

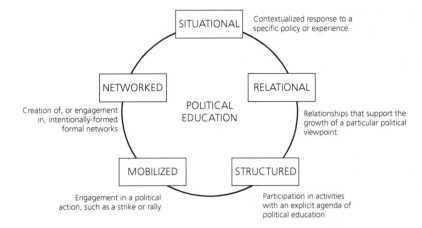

Figure 10.1 The five cultural processes of political education.

development through the creation of, or engagement in, intentionally-formed formal networks.

In this findings section, we identify, describe, and provide evidence for each of these varied cultural processes of teacher political education. In so doing, we examine at least two incidences of teacher political education for each form of political education, one from Chicago and one from Philadelphia, and use these to show the strong connections between school closures and their related processes and the growth of teachers' critical political analysis and perspectives. While each of these processes of political education has been evident in our research on the CORE and WE caucuses, they should not be understood as a finite or discrete list. Rather, we found that caucus organizing integrates multiple processes of political education, and that many of the teachers we interviewed discussed experiences aligning with several of these processes while discussing their own political development.

Situational Political Education

In reviewing the development of social justice caucuses in Chicago and Philadelphia, we noted that market-based reforms such as closures in many cases supported the political education of teachers and communities, developing the foundation for grassroots and rank-and-file organizations including social justice caucuses. Social justice unionist teachers frequently identified that witnessing or experiencing school closures was a significant factor in their decision to become politically involved in social justice caucuses.

Through situational political education, a teacher's critical political outlook develops in response to experiencing or witnessing a specific experience or policy. We identify this form of political education as situational, in that it is tied to a specific and contextualized event, experience, or policy that brings together individual interests and experiences with external situational factors and experiences. These external factors may take place suddenly or be sustained over time. Processes of situational political education include the experience or threat of school closure or its related processes—such as turnarounds, charter school expansion, and layoffs. Our data indicates that teachers in both Chicago and Philadelphia were politicized through situational factors.

In Chicago, school closures were a clear catalyst to teacher organizing, galvanizing the situational political education of caucus educators. The CORE caucus itself was created with the express purpose of fighting school closures and other market-based policies affecting public education. Erica,[1] one of the attendees at the caucus's first meeting, noted the connections between school closures and the formation of the caucus: "We didn't know exactly what we were going to do; we just we knew that we needed to do more to fight school closings and unjust firings, and we knew that the union was the biggest organization that could be tackling these issues in a meaningful way." She further noted that the work that community organizations were doing to fight school closures in solidarity with teachers in affected schools hadn't been enough to build "a broad resistance" so far, and that the union had not had the "wherewithal to organize mass demonstrations and really engage the broader membership" (Stark, interview, August 4, 2015). In this way, early caucus organizers saw their work as a natural extension of existing community and grassroots organizing against closures, with the potential to build effective mass movement through the considerable numbers and political power of the CTU's rank-and-file membership.

Looking back on the formation of CORE at the caucus's 2015 annual convention, Logan, one of the caucus's founding members, noted the ways in which the caucus aimed to fight closings and other policies that negatively affect their students: "when we got together, [...] we wanted a union that would stand up for kids, that was going to fight against school closings." He went on to contrast the previous union leadership's inaction surrounding school closings with the work CORE and CTU have done since then, noting that they had recently organized to successfully reopen a closed school (Stark, field notes, September 25, 2016).

For many of the founding members of CORE, the fight against school closures and other market-based reforms is both politically significant and deeply personal, building on their own experiences of market-based reforms in schools. Several Chicago organizers explicitly connected their political education to direct experiences of market-based education policies and reforms. Nicole, former special education teacher and CORE leader, discussed how she was politicized by her eighth grade student's decision to drop out after she learned that her school was closing: "Once we got word that we were really going to close, that's when she stopped showing up." While her student had been promised a placement in the charter school that would take over their closed public school the following year, the charter school reversed this acceptance after they were sent the student's individualized education plan (IEP). This experience politicized Nicole by allowing her to analyze the relationship between her students' experience and market-based reforms in Chicago. In realizing how closures and charter schools marginalized students with learning differences, she said to herself, "That's it. Gloves are off. I am going to fight charter schools to the death" (Stark, interview, May 30, 2015). For Nicole, losing a student was pivotal, leading her to shift her focus from teaching at a single school throughout her career to dedicating her efforts to education organizing (Stark, interview, May 30, 2015).

Another CORE organizer, James, was politicized through attending meetings hosted by the city's unelected board of education. He noted that he had not previously realized how those meetings were structured and how major board decisions were made. This understanding helped him theorize undemocratic processes as a whole, recognizing how school governance relates to privatization and the closure of schools, as well as how they relate to the marginalization of students of color (Stark, interview, May 30, 2015).

School closures have also played an important role in the history of teacher organizing in Philadelphia, galvanizing teachers to organize for educational justice through both grassroots and union organizations. As was the case in Chicago, teacher organizing and theorizing around closures initially began through grassroots networks and community organizations. Philadelphia's TAG has been especially central to this development.

For many teachers working within TAG, the wave of school closures in Philadelphia served as a point of political education. In a piece she published in *Perspectives on Urban Education,* TAG and WE organizer Anissa Weinraub (2013) noted that school closures were a "wake-up call" to teachers in the city. Since this wave of school closures, TAG organizers have continued to purposefully provide opportunities for educators to make sense of their own experiences, analyzing the relationship between market-based reforms and broader systems of inequality through reading groups and other activities. Most recently, TAG organizers created an opportunity for teachers to collectively attend a play and discussion focusing on school closures in Chicago (Teacher Activist Group, 2016).

Teachers in WE have similarly discussed the role of market-based reforms in the political education of Philadelphia's teachers. Another WE caucus organizer, Ben, reflected on the ways in which processes of charter school expansion and school turnover radicalized teachers within his school. In the year before he began teaching there, the school had been slated for charter school expansion, and teachers worked with parents and community organizations to successfully challenge this decision. In reflecting on the charter fight, he observed that "a lot of teachers who just otherwise thought they were going about their jobs suddenly were meeting after school every day to rally support for [our school] as a public school as opposed to a charter school" (Stark, Interview, 29 May 2016). When he was organizing the school to fight the district turnaround plan 2 years later, teachers were again "moved to action" when they realized that their union was not going to fight for their school (Stark, interview, May 29, 2016). This process has also been evident across the WE membership. At the 2016 election kickoff meeting, Stephen, an active WE organizer, reflected on his own political development as a result of school closures, noting that he had become politicized in the face of school closures and layoffs in his community. He also recognized the work of WE teachers who had been active organizers since they began fighting against school closures, noting that many educators in the room "were at every march" (Stark, field notes, January 27, 2016).

Together, the cases of teachers facing school closures in Chicago and Philadelphia indicate that teachers witnessing and experiencing what they perceived as unjust school closures developed an increasingly politicized and critical view. Teachers experiencing such threats, or witnessing threats to their students or colleagues, were often drawn to deepen their critical analysis of the political underpinnings to explain *why* the closure was taking place. They sought to develop an explanation for the feeling of injustice and this development of an explanation reinforced a critical viewpoint and perspective on school closures and their related processes.

Relational Political Education

While teachers are in many cases radicalized through their own experiences with market-based reforms such as school closures, they can also be politicized through their relationships with other teachers who have experienced or challenged these reforms. Moreover, they can be politicized through relationships with community or family members outside of their teaching careers, developing leftist political ideologies that in turn support their work within social justice caucuses. Teachers' critical political viewpoints may be expanded and deepened through engagement in these informal relational connections (Maton, 2016b; McAlevey, 2012; Tatum, 2003) and through one-on-one conversations (McAdam, 1982).

Through relational political education, a teacher's political development is tied to experiences of a friend or colleague, and new political analysis and perspectives are developed through relationships with others. Here, relational connections and learning often take place through a common experience or issue of concern, such as a threat to one's school or job. Through conversing and hearing about the viewpoints or experiences faced by another, broader or deeper political analysis is developed without necessarily requiring a direct experience of the phenomenon or policy. Processes of relational political education in this study include one-on-ones, mentorship, witnessing the layoff of a colleague, peer, or mentor, witnessing the effects of school closure on a student or family, and the development of a political analysis through discussions with friends, colleagues, or family. This study finds that both Chicago and Philadelphia social justice unionist teachers experienced political education as a result of relational experiences and connections.

For Chicago teachers active in CORE, relationships have been central both to their own political development and to the work they do within their caucus. Erica, one of the early members of the CORE caucus, was politicized by witnessing the layoffs of her mentor teacher and the head union delegate in her school, with the delegate losing her job for questioning previous layoffs. In discussing this experience, this organizer noted that it radicalized her by revealing the political nature of education organizing as well as the need for organized resistance to unjust policies: "[it] opened my eyes to the ways in which people who are critical can be targeted," she noted, which was "foundational in me being more involved in social justice work through the union" (Stark, interview, August 4, 2015). For Erica, the experience of seeing her experienced mentor teacher targeted helped her realize the potential stakes of organizing, while also cementing her resolve to engage in this work. From there, she took on the position of union leader within the fractured and traumatized staff within her school, ultimately going on to be one of the early members of CORE.

The growth of CORE can also be tied to relational political education. Erica met another founding member through the Chicago History Project in the 2005–2006 school year, coming together over shared experiences with market-based reforms such as school closures and mass layoffs (Stark, interview, August 4, 2015). For her, this relationship was a crucial step toward future engagement in education organizing, bringing her into "different circles" that would allow her to challenge the market-based education reforms that affected colleagues and the school. She further noted that other teachers were politicized through their relationships with teachers throughout the district, which fueled the growth of the caucus: "teachers were joining because they were realizing that if one school was threatened, they all were" (Stark, interview, August 4, 2015).

Relational political education was also central to the experiences of Nicole, the early CORE organizer whose student dropped out in response to her school being closed. While she had been closely following education politics in Chicago, she did not think that she had a place as an organizer in this struggle until she met two of the founding CORE members. She noted that they were "very open to anyone who was willing to do work," and that this openness was central to her decision to become an organizer herself (Stark, interview, May 30, 2015).

CORE organizers have continued to intentionally foster relational political education within their caucus membership, as well as in the union as a whole. CORE frequently hosts social events that allow teachers to develop solidarity with their colleagues across the district, including dinners and fundraisers. Their meetings also frequently include opportunities for teachers to develop friendships with the potential to foster future organizing. In one of the opening activities of their 2015 annual convention, CORE organizers led participants in paired listening exercises where each participant had the opportunity to share highlights from their teaching and organizing work. While this activity hones some of the concrete skills of organizing, such as one-on-one conversations and careful listening, it is also designed to allow participants to develop strong relationships with other organizers. One of the organizers leading the activity, Annette, discussed the relational dimensions of this activity, saying, "Even if this is your first time coming to a CORE meeting, you're going to have three new friends" (Stark, field notes, September 25, 2015).

Under CORE leadership, the CTU also fosters relational development through both social events for rank-and-file members and workshops dedicated to developing organizing skills. Social events include such informal activities as weekend camping trips with the CTU bike club, where CORE organizers, CTU staff, and adventurous rank-and-file members have the chance to informally share their school and political experiences (Stark, field notes, July 25–26, 2015). The union also provides opportunities for rank-and-file educators to develop the relational skills central to effective organizing through union workshops and extended learning opportunities such as a summer organizing program (Stark, interview, July 26, 2015). For many CORE organizers, developing relationships and having one-on-one conversations with teachers at every school are the building blocks of effective organizing (Stark, interview, May 30, 2015).

Philadelphia's WE similarly emphasizes relationships when organizing people to resist school closures and their related processes. WE hosts regular happy hours, organizes social events such as trips to plays and musical events, and most events include time for sharing food and socializing. WE also hosts ongoing trainings for members to practice and hone their skills at connecting with and politicizing colleagues and acquaintances about the causes and consequences of austerity and school closures. These trainings are largely concerned with enhancing participants' relationship-building skills. For example, at the Teacher Union Bootcamp training in

2014, attendees were provided with a handout titled "So you want to build teacher power at your school?: A practical checklist." The handout states:

> In the face of political and corporate forces that want to make teachers feel isolated and powerless, the first step to building teacher power is by strengthening the connections in our schools. The actual power of a teachers union does not come from the top; it is found within the work and commitment of the union's members in the schools. Things happen because we have developed a tight "web of relationships" within our schools and throughout the city that we can activate. (Maton, document, October 2, 2014)

In the training, members were encouraged to counter political and corporate experiences like layoffs, school charter school expansion and school closures, through building connections and relationships at their school site that would support teachers' deepened political viewpoints and critical analysis of policy trends. Attendees were asked to consider what kind of meetings already exist at their school, and to develop "additional creative fun ways to bring teachers together" that would enable "stronger community" within the school site. Relational political education is framed by WE's membership as a core means for supporting growth in organizational membership and future mobilization potential—in part to prepare for unexpected threats such as school closures.

Across both Chicago and Philadelphia, relational political education has supported the political development of both new and experienced organizers. Several organizers developed principled stances on education and social justice through their relationships with politically active mentors, peers, teachers, or family members. Likewise, several educators became politicized through their relationships with other social justice caucus organizers, and this form of political education is one of the central components of caucus organizing. In this way, relationship-building is seen by social justice unionists as a primary means through which to educate teachers, connect prospective members with the organization, and build mobilizing power to resist school closures and their related effects.

Structured Political Education

In our research into the organizing work of social justice caucuses, we find that caucuses purposefully provide opportunities for their members to engage in political education on the sociopolitical inequalities characterized by school closures. We further find that these learning opportunities support the ongoing political education of caucus members, as well as furthering the growth of the caucus by attracting new progressive and radical teachers. Structured political education provides teachers with the opportunity to develop new perspectives and viewpoints as they engage in individual and collective learning experiences. This political education is supported by intentional activities that take up varied pedagogical forms and functions and that explicitly seek to support the development of a critical viewpoint and perspective among attendees (Foley, 1999; Freire 1970; Maton, 2016a, 2016b). These activities tend to hold an explicit agenda to educate members, potential members, and allies. They range in the extent to which attendees are involved—some structured events seek highly active participant involvement, while others engage in a more passive approach to learner involvement. They also vary in the extent to which they are sustained over time, with some structured events asking for long-term commitment and participation by attendees and others taking place as stand-alone events.

Target audiences for educational events vary, with some social justice unionist caucus events designed to engage broad audiences such as local community members around a particular school, and others targeting a more distinct or tight group of attendees. These educational events take up varied forms in social justice unionist caucuses, including: book or topical discussion groups, inquiry groups, workshops, keynote talks, lectures, and film viewings. Our findings indicate that Chicago and Philadelphia both center structured approaches to building political education in connection with school closures. These spaces provide opportunities for members to make sense of school closures in light of broader political framings, such as critiques of neoliberalism or structural racism, and this sense-making supports the growth of political education among the social justice caucus membership.

Structured political education has been central to teacher activism and rank-and-file organizing against school closures and related reforms in Chicago. Within CORE and allied teacher activist groups, educators have had the opportunity to develop strong political analyses of market-based reforms as they relate to broader political processes such as neoliberalism and systemic racism. They have also had the opportunity to work collectively to develop a framework for their own organizing, encouraging new organizers to engage in their struggle, and providing them with the tools they need to be successful in doing so.

While our research focuses primarily on the work of labor organizations such as CORE and WE in supporting the political development of educators, it is important to recognize the links between CORE and allied organizations as they engage in structured political education to fight school closures in Chicago. Teachers for Social Justice (TSJ) is perhaps the strongest example of an allied organization dedicated to structured political education. TSJ organizers, faculty, and community members collaborated to develop an annual curriculum fair that features social justice workshops and reading materials, featuring presentations by CORE members such as a workshop on social justice unionism in 2008, the same year that CORE was founded (TSJ, 2008). They have also hosted ItAG (inquiry to action groups), which explore such topics as education for liberation and teaching for social justice (TSJ, 2009). Other organizations have proven crucial to structured political education of CORE and other members, as well. Nicole, an early CORE member, noted that her political development was linked to the *Catalyst Chicago* political magazine, where she followed debates of political struggles in Chicago (Stark, interview, May 30, 2015). She further recognized the role of community groups in supporting rank-and-file educators' political education, with parent activists sharing unreleased information about school closures and collaborating with teachers through such networks as the Chicago Grassroots Education Movement (GEM). Likewise, Chicago organizers frequently acknowledge the work of Labor Notes, a national organization supporting the labor movement through trainings and publications, in providing spaces for rank-and-file educators and other unionists to share organizing strategies (Stark, interview, May 30, 2016).

Within CORE itself, rank-and-file organizers have continued the tradition of linking education activism to political education. Indeed, an informal inquiry group was foundational to the creation of the caucus itself. Eight teachers met in an informal study group in 2008 to discuss Naomi Klein's *Shock Doctrine*, contextualizing school closures among other neoliberal reforms and discussing how to respond to their union's failure to combat closures head-on (Alter, 2013). This group included future CORE leader and CTU president Karen Lewis, as well as teachers active in organizing against Renaissance 2010 through grassroots and community organizations. Early CORE organizers participated in other reader circles, as well, including a circle on "lessons learned from the TWA rail strike in New York," leading them to discuss what would happen once they won positions in the union (Stark, interview, May 30, 2015). As CORE organizer and high school history teacher James noted, they also held a conference on budgeting and transparency that allowed rank-and-file educators to analyze the political dimensions of cuts and governance within their own schools (Stark, interview, May 30, 2015).

These teachers went on to found CORE with other education activists in June of 2008 (Alter, 2013). From there, CORE supported structured political education through community forums featuring students and teachers who had experienced school closures and charter school expansion firsthand. They also supported structured political education among rank-and-file teachers by "raising the right issues at the [union] meetings" in order to "raise awareness" as a CORE organizer, Nicole noted (Stark, interview, May 30, 2015).

While many of the original members of CORE were elected into CTU leadership in 2010, the caucus itself continues to provide spaces for structured political education at their meetings and annual convention. With 2 days of workshops and lectures, CORE's annual convention is a particularly potent space for political development. At the 2015 convention, CORE organizers created opportunities for political education on the history of CORE and labor organizing in Chicago. They also sponsored workshops where organizers could learn collectively, sharing strategies for such issues as developing a campaign, opting out of standardized testing, and using one-on-one conversations and practice strike votes to organize schools (Stark, field notes, September 25, 2015). CORE members' ongoing political development has also been supported by formal organizing training through both the CTU (Chicago Teachers' Union) and Labor Notes (Stark, interview, May 30, 2015).

In Philadelphia, WE tends to place a strong focus upon educational dimensions within its membership recruitment and mobilization. WE offers a range of explicit educational opportunities for its members, including: a yearly summer book club series, trainings to prepare teachers for specific aspects of recruitment and mobilization, lectures and talks, inquiry groups focused on particular topics and themes, film viewings, and more.

The summer book group series is framed by WE organizers as one of the most important pedagogical and structured events of the year. This educational book group series originated in Summer 2014 and continues every year with expanded and enhanced methods for organizing the groups, and is targeted toward WE members and supporters—including teachers, parents and community members. The books are chosen by caucus supporters and members through votes, and sometimes involve particular themes. In her description of the 2014 book groups, Riley (2015) reports that one intended function of the book groups is to politicize WE members. In the first year of the book groups, 2014, there was no identified central theme underlying the book series or the books chosen for group discussion. Rather, the nine books were selected by book group leaders, and tended to be responsive to political contexts perceived as shaping local public education (Maton, field notes, May 9, 2014). Most of the nine books tended to advance a framing of neoliberalism as the primary explanation for school closures, turnarounds, and charter school expansion. Thus, WE's book groups informally advanced critiques of neoliberalism as the primary lens for analyzing the causes and effects of school closures in the Summer of 2014.

Over time, the political framing of the caucuses for school closures was altered, deepened, and enhanced through posing new framings for understanding the cause of school closures. The books chosen for the 2015 summer book group series all centered around the notion of structural racism. This theme emerged from an inquiry group conducted for Maton's dissertation (Maton, 2016b) that was composed of WE teachers who were concerned with structural racism. Stemming from their work together in the group, the teachers proposed to WE their idea of extending their learning about race to the broader organization through the summer book series. This explicit engagement of WE members in sensemaking conversations about the links between neoliberalism and race contributed to the development of an analysis of school closures that locates such policy initiatives within interlinked systems of racial oppression and neoliberalism (Maton, 2016c).

Social justice union caucuses organize educational activities for prospective and existing members with the intention of building critical awareness of the reasons for and causes of school closures. The caucuses tended to take up a particular framing of the problem facing public education and local schools, and to center this framing within their design of pedagogical activities. The purpose of such activities in both Chicago and Philadelphia tend to center on increasing teachers' critical awareness and politicized analysis of neoliberalism and systemic racism. Discussion groups, talks, and other activities were formed in line with this intention for member political education.

Mobilized Political Education

People develop political viewpoints and analysis through their involvement in, or observations of, activist organizing and organized action (McAdam, 1982). Through mobilized political education, teachers engage in political actions and activities such as protests, campaigns, or other forms of resistance. Processes of action-based political education include: involvement in or observation of a protest, strike, rally, boycott; engagement in organizing actions or campaigns; and school-based organizing. While this engagement is generally direct, such as participating in a strike or rally, it can also include more remote forms of engagement, such as using social media to express solidarity from another city or school. We observed political education through actions among social justice unionist teachers in both Chicago and Philadelphia.

Within Chicago, teachers' political education has been fueled by the organizing work of CORE and the CTU. Despite the ongoing pressures of education reform policies, this work has had the potential to shape teachers' understanding of their own potential as organizers. This has been true in both mass mobilizations such as the Chicago Teachers' Strike as well as building-based mobilizations such as a test boycott.

For many teachers in Chicago and across the country, the 2012 teachers' strike represented a pivotal moment for social justice unionism. This was true for the organizers who led the strike, whose own political development continued as they realized their own capacity for mass mobilization and systemic change. Nicole recalled watching teachers and allies march through downtown Chicago wearing red CTU shirts. For her, seeing that "sea of red" t-shirts during the march was a "real turning point," enabling her to understand that CORE organizers were "on to something" bigger than they had anticipated (Stark, interview, May 30, 2016).

Building-based mobilizations in Chicago have proven equally important to teachers' political development. An active CORE organizer, Hannah, discussed how educators, students, and parents in her school were politicized through organizing against a mandated test. Drawing inspiration from the Seattle MAP boycott, this teacher had conversations with teachers and parents at her school about the necessity of organizing against unjust policies, noting that "strikes started illegally" and that they need to "fight back" (Stark, field notes, April 25, 2015). On a single day, teachers at this school distributed opt-out letters in a coordinated effort before their principal could realize what had happened. They further collaborated with parents at the school to determine how to respond to the new testing policies, discussing the testing calendar and developing strategies for parents to organize against the test in their communities. Through this organizing, the faculty in Hannah's building went on to take a unanimous vote to boycott the test, standing up to threats from multiple levels of school administration (Stark, field notes, April 25, 2015). This organizing galvanized teachers, parents, and students, with students standing up to their principal for "lying" about the test and continuing to organize in the years following the boycott (Stark, field notes, April 25, 2015).

Like any other successful political action, the teachers' strike and school boycott discussed in this section inspired hope among the organizers and participants. In the face of ongoing market-based reforms in Chicago, this hope can prove crucial for future organizing work. Successful actions such as these therefore represent an opportunity to counter the inaction that is often misinterpreted as apathy among educators. As Lucy, an experienced CORE organizer, noted at a national conference, "Apathy doesn't really exist. Apathy is fear and a feeling that you can't do anything" (Stark, field notes, April 2, 2016). By providing opportunities for teachers to realize that they can in fact "do something," organizers support the ongoing political education of rank-and-file teachers in Chicago.

We can see further mobilized political education in the example of the CTU's 27,000-member strike against austerity on April 1, 2016. As part of this strike, Chicago teachers marched in picket lines at their schools, participated in teach-ins and protests across the city, and gathered downtown for a mass rally and march through the rain. Rather than focusing solely on unjust labor and educational practices in Chicago Public Schools, the strike organizers developed coalitions with organizations fighting related struggles across the city: fast food workers leading "the fight for $15," faculty and staff members combating funding cuts at Chicago State University and Northeastern Illinois University, and organizers combatting racism through the Black Youth Project 100 and Assata's Daughters (Catalyst Chicago, 2016; Lydersen & Brown, 2016; Stark, field notes, April 1, 2016). This action spoke to the CTU's history of organizing for both educational and social justice in solidarity with community organizations. It also spoke to the political development this union has undergone since electing leadership from CORE, a caucus within the CTU that formed with the express purpose of challenging school closures in Chicago.

There were numerous examples of political education through mobilization among Philadelphia's social justice unionist teachers as they organized in response to market-based policy reforms including closures. Through their experiences organizing and participating in political actions, Philadelphia teachers developed an awareness of their own potential to take control of difficult situations, potentially changing the political landscape of their school or city in turn.

Some local educators found mobilizing to be a significant political learning experience both for learning about the possibilities in protest and for building understanding of the contexts in which practitioners may—and may not—exert influence in policy development. In describing her initial involvement in social justice unionist activism, a school district nurse named Claire identified a potential layoff due to funding cuts as influencing her to attend her first protest. Claire said that as a result of attending this single protest she "fell into" organizing weekly protests with another educator leader. She ended up taking primary responsibility for organizing weekly protests over a period of 22 consecutive weeks, and through the experience learned how to mobilize people, turn people out for protests, build support, and other activist skills.

Much of Claire's learning here was supported through the mentorship of a local ex-union president, who took her under his wing and taught her mobilizing and tactical techniques. Claire describes how she would meet with him for coffee, and "he would absolutely just teach me . . . he said every time, when you hold these rallies you have to bring someone into the rally so that that's growing the understanding of your issues. He was really like an organizer. And then you put those names on your list and you get to know people. It was 22 weeks of just working full time, but I would meet with him every week for like an hour." During these experiences of organizing the weekly protests, observing what worked and what did not work, and debriefing the protests with her mentor, Claire found that she was politicized into many new tactical techniques that allowed her to build increasingly strong leadership as an activist organizer (Maton, interview, Sept. 29, 2014).

It was also common for seasoned Philadelphia social justice unionist teachers to discuss how mobilizing contributed to their ongoing political education. Similar to the organizers leading the testing boycott in Chicago,

Ben, a WE organizer, noted that his school-based colleagues became increasingly politically engaged through building-based organizing. As a union delegate, he discussed the union contract frequently with teachers, noting that teachers were not required to go into meetings alone with their principal, especially when they feared bullying or harassment. He then began attending meetings with his colleagues, which in turn encouraged other teachers to attend meetings themselves. This change has proven significant for educators in his building, providing "a real source of strength in an otherwise tough situation" (Stark, interview, May 29, 2016). Through this action, the teachers in his building have developed a strong union presence that will enable them to continue organizing the next school year.

While teachers were in many cases politicized during their teaching careers, some educators were politicized through participation in social actions during their own schooling. As a high school senior, Ben had witnessed the potential to use organizing to effect political change through his participation in a student walkout. This walkout resulted in the end of his school principal's tenure and ushered in a new slate of board of education candidates. Reflecting on the success of this walk-out and its influence on his own political development, he noted, "student activism is a potent force. So, that was a lesson I got pretty quick" (Stark, interview, May 29, 2016).

Through their experiences organizing and participating in mobilizations, teachers and other stakeholders in Chicago and Philadelphia developed a strong political awareness of their own potential for social change. This was the case for experienced organizers who recognized the immense power of mass political mobilizations, as well as new organizers participating in fights against standardization and undemocratic governance at their schools.

Networked Political Education

Formal relational and organizational connections through intentionally-formed networks support political education (Stark, 2016a). Through networked political education, the political development of educators is supported by the creation of formal political networks, which in turn support both relational and organizational connections among organizers. This form of political education is of a sustained nature, in that it takes place over periods of time as relationships are formed and deepened across individuals and organizations. The creation of networks is often an advanced stage in political development, while at the same time networks can foster new processes of political development (Featherstone, 2008). Examples of networked political education include: interorganizational formal networks, interorganizational mentorship, and conferences sponsored or organized by a network. We found instances of networked political education across both contexts of Chicago and Philadelphia, and found that these instances involved both local networks within the city and national formal social justice unionist networks such as UCORE.

CORE organizers have been central to the development of national networks organizing against school closures, in particular UCORE. As one of the founding members of the network, James, discussed, UCORE formed as part of an effort to bring together teachers who are engaged in similar struggles in a wide range of political and labor contexts. In late 2012 and early 2013, CORE organizers realized that there was a need for support and guidance in burgeoning social justice caucuses across the United States. With this in mind, three CORE organizers drafted a letter inviting teacher organizers from across the country to come to Chicago in 2013 "with the purpose of turning your movement into a caucus to retake your union" (Stark, interview, May 30, 2015). From the perspective of Eleanor, another teacher organizing this conference, they realized that the only way they would be able to combat the attack on public education was through "national work" (Stark, interview, July 28, 2015).

Teachers from cities such as Chicago, Madison, New York City, Philadelphia, and St. Paul came to the initial, informal UCORE conference, which was expressly designed to meet the needs of union organizers with differing experience levels and political challenges (Stark, interview, 30 May 2015). For James, CORE teachers did not see themselves as the ones who "have the answers" at the conference, but instead conceptualized themselves as part of a "group that were willing to work with other people and bring all of our experiences to the table from across the states" (Stark, interview, May 30, 2015). This network met informally for a second year in Chicago in 2014, where they voted to form a network and developed their platform (Stark, interview, May 30, 2015). The following year, they met in Newark, NJ, creating spaces for organizers to share insights from their work across the country as well as allowing participants to brainstorm next steps for their movement (Stark, field notes, August 8, 2015).

In bringing together organizers from across the country, UCORE has also provided spaces to support the ongoing relational and structured political education of their members. Organizers frequently note the strong bonds they have developed with their peers in other cities, through both UCORE and grassroots networks such as Save Our Schools and United Opt Out (Stark, interview, July 21, 2015). Likewise, CORE organizers have been traveling across the country to offer support to new caucus organizers, developing strong relationships with other organizers. As Lucy notes, UCORE has a "group of people willing and ready to come and meet with you and have cups of coffee," emphasizing the informal and personal nature of mentorship within the network (Stark, field notes, February 27, 2015). CORE organizer James sees this networked, relational organizing as central to the national fight against market-based reforms and systems of inequality: "Because this hydra of privatization looks different and yet similar, it's making sure that we're giving a group of people some concentrated support for a while to get their stuff off the ground and get them going" (Stark, interview, May 30, 2015). This concentrated support has proven crucial for new caucuses in other cities, who have had the opportunity to collaborate with more established caucuses to develop tools and strategies, including reading lists for their inquiry groups and political learning opportunities (Stark, field notes, November 16, 2015).

Similar to Chicago, there were noteworthy examples of political education among Philadelphia social justice unionist teachers through individual and organizational involvement in the national social justice network, UCORE. Here, WE teachers found it significant to their political learning process to share organizing strategies for growing WE and challenging layoffs and closures. For example, seven social justice unionist educators—including Maton—from Philadelphia attended UCORE in the Summer of 2014. At the UCORE conference, WE members had the opportunity to attend workshops led by social justice unionist teachers from across the country and to network with social justice teachers from other cities. One attendee, Jonah, who was new to social justice unionism, reflected afterward that it was an important experience to observe how members of CORE worked together, as it posed a model for Philadelphia's organizing. Jonah said: "[it was] thrilling it was to see how well people in CORE work together, how diverse it was, that was really encouraging for feeling like WE is on track" (Maton, interview, September 14, 2014). Networking at this national conference provided WE members with the opportunity to observe the dynamics and relationships in similar caucuses, and to make decisions about how and when to model their rank-and-file organizing in Philadelphia after caucuses in cities like Chicago.

At the conclusion of the UCORE conference, WE attendees collectively wrote a document naming six "BIG LESSONS" learned at UCORE in Chicago. This document was distributed to the membership of WE more broadly, and was intended to share the experience of networking with those members who were unable to attend the conference. The lessons named in this document included descriptions of the significance of each of the following topics: organizing techniques and orientations; organizational structure; diversity; relationships with parents and communities; strength recognition in role assignment; and, goals for continued involvement in the national network (Maton, document, August 8, 2014). Together, these six "lessons" show that members were politicized through intentional and networked learning about the strategies, tactics, structures, and values of other organizations and their members. Members found it valuable to learn new organizing skills and tactics from caucuses engaged in similar fights against shrinking school districts and school closures.

Furthermore, WE attendees were conscious of the political learning opportunities afforded to them by the network. In the document, the sixth lesson was recorded as follows:

> *Staying Involved with the National Work:* We should devote some of our resources to bringing the energy of the weekend conference to Philadelphia. Share the lessons and excitement of CORE and other groups around the country who are fighting different sides of the same struggle all over the place. (Maton, document, August 8, 2014)

The social justice teachers who attended this conference identified the network of UCORE as a significant opportunity for learning from the knowledge of other caucuses, as well as a source for maintaining a sense of "excitement" and "energy" among local social justice active teachers, as they could learn of the broader national significance of their work through accessing the national network. Philadelphia educators felt that through accessing national networks, that they could build and maintain energy among the rank-and-file in the fight to resist austerity and school closure policies.

Together, Chicago's and Philadelphia's experiences show that networks pose an important politicizing experience for social justice unionist teachers. Teachers draw upon national and local networks to work more closely and strategically with area organizations, to learn from the wisdom and experiences of other caucuses, and to retain a sense of excitement and energy for their local organizing work.

DISCUSSION AND CONCLUSION

This chapter has shown that school closures and their related processes can support teacher political education. Through examining the case studies of Chicago and Philadelphia, we have shown that school closures foster multiple processes of political education. These cultural processes may be enacted within different contexts, such as the school closure site, grassroots organizing surrounding the closure, social justice unionist caucuses, informal social gatherings, or networks extending beyond the city. Likewise, they can include a range of cultural processes, including situational, relational, structured, mobilized, and networked political education. In analyzing the complex ways in which political education operates within social justice caucuses and among social justice organizers, this study contributes to broader discussions of the significance of school closures and the effects on education reform, tracing how closures galvanized organizing within both Chicago and Philadelphia. It further contributes to our understanding of how grassroots and labor organizations can further this political development by engaging in multiple processes of political education.

This chapter brings five cultural processes of political education together into a new framework (see Figure 10.1). We have shown that situational, relational, structured, mobilized, and networked political education work in distinct but interrelated ways to support the political education of teachers. While situational political education requires direct experience of a given policy such as school closures, the other processes of political education can unfold without direct experience of that policy. Through mobilized political education, for example, Chicago educators organized against school closures, layoffs, and austerity during the 2012 teachers' strike. While some of these teachers had directly experienced school closures and related policies, the majority of teachers were politicized through other processes, such as relational, structured, mobilized, or networked political education. In other instances, a single event or experience can speak to multiple processes of political education. In the case of the teacher, Ben, who organized against the turnaround of his school in Philadelphia, his colleagues were politicized through both their own experiences and their activities as a union. Over the course of discussions of their contract, one-on-one conversations, and organized political actions, they were able to deepen their political education as a staff, engaging in interrelated processes of structured, relational, and mobilized political education (Stark, interview, May 29, 2016).

By tracing these five processes of political education in the work of Chicago and Philadelphia organizers, this study sheds light on both the pedagogical and political dimensions of social movements. On the individual level, this framework offers insights into the ways in which direct and indirect experiences of market-based reforms can influence the political development of teachers and organizers. On the organizational level, this framework elucidates the ways in which social justice caucuses can galvanize and sustain the political development of rank-and-file teachers through social activities, learning experiences, political actions, and engagement in broader networks and social movements.

This work on political education and school closures holds significance for scholarship on labor history and social justice unionism. Through its analysis of the experiences that inspired and sustained CORE and WE organizers' political engagement, this study offers insights into the development of both teacher activists and social justice caucuses. In discussing the ways that individual experiences shaped the political perspectives of caucus organizers, this study contributes to our understanding of how perspectival changes among educators connect with their activism, political engagement, and union work. It also enriches our understanding of how and why teachers come to join social justice caucuses, contributing to the literature on the role of unions in teachers' professional lives. On the organizational level, this study confirms the developmental importance of caucuses' explicit focus on structured events, such as workshops, discussion groups, informal dinners, and organizer training sessions, as well as suggesting reasons why these experiences might be useful for larger labor organizations. Likewise, in tracing how these processes of political education intertwine to support the growth of social justice caucuses, this study offers insight into how social justice organizations maintain and build power over time.

The political education of teachers in Chicago and Philadelphia holds significant implications for both U.S. schooling and society. Teachers are in the unique position to develop strong relationships with hundreds of parents and students every year, in many cases crossing rigid social boundaries of race and class. Because of the often close and caring nature of these relationships, teachers' lives are deeply bound with the experiences of their students, and in particular their direct experiences of unjust educational and social policies. When a student's life is impacted by a social policy, whether it be criminalization, gentrification, housing insecurity, or the closure of their school, the teacher's classroom and—in many cases—political perspective is impacted in turn. Through grassroots networks and labor organizations such as CORE and WE, teachers have the potential to work in solidarity with the students and community members that they serve, and to galvanize broad, intersectional movements for educational and social justice. This broader political purpose is intentional for many caucus organizers, who see their work as a way to challenge systems of inequality such as neoliberalism and racism. As one WE organizer notes, teachers are "on the frontlines" of U.S. social policies and schools are "embedded" in the direction of society. As this organizer argues, teachers have the ability and the obligation to work toward a more equitable future for their students and communities: "it is very important that we start to articulate our vision for the future," rather than allowing those in power to "articulate this vision for us" (Stark, field notes, 22 October 2015).

NOTE

1. Pseudonyms have been used throughout the chapter to keep the identities of caucus organizers confidential.

REFERENCES

Alter, T. (2013). "It felt like community": Social movement unionism and the Chicago Teachers Union strike of 2012. *Labor: Studies in Working Class History of the Americas, 10*(3), 11–25.

Barker, C., & Krinsky, J. (2009). Movement strategizing as developmental learning. In H. Johnston (Ed.), *Culture, protest, and social movements* (pp. 209–225). Farnham, England: Ashgate.

Bernal, D. (1998). Using a Chicana feminist epistemology in educational research. *Harvard Educational Review, 68*(4), 555–579.

Bevington, D., & Dixon, C. (2005). Movement-relevant theory: Rethinking social movement scholarship and activism. *Social Movement Studies,* 4(3), 185–208.

Bradbury, A., Brenner, M., Brown, J., Slaughter, J., & Winslow, S. (2014). *How to jump-start your union: Lessons from the Chicago teachers.* Detroit, MI: Labor Notes.

Bulkley, K. E., Henig, J. R., & Levin, H. M. (Eds.). (2010). *Between public and private: Politics, governance, and the new portfolio models for urban school reform.* Cambridge, MA: Harvard Education Press.

Buras, K. L. (2014). *Charter schools, race, and urban space: Where the market meets grassroots resistance.* New York, NY: Routledge.

Caref, C., Hainds, S., Hilgendorf, K., Jankov, P., & Russell, K. (2012, November 30). *The Black and White of education in Chicago's public schools: Class, charters, & chaos: A hard look at privatization schemes masquerading as education policy.* Retrieved from https://www.ctulocal1.org/reports/black-white-chicago-education/

Casas-Cortés, M., Osterweil, M., & Powell, D. (2008). Blurring boundaries: Recognizing knowledge-practices in the study of social movements. *Anthropological Quarterly, 81*(1), 17–58.

Catalyst Chicago. (2016, April 1). CTU ends one-day strike with downtown rally. *The Chicago Reporter.* Retrieved from https://www.chicagoreporter.com/liveblog -april-1-ctu-strike/

Chabot, S. (2010). Dialog matters: Beyond the transmission model of transnational diffusion between social movements. In R. K. Givan, K. M. Roberts, & S. A. Soule (Eds.), *The diffusion of social movements: Actors, mechanisms, and political effects* (pp. 99–124). New York, NY: Oxford University Press.

Charmaz, K. (1983). The grounded theory method: An explication and interpretation. In R. M. Emerson (Ed.), *Contemporary field research* (pp. 109–126). Boston, MA: Little, Brown.

Chicago Teachers Union Foundation Library. (2016). Chicago Teachers Union Foundation. Retrieved from http://www.ctuf.org/resources/

Choudry, A. (2015). *Learning activism: The intellectual life of contemporary social movements.* Toronto, Canada: University of Toronto Press.

Choudry, A., & Kapoor, D. (2013). *Learning from the ground up: Global perspectives on social movements and knowledge production.* New York, NY: Palgrave Macmillan.

Chovanec, M. (2009). *Between hope and despair: Women learning politics.* Halifax, NS: Fernwood.

Cochran-Smith, M., & Lytle, S. L. (1999). Relationships of knowledge and practice: Teacher learning in communities. *Review of Research in Education,* 249–305.

Cohen, R. M. (2016, April 11). School closures: A blunt instrument. *American Prospect.* Retrieved from http://prospect.org/article/school-closures-blunt -instrument-0

Conway, J. (2011). Activist knowledges on the anti-globalization terrain. *Interface: A Journal For and About Social Movements, 3*(2), 33–64.

Cox, L. (2014). Movements making knowledge: A new wave of inspiration for sociology. *Sociology, 48*(5), 954–971.

Davis, J. E. (2002). *Stories of Change: Narrative and Social Movements.* Albany, NY: State University of New York Press.

DeJarnatt, S. (2014, August 5). *Community losses: The costs of education reform.* 45 University of Toledo Law Review 579 (2014); Temple University Legal Studies Research Paper No. 2014-36. Available at SSRN: https://ssrn.com/abstract=2476612

de la Torre, M., & Gwynne, J. (2009). *When schools close: Effects on displaced students in Chicago Public Schools. Research report.* Chicago, IL: Consortium on Chicago School Research.

della Porta, D., & Diani, M. (1999). *Social movements: An introduction.* Oxford, England: Oxford Press.

Diani, M. (1996). Linking mobilization frames and political opportunities: Insights from regional populism in Italy. *American Sociological Review,* 61, 1053–1069.

Emerson, R. M., Fretz, R. I., & Shaw, L. L. (1995). *Writing ethnographic fieldnotes.* Chicago, IL: University of Chicago Press.

Eyerman, R., & Jamison, A. (1991). *Social movements: A cognitive approach.* University Park: Pennsylvania State University Press.

Featherstone, D. (2008). *Resistance, space, and political identities: The making of global networks.* West Sussex, England: Wiley-Blackwell.

Foley, G. (1999). *Learning in social action: A contribution to understanding informal education.* London, England: Zed Books.

Foley, G. (2001). Radical adult education and learning. *International Journal of Lifelong Education, 20*(1), 1–2.

Freire, P. (1970). *Pedagogy of the oppressed.* New York, NY: Seabury.

Geertz, C. (1973). *The interpretation of cultures: Selected essays.* New York, NY: Basic Books.

Goodwin, J., Jasper, J. M., & Polletta, F. (2001). *Passionate politics: Emotions and social movements.* Chicago, IL: The University of Chicago Press.

Hall, B. L., & Clover, D. E. (2005). Social movement learning. In L. M. English (Ed.), *International Encyclopedia of Adult Education* (pp. 584–589). New York, NY: Palgrave Macmillan.

Hall, B. H., Clover, D. E., Crowther, J., & Scandrett, E. (2012). Introduction. In B. H. Hall, D. E. Clover, J. Crowther, & E. Scandrett (Eds.), *Learning and education for a better world: The role of social movements* (pp. ix). Rotterdam, Netherlands: Sense.

Holst, J. D. (2002). *Social movements, civil society, and radical adult education.* Westport, CT: Bergin and Garve.

Horton, M., & Freire, P. (1990). *We make the road by walking: Conversations on education and social change.* Philadelphia, PA: Temple University Press.

Hosseini, S. A. H. (2010). Activist knowledge: Interrogating the ideational landscape of social movements. *The International Journal of Interdisciplinary Social Sciences, 5*(5), 339–357.

Howard, P. N. (2002). Network ethnography and the hypermedia organization: New media, new organizations, new methods. *New Media and Society, 4*(4), 550–574.

Institute on Metropolitan Opportunity. (2014, October). Charter schools in Chicago: No model for educational reform. *University of Chicago Law School.* Retrieved from https://www1.law.umn.edu/uploads/e9/5d/e95d8af0fa0673c39aac013df6d3d56d/Chicago-Charters-FINAL.pdf

Jack, J., & Sludden, J. (2013). School closings in Philadelphia. *PennGSE Perspectives on Urban Education, 10*(1). Retrieved from http://www.urbanedjournal.org/archive/volume-10-issue-1-summer-2013/school-closings-philadelphia

Johnson, S. M., Kraft, M. A., & Papay, J. P. (2012). How context matters in high-need schools: The effects of teachers' working conditions on their professional satisfaction and their students' achievement. *Teachers College Record, 114*(1), 1–39.

Johnston, H. (1995). *Social movements and culture.* Minneapolis: University of Minnesota Press.

Journey for Justice Alliance. (2014). *Death by a thousand cuts: Racism, school closures, and public school sabotage.* Retrieved from http://www.j4jalliance.com/wp-content/uploads/2014/02/J4JReport-final_05_12_14.pdf

Kelley, D. (2015, February 18). Philadelphia approves five new charter schools. *The Public School Notebook.* Philadelphia, PA. Retrieved from http://www.reuters.com/article/us-usa-philadelphia-charter-schools-idUSKBN0LM10R20150219

Khalek, R. (2013, September 12). The "systematic murder" of Philadelphia public schools. *Truthout.* Retrieved from http://www.truth-out.org/news/item/18610-the-systematic-murder-of-philadelphia-public-schools

Kincheloe, J. L. (2005). *Critical constructivism primer.* New York, NY: P. Lang.

Kincheloe, J. L., McLaren, P., Steinberg, S. R., & Monzó, L. (2017). Critical pedagogy and qualitative research: Advancing the bricolage. In N. K. Denzin & Y. S. Lincoln (Eds.), *The SAGE handbook of qualitative research* (5th ed., pp. 235–260). Thousand Oaks, CA: SAGE.

Lamont, M., Beljean, S., & Clair, M. (2014). What is missing? Cultural processes and causal pathways to inequality. *Socio-economic Review, 12*(3), 573–608. doi:10.1093/ser/mwu011

Larsen, M. F. (2014). Does closing schools close doors? [Working Paper]. Retrieved from http://www.tulane.edu/~mflarsen/uploads/2/2/5/4/22549316/mflarsen_schoolclosings

LeCompte, M. D., & Schensul, J. J. (1999). *Designing and conducting ethnographic research: An ethnographer's toolkit.* Lanham, MD: AltaMira Press.

Lipman, P. (2011). *The new political economy of urban education: Neoliberalism, race, and the right to the city.* London, England: Routledge.

Lydersen, K., & Brown, E. (2016, April 1). Chicago teachers go on strike, shutting down nation's third-largest school system. *The Washington Post.* Retrieved from https://www.washingtonpost.com/news/education/wp/2016/04/01/chicago-teachers-to-strike-friday-shutting-down-nations-third-largest-school-system/

Marshall, C., & Rossman, G. (2011). *Designing qualitative research* (5th ed.). Washington, DC: SAGE.

Maton, R. (2016a). WE learn together: Philadelphia educators putting social justice unionism principles into practice. *Workplace: A Journal for Academic Labor, 26,* 5–19.

Maton, R. (2016b). *Learning racial justice: Teachers' collaborative learning as theory and praxis.* Philadelphia: University of Pennsylvania.

Maton, R. (2016c). *Learning, national ideology, and grassroots organizing: Teacher organizing through inquiry in Philadelphia.* Washington, DC: American Educational Research Association.

McAdam, D. (1982). *Political process and the development of black insurgency, 1930–1970.* Chicago, IL: University of Chicago Press.

McAlevey, J. (2012). *Raising expectations (and raising hell): My decade fighting for the labor movement.* Brooklyn, NY: Verso.

National Alliance for Public Charter Schools. (2019). *Measuring up to the model: A ranking of state public charter school laws, 2019.* Retrieved from https://www .publiccharters.org/ranking-state-public-charter-school-laws-2019

Opportunity to Learn Campaign. (2013). *The color of school closures.* Retrieved from http://www.otlcampaign.org/blog/2013/04/05/color-school-closures

Patton, M. Q. (1980). *Qualitative evaluation methods.* Beverly Hills, CA: SAGE.

Peterson, B. (1997). We need a new vision of teacher unions. *Rethinking Schools, 11*(4). Retrieved from http://www.rethinkingschools.org/special_reports/ union/un11_4.shtml

Picower, B., & Mayorga, E. (Eds.). (2015). *What's race got to do with it? How current school reform policy maintains racial and economic inequality.* New York, NY: Peter Lang.

Polletta, F. (2006). *It was like a fever: Storytelling in protest and politics.* Chicago, IL: The University of Chicago Press.

Prior, L. (2002). *Using documents in social research.* London, England: SAGE.

Research for Action. (2013). *Issue brief: School closings policy.* Pennsylvania Clearinghouse for Education Research (PACER). Retrieved from http://8rri53pm0 cs22jk3vvqna1ub-wpengine.netdna-ssl.com/wp-content/uploads/2015/10/ RFA_PACER_School_Closing_Policy_March_2013.pdf

Rich, M., & Hurdle, J. (2013, Mar. 8). Rational decisions and heartbreak on school closings. *The New York Times.* Retrieved from http://www.nytimes.com/2013/ 03/09/education/rational-decisions-and-heartbreak-on-school-closings .html?_r=0

Riley, K. (2015). Reading for change: Social justice unionism book groups as an organizing tool. *Perspectives on Urban Education, 12*(1), 70–75.

Robertson, S. L. (2008). "Remaking the World": Neoliberalism and the Transformation of Education and Teachers' Labor. In M. Compton & L. Weiner (Eds.), *The Global Assault on Teaching, Teachers, and their Unions Stories for Resistance* (pp. 11–27). New York, NY: Palgrave Macmillan.

Saltman, K. J. (2010). Urban school decentralization and the growth of "portfolio districts." *The Great Lakes Center for Education Research and Practice.* Retrieved from http://epicpolicy.org/publication/portfolio-districts

The Schott Foundation for Public Education. (2013). *The color of school closures.* Retrieved from http://schottfoundation.org/blog/2013/04/05/color-school -closures

Shamir, R. (2008). The age of responsibilization: On market-embedded morality. *Economy and Society, 37*(1), 1–19.

Spindler, G., & Spindler, L. (1997). Cultural process and ethnography. In G. S. Spindler, *Education and cultural process: Anthropological approaches.* Prospect Heights, IL: Waveland Press.

Spradley, J. P. (1979). *The ethnographic interview.* New York, NY: Holt, Rinehart, and Winston.

Stark, L. (2016a). *Organizing for social justice: Social justice caucuses and the development of national solidarity networks.* Washington, DC: American Education Research Association.

Stark, L. W. (2016b). *"Vitally important and inextricably linked": Toward an ethics of social justice unionism.* Seattle, WA: American Educational Studies Association.

Stern, M., & Brown, A. (2016). "It's 5:30. I'm exhausted. And I have to go all the way to f*%#ing Fishtown.": Educator depression, activism, and finding (armed) love in a hopeless (neoliberal) place. *The Urban Review, 47*(5), 333–354.

Street, P. L. (2005). *Segregated schools: Educational apartheid in post-civil rights America.* London, England: Routledge.

Stringer, E. T. (2007). *Action research: A handbook for practitioners* (3rd ed.). Thousand Oaks, CA: SAGE.

Tarlau, R. (2014). From a language to a theory of resistance: Critical pedagogy, the limits of 'framing,' and social change. *Educational Theory, 64* (4), 369–392.

Tarrow, S. (2010). Dynamics of diffusion: Mechanisms, institutions, and scale shift. In R. K. Givan, K. M. Roberts, & S. A. Soule (Eds.), *The diffusion of social movements: Actors, mechanisms, and political effects* (pp. 204–219). Cambridge, England: Cambridge University Press.

Tatum, B. (2003). *"Why are all the black kids sitting together in the cafeteria?": And other conversations about race.* New York, NY: Basic Books.

Teacher Activist Group. (2016, February 1). *'Exit strategy' at Philadelphia theatre company.* Retrieved from http://tagphilly.org/exit-strategy-at-philadelphia-theatre-company/

Teachers for Social Justice. (2008, February 22). 2008 teachers for social justice curriculum fair recap. Retrieved from http://www.teachersforjustice.org/2008/02/teaching-for-social-justice-curriculum.html

Teachers for Social Justice. (2009, December 31). Kicking off inquiry to action groups. Retrieved from http://www.teachersforjustice.org/2009/12/kicking-off-inquiry-to-action-groups.html

Uetricht, M. (2014). *Strike for America: Chicago teachers against austerity.* New York, NY: Verso Books.

U.S. Department of Education. (2009). *Race to the top program: Executive summary.* Retrieved from http://www2.ed.gov/programs/racetothetop/executive-summary.pdf

Valencia, R. R. (1984). *School closures and policy issues.* Policy Paper No. 84-C3. Retrieved from ERIC database. (ED323040)

Weiner, L. (2012). *The future of our schools: Teachers unions and social justice.* Chicago, IL: Haymarket Books.

Weinraub, A. (2013). Why teachers must join the fight for public education now. *Perspectives on Urban Education, 10*(1), 1–4.

Welk, M. (2010, January 10). Timeline: A brief history of charters. *The Public School Notebook.* Philadelphia, PA. Retrieved from http://thenotebook.org/articles/2010/06/10/timeline-a-brief-history-of-charters

Wolcott, H. F. (1987). On ethnographic intent. In G. Spindler & L. Spindler (Eds.), *Interpretive Ethnography of Education: At Home and Abroad* (pp. 37–60). Hillsdale, NJ: Erlbaum.

Wolcott, H. F. (1999). *Ethnography: A way of seeing*. Walnut Creek, CA: AltaMira Press.

CHAPTER 11

CLOSING COSTS

Examining the Impact of School Closures on African-American Students' Educational Outcomes

Richard O. Welsh
University of Georgia

Shafiqua Little
University of Georgia

ABSTRACT

School closures result in changing schools and student mobility is associated with a negative impact on educational outcomes unless students switch to higher quality schools. Given the prevalence of school closures in urban cities with high concentrations of low-income and minority students, the effects of student mobility due to school closures is an important issue with substantial education and social equity policy implications. This chapter provides a comprehensive review of the empirical evidence on the impact of student mobility due to school closures on African American students' cognitive (for e.g., test scores) and noncognitive (for e.g., social and emotional well-being) outcomes. It describes the prevalence of school closure-related student mobil-

Shuttered Schools, pages 325–351
Copyright © 2019 by Information Age Publishing

ity and examines the choices and constraints involved in enrolling in a new school. It then details the impact of these school changes on educational outcomes. The effects of school closures from the perspective of receiving schools (for e.g., challenges for school personnel and teachers) are also explicated. Empirical evidence from post-Katrina New Orleans on whether the lowest performing schools in a portfolio district are closed complements the integrative review of the extant literature on school closures. The chapter concludes with a discussion of how education policy may mitigate some of the disruptive effects associated with student mobility related to school closures and directions for future research.

Student mobility, or the movement of students between schools, presents both a challenge and an opportunity for urban school districts. Even though student mobility may facilitate access to higher quality schools, especially for low-income and minority students, the majority of the extant literature has found that changing schools is associated with a decline in test scores as well as a higher likelihood of grade retention and dropout (Institute of Medicine and National Research Council, 2010; Kerbow, 1996; Mehana & Reynolds, 2004; Reynolds, Chen, & Herbers, 2009). Indeed, several challenges are associated with student mobility such as forming new relationships and adjusting to different academic norms (Rumberger, Larson, Ream, & Palardy, 1999; South, Haynie, & Bose, 2007; Welsh, 2016a). However, several scholars posit that transferring to higher quality schools may offset and outweigh the disruptive effects of student mobility and lead to a net positive impact on students' educational outcomes (Engberg, Gill, Zamarro, & Zimmer, 2012; Hanushek, Kain, & Rivkin, 2004; Temple & Reynolds, 1999).

Student mobility may occur for a variety of reasons (Rumberger, 2015; Welsh, 2016a; Welsh, Duque, & McEachin, 2016). Promotional school changes generally occur as students switch from elementary to middle schools and then from middle to high schools. Nonstructural school changes occur when students switch schools on their own accord such as moving from one elementary school to another. This may be due to a multitude of reasons ranging from job loss or promotion that prompts changes in residence or the search for a better fit school or particular schooling programs such as magnet schools or career academies. Some school changes may be initiated by schools and districts such as school closures or discipline-related mobility. School closures provide a somewhat unique reason for switching schools given that it is imposed by an external agency and may be accompanied by a stigma for students hailing from the closed school (Kirshner, Gaertner, & Pozzoboni, 2010).

In recent decades, several large urban school districts nationwide such as Chicago, Philadelphia, and Detroit have initiated student mobility through school closures (Brummet, 2014; de la Torre & Gwynne, 2009b; Lipman & Person, 2007; Rumberger, 2015; Steiner, 2009). Closing schools is typically attributed to decreasing enrollments (this is largely due to depopulation in some urban neighborhoods), fiscal reasons (shrinking budgets or deficits), academic reasons (below average academic performance), or nonacademic reasons (condition of school facilities or school buildings are underused; Brummet, 2014; de la Torre, Gordon, Moore, & Cowhy, 2015; de la Torre & Gwynne, 2009b; Engberg et al., 2012; Rumberger, 2015; Steiner, 2009; Sunderman & Payne, 2009). School closings have also evolved a way for urban school districts to address consistently low-performing schools (Lipman & Haines, 2007; Maxwell, 2006; Olson, 2006). The passage of the No Child Left Behind (NCLB) Act in 2001 ushered in an era where schools could be sanctioned with closure as an option for not making Adequate Yearly Progress (AYP) for several consecutive years (Steiner, 2009; Sunderman & Payne, 2009). Under the Obama administration, there were also demands from the federal government to close consistently low-performing schools (Gewertz, 2009). The School Improvement Grant program (a part of the American Recovery and Reinvestment Act in 2009) buttressed this federal position by providing significant funding to support school closures (Steiner, 2009; Sunderman & Payne, 2009).

School closures are undergirded by a few assumptions. It is presumed that closing schools will allow students in under-enrolled or chronically low-performing schools to switch to higher quality schools and thus improve students' educational outcomes. The overarching tenet of school closings is improving the educational environment of students in underperforming schools. School closures may also allow districts to reallocate scarce resources to the remaining schools in hopes of enhancing school quality. In some instances, school closures are viewed as an important component of broader district reform and improvement plans rather than to directly improve student achievement (Steiner, 2009). Schools can be closed solely because of the financial exigencies in a district.

Given the prevalence of school closures in cities with high concentrations of low-income and minority students, the effects of student mobility due to school closures is an important issue with substantial education and social equity policy implications. One of the major consequences of school closings in urban districts is the impact on the educational outcomes of low-income and minority students, who tend to be concentrated in these districts. Prior research has found a relationship between student mobility and achievement gap and suggests that student mobility may play an important role in educational inequality in urban school districts (Welsh, 2016b). It is plausible that school closures may contribute to the racial achievement gap and inequalities in educational opportunities, experience and outcomes. Few studies have reviewed the research on school closures and the effects of this policy on students', schools, and neighborhoods. In an information brief, Sunderman and Payne (2009) provided a brief overview of studies up to 2009 that examine whether school closures are helpful or harmful. Since this review, several published empirical journal articles and reports have examined the effects of school closures. The ongoing increase in school closures and the equity implications associated with this phenomenon stemming from the disproportionate effect on African American and low-income students make it an opportune and important moment to take stock of the existing body of knowledge and highlight areas for future research.

This chapter provides a comprehensive review of the empirical evidence on the impact of student mobility due to school closures on cognitive (for e.g., test scores) and noncognitive (for e.g., social and emotional well-being) outcomes with a particular focus on African American students. It encompasses published empirical articles and reports between 2006 and 2016. We complement the integrative overview of the extant literature on the prevalence and effects of school closures with an empirical analysis of school closures in post-Katrina New Orleans. In total, our analysis addresses two main research questions: (a) Are school closures helpful or harmful for student achievement, especially that of African American students?; and (b) Are the lowest performing schools in a portfolio district typically closed?

We address both research questions using a combination of a primarily integrative review of the extant literature complemented by an empirical analysis of data from post-Katrina New Orleans. In order to address the first research question, we focus on the literature examining student mobility due to school closures and the estimated effects associated with changing schools due to school closures. Previous studies have provided a comprehensive review of student mobility in general (Rumberger, 2015; Welsh, 2016a) but none have focused exclusively on student mobility due to school closures with a particular focus on educational equity. There is a need for a rigorous assessment of the impact of school closures especially as it relates to the subgroups the intervention targets (Kemple, 2015). To date, only one other study has empirically examined school closures in New Orleans (Bross, Harris, & Liu, 2016b), a context widely regarded as a national exemplar of school reform. Our analysis of school closures in post-Katrina New Orleans acknowledges two distinct phases of the reforms. The first phase occurred in the seven years immediately succeeding the implementation of the portfolio management model (PMM) and the second phase began in 2012 and is still ongoing. Bross et al (2016b) examined school closures from 2008–2014, inclusive of both phases, whereas this empirical analysis focuses on the first phase. Little attention has been paid to the identification and selection of schools for closure in the PMM. In order to address the second research question, we use a set of graphical analyses to examine the patterns of schools' math value-add across closure status (the patterns are similar for ELA, thus for brevity's sake, we only present math results).

Resulting insights from both questions provide a better sense of two key policy issues: (a) the effects associated with school closures, especially for the students most affected by these changes; and (b) the process of identifying and selecting schools to be closed. In totality, the analysis contributes to the student mobility, school closure and educational equity literatures.

We argue that there is a mismatch between theory and reality that appears to result in school closures ultimately harming the students it is intended to help. In theory, school closures should provide access to higher quality schools for students in chronically low-performing schools. African American students are disproportionately concentrated in these schools, especially in urban school districts. Thus, it is presumed that school closures can improve the educational outcomes of African American students by transferring these students from low to higher quality schools. A review of the extant literature and empirical evidence from the post-Katrina New Orleans case presented in this chapter suggest that even though some of the lowest performing schools are typically closed, students tend to transfer to similar quality schools. Overall, students that experience student mobility related to school closures pay the costs of switching schools but do not appear to receive the purported benefits. Although disruption is necessary to improve persistently low-performing schools, policymakers should be careful to ensure that the interventions do not cause more harm than good.

In what follows, we first describe the prevalence of school closure-related student mobility and examine the choices and constraints involved in enrolling in a new school. Next, we detail the impact of these school changes on educational outcomes. The effects of school closures from the perspective of receiving schools (for e.g., challenges for school personnel and teachers) are also explicated. The chapter concludes with a discussion of how education policy may mitigate some of the disruptive effects associated with student mobility related to school closures and directions for future research.

THE POST-KATRINA NEW ORLEANS CASE

Within the last decade, the portfolio model in urban school reform has emerged nationwide as a strategic approach to public education in numerous major cities. Portfolio districts are characterized by the combination of several school providers, including traditional public schools and charter schools, and a rigorous performance-based accountability system (Bulkley, Henig, & Levin, 2010). Though reforms vary by location, there are commonalities among portfolio districts including: the contracting of schooling services to various public and private providers; the use of market mechanisms to increase competition among public schools, standards and performance accountability with the closing of failing schools, and the provision of a variety of educational options to families (Bulkley et al., 2010). There are more than 40 cities nationwide that apply some version of the portfolio strategy (Lake & Campbell, n.d.).

Education reforms in post-Katrina New Orleans have garnered significant national and international attention. It is widely viewed as important model of urban education intended to improve chronically low-performing schools and districts, and has piqued the interest of policymakers nationwide. Overall, New Orleans went from a traditional school district to a majority charter school district. The PMM in post-Katrina New Orleans is an unprecedented and comprehensive package of reforms. The underpinnings of these policies are test-based accountability and market-based accountability. The majority of public schools in post-Katrina New Orleans are publicly funded, privately operated schools that are held to strict accountability standards based primarily on students' test scores. New Orleans leads the nation in the percentage of public school students enrolled in charter schools with more than 95%. There is a wide variety of educational options and there is also variety within charter management organizations (CMOs). School closures, or closing schools to improve student achievement is a central part of the PMM. Akin to a financial portfolio, the underlying mantra of the PMM is continuous improvement. Effective schools are expanded and ineffective schools are closed. In post-Katrina New Orleans, the first set of closures began in the 2009–2010 school year (Ferguson, 2014). That year four schools were closed in the special state-administered Recovery School District (RSD; Ferguson, 2014). At the close of the 2010–2011 school year, a total of 9 RSD schools were closed (Ferguson, 2014).

Post-Katrina New Orleans is the most prominent example of the PMM. We use the New Orleans case to examine school closures in a portfolio district. There is little research on the relationship between charter schools (especially those in the PMM) and school closures. Although post-Katrina school closures in the PMM present an extraordinary case that may be difficult to compare across districts, the PMM in New Orleans is often hailed as a model of urban education, thus a better understanding of school closures in this portfolio district has significant national policy implications.

PREVALENCE OF SCHOOL CLOSURE-RELATED MOBILITY

School closings are prevalent across districts in the United States[1] Even though the number of annual school closures has fluctuated in recent decades, school closings have increased over time. There were 1,840 school closures in the 2011–2012 academic year compared to 1,193 in 2000–2001 (National Center for Education Statistics, 2015). Between 2000 and 2010,

70 urban school districts closed schools, with an average of 11 schools per district (Engberg et al., 2012). Table 11.1 illustrates the prevalence of school closures in large urban centers in the past decade.[2] It demonstrates that school closures have become somewhat commonplace. For instance, in 2013, Philadelphia approved a plan to close 23 public schools or 10% of the district's schools (Hurdle, 2013). Collectively, the urban cities listed in Table 11.1 had more than 1,000 school closures between 2000–2016 affecting thousands of displaced students. Of those cities, Detroit experienced the most school closures. Districts such as Chicago have implemented multiple rounds of school closings.

Regardless of the cause of student mobility, African American students typically have the highest mobility rates among ethnic groups. For example, in Chicago, among ethnic groups, African Americans had the highest mobility rates and the gap in mobility rates increased over time (de la Torre & Gwynne, 2009a). Although a relatively small proportion of students are compelled to switch schools due to school closures (for example, less than 1% in Chicago; Rumberger, 2015), the students affected by school closures are disproportionately African American (Lipman & Haines, 2007; Maxwell, 2006). Students displaced due to school closures are more likely to be: recipients of free and reduced price lunch, enrolled in special education, too old for their grade and African American (Brummet, 2014; de la Torre et al., 2015). For instance, de la Torre and colleagues (2015) found that nearly 90% of students who changed schools due to school closings were

TABLE 11.1 School Closures in Urban Centers: 2000–2016

City/State	Year	Number of Schools Closed	Reasons
Chicago, IL	2001–2009; 2013	44; 47	Declining student enrollment (underutilization); academic performance
Philadelphia, PA	2012; 2013	6; 23	Budget deficit and underused schools
New York, NY	2002–2012; 2013	140; 22	
Washington, DC	2008; 2013	23; 15	
New Orleans, LA	2005	120	Hurricane Katrina
Pittsburgh, PA	2006	22	Underperformance; reduction of excess capacity
Michigan (majority of the school closings were in the Detroit Metropolitan Area)	2006–2009	246	Declining student enrollment
Denver, CO	2007	13	Underperformance
Hartford, CT	2007	4	Underperformance

African American (de la Torre et al., 2015). Students affected by closures also tend to perform below district and state average (Brummet, 2014). Brummet (2014) found that the characteristics of students displaced by school closures reflect the demographics of urban districts with high concentration of low-income and minority students. de la Torre et al. (2015) reported that families of displaced students were more likely to change residences in the year before school closures. Overall, the extant literature indicates that students affected by school closures are generally vulnerable students in a school district such as low-income students, those with instability in housing and African American students. The disruptive costs of sorting due to school closures in urban districts are largely borne by African American students.

CHOICES AND CONSTRAINTS

Closing schools is a difficult and politically charged decision often avoided by school districts (Steiner, 2009). School closures generally occur in two main ways: (a) the district shutters the school building and displaced students and staff are transferred to another school, and (b) the school is closed but reopened under new leadership (e.g., converting to charter schools; Steiner, 2009; Sunderman & Payne, 2009). Districts that close schools generally have exhausted other reforms and interventions over several years (Steiner, 2009). Most districts do not decide on school closings until the spring of the final year the school is open (Brummet, 2014).

Typically, students are assigned to new schools after school closings. In some cases, parents may switch residences or capitalize on school choice policies, however, school closures do not substantially change parents' choice of schools in a district (Brummet, 2014). There is little research on the choice and underlying reasoning of the destination schools for students displaced by school closures. The empirical evidence indicates that proximity to home, quality, and the safety of the receiving schools as well as existing connections to friends and staff are pertinent considerations for families displaced by school closings (de la Torre et al., 2015). There were also families who presumed that the only option was to enroll their children into the designated school or experienced barriers getting into other schools in the district (de la Torre et al., 2015). More importantly, de la Torre et al. (2015) found that closeness to home was the main reason displaced students enrolled in lower quality schools instead of designated schools. In these cases, distance superseded academic and safety reasons. This implies that the choices of destination schools of displaced students were influenced by family and economic circumstances.

FINDINGS

RQ1: Are school closures helpful or harmful for student achievement, especially that of African American students?

Conceptually, the effect of student mobility due to school closures has a considerable degree of "push" and "pull." Student mobility introduces discontinuity in learning environments and disrupts stability (Institute of Medicine and National Research Council, 2010; Reynolds et al., 2009; Temple & Reynolds, 1999). Changing schools disrupts and weakens peer relationships, lowers social ties and school attachments as well as engagement in school and community, and increases the risk of underachievement (Astone & Mclanahan, 1994; Coleman, 1988; Pribesh & Downey, 1999; Ream, 2005; South et al., 2007; Swanson & Schneider, 1999; Teachman, Paasch, & Carver, 1996). Research has also found that mobile students experience challenges in making new friends and acclimating socially to a new school environment (Rumberger et al., 1999). However, students that change schools due to school closures may end up in schools with a substantial proportion of students from the closing school. In addition, student mobility may also disrupt relationships with teachers (Rumberger et al., 1999). Nevertheless, school closures may afford students the opportunity to switch from low-performing to better schools and more beneficial peers and teachers. Thus, whether school closures have a negative or positive impact is an important yet open empirical question.

Table 11.2 presents the location, methods, and results from empirical studies on the impact of school closings on students' educational outcomes. There is relatively little evidence on the impact of school closing policies on students' educational outcomes. Overall, the evidence on the effect of school closings on students' outcomes is mixed and suggests that the ultimate impact of school closures on student achievement depends on the quality of the closing and receiving schools. Students that transfer to higher quality schools and students that exit poor performing schools (relative to nearby schools) appear to benefit the most from school closures.

In most cases, studies examining student mobility due to school closures have found that this type of structural mobility is associated with adverse student outcomes. Using a combination of quantitative and qualitative methods, Kirshner and colleagues (2010) found that mobile students experienced several challenges after school closure such as forming new relationships and adjusting to different academic norms and expectations.

In their quantitative study of elementary school closings in Chicago, de la Torre and Gwynne (2009b) found mixed results—test scores of displaced students declined in the year of the closure announcement but improved in subsequent years. De la Torre and Gwynne (2009b) estimated the effect of school closures by comparing displaced students to similar students

TABLE 11.2 The Impact of School Closures on Students' Outcomes: Empirical Studies, 2006–2016

Study	City/State	Methods	Results
Brummet (2014)	Michigan	Quantitative methods: Dynamic treatment specifications with controls for student characteristics and student and year fixed effects.	School closings did not have persistent negative effects on displaced students. Students in relatively lower quality schools that closed had achievement gains. School closures had a negative spillover effect on receiving schools.
de la Torre and Gwynne (2009)	Chicago, IL	Quantitative methods: Propensity score matching that matched closing schools to similar schools, HLM to analyze student achievement, logistic model for non-academic outcomes.	Most students leaving closing schools transferred to similar low-achieving schools. Displaced students were more likely to change schools a second time after leaving for a school closure. Students who transferred to a higher-achieving school had larger gains in reading and math relative to students who transferred to lower-achieving schools.
Engberg et al. (2012)	Anonymous Urban District	Quantitative methods: Instrumental variables with controls for student characteristics.	School closures had negative effects on test scores and attendance, but these effects were lessened or offset when students switched to higher-performing (value-added) schools. There was no evidence of adverse effects on students in receiving schools.
Imberman et al. (2012)	Houston, TX and Louisiana	Quantitative methods: Value-added specification with controls for student characteristics as well as grade, year and school fixed effects.	The inflow of evacuees had little impact on incumbent students' achievement in Louisiana and no effect in Houston (there was a negative effect on attendance and behavior). There is evidence that all students benefit for high-achieving peers. There was little impact on the student mobility of incumbents in Houston in response to the inflow of evacuees.
Sacerdote (2012)	New Orleans, LA	Quantitative methods: OLS regression model with controls for student characteristics and grande and year fixed effects; difference-in-differences regression.	Students who were forced to switch schools due to the hurricanes had substantial declines in test scores in the first year after the disaster but experienced achievement gains by the third and fourth years. Academic gains were concentrated among low achieving students.
Lipman and Person (2007)	Chicago, IL	Qualitative methods: Interviews with teachers, parents, administrators, and students	Receiving schools experience lack of resources as well as a disrupting and demoralizing climate. Teachers posited that the influx of displaced students adversely affected all students. There was a lack of consultation with the school community regarding closures.

(continued)

TABLE 11.2	The Impact of School Closures on Students' Outcomes: Empirical Studies, 2006–2016 (cont.)		
Study	City/State	Methods	Results
Kirshner et al. (2010)	Large urban high school in the western United States	Mixed methods: Quantitative and qualitative, quantitative analyses for academic performance and open-ended surveys for students' experiences with closure and transitioning to new schools and HLM	Test scores of displaced students declined after the school closure and dropout rates increased. School closures were associated with disruptions in relationships and declines in student achievement. School closings add to the stress of students already dealing with the challenges of urban poverty.
Barrow et al. (2012)	Chicago, IL	Quantitative methods:	Students displaced by school closures experience persistent decline in test scores.
Carlson and Lavertu (2016)	Ohio	Quantitative methods: Regression Discontinuity Design that compares students in charter schools that closed with similar charter schools just above the criteria for closure	Closing low-performing charter schools results in achievement gains for displaced students.
Young et al. (2009)	Chicago, Il	Quantitative methods: Matching techniques	School closures had no significant impact on student achievement.
Bross et al. (2016a)	Louisiana	Quantitative methods: Matched sample difference-in-difference identification	School closures had the most positive affect when schools were phased out instead of abruptly closed.
Bross et al. (2016b)	Louisiana	Quantitative methods: Matched difference-in-difference	School closures had a minimal effect (positive or negative) on students that were enrolled during the phase out process.
Kemple (2015)	New York City	Quantitative methods: Comparative interruptive time series (CITS)	With respect to rising 9th graders, school closures increase the likelihood that students would enroll in a higher performing school and receive a New York State Regents diploma.
Kemple (2016)	New York City	Quantitative methods: Comparative interruptive time series (CITS)	School closures led to lower GPAs and attendance and decreased the likelihood of graduation and college enrollment.
Larsen (2014)	Milwaukee, WI	Quantitative methods: Difference-in-difference	

Note: OLS = ordinary least squares; HLM = hierarchical linear model in similar schools that remained open. De la Torre and Gwynne (2009b) also found that the effect of school closures depended on the characteristics of the receiving school: students who moved to higher quality new schools performed better than those who moved to lower quality new schools. However, in Chicago, the majority of students transferring out of closing schools switched to low-performing schools (de la Torre & Gwynne, 2009b). In other words, many displaced students end up in schools with similar student composition and academic performance. De la Torre and Gwynne (2009b) also highlighted that closure-related mobility begets more student mobility—displaced students were more likely to switch schools a second time. Using similar matching techniques, Young and colleagues (2009) examined how Renaissance 2010 (an initiative to close roughly 70 schools and open 100 new schools by 2010) influenced the academic performance of displaced students. Young et al. (2009) found that school closures had no significant effects—displaced students have similar academic performance as the matched comparison group.

Using data from an anonymous urban district, Engberg and colleagues (2012) found that school closures had negative effects on test scores but these effects were lessened or offset when students switched to higher-performing schools. In Michigan, Brummet (2014) found that school closures had no consistent impact on the achievement of displaced students: there was no effect on reading and a significant negative effect in math 1 year prior to closure (–0.04SD), year of closure (–0.06SD), and 1 year after closure (–0.07SD). Using a regression discontinuity design, Carlson and Lavertu (2016) found that the closing of charter schools in Ohio resulted in achievement gains and that these gains are partly attributed to an increase in school quality.

Similar to Engberg et al. (2012) and de la Torre (2009b), the findings of Brummet (2014) reinforced the importance of the quality of receiving schools—students who switched to better schools experienced a positive impact on achievement. The trajectories of schools chosen to be closed may also influence the impact of school closures. Brummet (2014) found that students who exited low-performing closing schools experienced positive effects on achievement.

There is mixed evidence on whether the effects of displacement fade out over time. Some studies have found that the impact of school closure on student achievement disappear over time (Brummet, 2014; de la Torre & Gwynne, 2009b; Sacerdote, 2012) whereas Engberg et al. (2012) found that the adverse effects of school closings on test scores were persistent over time (Engberg and colleagues (2012) found that the negative effect on attendance disappears after the first year in the new school). The extent of displacement in cohorts may also affect the impact of school closures. There are temporary positive effects when students from a closing school move to the same receiving school but these effects fade after 2 years (Brummet, 2014).

The underlying mechanisms of school closures are similar to those of student mobility. Parents and students grapple with a sense of loss when schools are closed as strong bonds are broken and new school environments prove difficult to navigate. Lipman and Haines (2007) found that displaced students and families experienced social dislocation upon the closing of community schools. Kirshner and colleagues (2010) highlighted that students generally viewed closures "as an unwanted and externally imposed mandate rather than a strategic opportunity" (p. 419). Forming new relationships with peers and adults and overcoming stereotypes associated with the closed schools make the transition challenging (Kirshner et al., 2010). Another important explanatory factor is the role of receiving schools where displaced students enroll after closure.

The outcomes produced by school closures are contingent on several factors. Bross et al. (2016a) suggested that school closures proved most helpful to students at the elementary level or when conducted via a phase out process rather than abruptly closing. Kemple (2015, 2016) shared commonalities with the findings of Bross et al. (2016a) as it pertained to correlations between school closures and student achievement. Similar to Bross et al. (2016a), Kemple (2015) found that school closures had a minimal effect on students when they were apart of phase out processes. With respect to rising 9th graders, Kemple (2016) found that school closures increased the likelihood that students would enroll in a higher performing school and receive a New York State Regents diploma. Larsen (2014) highlighted different outcomes in his examination of school closures at the high school level. Larsen (2014) found that school closures yielded lower GPAs and attendance and decreased the likelihood of graduating and/or college attendance. As it stands studies pertaining to school closures highlight the overwhelming proportion of African American students affected by school closures however they do not place emphasis or focus specifically on African American students. The lack of explicit emphasis could be attributed to the fact that research already acknowledges that school closures disproportionately impact African American students. In the next section, this chapter describes the challenges and struggles of these schools in integrating displaced students.

The Effects of School Closures on Non-Mobile Students and Schools

The disruptive effects of school closures may extend beyond displaced students. Student mobility may also affect nonmobile students in receiving schools. When mobile students change schools due to school closings, the composition of the receiving school also changes. Students at the receiving school may suffer a cumulative negative impact as faculty and administrators adjust curriculum and activities or as relationships with peers are altered as the composition of classes change. This negative externality, or costs borne by students who did not switch schools, arises as high student turnover introduces discontinuities in the learning environment of all students (both mobile and nonmobile) and may disrupt teaching and curriculum development (Alexander, Entwisle, & Dauber, 1996; Hanushek et al., 2004; Institute of Medicine and National Research Council, 2010; Kerbow, 1996; Raudenbush, Jean, & Art, 2011; Reynolds et al., 2009; Rumberger, 2003; Rumberger et al., 1999).

Only two studies have estimated these mobility externalities (spillover effects), or the impact of the rate of students entering a school on student achievement (Hanushek et al., 2004; Raudenbush et al., 2011). Hanushek and colleagues (2004) highlighted that the effect of student mobility on nonmobile students disproportionately affects poor minority students who are more likely to attend schools with high mobility rates. Raudenbush et al. (2011) found similar results and effect size with respect to school-level mobility ($d = -.03$) as well as evidence of grade-level and cumulative effects associated with the within year in-migration rate. Additionally, South and colleagues (2007) found that nonmobile students in high mobility schools have higher dropout rates, lower levels of school attachment, and lower academic performance.

Unlike previous studies on school closures that examined spillover effects (Engberg et al., 2012; Imberman, Kugler, & Sacerdote, 2012), Brummet (2014) found that there is a negative spillover of school closures, or school closings lower the student achievement of incumbent students in schools that displaced students transfer to. Brummet (2014) also found that school closures had persistent negative spillover effects on receiving schools. In other words, the achievement of students in receiving schools was adversely impacted by the closing of nearby schools for several years. Spillover effects are also dependent on the quality of the closing schools and were larger for students displaced from lower quality schools (Brummet, 2014). Lipman and Person (2007) found that receiving schools had limited staff, resources, professional support and preparation to effectively accommodate and integrate displaced students. Interviewees also highlighted that school closures may also adversely affect school discipline and safety in receiving schools (Lipman & Person, 2007).

School closures also result in teacher mobility as teachers are also displaced from schools that are shut down. Although some districts may have placement policies driven by teachers' preferences, displaced teachers are typically placed in another school based on districts' transfer policies

(Brummet, 2014). Staff in schools that receive a considerable number of students from closing schools can experience increase in stress due to the lack of resources for the integration of new, incoming students (de la Torre & Gwynne, 2009a).

Evidence From Post-Katrina New Orleans

We use a 5 year panel of student-level data from 2006–2007 through 2010–2011 for all public schools within the portfolios of the special state-administered RSD, the locally elected Orleans Parish School Board (OPSB) and the BESE.[3] The data set contains demographic information and students' annual math and English Language Arts (ELA) test scores for each student who attended charter schools and traditional public schools in both sectors. Demographic data includes indicators for students' race/ethnicity (Black, Hispanic, Asian, and White), free and reduced price lunch (FRPL) status, special education status, English language learner (ELL) status and gifted and talented (GATE) status. We standardize test scores for students in Grades 3 through 10 by grade and year, relative to the school mean, as well as relative to the district (all public schools regardless of type or sector) mean.[4] Unique student identifiers in the data set allow us to match students to schools in each year and determine which students were not in the same school in consecutive years. The estimation strategies used to compare school performance across the school types and sectors is similar to those used in prior work (McEachin, Welsh, & Brewer, 2016).

Table 11.3 shows that students that switch schools due to school closures are predominantly low-income and African American. Most of these students were enrolled in RSD non-charter schools. These students were also performing nearly a half a standard deviation below the district average in ELA and math. Prior research has established that mobile students are significantly different from nonmobile students on all observable characteristics (Welsh, 2016a). Table 11.3 also shows that mobile students vary significantly by the reasons for mobility. In this case, students that switch schools due to school closures have statistically significant differences with nonstructural movers (students that switch schools on their own accord) across all demographic and achievement characteristics expect Hispanic, gender, and special education status.

Estimation of the impact of student mobility due to school closures in the first phase is limited by sample size. In the data, most school closures occurred in the final year of the panel, thus limiting the ability to follow these students over time. The sample is less than a thousand students that switch schools due to school closures.

TABLE 11.3   Characteristics of Mobile Students, School Closure-Related and Non-Structural Mobility

Student Characteristics	School Closures	Non-Structural	Difference
Black	0.98	0.95	0.03**
	(0.15)	(0.22)	
Hispanic	0.01	0.01	0.0001
	(0.12)	(0.12)	
White	0.008	0.02	−0.014**
	(0.09)	(0.14)	
Asian	0	0.01	−0.01**
	0	(0.11)	
Male	0.49	0.51	−0.02
	(0.50)	(0.50)	
Special Education	0.07	0.06	0.006
	(0.25)	(0.23)	
Gifted	0.02	0.05	−0.03***
	(0.13)	(0.21)	
FRPL	0.90	0.88	0.02*
	(0.29)	(0.33)	
Charter	0.12	0.65	
	(0.33)	(0.48)	
TPS	0.88	0.35	
	(0.33)	(0.48)	
ELA	−0.52	−0.06	−0.46***
	(0.99)	(1.01)	
MATH	−0.47	−0.06	−0.41***
	(0.96)	(1.01)	

RQ2: Are the lowest performing schools in a portfolio district typically closed?

Deciding which schools to close is a complicated process and schools that are closed are not always the lowest-performing schools in a district (Brummet, 2014). Test scores, schooling environment, location, and enrollment are also considered. Even for performance-related school closures, it is challenging for districts to develop an objective, transparent, and fair criteria for closing schools and clearly explicate the rationale for school closures to the public (Steiner, 2009). District leaders typically aim to involve several stakeholders, especially neighborhood constituents, in hopes of defusing the contentious nature of school closings (Steiner, 2009). However, lack of consultation and sidestepping families, teachers, and community organizations have been reported as common in the closure process (Lipman & Person, 2007). The existing evidence indicates that the majority of school closings are low-performing schools within a district (Brummet, 2014; Carlson & Lavertu, 2016; Engberg et al., 2012; Kemple, 2015; Steiner, 2009). Research suggests that the harm yielded to neighborhoods as a result of school closures extend beyond the direct responsibility of educating children (Bross et al., 2016a). Hence such, closure decisions are considered extremely controversial especially as it pertains to how the selection process occurs (Bross et al., 2016a; Kemple, 2015).

Using data from New Orleans, in Figure 11.1 we plot each school's value-add and confidence interval by school type and sector. These plots illustrate if and how many, schools' value-add is significantly different from the districts' grand mean, and how these patterns vary within and between school types and sectors. The results show that while the majority of the RSD direct-run schools have a math value-add below the district average, a nontrivial share are within the district average with a few above the average.

Although rigorous information about central tendencies across certain types of schools is certainly useful, the PMM posits that government officials will use performance data in future contracting decisions (e.g., deciding which schools to reward, and which to close). Hence, the use of performance and other data to close low performing schools is an important

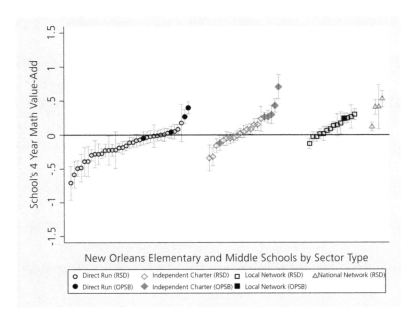

Figure 11.1   The distribution of schools' math value-add by school type and sector.

aspect of school choice policies such as the PMM. The RSD closed seven low performing schools in our sample in 2010–2011. Figures 11.2 and 11.3 show that all closed schools fell in the "low growth, low attainment" category and had some of the highest concentration of low-income students in the district. Finally, we compare the math value-add of these closed schools against the rest of our sample of New Orleans schools. In Figure 11.4, we plot schools math value-add with 95% confidence intervals, grouping schools by closure status. Figure 11.4 shows that although the closed schools were near the bottom of the district performance, they were not the seven lowest in the district. In fact, two of the closed schools have value-add that is indistinguishable from the district mean.

The results indicate that that value added estimates is not the only criterion for closing schools. In other words, academic performance is important but not the sole consideration in closing schools. Overall, in post-Katrina New Orleans, the lowest performing schools are the ones being closed. However, it is worth developing a rich set of performance metrics beyond simply using math and ELA achievement levels and growth, especially when deciding which schools to close. Although the schools closed during the panel of this had some of the lowest math value-add, they may

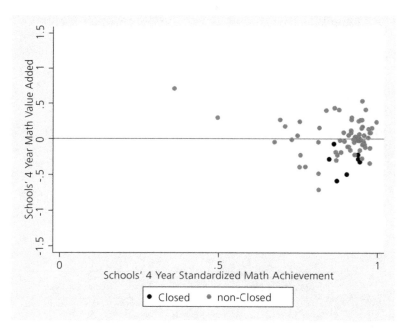

Figure 11.2 The distribution of schools' math value-add and achievement by school closure status.

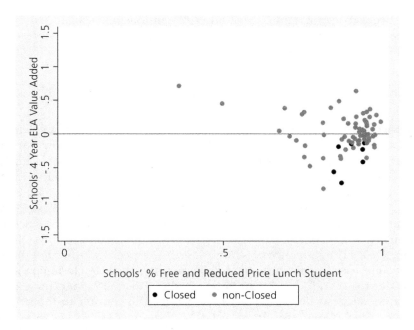

Figure 11.3 The distribution of schools' math value-add by school closure status and schools percent of low-income students.

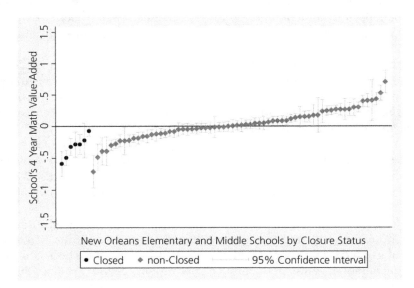

Figure 11.4 The distribution of schools' math value-add by school closure status.

have been strong on a number of other dimensions that are more difficult to measure. Nevertheless, school closures create tension and fissures with and within the community.

DISCUSSION

School closures are a controversial policy issue across districts in the United States. On the one hand, increasingly popular education reforms such as the PMM posit school closures as a way to improve student achievement (Bulkley et al., 2010). On the other hand, families, teachers, school staff, and community leaders generally oppose school closures (Brummet, 2014; de la Torre et al., 2015). Consequently, the effects of school closures on students' educational outcomes have important policy implications. School closures may affect the most at-risk students in a school district (de la Torre et al., 2015). The influence of school closings is especially important for African American students who tend to be most impacted by closing policies. In order for school closures to improve student achievement, the extant literature suggests that displaced students need to transfer to higher-performing schools than the closing school, however, relatively few displaced students switch to better schools. Opponents of school closures fear that displaced students may not end up in better schools and instead transfer to worse schooling environments and experience the transactions costs of switching schools (de la Torre et al., 2015). Given that school closures are not beneficial to student learning unless students switch to better schools, the existing stock of higher quality schools in a district is operative in the efficacy of school closings.

School closures have considerable equity implications. The burden typically falls on low-income and minority students (especially African American students) who are concentrated in low-performing schools or schools in depopulating neighborhoods. In some instances, school closures may be interpreted as "racist and part of a broader process of gentrification" (Kirshner et al., 2010, p. 419). Community groups contend that school closures tend to discriminate against African American students who are typically the overwhelming majority of students in urban schools (Hurdle, 2013). Indeed, in January 2013, activists from six cities filed a civil-rights complaint with the Department of Education.

Closing schools may have broader effects beyond the displaced students. There is mixed evidence on whether there are negative spillover effects for students in receiving schools. Teachers are also displaced by school closures. Closing schools may also destabilize neighborhoods (de la Torre et al., 2015). For instance, in Chicago, school closings in 2013 were concentrated in the South and West sides—neighborhoods with substantial levels of poverty, crime, and unemployment that is depopulating (de la Torre et al., 2015). Critics of school closures posit that closings will likely create further instability in already unstable neighborhoods. Traditionally, schools are important institutions in the ethos and social fabric of communities and neighborhoods.

It is interesting to note that declining enrollment at public schools, a common cause for school closures, is increasing as more students choose to enroll in charter schools. For instance, in Philadelphia, the number of public school students attending charter schools doubled between 2004–2005 and 2011–2012 while 23 traditional public schools were closed in 2013 (Hurdle, 2013). Opponents of charter schools posit that these publicly-financed, privately-operated schools are harmful for traditional public schools.

School finance is also a major consideration in school closures. As school districts continue to navigate state budget cuts (schools are typically financed by 10% federal funds, 45% state funds, and 45% local funds), it is plausible that school closures will continue to increase over time. Fiscal reasons in addition with incentives from the federal government to shutter low-performing schools will play a significant role in reshaping public education in the coming decades.

School closures also raise important questions about the efficacy of educational reform efforts. Districts across the United States have invested significant resources into interventions such as professional development in hopes of significantly improving schools and ultimately avoiding closure. The inability of these measures to transform persistently low-performing schools is an important root cause of school closures.

Policy Implications

The findings of this chapter highlight a few policy implications. Rumberger (2015) posits that if school closures cannot be avoided, policymakers ought to consider programs and support that may reduce the burden of transitions. The results of this study suggests that targeted programs and support for African American students may also be appropriate given that this subgroup is most affected by school closures. Kirshner et al. (2010) highlighted that support and help were lacking for displaced students at their new schools. It would be beneficial for students to create engagement programs that help with social adjustment and foster academic and extracurricular involvement in the new school environment. Mentoring, differentiated instruction and individualized learning may aid students in the classroom whereas buddy programs may help immersion in the school community.

Second, it is prudent for policymakers to provide more resources and support for nearby schools that may also bear the burden of school closures. There is suggestive evidence that school closures also affect students in nearby schools that receive displaced students. Thus, it is important to ease the transition of school closures for both the mobile student as well as the receiving school. Preparation time at the receiving school is a challenge, thus district officials may consider providing these schools with additional staff and administrators in the summer and initial year of the school closure to help satisfy the needs of incoming students.

Directions for Future Research

There are several directions for future work on school closures to aid the existing understanding. First, few studies have estimated the conditional effects of student mobility due to school closures (how changing schools may affect different students differently) with a specific focus on African American students (Kirshner et al., 2010; Lipman & Haines, 2007). It is likely that the overall school closure effect is fairly representative of the closing costs for African American students given that the overwhelming majority of students affected by school closures are African American. No prior study has disentangled the effect of changing schools due to school closings into the transactions costs versus the school quality effect. The nascent literature on the effects of school closures can be bolstered by explicitly focusing on African American students and disentangling the transactions costs experienced by these mobile students from the effects of changing schools attributed to school quality. Only one previous mobility study has separated the transactions costs associated with switching schools from the impact of switching to higher quality schools (Hanushek et al., 2004).

Second, learning more about the nature of transactions costs incurred by families and students, especially in the transition year can aid policymakers in crafting school closure policies. In addition, a better understanding of families' demand for destination schools upon the closure of schools is also needed. Similarly, although school closures affect elementary through high schools, the majority of studies investigating school closures focus on the elementary and middle school levels, thus there is little evidence on high school closings. In addition, most studies also focus on student achievement or cognitive outcomes, thus there is a need for research that examines how school closures affect noncognitive outcomes such as students' behavior and attendance or how students fare socially and behaviorally following displacement due to school closures. Ultimately, it would be insightful to expand outcomes to higher education and labor market outcomes, or examine the impact of school closures on wages and post-secondary outcomes.

Third, few studies have focused on charter school closures (Carlson & Lavertu, 2016). Charter schools that do not meet performance requirements are likely to be closed. Charter schools are a fast growing schooling option, thus a better understanding of the effects associated with the closure of these schools has important policy implications.

Fourth, teacher mobility due to school closures especially issues pertaining to African American teachers is relatively unexplored. Teachers are also displaced when a school is closed and generally transfer to another school in the district. Students are usually placed in nearby schools but teachers can be transferred throughout the district (Brummet, 2014). In some instances, such as Philadelphia, other staff members lose their jobs when schools are closed (Hurdle, 2013). More research is needed on the effects of school closures on teacher labor markets, especially teacher mobility and retention in urban school districts. It also important to learn more about how school closures may affect other staff members and administrators such as principals.

Fifth, there is a need for more research on the benefits of closing schools for districts as there are lingering questions on the effectiveness of closing schools. A 2011 study by the Pew Charitable Trusts found that districts did not benefit financially from selling buildings from closed schools in declining neighborhoods where property values may be on the decline. A study by Research for Action highlighted that typically districts that close schools save money through the reduction of payrolls. Thus if teachers are not fired, there may not be windfall savings. School closures impose considerable costs in the short run on students, families, staff, and teachers without clear indications of long-term benefits for districts. Additionally, there are also expenses involved in school closures such as transportation costs for displaced students. Steiner (2009) highlighted that there are several collective bargaining and legal issues that are complex and require considerable time to resolve. Hence, a cost-benefit analysis of school closures is needed to help clarify the mechanisms of savings and whether these are worth the toll on students and families.

Finally, the costs of school closures likely extend beyond the students in a school. Thus, it is pivotal to learn more about the effects of school closures on neighborhoods, in particular predominantly African American neighborhoods and communities that may be disproportionately affected by school closings.

NOTES

1. School closure is one of several options for school turnarounds (de la Torre & Gwynne, 2009b). Schools may also be reconstituted (staff are replaced but students remain at the same school) or converted (divided into small schools). School closures occur when staff and students are transferred to new schools.

2. Urban districts can be generally defined by size or the prevailing social and economic conditions. For instance, urban school districts may be defined as being located in cities with a population greater than 250,000 and student enrollments of more than 35,000 (Council of the Great City Schools, 2013). In essence, urban school districts are the melting pot of cultures and communities—densely populated, epicenters of commerce that attract a diverse set of people of varying ethnic, racial, linguistic, and geographic origins. Urban school districts can also be defined by the concentration of inequality and evolving economic conditions characterized by poverty, segregation, and under-resourced schools (Milner & Lomotey, 2014).

3. As of 2010–2011 school year, there were roughly 65,000 students in 88 public schools in New Orleans including: 6 OPSB traditional public schools, 11 OPSB charter schools, 46 RSD Charter schools and 23 RSD traditional public schools. Special education students constitute a small proportion—9% in 2010–2011. However, the percentage of special education student increased throughout the post-Katrina era from 4% in 2006–2007 to 9% in 2010–2011.

4. State standardized tests include: the Louisiana Educational Assessment Program (LEAP) administered to 4th and 8th graders in mathematics, English Language Arts (ELA), science and social studies; the high stakes Graduation Exit Exam (GEE) administered in Grades 10 and 11; and the Integrated Louisiana Educational Assessment Program (iLEAP) administered in Grades 3, 5, 6, and 7 (LDE, 2012). The results categorize students in one of five achievement levels: Unsatisfactory, Approaching Basic, Basic, Mastery, or Advanced. A basic classification is generally considered passing the test.

REFERENCES

Alexander, K. L., Entwisle, D. R., & Dauber, S. L. (1996). Children in motion: School transfers and elementary school performance. *Journal of Educational Research*, *90*(1), 3–12. http://doi.org/10.1080/00220671.1996.9944438

Astone, N. M., & Mclanahan, S. S. (1994). Family structure, residential mobility, and school dropout: A research note. *Demography*, *31*(4), 575–584. http://doi.org/10.2307/2061791

Barrow, L., Park, K., & Schanzenbach D. W. (2012). Assessing the impact on students of closing persistently failing schools.

Bross, W., Harris, D. N., & Liu, L. (2016a). *The effects of performance-based school closures and charter takeover on student performance.* Retrieved from http://education researchalliancenola.org/files/publications/Bross-Harris-Liu-The-Effects -of-Performance-Based-School-Closure-and-Charter-Takeover-on-Student -Performance.pdf

Bross, W., Harris, D. N., & Liu, L. (2016b). *Extreme measures: When and how school closures and charter takeovers benefit students.* Retrieved from http://education researchalliancenola.org/files/publications/Education-Research-Alliance -New-Orleans-Policy-Brief-Closure-Takeover.pdf

Brummet, Q. (2014). The effect of school closings on student achievement. *Journal of Public Economics, 119*, 108–124. http://doi.org/http://dx.doi.org/10.1016/j .jpubeco.2014.06.010

Bulkley, K., Henig, J., & Levin, H. (2010). *Politics, governance, and the new portfolio models for urban school reform: Between public and private.* Cambridge, MA: Harvard Education Press.

Carlson, D., & Lavertu, S. (2016). Charter school closure and student achievement: Evidence from Ohio. *Journal of Urban Economics, 95*, 31–48.

Coleman, J. (1988). Social capital in the creation of human capital. *American Journal of Sociology, 94*, S194–S120. http://doi.org/10.1086/228943

Council of the Great City Schools. (2013). *Fact sheet.* Washington, DC: Author. Retrieved from https://www.cgcs.org/domain/24

de la Torre, M., Gordon, M., Moore, P., & Cowhy, J. (2015). *School closings in Chicago: Understanding families' choice and constraints for new school enrollment.* Chicago, IL: Consortium on Chicago School Research, University of Chicago.

de la Torre, M., & Gwynne, J. (2009a). *Changing schools: A look at student mobility trends in Chicago Public Schools since 1995.* Chicago, IL: Consortium on Chicago School Research, University of Chicago.

de la Torre, M., & Gwynne, J. (2009b). *When schools close: Effects on displaced students in Chicago public schools.* Chicago, IL: Consortium on Chicago School Research, University of Chicago.

Engberg, J., Gill, B., Zamarro, G., & Zimmer, R. (2012). Closing schools in a shrinking district: Do student outcomes depend on which schools are closed? *Journal of Urban Economics, 71*(2), 189–203. http://doi.org/10.1016/j.jue.2011.10.001

Ferguson, B. (2014). Closing schools, opening schools and changing school codes: Instability in the New Orleans Recovery School District. Retrieved from http://www.researchonreforms.org/html/documents/RSDClosingOpening ChangingCodes.pdf

Gewertz, C. (2009). Duncan's call for school turnarounds sparks debate. *Education Week.* Retrieved from http://files.maverickleadership.com/duncans_call_ for_school_turnarounds_sparks_debate.pdf

Hanushek, E. A., Kain, J. F., & Rivkin, S. G. (2004). Disruption versus Tiebout improvement: The costs and benefits of switching schools. *Journal of Public Economics, 88*(9–10), 1721–1746. http://doi.org/10.1016/S0047-2727(03)00063-X

Hurdle, J. (2013). Philadelphia officials vote to close 23 schools. *New York Times.* Retrieved from http://www.nytimes.com/2013/03/08/education/philadelphia -officials-vote-to-close-23-schools.html

Imberman, S., Kugler, A., & Sacerdote, B. (2012). Katrina's children: Evidence on the structure of peer effects from hurricane evacuees. *American Economic Review, 102*(5), 2048–2082. http://doi.org/http://dx.doi.org/10.1257/aer.102 .5.2048

Institute of Medicine and National Research Council. (2010). *Student mobility: Exploring the impacts of frequent moves on achievement: Summary of a workshop* (A. Beatty, Rapporteur). Washington, DC: The National Academies Press.

Kemple, J. (2015). *High school closures in New York City: Impacts on students' academic outcomes, attendance, and mobility.* New York, NY: The Research Alliance for New York City Schools.

Kemple, J. J. (2016). School closures in New York City: Did students do better after their high schools were closed? *Education Next, 16*(4), 66–75.

Kerbow, D. (1996). Patterns of urban student mobility and local school reform. *Journal of Education for Students Placed at Risk, 1*(2), 147–169. http://doi.org/10.1207/s15327671espr0102_5

Kirshner, B., Gaertner, M., & Pozzoboni, K. (2010). Tracing transitions: The effect of high school closure on displaced students. *Educational Evaluation and Policy Analysis, 32*(3), 407–429. http://doi.org/10.3102/0162373710376823

Lake, R., & Campbell, C. (n.d.). *Portfolio school districts: Transforming urban education in America.* Seattle, WA: Center for Reinventing Public Education. Retrieved from https://www.pie-network.org/uploads/media_items/rl-portfolio-school-districts.original.pdf

Larsen, M. (2014). Does closing schools close doors? The effect of high school closures on achievement and attainment. Retrieved from http://www.tulane.edu/~mflarsen/uploads/2/2/5/4/22549316/mflarsen_schoolclosings.pdf

Lipman, P., & Haines, N. (2007). From accountability to privatization and African American exclusion: Chicago's "Renaissance 2010." *Educational Policy, 21*(3), 471–502.

Lipman, P., & Person, A. (2007). *Students as collateral damage: A preliminary study of Renaissance 2010 school closings in the Midsouth.* Chicago, IL.

Maxwell, L. (2006, March 14). City districts tackle round of school closings. *Education Week.* Retrieved from https://www.edweek.org/ew/articles/2006/03/15/27close.h25.html

McEachin, A., Welsh, R. O., & Brewer, D. J. (2016). The variation in student achievement and behavior within a portfolio management model: Early results from New Orleans. *Educational Evaluation & Policy Analysis, 38*(4). https://doi.org/10.3102/0162373716659928

Mehana, M., & Reynolds, A. J. (2004). School mobility and achievement: A meta-analysis. *Children and Youth Services Review, 26*(1), 93–119. http://doi.org/10.1016/j.childyouth.2003.11.004

Milner, H. R., IV & Lomotey, K. (2014). *Handbook of urban education.* New York, NY: Routledge.

National Center for Education Statistics. (2015). *Digest of Education Statistics, 2013.* Washington, DC: U.S. Department of Education.

Olson, L. (2006, September 15). As AYP bar rises, more schools fail: Percent missing NCLB goals climbs amid greater testing. *Education Week.* Retrieved from https://www.edweek.org/ew/articles/2006/09/20/04ayp.h26.html

Pribesh, S., & Downey, D. (1999). Why are residential and school moves associated with poor school performance? *Demography, 36*(4), 521–534. http://doi.org/10.2307/2648088

Raudenbush, S. W., Jean, M., & Art, E. (2011). Year-by-year and cumulative impacts of attending a high-mobility elementary school on children's mathematics achievement in Chicago, 1995 to 2005. In G. J. Duncan & R. Murnane (Eds.), *Whither opportunity? Rising inequality, schools, and children's life chances* (pp. 359–376). New York, NY: Russell Sage Foundation.

Ream, R. K. (2005). Toward understanding how social capital mediates the impact of mobility on Mexican American achievement. *Social Forces, 84*(1), 201–224. http://doi.org/10.1353/sof.2005.0121

Reynolds, A. J., Chen, C.-C., & Herbers, J. E. (2009, June). *School mobility and educational success: A research synthesis and evidence on prevention.* Paper presented at the workshop on the impact of mobility and change on the lives of young children, schools, and neighborhoods, Washington, DC.

Rumberger, R. W. (2003). The causes and consequences of student mobility. *Journal of Negro Education, 72*(1), 6–21. http://doi.org/10.2307/3211287

Rumberger, R. W. (2015). *Student mobility: Causes, Consequences and Solutions.* Boulder, CO: National Education Policy Center. Retreived from https://nepc.colorado .edu/publication/student-mobility

Rumberger, R. W., Larson, K. A., Ream, R. K., & Palardy, G. J. (1999). *The educational consequences of mobility for California students and schools.* Berkeley, CA: Policy Analysis for California Education.

Sacerdote, B. (2012). When the saints go marching out: Long-term outcomes for student evacuees from Hurricanes Katrina and Rita. *American Economic Journal: Applied Economics, 4*(1), 109–135.

South, S. J., Haynie, D. L., & Bose, S. (2007). Student mobility and school dropout. *Social Science Research, 36*(1), 68–94. http://doi.org/10.1016/j.ssresearch .2005.10.001

Steiner, L. (2009). *Tough decisions: Closing persistently low-performing schools.*

Sunderman, G., & Payne, A. (2009). *Does closing schools cause educational harm? A review of the research.*

Swanson, C., & Schneider, B. (1999). Students on the move: Residential and educational mobility in America's Schools. *Sociology of Education, 72*(1), 54–67. http://doi.org/10.2307/2673186

Teachman, J., Paasch, K., & Carver, K. (1996). Social capital and dropping out of school early. *Journal of Marriage and the Family, 58*(3), 773–783. http://doi. org/10.2307/353735

Temple, J., & Reynolds, A. J. (1999). School mobility and achievement: Longitudinal findings from an urban cohort. *Journal of Social Psychology, 37*(4), 355–377. http://doi.org/10.1016/S0022-4405(99)00026-6

Welsh, R. O. (2016a). School hopscotch: A comprehensive review of K–12 student mobility in the United States. *Review of Educational Research.* Retrieved from https://doi.org/10.3102/0034654316672068

Welsh, R. O. (2016b). Student mobility, segregation and achievement gaps: Evidence from Clark County, Nevada. *Urban Education, 53*(1). Retrieved from https://doi.org/10.1177/0042085916660349

Welsh, R. O., Duque, M., & McEachin, A. (2016). School choice, student mobility, and school quality: Evidence from post-Katrina New Orleans. *Education Finance and Policy, 11*(2), 150–176.

Young, V., Humphrey, D., Wang, H., Bosetti, K., Cassidy, L., Wechsler, M., . . . Schanzenbach, D. (2009). *Renaissance schools fund-supported schools: Early outcomes, challenges, and opportunities.* Menlo Park, CA.

CONCLUSION

EDUCATION REFORM IN THE RACIAL STATE

The Costs of School Closures for Marginalized Communities

Ebony M. Duncan-Shippy
Washington University in St. Louis

Shuttered Schools: Race, Community, and School Closures in American Cities is a critical examination of 21st century school closure in the United States. Its chapters evaluate the causes, processes, structures, and consequences of school closure in districts across the nation. It examines ways that shifts in the social, economic, and political contexts of education inform closure decision and practice in meaningful ways. With topics ranging from gentrification and redevelopment to student experiences with school loss, research presented in this text moves beyond achievement outcomes; it incorporates varied methods (e.g., case studies, interviews, regression techniques, and textual analysis) in order to carefully contextualize the largely urban phenomenon of school closures. In this way, contributors examine ways in which closures have considerable impacts beyond school walls.

Shuttered Schools, pages 353–357

In concluding *Shuttered Schools*, it is important to consider what its contributions reveal about the intended and unintended consequences of closure for students, families, and communities. Several key themes emerge from the studies included in *Shuttered Schools*. First, these original works interpret closures against the backdrop of growing inequality in school contexts. Whether through an emphasis on the historical foundations of educational inequity (e.g., Kang & Slay, Chapter 4; Galletta, Chapter 6) or its relationship to neighborhood characteristics (e.g., Davis et al., Chapter 3; Syeed, Chapter 5; Brazil, Chapter 8), work in *Shuttered Schools* consistently demonstrates that school closures are rooted in ecological and institutional contexts with rampant inequality. Whether driven by redevelopment and gentrification or by education policies, changes in school communities have considerable effects on local educational landscapes. For example, Brazil demonstrates that schools closures depress property values, with stronger negative effects in areas with more African American residents. In contrast, school closures in White residential areas actually increase housing values. Other chapters also provide insight into how race and class intersections shape local school closure processes. Davis and colleagues (Chapter 3) conclude, for example, that segregated housing and demographic patterns in Atlanta explain differences in school closure rates across communities. Work from Syeed and Galletta (Chapter 5 and Chapter 6) underscores some of the ways that gentrification and redevelopment exacerbate racial and socioeconomic inequality, by fostering antagonism, conflict, displacement, and dispossession in local communities.

Second, contemporary school closure is associated with other educational policies that are often color- and class-blind, and as such, hurt students and communities (Noguera & Pierce, 2016). From No Child Left Behind and Race to the Top, to state takeover of local districts and mayoral control of schools, recent education policies reinforce social inequalities. Lowery (Chapter 7) demonstrates that district leaders often made colorblind decisions in North Little Rock, ignoring the impact of racial inequality in the lives of students in the district. Kang and Slay (Chapter 4) also point out that recent district restructuring efforts preserve educational inequality in the metropolitan Detroit context—rather than dismantle its racially disparate and unequal schooling systems.

Other studies find that district closure practice devalues civic engagement and fosters a distrust of government officials among constituents. Other research reveals that residents and teachers alike are skeptical of district leaders, and often challenge closure practice in local communities (e.g., Nuamah, Chapter 9; Stark & Maton, Chapter 10). Third, despite justifications that school closures are in the spirit of equitable education reform, research in this text demonstrates that these decisions rarely benefit students. While evidence suggests that low academic performance may be a factor in some school closure decisions (e.g., Duncan-Shippy, Chapter 2; Welsh & Hill, Chapter 11), shortsighted policy responses to the social foundations of the problems affecting schools appear only to exacerbate educational challenges.

Nearly all of the chapters in *Shuttered Schools* demonstrate that the state advances closures in racially disparate ways. To this end, school closures represent a project of the racial state in urban communities across the United States. The racial state, which has contextual, institutional, and ideological components, is a key concept for understanding the reproductive power of race in public life. Race is inherent to the state, which is "composed of *institutions*, the *policies* they carry out, the *conditions and rules* which support and justify them, and the *social relations* in which they are embedded" (emphasis in original, Omi & Winant, 1994, p. 82). In other words, the state is an institution comprised of organizations that carry out policies, support its projects, practices, and justify its actions through rules and procedures (Goldberg, 2001; Omi & Winant, 1994). Implicit and explicit racial interests, entanglement with racial politics, interaction with identity processes, and embeddedness in broader racial contexts imbue the state and its action with racial meaning and significance (Goldberg, 2001; Omi & Winant, 1994; Tilly, 1999).

With respect to context, the state operates both socially and culturally (Goldberg, 2001; Jung & Kwon, 2013; Omi & Winant, 1994), such that institutional and ecological considerations become important for understanding the racial ramifications of state action. Because it operates in these broader contexts, state procedures, practices, and policies produce racially disparate patterns and perpetuate inequality within social institutions (Better, 2008; Haas, 1992). Although institutions and their policies are not always *explicitly* racial, the outcomes of such institutional policies in racialized contexts create and protect racial privilege and power through disadvantaging and exploiting members of non-White racial groups. As such, decisions that harm some racial groups often flow from following laws, policies, and procedures that are not necessarily racist in design or intent (Taylor & Clark, 2009). In other words, so-called race-neutral or race-blind policies still have racialized consequences when implemented.

From a racialization perspective, the state influences the operation of public schools, such that access to resources, experiences in public spaces and organizations, and outcomes have racially disparate patterns. In addition, it allocates social resources in ways that inequitably benefit those with racial privilege at the expense of other groups (Better, 2008; Carmichael & Hamilton, 1967; Taylor & Clark, 2009). As such, state-run education reproduces hierarchy and stratification, materializing as racial disparities in the distribution of social status and other immaterial and material resources. The state is not only responsible for public schools as state organizations, but also for the ways it allows social conditions to corrupt the objectives and operation of public education. Thus, the racial state bridges ecological and institutional factors shaping closure processes and outcomes. Contemporary school closures represent yet another way that state policies and practices interact with social contexts to reproduce inequity.

While this interdisciplinary volume offers original research on school closure, there are several ways to advance scholarship on this topic. In current educational policy contexts, parents are stakeholders who have the burden of navigating increasingly complex educational landscapes—which closures further complicate. In addition, parents represent the primary group to which education officials are accountable. Although some authors include parent perspectives (e.g., Syeed, Chapter 4; Lowery, Chapter 7; and Nuamah, Chapter 9), future work should centralize their voices. In addition, researchers should track students and families with firsthand closure experience. Galletta (Chapter 6), for example, captured the voices of students displaced by closures in Cleveland. Additional studies are necessary to document the resultant short- and long-term impacts that these decisions have on the lives of marginalized youth. Furthermore, while *Shuttered Schools* focuses on closure in African American communities and schools, it is essential to expand analyses to include other racial groups. Studies should also consider the extent to which intersecting systems of socioeconomic status and ethnicity potentially affect school closure patterns—in this respect, comparative approaches will be particularly illuminating. Finally, education researchers should consider whether school closure produces any benefits. Despite justifications for school closure that claim to be in the spirit of reform, recent research demonstrates that these decisions rarely benefit students. However, the decision to shutter schools might benefit other stakeholders (e.g., school districts, new charter schools).

Studies in *Shuttered Schools* demonstrate that the impacts of shuttering schools are neither colorblind nor class-neutral, but indeed interact with social contexts in ways that reify existing social inequalities in education. In particular, they speak to the racially disproportionate impacts of school loss on African American students. Racially specific school closure consequences are testament to a long history of racial stratification, which deprives African American students of equitable educational access, experiences, and outcomes. In racialized contexts, social institutions like public education reproduce racial hierarchy and stratification (Lewis & Diamond, 2015), materializing as racial disparities in the lives of youth. *Shuttered Schools* demonstrates that countless factors exacerbate inequality in predominantly African American school communities where closures are common. Economic and social challenges cause institutions to fail, but the state uses closures to construct Black need, and then positions itself to "save" Black youth in these communities. Black youth are not needy, but they are often marginalized. Rather than address the social conditions fundamental to their marginalization, myopic policy responses like school closure reinforce the social construction of Black need, and facilitate state activity in resource-strapped districts. As such, school closure appears to benefit the State, enhancing its local presence and power rather than disrupting the cycles of social marginality and immobility that hurt young people. Rather than reform education, closure decisions further deprive young people of the educational change they truly deserve.

REFERENCES

Better, S. (2008). *Institutional racism: A primer on theory and strategies for social change* (2nd ed.). Lanham, MD: Rowman & Littlefield.

Carmichael, S., & Hamilton, C. V. (1967). *Black power: The politics of liberation.* New York, NY: Random House.

Goldberg, D. T. (2001). *The racial state.* Malden, MA: Blackwell.

Haas, M. (1992). *Institutional racism: The case of Hawai'i.* Westport, CA: Praeger.

Jung, M.-K., & Kwon, Y. (2013). Theorizing the US racial state: Sociology since racial formation. *Sociology Compass, 7*(11), 927–940.

Lewis, A. E., & Diamond, J. B. (2015). *Despite the best intentions: How racial inequality thrives in good schools.* Oxford, England: Oxford University Press.

Noguera, P. A., & Pierce, J. C. (2016). The (evasive) language of school reform. *Educational Leadership,* 74–78.

Omi, M., & Winant, H. (1994). *Racial formation in the United States: From the 1960s to the 1990s* (2nd ed.). New York, NY: Routledge.

Taylor, D. L., & Clark, M. P. (2009). "Set up to fail": Institutional racism and the sabotage of school improvement. *Equity & Excellence in Education, 42*(2), 114–129.

Tilly, C. (1999). *Durable Inequality.* Berkeley: University of California Press.

ABOUT THE EDITOR

Ebony M. Duncan-Shippy is an assistant professor in the Department of Education at Washington University in St. Louis. As a sociologist, she examines the racial contexts of education in the United States. She is especially interested in the ways that educational policies and practices affect the lives of students living and learning in the margins of society.

ABOUT THE CONTRIBUTORS

Noli Brazil is an assistant professor at the University of California, Davis. His research utilizes quantitative methods and geospatial techniques to understand the intersection of school and neighborhood environments and their impacts on adolescent outcomes.

Tomeka Davis, PhD, is associate professor of Sociology at Georgia State University. Her research interests include the sociology of education, race, and social inequality.

Anne Galletta is a professor at the College of Education and Human Services at Cleveland State University. Her research interests include attention to social relations as well as structural violence and liberatory impulses within public institutions.

Leanne Kang is an assistant professor in the College of Education at Grand Valley State University. She received her PhD in Educational Foundations and Policy at the University of Michigan. She was an English teacher in an urban school district in New Jersey.

Shafiqua Little is a doctoral candidate in the Educational Administration and Policy Department at the University of Georgia. Her research focuses on K–12 education policy, charter schools, and school discipline.

Kendra Lowery, PhD, is an assistant professor and program director in Educational Leadership at Ball State University. Kendra's research interests include examining leadership practices that contribute to social justice with a focus on racial equity, cross-racial dialogues; and school de/segregation.

Rhiannon Maton, PhD is an assistant professor of Foundations and Social Advocacy at State University of New York College at Cortland. Her research examines teacher learning and leadership, and stakeholder engagement in policy systems and processes. She has previously published in several edited volumes and academic journals, including *Curriculum Inquiry, Critical Studies in Education,* and *Policy Futures in Education.*

Sally A. Nuamah is an assistant professor at Duke University's Sanford School of Public Policy. She is the founder of the TWII Foundation HerStory Girls Scholarship, and author of *How Girls Achieve* (Harvard University Press, 2019).

Deirdre Oakley, PhD, is professor of sociology at Georgia State University. Her research focuses on urban sociology and inequality. She is currently Editor in Chief of *City and Community*, the flagship journal of the Community and Urban Sociology section of the American Sociological Association.

Dr. Kelly Slay is an inaugural President's Postdoctoral Fellow in the College of Education at the University of Maryland–College Park and affiliate faculty in the Center for Diversity and Inclusion in Higher Education. Her interdisciplinary research explores issues of race, diversity, and inclusion in K–12 and higher education. Slay's research has been published in *Educational Policy* and *Teachers College Record* and is forthcoming in the *Review of Higher Education.*

Lauren Ware Stark is a doctoral candidate specializing in the Cultural Sociology of Education and Critical Policy Studies at the University of Virginia. She earned a master's degree in French Studies at the University of Pennsylvania and spent eight years teaching secondary English, French, and Humanities in public schools in Delaware, Texas, and Washington. Her research interests include critical pedagogy and social justice education, teachers' work and teachers' unions, and teacher and student engagement in social movements.

Shanae Stover is a graduate student at Georgia State University. Her dissertation focuses on race and health disparities among African American adults reared in poverty.

Esa Syeed is an assistant professor of Sociology at California State University-Long Beach. He collaborates with communities to conduct research that informs educational justice work.

Richard O. Welsh is an assistant professor of educational administration and policy at the University of Georgia. His research focuses on the economics of education, K–12 education policy, and international comparative education.

CPSIA information can be obtained
at www.ICGtesting.com
Printed in the USA
BVHW042004111019
560917BV00005B/27/P

9 781641 136082